Elections in Pennsylvania

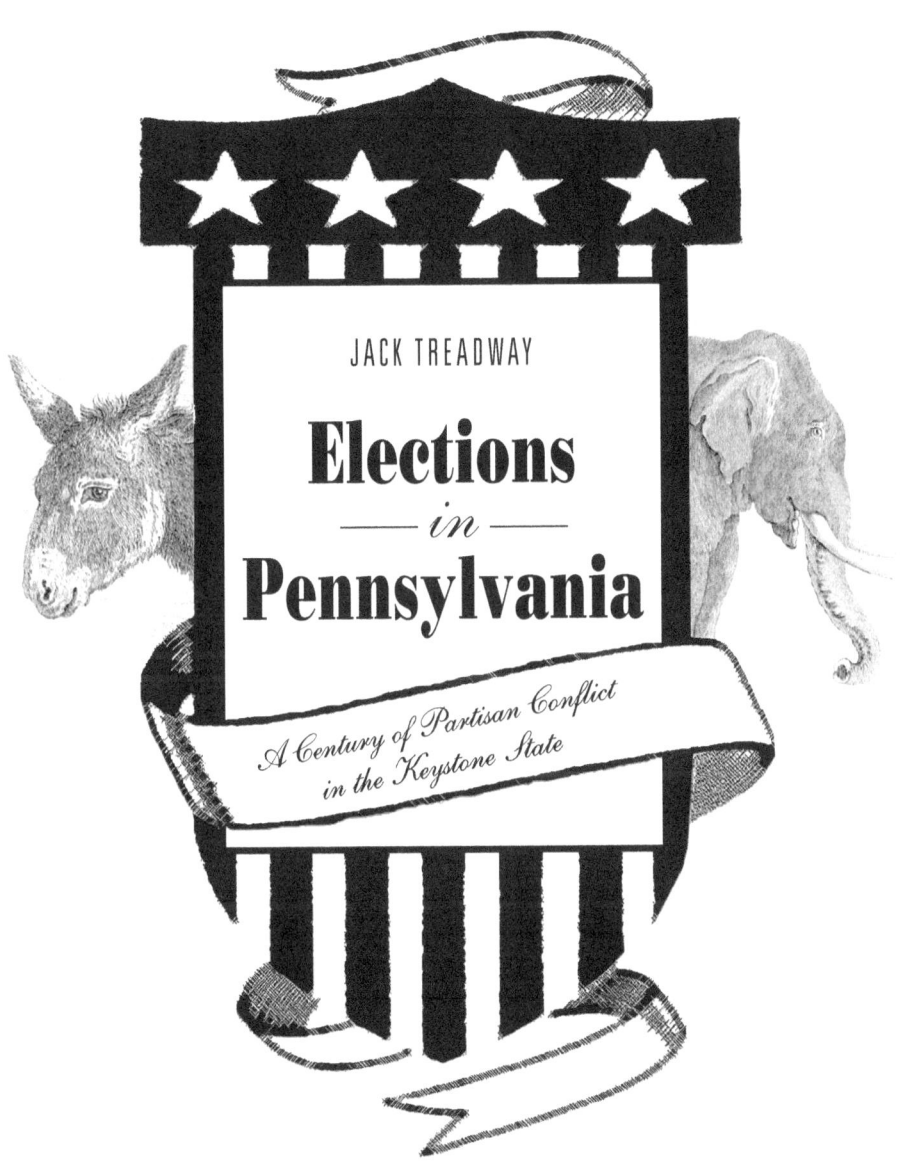

Elections in Pennsylvania

A Century of Partisan Conflict in the Keystone State

JACK TREADWAY

The Pennsylvania State University Press
University Park, Pennsylvania

Library of Congress Cataloging-in-Publication Data
Treadway, Jack M.
Elections in Pennsylvania : a century of partisan conflict in the Keystone State / Jack Treadway.
p. cm.
Includes bibliographical references and index.
ISBN 978-0-271-05861-0 (pbk : alk. paper)
1. Elections—Pennsylvania—History–20th century.
2. Elections–Pennsylvania—History—20th century—Statistics.
I. Title.

JK3692.T74 2005
324.9748'043—dc22
2005011938

Copyright © 2005 The Pennsylvania State University
All rights reserved
Printed in the United States of America
Published by The Pennsylvania State University Press,
University Park, PA 16802-1003

The Pennsylvania State University Press is a member of the Association of American University Presses.

It is the policy of The Pennsylvania State University Press to use acid-free paper. This book is printed on stock that meets the minimum requirements of American National Standard for Information Sciences—Permanence of Paper for Printed Library Material, ANSI Z39.48–1992.

For Bonnie

Contents

Preface and Acknowledgments ix

Tables and Figures xi

Introduction xxi

1 Pennsylvania Then and Now 1

2 A Century of Electors 24

3 Legislative Elections 50

4 Legislative Careerism 80

5 Statewide Elections 96

6 Primary Elections 136

7 Patterns of Partisanship 158

8 In Perspective 192

9 Postscript 208

Appendix 217

References 285

Index 291

Preface and Acknowledgments

The genesis of this book was a conference paper I wrote several years ago. Much had been written regarding the dramatic increases in the reelection rates and margins of victory among incumbent legislators since 1960. I decided to attempt to put those trends in historical perspective. I examined Pennsylvania General Assembly elections between 1900 and 1998 and discovered that not all of the trends discussed in the literature were unique to the post-1960 era; some had been present since the turn of the twentieth century. These initial findings led me to expand the scope of the study to all include all state level elections, except judicial elections, held in Pennsylvania during the twentieth century. The results of the expanded study are presented in this book. I hope that it will help readers to understand better the dynamics of state elections, particularly those in Pennsylvania.

A number of people made significant contributions to the final draft of *Elections in Pennsylvania*. Two anonymous reviewers provided constructive criticism and offered a number of suggestions that made the finished product much better. The copyeditor, Andrew Lewis, significantly improved the manuscript. The maps were produced by Damian Carabello, a graduate student at Kutztown University. The staff at Penn State Press has been gracious, efficient, and professional throughout the process. I have worked with the Director of the Press, Sanford G. Thatcher, for the past two years. His encouragement and advice have been invaluable. Jennifer Norton, Design and Production Manager, Cherene Holland, Managing Editor, and Patricia Mitchell, Production Coordinator, all provided expertise and advice that made the book better. I assume responsibility for any deficiencies that remain.

The biggest debt of gratitude goes to my family. My wife, Bonnie, and our children, Justin and Tara, all help to create a loving environment in which it is possible to complete a project such as this. I am grateful to Bonnie for much more than that, which is why the book is dedicated to her.

Tables and Figures

TABLES

1.1 Philadelphia's black population as a percentage of state total   5
1.2 Number of multimember districts and number of representatives elected from multimember districts, selected years   15
1.3 Percentage urban of the forty-seven counties with populations less than the House ratio, 1900   16
2.1 Registered voters as a percentage of the voting age population (VAP), 1926–1998   26
2.2 Independents among the American electorate, 1952–1998 (percentage)   26
2.3 Republican and Democratic registration as a percentage of total registration, selected years, 1925–1998   27
2.4 Total number of registered Democrats and Republicans, 1925–1998, and registered voters as a percentage of the voting age population (VAP)   34
2.5 A comparison of the mean Republican and Democratic vote for selected offices with the mean Republican and Democratic registration, statewide, for both majority and minority status, 1925–1998   35
2.6 The turnout-loyalty index for governor, by decade, 1920s–1990s   36
2.7 The turnout-loyalty index for president, by decade, 1920s–1990s   36
2.8 Voter turnout in presidential and gubernatorial elections, as a percentage of voting age population (VAP), 1900–1998   39

2.9 Percentage increase or decrease in voter turnout for presidential and gubernatorial elections for three eras: 1900–1948, 1950–1968, 1970–1998   40
2.10 Voter turnout in presidential and gubernatorial elections, as a percentage of registered voters, 1926–1998   41
2.11 Mean partisanship consistency index and percentage of split results, by decade, 1900–1998   44
2.12 Split-ticket voting examined by the incidence of close elections, by decade, 1900–1998   46
2.13 The recalculated partisanship consistency index, by decade, 1900–1998   47
3.1 Percentage of incumbents running for reelection, by chamber and decade, 1900–1998   55
3.2 Percentage of incumbents winning reelection, by chamber and decade, 1990–1998   56
3.3 Mean rate of membership turnover, by chamber and decade, 1900–1998   58
3.4 Percentage of safe House seats, by decade and category of winner, 1900–1998   59
3.5 A comparison of the percentage of safe House seats, by category of winner, from 1900 to 1928 and from 1960 to 1998   59
3.6 Percentage of safe Senate seats, by decade and category of winner, 1900–1998   60
3.7 A comparison of the percentage of safe Senate seats, by category of winner, from 1900 to 1928 and from 1960 to 1998   60
3.8 Percentage of voters registered with dominant party, by chamber, 1995–1996   62
3.9 Percentage of contested House candidates, by type of candidate and decade, 1900–1998   63
3.10 Percentage of contested Senate candidates, by type of candidate and decade, 1900–1998   63
3.11 Percentage of safe House and Senate seats, by decade and category of winner, in all (contested) races, 1970–1998   63
3.12 The relationship between electoral marginality and incumbent defeat, by chamber and decade, 1900–1998   64
3.13 The relationship between the majority party's statewide share of the vote for Pennsylvania House candidates and the share of House seats won, 1900–1998   67

3.14 The relationship between the majority party's statewide share of the vote for Pennsylvania House candidates and the share of House seats won, 1900–1964 and 1966–1998   67
3.15 Percentage of congressional incumbents running for reelection, by decade, 1900–1998   69
3.16 Percentage of congressional incumbents winning reelection, by decade, 1900–1998   70
3.17 Percentage of safe congressional seats, by decade and category of winner, 1900–1998   71
3.18 Percentage of contested congressional candidates, by type of candidate and decade, 1900–1998   72
3.19 Percentage of safe congressional seats, by decade and category of winner, in all (contested) races, 1970–1998   73
3.20 The relationship between electoral marginality and congressional incumbent defeat, by decade, 1900–1998   74
3.21 The relationship between the majority party's statewide share of the vote for congressional candidates and the share of congressional seats won, 1990–1998   75
3.22 A comparison of the percentage of safe House and Senate seats, by category of winner, 1900–1928, 1930–1958, and 1960–1998   77
3.23 A comparison of the percentage of safe congressional seats, by category of winner, 1900–1928, 1930–1958, and 1960–1998   79
4.1 Percentage of members of the Pennsylvania House of Representatives serving selected terms of office, and mean tenure, by decade elected, 1900–1985   83
4.2 Percentage of members of the Pennsylvania Senate serving selected terms of office, and mean tenure, by decade elected, 1900–1985   84
4.3 Percentage of members of the Pennsylvania congressional delegation serving selected terms of office, and mean tenure, by decade elected, 1900–1985   85
4.4 A comparison of mean rates of tenure (in years) for members of the General Assembly and members of the Pennsylvania congressional delegation, by decade elected, 1900–1985   87
4.5 Mean rates of tenure and mean rates of incumbent reelection success for members of the General Assembly and members of the Pennsylvania congressional delegation, 1990–1998   88
4.6 A comparison of the previous political backgrounds of members of the Pennsylvania House of Representatives, 1901 and 1995   90

4.7 A summary of the previous political backgrounds of members of the Pennsylvania House of Representatives, 1901 and 1995   90
4.8 A comparison of the previous political backgrounds of members of the Pennsylvania Senate, 1901 and 1995   92
4.9 A summary of the political backgrounds of members of the Pennsylvania Senate, 1901 and 1995   92
4.10 The mean and median age of members of the General Assembly at the time of their initial election, 1901 and 1995   94
5.1 The ten most Republican and ten least Republican counties in gubernatorial elections, 1900–1998   98
5.2 The ten most Republican and ten least Republican counties in gubernatorial elections, 1910–1918   99
5.3 The ten most Republican and ten least Republican counties in gubernatorial elections, 1920–1928   100
5.4 The ten most Republican and ten least Republican counties in gubernatorial elections, 1930–1938   102
5.5 The ten most Republican and ten least Republican counties in gubernatorial elections, 1940–1948   103
5.6 The ten most Republican and ten least Republican counties in gubernatorial elections, 1950–1958   104
5.7 The ten most Republican and ten least Republican counties in gubernatorial elections, 1960–1968   106
5.8 The ten most Republican and ten least Republican counties in gubernatorial elections, 1970–1978   107
5.9 The ten most Republican and ten least Republican counties in gubernatorial elections, 1980–1988   108
5.10 The ten most Republican and ten least Republican counties in gubernatorial elections, 1990–1998   109
5.11 The ten most Republican and ten least Republican counties in presidential elections, 1900–1908   111
5.12 The ten most Republican and ten least Republican counties in presidential elections, 1910–1918   112
5.13 The ten most Republican and ten least Republican counties in presidential elections, 1920–1928   113
5.14 The ten most Republican and ten least Republican counties in presidential elections, 1930–1938   114
5.15 The ten most Republican and ten least Republican counties in presidential elections, 1940–1948   116

5.16 The ten most Republican and ten least Republican counties in presidential elections, 1950–1958   117
5.17 The ten most Republican and ten least Republican counties in presidential elections, 1960–1968   118
5.18 The ten most Republican and ten least Republican counties in presidential elections, 1970–1978   119
5.19 The ten most Republican and ten least Republican counties in presidential elections, 1980–1988   121
5.20 The ten most Republican and ten least Republican counties in presidential elections, 1990–1998   122
5.21 Number of counties won by Republican and Democratic candidates, in gubernatorial and presidential elections, 1900–1998   123
5.22 Counties that ranked among the ten most Republican counties in gubernatorial elections, and the decade(s) they achieved that ranking, 1900–1998   124
5.23 Counties that ranked among the ten most Republican counties in presidential elections, and the decade(s) they achieved that ranking, 1900–1998   126
5.24 Counties that ranked among the ten least Republican counties in gubernatorial elections, and the decade(s) they achieved that ranking, 1900–1998   127
5.25 Counties that ranked among the ten least Republican counties in presidential elections, and the decade(s) they achieved that ranking, 1900–1998   129
5.26 Democratic victories in statewide elections, by category and decade, 1900–1998   131
5.27 Democratic victories, by category, before and after 1960   132
5.28 Mean Democratic vote for president, governor, and U.S. senator in six counties, by decade, 1970–1998   133
5.29 Mean Democratic vote for president, governor, and U.S. senator in six counties, by county, 1970–1998   134
6.1 The percentage of the vote received by the winning candidate (and the number of contestants) in gubernatorial and senatorial primaries, by party and year, 1926–1998   140
6.2 A summary of gubernatorial primary elections, by party and selected variables, 1926–1998   141
6.3 A summary of U.S. Senate primary elections, by party and selected variables, 1926–1998   142

6.4 The percentage of contested congressional and Pennsylvania General Assembly primaries, by type of candidate, office, and decade, 1972–1998   144
6.5 The percentage of opposed congressional and General Assembly candidates who received at least 60 percent of the primary vote, by type of candidate, office, and decade, 1972–1998   145
6.6 The relationship between Pennsylvania Senate incumbents who received less than 60 percent of the vote in a primary election and the vote in the previous and subsequent general elections, by decade, 1972–1998   146
6.7 The relationship between congressional and Pennsylvania House incumbents who received less than 60 percent of the vote in a primary election and the vote in the previous and subsequent general elections, by decade, 1972–1998   147
6.8 The incidence of primary election defeat for congressional and General Assembly incumbents, by decade, 1972–1998   148
6.9 The relationship between contested and uncontested primaries for the Pennsylvania House of Representatives and the vote in the general election, by party and decade, 1972–1998   149
6.10 The relationship between partisanship and urban-rural categories among Pennsylvania House of Representatives districts, 1990–1998   151
6.11 The incidence of contested primaries among urban-rural categories, Pennsylvania House of Representatives, 1900–1998   151
6.12 The relationship between incumbency and urban-rural categories, Pennsylvania House of Representatives, 1990–1998   151
6.13 The relationship between contested and uncontested primaries for the Pennsylvania House of Representatives and the vote in the general election, by party and urban-rural classification, 1990–1998   153
6.14 Percentage voter turnout in primaries, and the difference between primary and general election turnout, in gubernatorial primaries, 1926–1998   155
7.1 A comparison of the mean Republican share of the vote in given elections with the mean Republican share of the vote in the four previous elections, for gubernatorial and presidential elections, 1900–1998   163
7.2 Coefficients of correlation between Republican voting in gubernatorial elections, 1922–1942   165

7.3   Coefficients of correlation between Republican voting in presidential elections, 1920–1940   166
7.4   A comparison of the mean Republican share of the vote in given elections with the mean Republican share of the vote in the four previous elections, for Pennsylvania and U.S. Houses of Representatives, 1900–1998   168
7.5   Mean percentages urban, foreign born, and African American for all Republican and all Democratic counties, by decade, for gubernatorial elections, 1900–1998   169
7.6   Mean percentages urban, foreign born, and African American for all Republican and all Democratic counties, by decade, for presidential elections, 1900–1998   169
7.7   The relationship between county urbanization and Republican vote for governor, by decade, 1900–1998   171
7.8   The relationship between county urbanization and Republican vote for president, by decade, 1900–1998   171
7.9   Pennsylvania counties, categorized by level of competition in gubernatorial elections, 1902–1998   174
7.10 Decades in which the change in partisanship became permanent for counties that became more Republican or more Democratic in gubernatorial elections, 1900–1998   175
7.11 Pennsylvania counties, categorized by level of competition in presidential elections, 1900–1996   178
7.12 Decades in which the change in partisanship became permanent for counties that became more Republican or more Democratic in presidential elections, 1900–1998   179
7.13 Counties with different classifications in gubernatorial and presidential elections, 1900–1998   182
7.14 A profile of Republican and Democratic House districts, with selected variables, 1996   183
7.15 A profile of Republican and Democratic Senate districts, with selected variables, 1996   185
7.16 Home counties or areas of Pennsylvania governors, 1900–1998   186
7.17 Home counties or areas of U.S. senators from Pennsylvania, 1914–1998   187
7.18 Home counties or areas of Pennsylvania statewide officials, 1900–1998   188

7.19 Home counties or areas of Pennsylvania governors, U.S. senators from Pennsylvania, and Pennsylvania statewide officials, 1900–1998   189

FIGURES

2.1 Counties with more than ten percent of voters not registered as Republicans or Democrats, 1925   29

2.2 Counties with more than ten percent of voters not registered as Republicans or Democrats, 1998   30

2.3 Counties with more than ten percent of voters not registered as Republicans or Democrats in both 1925 and 1998   32

5.1 Republican and Democratic counties in gubernatorial elections, 1900–1908   98

5.2 Republican and Democratic counties in gubernatorial elections, 1910–1918   99

5.3 Republican and Democratic counties in gubernatorial elections, 1920–1928   100

5.4 Republican and Democratic counties in gubernatorial elections, 1930–1938   101

5.5 Republican and Democratic counties in gubernatorial elections, 1940–1948   103

5.6 Republican and Democratic counties in gubernatorial elections, 1950–1958   104

5.7 Republican and Democratic counties in gubernatorial elections, 1960–1968   105

5.8 Republican and Democratic counties in gubernatorial elections, 1970–1978   107

5.9 Republican and Democratic counties in gubernatorial elections, 1980–1988   108

5.10 Republican and Democratic counties in gubernatorial elections, 1990–1998   109

5.11 Republican and Democratic counties in presidential elections, 1900–1908   110

5.12 Republican and Democratic counties in presidential elections, 1910–1918   112

5.13 Republican and Democratic counties in presidential elections, 1920–1928   113

5.14 Republican and Democratic counties in presidential elections, 1930–1938   114
5.15 Republican and Democratic counties in presidential elections, 1940–1948   115
5.16 Republican and Democratic counties in presidential elections, 1950–1958   117
5.17 Republican and Democratic counties in presidential elections, 1960–1968   118
5.18 Republican and Democratic counties in presidential elections, 1970–1978   119
5.19 Republican and Democratic counties in presidential elections, 1980–1988   120
5.20 Republican and Democratic counties in presidential elections, 1990–1998   122
7.1 Index of Republican and Democratic counties in gubernatorial elections, 1902–1998   177
7.2 Distribution of counties according to competition in presidential elections, 1900–1996   181

Introduction

The last four decades of the twentieth century produced a significant amount of academic research that has greatly enhanced our understanding of electoral dynamics and individual voting behavior. As has always been the case, the bulk of the research focused on national elections. Nevertheless, the sharp increase in research at the state level has added much to our knowledge about state elections, particularly state legislative elections.

Of particular importance to our understanding of legislative elections was the release in 1990 of computer files created by the Inter-University Consortium for Political and Social Research (ICPSR) at the University of Michigan. The initial files covered general elections in almost all states and primary elections in fourteen southern and border states for the election years 1968–86. The files have been updated every two years. A number of scholarly articles were published following the release of the files.

Some of the authors supplemented the ICPSR data with data from earlier years (Jewell 1994).

Despite these recent efforts, much remains to be done. Many aspects of state legislative elections have received no or only cursory examination (Jewell 1994). While gubernatorial elections have been analyzed by a number of state government scholars, elections for other statewide offices have received little attention. A more significant deficiency, in my opinion, is the dearth of studies examining elections from a historical perspective. Dealing with that shortcoming is the primary goal of this book.

Most of the election studies chronicle the changes that have transpired since the early 1960s. While this research has greatly expanded our understanding of the electoral process, it begs an important question—namely, are the trends of the past four decades unique? If they are, then we have, indeed, witnessed some significant changes during the last forty years. But if they are not, then the current patterns may not be all that different from those of the past, in which case, the 1960s may not be the best baseline for at least some areas of electoral research.

The basic premise of this book is that contemporary electoral dynamics and trends must be put into historical perspective. One cannot assume that current trends are unprecedented. A historical analysis may reveal that particular electoral patterns, assumed to be a byproduct of the contemporary political environment, may, rather, be a continuation of a longer-term trend or a reversion to a standard that was prevalent decades ago.

This book will provide a historical perspective by examining the more than thirteen thousand general elections and more than six thousand primary elections for president, governor, U.S. senator and representative, statewide offices, and members of the Pennsylvania General Assembly that took place in Pennsylvania between 1900 and 1998. This approach will allow us to distinguish between longer-term trends and unique contemporary patterns. It is my conviction that to understand and appreciate fully contemporary electoral patterns and arrangements, one must understand what existed before. Trends do not exist in a historical vacuum—placing them in the proper historical context is crucial to assessing their ultimate significance.

The basic goal of this book is to develop a series of generalizations regarding electoral dynamics and voting based on a comprehensive set of elections over the course of a century. It is hoped that this detailed case study will offer some useful insights into the changing character of electoral competition and voting in Pennsylvania during the twentieth century.

INTRODUCTION ★ xxiii

The most obvious limitation of this study is that the findings do not necessarily apply to other states. However, there is no reason to believe that elections in Pennsylvania are completely unlike those in the other forty-nine states and that nothing that is learned from this research is applicable outside its borders.

Chapter 1, "Pennsylvania Then and Now," chronicles the economic, social, and political changes that took place in the state during the twentieth century and discusses the impact of the Republican statewide political machine during the first decades of the century.

Chapter 2, "A Century of Electors," details trends in voter registration and turnout and discusses the incidence of independence among voters and the increasing incidence of split-ticket voting.

Chapter 3, "Legislative Elections," examines in detail General Assembly and congressional elections. Among the topics included are the percentage of incumbents running for reelection, the reelection rates of incumbents, the incidence of marginal districts, the percentage of contested elections, electoral marginality and the incidence of defeat, and the relationship between vote share and seats won.

Chapter 4, "Legislative Careerism," focuses on changes in the level of professionalism among Pennsylvania state legislators and members of the state's delegation to the U.S. House of Representatives and summarizes the political backgrounds of members of the General Assembly who were serving in 1901 and 1995.

Chapter 5, "Statewide Elections," analyzes twentieth-century elections for governor, president, U.S. senator, and statewide offices. It also provides detailed county voting patterns for gubernatorial and presidential elections for each decade and for the entire century, discusses the varying Democratic fortunes in statewide elections, and treats in detail the Democrats' persistent inability to elect U.S. senators.

Chapter 6, "Primary Elections," examines competition and voter turnout in primary elections for governor, U.S. senator, congressional representative, and the state legislator. The chapter examines the potential influence of incumbency, prospects for general election success, urban-rural differences, and majority-minority party status on the level of primary competition and analyzes trends in primary election voter turnout and the difference between primary and general election turnout.

Chapter 7, "Patterns of Partisanship," treats a variety of electoral patterns. It attempts to determine when the New Deal realignment occurred in Pennsylvania; examines the changing relationship between urbanism, racial and ethnic diversity, and the Republican vote; categorizes all sixty-seven counties according to their level of competition in gubernatorial and presidential elections during the twentieth century; profiles contemporary Republican and Democratic state legislative districts; and finally, presents a summary of the home counties of all those individuals who served as governors, U.S. senators, and statewide officeholders.

Chapter 8, "In Perspective," summarizes a century of partisan conflict and reviews the findings contained in the previous chapters. It shows that some recent trends, hailed as significant departures from the past, are less significant than is contended. Some of these patterns are simply the past revisited.

Chapter 9, "Postscript," updates the twentieth-century trends through the 2000 and 2002 elections.

It is hoped that this study of twentieth-century Pennsylvania elections can further our understanding of state elections in general. If this approach proves useful, perhaps others will conduct similar studies in other states. Additional comparative data will allow us to better understand which patterns are common to a variety of states as well as which are unique to particular states. I remain convinced that more historical data can only increase our understanding of contemporary elections in the American states.

PENNSYLVANIA THEN AND NOW

Since the founding of the Republic, Pennsylvania has lived up to its appellation as the Keystone State. The state's contributions to the industrial, agricultural, social, artistic, religious, and political well-being of the nation have been extensive and continuous. The state is large, and its people and politics are as varied as its geography. For more than two hundred years, Pennsylvania has produced individuals and ideas that have had major impacts on the nation's political history. Pennsylvania politics clearly is worth studying. Greater knowledge about Pennsylvania politics should lead to a better understanding of state-level politics in rest of the country.

It would be premature to examine twentieth-century elections in Pennsylvania before reviewing the state's social, economic, and political environments and how they have been altered during the past one hundred years. As might be expected, all aspects of life in Pennsylvania were dramatically transformed during the twentieth century. In many respects,

Pennsylvania reached its political and industrial apogee in 1900. While the state is still a force politically and economically, it has declined in both areas according to a number of key indicators.

The Social Setting

As Pennsylvanians ushered in the twentieth century, they were filled with hope and optimism. According to the Philadelphia *North American,* it was "the beginning of a greater era to come." In the Philadelphia *Public Ledger,* George Childs wrote: "This is the century of freedom. Political, industrial, and intellectual swaddling clothes have been torn from man, and the individual stands forth, feeling that he is somewhat conscious of his power and stimulated by the knowledge that the door of opportunity stands wide open" (Beers 1980, 15). Surveying the social and economic situation in Pennsylvania at the time, one saw few reasons to be dissuaded from such a sanguine point of view.

Population

Pennsylvania was the second-largest state in 1900, with 6,302,115 inhabitants; the population had increased to 12,281,054 people by 2000, ranking Pennsylvania fifth among the states. At the turn of the century, Philadelphia was the nation's third-largest city, with a population of 1,293,697; Pittsburgh was the seventh-largest city, with a population of 452,000. By 2000, Philadelphia totaled 1,517,550 residents and Pittsburgh 389,879, ranking them fifth and fifty-second. Both Philadelphia (2,071,605) and Pittsburgh (676,806) recorded their largest populations in the 1950 census. Over the course of the century, Philadelphia's population increased by 23 percent while Pittsburgh's declined by 18 percent. The state's two major cities housed 28 percent of the state's population in 1900, compared with 15 percent in 2000. Thus, while their political importance remains crucial, especially for Democratic candidates, their relative importance has been lessened somewhat.

The last fifty years have seen Philadelphia and Pittsburgh suffer significant population losses. Mirroring the trend nationwide, residents have fled the cities for the surrounding suburbs. This has resulted in dramatic rates of growth in many suburban areas within the Philadelphia and Pittsburgh metropolitan areas, especially the former. However, not all growth, especially in recent years, occurred in the Philadelphia and Pittsburgh metropolitan areas. Indeed, the highest rates of growth between 1990 and 2000 were in Pike (65.6 percent), Monroe (44.9 percent), and Wayne (19.5 percent) Counties, located in the northeast corner of the state on the New York border.

In 1900, the two metropolitan areas accounted for 47 percent of the state's population; by 2000, this had increased to 51 percent. Further evidence of the higher rates of population growth in the suburban areas is provided by a comparison of the growth rates for Philadelphia and Allegheny Counties and the remaining counties in the two metropolitan areas. The rate of population growth over the course of the century was 17 percent for Philadelphia County and 65 percent for Allegheny County; the rates of growth for the other counties in the two metropolitan areas were 82 percent and 125 percent. By the end of the century, suburban residents in the two major metropolitan areas had become powerful blocks of voters in both national and state elections.

Over the course of the twentieth century, the state became increasingly more urbanized. Fifty-five percent of the population lived in urban places in 1900, compared with 77 percent in 2000. Older citizens have also become a more significant portion of the population. Currently, 16 percent of the population is sixty-five or older. Only Florida has a larger proportion of senior citizens in its population.

Ethnicity

Population diversity has long been one of the state's distinguishing characteristics. In 1900, 16 percent of Pennsylvania's population was foreign born; the figure was 4 percent at the end of the century. What has changed has been the countries of origin and the exact ethnic mix. From 1790 to 1840 the overwhelming majority of immigrants came from Great Britain and Ireland. Until 1840, the three predominant ethnic groups were the English, the Germans, and the Scotch-Irish. The volume of immigrants settling in the state increased dramatically around 1840. During the next fifty years, the Irish constituted the major immigrant group, followed by the Germans. By 1890, the Irish were the largest foreign-born group, slightly edging out the Germans (Dunaway 1948, 527–30).

After 1890 the face of immigration changed, with immigrants from northern Europe being supplanted by groups from southern and eastern Europe. The predominant elements in the new wave of immigration were the Italians, the Poles, the Czechs, the Russians, and the Austrians. Members of these newer groups settled in the coal regions and the major urban centers, seeking employment in the mines, knitting mills, and factories (Klein and Hoogenboom 1973, 317). As the immigrants dispersed throughout the state, ethnic enclaves were created:

> In 1920 natives of Russia were the largest immigrant group in Philadelphia, with Irish and Italians vying for second place; Poles the largest group in Allegheny, Luzerne, Lackawanna, and Schuylkill Counties and in the cities of Wilkes-Barre and Chester; Italians in Washington, Fayette, and Montgomery Counties and in the city of Scranton; natives of Austria in Westmoreland and Cambria Counties and in Johnstown; Hungarians in Northampton County and the cities of Bethlehem and McKeesport; Irish in Delaware County; Yugoslavians in Beaver County; and Germans in Erie County and in the cities of Pittsburgh and Erie. Italians and Germans very nearly shared the lead with Poles in Allegheny County. Almost half the 30,000 Lithuanians in Pennsylvania located in Schuylkill and Luzerne Counties; Czechoslovakians were second and third in Washington and Fayette Counties, respectively, while Welshmen were second to the Poles in Wilkes-Barre. (Klein and Hoogenboom 1973, 317)

Among contemporary Pennsylvanians, German is the predominant ancestry. More than six million residents of the state trace their ancestry back to Germany. The second most common ancestral home is Ireland, claimed by nearly two million inhabitants. The next group is the Italians (1.4 million), followed by the English (966,373), Polish (824,146), Hispanic (394,088), Slovak groups (243,009), and Scotch-Irish (218,173) (U.S. Bureau of the Census 2001).

Race

Three percent of the state's population was African American in 1900; that percentage had more than tripled to 10 percent by 2000. African Americans have never been evenly distributed throughout the state. A disproportionate share of the African American population has always lived in Philadelphia (see Table 1.1). Philadelphia's percentage has never dipped below 40 percent, and for the past fifty years it has been approximately

Table 1.1 Philadelphia's black population as a percentage of state total

Census	Philadelphia's percentage
1900	39.9
1910	43.6
1920	49.3
1930	50.9
1940	53.4
1950	57.2
1960	62.2
1970	64.3
1980	61.1
1990	58.0
2000	53.5

SOURCE: Figures calculated by the author from data for each census from 1900 to 2000 in U.S. Bureau of the Census, *Census of Population, Pennsylvania, General Population Characteristics* (Washington, D.C.: U.S. Government Printing Office).

60 percent. Sixty-seven percent of Pennsylvania's African American population currently resides in either Philadelphia or Allegheny Counties. Moreover, 77 percent of all Pennsylvania's African American population lives in only six counties (Allegheny, Chester, Dauphin, Delaware, Montgomery, and Philadelphia).

Religion

Religious diversity has always been a Pennsylvania hallmark. The Charter of Privileges in 1701 "gave as impregnable a guarantee of religious liberty as has ever been written" (Klein and Hoogenboom 1973, 228). The waves of immigration that fostered population diversity likewise gave rise to religious diversity. Since the founding of the colony, Lutherans and Presbyterians have had a strong presence in Pennsylvania. Other denominations had their numbers enhanced by groups arriving later. By 1870, Methodists had become a major Protestant denomination. Since 1832, the Roman Catholic Church has been the fastest growing denomination in the state. The Catholic population was swelled by immigrants from Ireland, Italy, and the Austro-Hungarian Empire. After 1890 immigrants from eastern and southeastern Europe established the Greek Orthodox and the Russian Orthodox Churches (Dunaway 1948, 631).

Pennsylvanians continue to be a religious people. It is estimated that 64 percent of the population adheres to a religious faith. This places Pennsylvania among the top ten states in terms of religious worshippers (*Pennsylvania Manual* 2001, 1–31). The Roman Catholic Church is by far the state's largest religious denomination; its 3.9 million members represents 32 percent of the state's population. With more than 750,000 members each, the two largest Protestant denominations are the Lutherans and the United Methodists. Presbyterians number approximately 500,000. Three other Protestant denominations—the United Church of Christ, the Episcopal Church, and the American Baptists—each have more than 100,000 members (*Pennsylvania Manual* 2001, 1–31).

The predominantly African American denominations include the African Methodist Episcopal and A.M.E. Zion Churches and two National Baptist Conventions. There are also a sizable number of smaller Protestant denominations, including Pentacostals, the Assemblies of God, the Christian Scientists, the Mormons, Seventh-Day Adventists, Jehovah's Witnesses, Disciples of Christ, the Church of the Brethren, the Nazarene Church, the Evangelical Congregational, and the Church of God (*Pennsylvania Manual* 2001, 1–31).

While there are no reliable estimates of membership in the twenty-one Eastern Orthodox churches, one source estimates that membership in the Greek Orthodox Church is only slightly less than that of the Presbyterians. This would make it the fifth-largest denomination in the state (Bradley et al. 1992). There are about 63,000 Orthodox, Reconstructionist, Conservative, and Reform Jews. The secular Jewish population is estimated to be 347,000. The Quakers had only 13,174 adherents in 1980. The Mennonites and the Amish, who gave rise to the term "Pennsylvania Dutch," have seen their numbers significantly diminished and are struggling to preserve their traditional ways in a rapidly changing society (*Pennsylvania Manual* 2001, 1–31).

Income

Pennsylvania has been a reasonably wealthy state for the past century. In 1929, the state ranked thirteenth in income, with a per capita average of $775. By 2002, that figure had increased to $31,663, while the state's rank had slipped slightly to fifteenth. At present, six of the ten wealthiest counties fan out northward from Philadelphia. Four of these counties (Bucks, Delaware, Montgomery, and Chester) are Philadelphia suburbs, while the other two (Lehigh and Berks) are immediately to the north of those suburbs. Most of the poorest counties are in the center of the state.

Eleven percent of Pennsylvanians lived below the poverty level at the end of the century. There are significant variations by gender, race, and age. For females, the rate is 13 percent; for males, 9 percent. Hispanics have the highest rate (36 percent), followed by African Americans (29 percent), Asian and Pacific Islanders (19 percent), and whites (9 percent) (Kennedy 1999, 24).

For children under eighteen, the poverty rate is 14 percent. However, 45 percent of African American children from birth to age four live in poverty, as do 51 percent of Hispanic children (Kennedy 1999, 24). For citizens age eighteen and older, the figure is 10 percent; for those sixty-five and older, the rate is 9 percent (U.S. Bureau of the Census 2001).

The Economic Setting

Coal and Coke

Pennsylvania has been one of the leading coal-producing states for more than 150 years. For much of that time, Pennsylvania led the nation in the production of coal. The anthracite region covers approximately 480 square miles in the northeastern part of the state. The area encompasses eleven counties, with Luzerne County accounting for the most production. The bituminous coal area blankets 15,880 acres in the western part of the state. Coal deposits are found in every county west of the Allegheny Mountains and in several areas east of the mountains. Coal is mined in twenty-five of the counties in this vast area (Dunaway 1948, 612–20).

Anthracite production totaled 51,221,353 tons in 1900, while bituminous production was 79,318,362 tons. The combined anthracite and bituminous production represented 57 percent of the nation's total coal production. Since then, production has declined precipitously. In 1999, 73.4 million tons of bituminous coal and 5.6 tons of anthracite coal were mined in the state (*Pennsylvania Statistical Abstract* 2001, 260). Only 6 percent of the national coal output currently originates in Pennsylvania. The state now ranks fourth in production, trailing Wyoming, West Virginia, and Kentucky. In fact, Wyoming's production is more than four times that of Pennsylvania. Between 1970 and 1995, national production increased 71 percent, while production in Pennsylvania declined by 22 percent

(*Pennsylvania Manual* 2001, 1–28). The tremendous decline in production has had a deleterious effect on employment in the industry. At the turn of the century, three of five coal miners in the country worked in Pennsylvania mines. In 1960, the industry had more than 52,000 employees; that figure had declined to 9,500 by 1996 (*Pennsylvania Statistical Abstract* 1999, 259).

Anthracite had been used to smelt iron since the 1840s, but by the 1880s coke made of bituminous coal had supplanted it. The commercial production of coke was begun in 1841 in the Connellsville coke district in Westmoreland and Fayette Counties. Seventy percent of the national output was manufactured in Pennsylvania in 1907. By 2000, the state accounted for only 6 percent of the nation's coal and coke production (*Pennsylvania Manual* 2001, 1–28).

Steel

Pennsylvania has been synonymous with the steel industry for more than a century. In 1900, 60 percent of the nation's steel was fabricated in Pennsylvania. It is estimated that the Carnegie Steel Corporation produced between 25 and 30 percent of the nation's steel, including 50 percent of the structural steel and armor plate, and 30 percent of the rails fabricated in the country (Klein and Hoogenboom 1973, 307). Carnegie sold his company in 1901 to the United States Steel Corporation, organized by J. P. Morgan. The steel industry was concentrated primarily in the western part of the state, but there were also important centers in Bethlehem, Harrisburg, Lewistown, Carlisle, and Morrisville.

During the past four decades, the steel industry in Pennsylvania has been devastated. Bethlehem Steel closed its doors during the 1990s. Pennsylvania's share of total production has plummeted to 7 percent, although the state still leads the nation in specialty steel production (*Pennsylvania Manual* 2001, 1–27).

Agriculture

Agriculture has always been an integral part of Pennsylvania's economy. The twentieth century witnessed dramatic changes within the agricultural sector. At the beginning of the century, there were 224,000 farms in the state, a number that had diminished to 58,209 by 2002. The farm population declined from 1,183,000 to 117,119. Total farm land was more than halved, decreasing from 19,371,000 acres to 7,700,000 acres. The average farm size went from 86 acres to 133 acres; the disappearance of a significant number of small family farms has actually increased the size of the average farm. The total value of farm products was $10 million in 1925; by 2002, the figure was $4.3 billion. Of the latter amount, $1.3 billion came from crops and $2.9 billion came from livestock (*Pennsylvania Statistical Abstract* 1902; 2004). The state ranks nineteenth in total farm income.

The state's farmers produce an impressive variety of crops. Cereals and livestock were the mainstays of the original settlers. In 1902, the state ranked third in the production of potatoes, and sixth in hay and wool. Currently, Pennsylvania ranks in the top ten in such varied crops as milk, poultry, eggs, ice cream, pears, apples, grapes, cherries, sweet corn, potatoes, mushrooms, tomatoes, cheese, maple syrup, cabbage, snap beans, Christmas trees and floriculture crops, pretzels, potato chips, sausage, wheat flour, and bakery products. In livestock, the state ranks fourth in cows, fifteenth in hogs and pigs, and seventeenth in total cattle (*Pennsylvania Manual* 2001, 1–29). The top commodities, in order of marketing receipts are dairy products, cattle, mushrooms, and greenhouse (*Almanac of the 50 States* 2004, 313).

Manufacturing

A century ago, Pennsylvania was a leader in a vast and varied array of industries. It led the nation in the manufacturing of textiles and clothing, especially worsteds and silks. The state produced half the nation's natural gas and was also the leader in the tanning of leather, tinmaking, ice cream, and chocolate. In addition, Pennsylvania manufactured half the steam locomotives built in 1900, was second in the production of metalworking and pumping machinery, was second in the printing and publishing industry, was third in automobile production, and was fourth in lumbering (Beers 1980, 15–17; Klein and Hoogenboom 1973, 343–45).

The state's economy has been dramatically transformed, especially during the past three decades. The reversals in the coal and steel industries have already been documented. Serious job losses have also been sustained by clothing manufacturers and knitting mills. More than 600,000 manufacturing jobs have been lost in Pennsylvania since 1970. Approximately 30 percent of the state's workers were employed in manufacturing jobs in 1970; by 2000, that figure was 16 percent.

Offsetting the loss of manufacturing jobs has been the creation of jobs in the service sector. Service industries are now the state's leading employer, accounting for 34 percent of the state's workforce. Within this sector, the biggest gains have been in the medical and health-related fields, including hospitals, nursing homes and personal care facilities, and residential and home health-care services (Kennedy 1999, 16). The wholesale and retail trade sector is now the state's second leading employer (22 percent).

Pennsylvania has also become one of the leading technology states. The American Electronic Association ranked Pennsylvania eighth in their 2002 Cyberstates update. The state currently employs nearly 194,000 high-tech workers and has added almost 40,000 high-tech jobs since 1995. Pennsylvania's high-tech exports amounted to $3.8 billion in 2001, accounting for 22 percent of the state's exports. Pennsylvania ranked twelfth among the states and is home to nine thousand high-tech establishments. Among the states, it is currently fourth in consumer electronics manufacturing employment, fifth in industrial electronics manufacturing employment, and ninth in total high-tech employment. In addition, Pennsylvania has the largest concentration of tissue engineering firms in the nation (American Electronic Association 2002).

The transformation of the state's economy has had a notable impact on many workers. The lost manufacturing jobs paid significantly higher wages than the service sector jobs that replaced them. Unskilled and semi-skilled workers who previously could secure well-paying manufacturing jobs must now compete for low-paying service jobs. Numbers of workers have also lost their jobs as industries have closed down or moved to other, often southern, states. Some of these workers were given the option of relocating when the industry moved; others simply found themselves facing unemployment. In addition to having to adjust to jobs that pay less, many of these workers also face the prospect of retraining to acquire the skills required in the newer jobs. The past twenty years has been a difficult period for many Pennsylvanians.

In addition to the industries previously discussed, there are several others that are important contributors to the contemporary economy. The state is a leader in the cement industry, producing more than 10 percent of the national total. Also notable is the production and distribution of chemicals and electrical machinery and equipment.

In 1900, the state's annual gross product was $7.2 billion, which was about 10 percent of the national total. By 2002, that figure had escalated to $408.0 billion. However, Pennsylvania now accounts for only 4 percent of the national total.

The Political Setting

At the beginning of the twentieth century, the GOP had a virtual stranglehold on the Pennsylvania political system. Republicans could be found in the governor's office, all other statewide offices, and most mayor's offices. The GOP had a 164 to 84 advantage in the General Assembly and dominated the congressional delegation 26 to 4 and controlled forty-two of the sixty-seven counties. The Democrats' fortunes would not soon improve. Between 1900 and 1932, only two of sixty-three Democratic candidates running statewide were victorious. As late as 1925, the Republicans controlled fifty-eight counties. The Democrats took control of Pittsburgh in 1933; the Republicans had dominated the city for sixty-six of the previous eighty years. The Democrats did not wrest control of Philadelphia until 1951, ending eighty-one consecutive years of GOP dominance.

Since the late 1950s, Pennsylvania has become a two-party state. After the 1998 elections, the Republicans had a 30–20 advantage in the state Senate and a 103–100 edge in the state House. Within the congressional delegation, eleven seats were held by Republicans and ten by Democrats. The Democrats had a 400,000 plurality among registered voters; however, the GOP still controlled forty-seven of the sixty-seven counties.

The Republican Political Machine

Between 1867 and 1921, the Republican Party in Pennsylvania operated the most efficient statewide machine in America. The machine was presided over, in turn, by Simon Cameron, Matthew Quay, and Boies Penrose. The organization put together by Cameron was an alliance of municipal and county machines, each concerned with its own particular interests (Evans 1966, 13). Occasionally, the local leaders defied the state leadership. Rural leaders tended to be more loyal to the statewide machine than their urban counterparts were (Klein and Hoogenboom 1973, 361). The key local organizations were the Republican machines in Philadelphia and Pittsburgh. The Cameron-Quay-Penrose machine controlled statewide nominations and elections for federal, state, and municipal offices. During much of this era, the machine was abetted by a fragmented Democratic Party with a penchant for taking the wrong side on many of the significant issues of the day.

During the reigns of Quay and Penrose, the machine was even able to control Democratic nominations. In many parts of the state the Republican machine would offer Democratic leaders money and a few jobs in return for their quiescence. Even in Philadelphia in the early 1930s this was still the case. The Democratic city chairman, John O'Donnell, desisted from battling the GOP machine headed by William S. Vare for control of the city in return for a few patronage positions. In return for the Democrats' tepid efforts to mobilize their voters, Vare would register enough of his own men as Democrats to ensure that O'Donnell would receive enough votes in the primary to retain his position. Moreover, when the Democratic City Committee met to select its slate of candidates they would wait for a messenger from Vare to arrive with a list of names he wanted chosen, then ratify it. Vare even paid the rent for the Democratic Party headquarters (Keller 1960, 103–5).

Further illustrating the pathetic plight of the Democrats, in 1930 Lawrence H. Rupp, the Democratic candidate for governor, withdrew from the campaign to focus on becoming the Grand Exalted Ruler of the Elks (Klein and Hoogenboom 1973, 455).

Simon Cameron, Lincoln's first secretary of war, founded the Republican dynasty that ruled Pennsylvania for the next half century. The wealthy businessman, who originally entered politics as a Democrat when that party controlled the state, began his reign as boss in 1867, one year after having been elected to the U.S. Senate for a second time. At the peak of his power in 1877, Cameron resigned his Senate seat so that his son Donald could be elected in his place.

Donald Cameron thus became the titular head of the Republican Party in 1877. The real leader of the party, however, was Matthew Quay. Quay had been a trusted lieutenant of the elder Cameron. Quay had served with distinction during the Civil War and had been military secretary for Governor Andrew Gregg Curtin. Entering politics after the war, he had served in the state House, as secretary of the commonwealth under two governors, as chairman of the Republican state committee, and as state treasurer. He was elected to the U.S. Senate in 1887. He was chosen as the Republican national chairman in 1888 and directed the presidential campaign of Benjamin Harrison. He was primarily responsible for Harrison's victory. For the next two decades, Quay was not only the boss of the Pennsylvania party, but also a force in national Republican politics (Dunaway 1948, 456–78).

The magnitude of Quay's power was made manifest during his attempt to win reelection to the Senate, beginning in 1899. The People's Bank of Philadelphia, which had long been a depository for state funds, failed in

1898. It was revealed that its cashier and Quay had been speculating with state monies; in fact, Quay, not the state, had been receiving the interest on the state's accounts. He was arrested and indicted on charges of misappropriation of state funds. When the state legislature met in January 1899 to select a senator, Quay was still on trial. The legislators finally adjourned on April 20, after failing to elect a senator after sixty-six ballots (Klein and Hoogenboom 1973, 365).

The following day a jury acquitted Quay, and within an hour Governor William A. Stone, Quay's man in the statehouse, appointed him to fill the unexpired Senate term. Quay's opponents carried their fight to the Senate, and, that body refused to seat him by a vote of 33 to 31. Quay returned to the state determined to help elect a more sympathetic legislature. When the next session of the General Assembly convened in January 1901, however, his opponents still commanded a majority. Nonetheless, Quay was able to engineer his election "by bribing two Democrats of easy virtue." He retained control of the machine until his death three years later (Dunaway 1948, 468–69).

Boies Penrose became the leader of the Cameron-Quay machine upon the death of Matthew Quay in 1904. He was a bright young man who graduated with honors from Harvard. After briefly practicing law, he was elected to the state House at age twenty-four. At twenty-six, he became the youngest state senator, and at twenty-nine the youngest president pro tempore of the state Senate. In 1897, at age thirty-six, he was elected to the U.S. Senate, succeeding Donald Cameron. He held that position for the next twenty-four years, directing political affairs in Pennsylvania and looking after the state's interests.

Penrose perpetuated the machine practices initiated by his predecessors. He was, however, more systematic than Cameron and Quay had been. He preached to local party officials the necessity of electing politicians who would be loyal to the machine (Klein and Hoogenboom 1973, 414). Penrose died on New Year's Eve in 1921. Because he had not trained a successor, his death marked the end of the organization begun more than fifty years earlier by Simon Cameron.

The General Assembly

Under the provisions of the Constitution of 1874, the Pennsylvania legislature in 1900 consisted of a Senate of 50 members and a House of 204 members. One-half of the senators were elected every even year, along with all of the representatives. Senators served four-year terms; representatives served two-year terms. The General Assembly met once every two years, convening on the first Tuesday in January of every odd year.

The apportionment provisions detailed in the constitution bore little resemblance to the contemporary standard of "one person, one vote." For representation in the Senate, the state was to be divided into fifty districts of compact and contiguous territory, with each district electing one senator. The ratio of senatorial representation was determined by dividing the state's population by fifty. Each county was awarded a number of districts equal to its number of ratios, with an additional district for a surplus exceeding three-fifths of a ratio. Under this arrangement, Philadelphia County had eight districts, and Allegheny County had four. Some districts covered two or three counties; no county could constitute a separate district unless its population was equal to three-fourths of a ratio, except that in cases where the adjacent counties were entitled to constitute separate districts a county could have a senator if its population exceeded one-half of a ratio.

The ratio for the House was the population of the state divided by two hundred. Every county containing fewer than five ratios was entitled to one representative for every full ratio, and an additional representative when the surplus exceeded one-half of a ratio; each county was entitled to at least one representative. Every county that had more than five ratios was entitled to a representative for every full ratio. Every city that had a population equal to a ratio separately elected its share of the representatives allotted to the county in which it was situated. Every city entitled to more than four representatives, and every county with a population greater than 100,000, was to be divided into districts, with each district electing its proportion of the representatives according to its population, but no district was allowed to have more than four representatives. Under these guidelines, Philadelphia had thirty-nine representatives.

The use of multimember districts persisted until the 1966 election; they were eliminated by that year's reapportionment plan. The number of multimember districts and the number of House members elected from such districts varied during the twentieth century (see Table 1.2). Fifty-three representatives were elected from multimember districts in 1900, while ninety-three were elected in 1964, the last election before their elimination. As the century progressed, the percentage of representatives elected from multimember districts increased.

Table 1.2 Number of multimember districts and number of representatives elected from multimember districts, selected years

	Magnitude of District				
Year	Two members	Three members	Four members	Total	Total as a percentage of the Pennsylvania House
1900	17	5	1	53	26%
1920	37	11	2	115	55%
1964	29	5	5	93	44%

SOURCE: Figures calculated by the author from data in *The Pennsylvania Manual*, selected volumes.

The strict partisanship of earlier generations of voters, coupled with multimember districts, made it virtually impossible for the minority party to capture any seats in these districts. In his classic study *Party and Representation,* Frank Sorauf (1963, 27) reported that there were split results in one district in 1954, no districts in 1956, and three districts in 1958. The present data confirm that this was the case going back to 1900. In fact, this pattern can be expanded to include all counties electing more than one representative. Rarely did the vote totals among the majority party candidates vary by more than a few dozen votes, if that many. Not only did the majority party dominate multimember districts, but also they dominated entire counties in elections for members of the House. For most of the past century, as we will see, strict partisanship prevailed among Pennsylvania voters, especially in legislative elections.

Significant malapportionment existed in the General Assembly at the turn of the century. Some of the problem, of course, could be attributed to partisan politics. But some of it was due to the constitutional provisions just discussed. According to the constitution, no city or county could have more than one-sixth (16.7 percent) of the total number of senators. This resulted in Philadelphia and Allegheny Counties being underrepresented. Philadelphia County had 20.5 percent of the state's population but with eight senators, only 16 percent of the Senate; Allegheny County was home to 12.3 percent of the state's residents, but it had only four senators (8.0 percent). In a well-apportioned legislature, Philadelphia County would have had ten senators, and Allegheny County six.

The level of malapportionment was dramatically worse in the House. In 1900, the ratio for the House was 30,893. The districts ranged in population from 7,048 to 59,113. The median district contained 25,172 individuals.

Table 1.3 Percentage urban of the forty-seven counties with populations less than the House ratio, 1900

	Percentage urban					
	0–9%	10–19%	20–29%	30–39%	40–49%	50%+
Number of counties	13	9	11	6	3	5

SOURCE: Figures calculated by the author from data in U.S. Bureau of the Census, *1900 Census of Population, Pennsylvania, General Population Characteristics* (Washington, D.C.: U.S. Government Printing Office, 1900), 41–42.

The fact that the largest district had more than eight times the population of the smallest district broadly suggests that a problem existed with regard to apportionment. A more detailed analysis reveals the magnitude of the problem.

Forty-seven counties had populations that fell below the ratio, yet the constitution guaranteed each of them a representative. This requirement precipitated a large degree of malapportionment. As was the case in other states prior to the involvement of the U.S. Supreme Court in the 1960s, malapportionment in Pennsylvania advantaged rural areas and disadvantaged urban areas. Table 1.3 shows clearly the rural nature of the forty-seven counties with populations below the ratio. Thirty-three of the forty-seven were less than 30 percent urban; a total of sixty representatives (29 percent) were elected from these counties. Only five counties in this group were more than 50 percent urban.

The other major source of malapportionment was introduced by the constitutional stipulation that counties with populations that exceeded the five-ratio mark would only receive representatives for every full ratio. Eight counties were in this category (Allegheny, Philadelphia, Luzerne, Lackawanna, Schuylkill, Lancaster, Berks, and Westmoreland). Philadelphia, Lackawanna, and Allegheny Counties were the three most urbanized in the state; they held 36 percent of Pennsylvania's population. Collectively, these eight counties had 50.3 percent of the state's population, but only 42.2 percent of the House seats. Early in the century, the Pennsylvania legislature was severely malapportioned. Rural counties were the big winners, and urban counties were the big losers. That problem would not be alleviated until the reapportionment of 1966.

Under the Constitution of 1968, the General Assembly became a two-year, continuously meeting body and the membership of the House was fixed at 203. Thus, the current legislature meets annually, and consists of

50 senators and 203 representatives. The four-year terms for senators and two-year terms for representatives have remained consistent over the course of the century.

The Executive Branch

At the beginning of the century, voters elected the governor, lieutenant governor, auditor general, treasurer, and secretary of internal affairs separately, and the governor appointed the attorney general. Both the governor and lieutenant governor were elected for four-year terms and could not succeed themselves. The treasurer was elected for a two-year term, and the auditor general a three-year term; they also were prohibited from serving consecutive terms. The secretary of internal affairs was elected for a term of four years, with no prohibition on reelection.

Beginning with the 1912 election, the terms of the treasurer and auditor general were extended to four years. The secretary of internal affairs was last elected in 1966, and the department was broken up in 1968. The attorney general became an elected official beginning with the 1980 election. The governor and lieutenant governor were last elected separately in 1966; beginning with the 1970 election, they were elected as a team in the general election. However, there still are separate primaries for the two offices.

By the end of the century, Pennsylvania general election voters were electing a governor–lieutenant governor ticket, an attorney general, an auditor general, and a treasurer. All serve four-year terms. The Constitution of 1968 makes all of these officials eligible for one successive reelection.

Nominations

Both the direct primary and convention were used to nominate candidates early in the twentieth century. The genesis of the direct primary was the caucus. The caucus was the original method of nominating candidates in this country. At the local level it consisted of party leaders, who met in a tavern or home and constructed the local slate of candidates. At the state level a legislative caucus, consisting of all the legislators from a particular party, would meet and select the party's candidates for the statewide offices. Gradually, the caucus was transformed into an irregular meeting of party members, and then into a regularly scheduled meeting called by party leaders. These meetings were only held at the local level and came to be known as primaries—so-called because they were the first step in the election process. They were used to nominate candidates for local offices, and, later, to nominate delegates to higher-level conventions (Tanger, Alderfer, and McGeary 1950, 22).

The Democratic Party of Crawford County, Pennsylvania, held the first direct primary in 1842; they were joined by the Crawford County Republicans in 1860 (Crotty 1977, 203). In fact, a century ago, at least in Pennsylvania, the direct primary was referred to as the Crawford County System. The direct primary spread from Crawford County to other Pennsylvania counties and westward to Ohio and other states. The primary was first recognized by the Pennsylvania legislature in 1871 when it passed regulations for the primary in Lancaster County. The legislation provided that the primary could be adopted by party officials or members, but once adopted, it became binding. The first statewide primary law was adopted in 1881. It prohibited fraudulent practices on the part of election officials. These initial laws applied to primaries in general, not direct primaries specifically (Tanger, Alderfer, and McGeary 1950, 24–25).

In 1900, local voters met in precincts to hold primary elections. The voters nominated local candidates and elected delegates to the county convention. County officers were nominated either by the direct primary or by a county convention. At the state level, a convention was used. The convention elected the state committee, which consisted of a representative from each county; in reality, however, each county delegation selected its own representative. The convention also adopted a state party platform. Finally, the convention nominated candidates for the statewide offices (Hinsdale and Hinsdale 1899, 234–35).

According to the Ballot Reform Act of 1892:

> Any convention of delegates or primary meeting of electors or caucus held under the rules of a political party or any board authorized to certify nominations representing a political party, which at the election next preceding polled at least two per cent of the largest entire vote for any office cast in the State, or in the electoral district, or division thereof, for which such primary meeting, caucus, convention, or board desires to make or certify nominations, may nominate one candidate for each office which is to be filled in the State, or in the said district or division, at the

next ensuing election by causing a certificate of nomination to be drawn up and filed as hereinafter provided. (Hinsdale and Hinsdale 1899, 235–36)

The statute also provided for the nomination of candidates by circulating nominating petitions.

Pennsylvania adopted a mandatory, statewide direct primary law in 1913. From the beginning, the state has employed a closed primary. Originally, voters had to tell election officials what party they planned to vote with. The law did away with all meetings of political parties to nominate candidates. However, local parties continued to hold caucuses to reduce the number of candidates and to select the candidates whom they wanted to support.

As the century began, the constitution provided for two election days. Local officials were elected on the third Tuesday in February; county officials, officials elected by districts (judges and legislators), statewide officials, and national officials were chosen on the first Tuesday after the first Monday in November. Shortly thereafter, the dates were altered. The general election was held on the first Tuesday after the first Monday in November in even-numbered years; on this date, state and national officials were selected. The municipal election was held on the first Tuesday after the first Monday in odd-numbered years; at this time, local officials, including local judges, were elected. The primary schedule was also modified. The spring primary was held on the second Saturday in April, in even years, to select candidates for the general election. The fall primary was held on the last Saturday in September, in odd-numbered years, to chose candidates for the municipal election.

Today, all candidates are nominated in a direct primary, held on the third Tuesday in May, except in presidential election years when it is held on the third Tuesday in April. A general election (there is no longer an election specifically titled the municipal election) is held every November. State and national officials are elected in a general election in even-numbered years, local officials in a general election in odd-numbered years.

Pennsylvania continues to have strong parties that play a significant role in the nomination process. Legislative candidates frequently report that party leaders recruited them to run for office (Kennedy 1999). Both major party organizations endorse legislative and statewide candidates. Endorsed candidates benefit from reduced competition, organizational campaign assistance, and better access to funding. Increasingly, much of the assistance is being provided by the parties' legislative campaign committees. Owing to such advantages, endorsed candidates typically win.

Qualifications for Voting

At the beginning of the twentieth century, suffrage was available to all male citizens of at least twenty-one years of age. Extensive residency requirements also existed. Prospective voters had to have been citizens of the United States for at least one month, and residents of Pennsylvania for at least one year preceding the date of the election; however, if the individual had previously been a qualified voter or native-born citizen of the state and had moved from the state and then returned, the residency requirement was reduced to six months. In addition, he must have resided in his voting district for at least two months preceding the election.

If the prospective voter was twenty-two or older, he must have paid a state or county tax not more than two years nor less than one month before the election. If the person was between the ages of twenty-one and twenty-two, he could "vote on age" without previously having paid taxes.

Pennsylvania's male voters had twice defeated a statewide referendum on women's suffrage, in 1889 and 1915. Women had been allowed to run for seats on school boards (but not for any other offices) since 1874, but they had not been allowed to vote. Women nationally were granted the right to vote by the Nineteenth Amendment, ratified in August 1920. In Pennsylvania and some other states, the provisions of the amendment were not implemented in time to allow women to vote in the 1920 election. Thus, the first election in which Pennsylvania women participated was in 1922.

The last major group to be admitted to the electorate was young voters. The Voting Rights Act of 1970 had granted individuals between the ages of eighteen and twenty-one the right to vote in all elections. In *Oregon v. Mitchell* (1970), The U.S. Supreme Court ruled that Congress had the power to grant the right to vote in national elections, but not state elections. The Twenty-Sixth Amendment, ratified in 1971, granted all citizens eighteen years of age and older the right to vote in all elections. This group of voters participated for the first time in Pennsylvania in the 1972 election.

Today, Pennsylvania has only a thirty-day state residency requirement. Citizens who are at least eighteen and satisfy the residency requirement are eligible to vote.

Voter Registration

The first registration law in Pennsylvania was passed in 1836. It directed the assessors in Philadelphia to compile lists of registered voters (Tanger and Alderfer 1939, 38–39). The Registry Act of 1869 gave the Republican machine complete control over registration in Philadelphia. This legislation gave the machine-dominated Board of Alderman the power to appoint election officials who, in turn, revised and certified the lists of qualified voters prepared by the assessors. By mere challenge, these officials could exclude any name from the list of registered voters. The burden of proof rested with the individual being challenged. Reinstatement by a court order was possible, but the legal process was lengthy and expensive, and reinstatement rarely occurred before the election (Evans 1966, 76). The Registry Act of 1869 was voided by a requirement in the Constitution of 1874 that all registration and election laws be uniform throughout the state. This provision was enacted into law by the Uniform Elections Act of 1874.

Under this law it was the responsibility of the township or ward property assessor to compile the list of registered voters. These officials were required to visit, as soon as possible after the first Monday in May and the first Monday in December, every residence in their districts to determine how many individuals in each residence were qualified voters. Each assessor was to make up a registry list and post a copy of this list on the door of the polling place. At stated hours, each assessor was to be at his home to hear complaints and make corrections. The completed, revised lists were then given to the county commissioners. The commissioners put the lists into alphabetical order and gave two copies to each of the election boards. One of the lists was called the ballot check list and was used to check off the names of the voters as they received their ballots; the second list, called the voting check list, was used to check off the names of the voters as they voted (Hinsdale and Hinsdale 1899, 229).

During this time, fraud was a constant problem. The names of dead people regularly appeared on registration lists (including some of the founding fathers). A citizens committee in Philadelphia in 1904 estimated that between fifty and eighty thousand fraudulent names appeared on the assessors' lists (Beers 1980, 35). Repeat voting was also a frequent occurrence. To attempt to curb these problems, personal registration was prescribed for first- and second-class cities in 1906, and third-class cities in 1911.

Legislation passed in 1937 established a statewide system of personal, permanent registration. According to the law, voters were to appear personally before registration commissions on designated dates prior to the 1937 fall primary. Even if an individual had been a registered voter, he or she had to appear in person or lose the right to vote. Assessors were no longer going to visit individual residences. In third-class cities, boroughs, towns, and townships, the county commissioners were designated as the registration commission. In Philadelphia, Pittsburgh, and Scranton, registration commissions were appointed by the governor (Tanger and Alderfer 1939, 39).

The basic registration lists were derived from these personal appearances before the commissions. Names would be added to the lists as others became eligible to vote; names would be deleted if people died, moved, or failed to vote for a certain number of years. Voters were required to declare a partisan affiliation or register as an independent. Registration was permanent as long as voters did not change their partisanship, move, or fail to vote with the required frequency.

The current system of registration still requires that voters declare a partisan affiliation. But the National Voter Registration Act of 1993 has altered the process in all of the states. Voters in every state can now register by mail as well as at motor vehicle departments and other state agencies. The legislation also makes it more difficult to drop voters from the rolls because they have failed to vote within a prescribed period of time (it was two years in Pennsylvania prior to the act).

Summary

The social, economic, and political environments in Pennsylvania have all been significantly altered during the past century. The state's population is considerably larger and more urbanized. Ethnic diversity has been reduced, while racial diversity has increased. Pennsylvania continues to be characterized by religious diversity. Philadelphia and Pittsburgh remain the two major cities, and their political significance, especially for Democratic candidates, remains crucial.

The economy has been dramatically transformed. The coal and steel industries have declined precipitously. The manufacturing sector has also been hard hit; many jobs have been lost to plant closings and to industries relocating to other states. Manufacturing jobs have been replaced primarily by service jobs. The state, however, has also added a significant number of jobs in high-tech industries. Pennsylvania has become one of the leading technology states. Farm land and farming jobs have also been lost. Still, agriculture remains an important part of the state's economy.

Over the course of the twentieth century, Pennsylvania became much more competitive politically. A statewide Republican machine dominated Pennsylvania politics until the advent of the New Deal. Today, both parties are competitive at the state level. The well-apportioned state legislature of the past few decades bears little resemblance to its malapportioned turn-of-the-century ancestor. The suffrage has been notably expanded, with the addition of women and young voters. Registration and voting requirements have been altered and made more lenient.

The context within which elections take place is crucial. It influences all aspects of the electoral process. It is reasonable to assume that as it changes so too will dimensions of the electoral process. The rest of the book will be devoted to documenting how election dynamics have changed during the past century.

A CENTURY OF ELECTORS

The past one hundred years have witnessed important transformations in the Pennsylvania electorate. When the century began, the franchise was available only to males twenty-one and older. By the end of the millennium, the eligible electorate included all citizens eighteen and older. This change more than doubled the pool of potential voters. Such an alteration could be expected to have a significant impact on a political system. For one thing, millions of voters with no tradition of voting were admitted to the electorate; this could have a substantial effect on rates of turnout. It is also reasonable to assume that women and young people might view the parties and issues differently from the traditional male voters; this could have important consequences for party identification and voting behavior. Indeed, recent evidence suggests that such is the case (Niemi 1981; Flanigan and Zingale 2002; Miller and Shanks 1996).

This chapter will examine a number of issues related to registration and turnout. Included will be discussions of the levels of voter registration, of turnout, of independence among voters, and of split-ticket voting. It will become apparent that consequential changes have taken place in all these areas.

Registration

Percentage Registered

Table 2.1 displays the percentage of voting age residents who were registered to vote in presidential and gubernatorial elections from 1926 to 1998.[1] Through the 1960s, the rate was consistently between 70 and 80 percent, with the notable exceptions of 1926 and 1930. From 1970 to 1994 the percentage of registered voters began a slow, but not consistent, decline. In the late 1990s there was a notable increase in registration rates, with the percentages returning to the levels attained in earlier decades. This was due to the impact of the National Voter Registration Act of 1993, which made registration much easier. Whether the individuals who took advantage of the simplified procedures actually voted will be examined later in this chapter.

Independents

The percentage of Americans who declared themselves to be independents increased dramatically during the 1960s, especially following the 1964 presidential election (see Table 2.2). While some older voters came loose from their partisan moorings, the increase in independence was primarily attributable to younger voters; a newer generation of voters entered the electorate with weaker party ties than previous generations (Miller and Shanks 1996). Much was made of this movement away from partisanship; some even wrote of "party dealignment" (Burnham 1970; Nie, Verba, and Petrocik 1976).

Table 2.2 reports the total number of independents as well as the number of pure independents among the American electorate between 1952 and 1998. Total independents includes the pure independents plus the independents who lean toward the Republicans or Democrats. Pure independents are individuals who profess no partisan affiliation at all.

---

1. The Election Bureau in the Secretary of State's Office has registration figures dating back only to 1925.

Table 2.1 Registered voters as a percentage of the voting age population (VAP), 1926–1998

Year	Presidential elections	Gubernatorial elections	Year	Presidential elections	Gubernatorial elections
1926		63.9	1964	80.7	
1928	78.8		1966		77.7
1930		62.3	1968	78.9	
1932	69.2		1970		68.3
1934		74.1	1972	74.0	
1936	86.9		1974		68.9
1938		82.2	1976	72.4	
1940	79.0		1978		73.0
1942		72.6	1980	65.8	
1944	71.8		1982		65.2
1946		73.3	1984	70.9	
1948	70.1		1986		66.9
1950		68.1	1988	67.2	
1952	76.3		1990		62.3
1954		73.7	1992	65.9	
1956	77.5		1994		64.7
1958		77.1	1996	74.9	
1960	80.1		1998		79.8
1962		79.9			

SOURCE: Figures calculated by the author from data in *The Pennsylvania Manual* and *Statistical Abstract of the United States,* selected volumes.

Table 2.2 Independents among the American electorate, 1952–1998 (percentage)

Year	Total independents	Pure independents	Year	Total independents	Pure independents
1952	23	6	1976	37	15
1954	22	7	1978	38	14
1956	23	9	1980	34	13
1958	19	7	1982	30	11
1960	23	10	1984	34	11
1962	21	8	1986	33	12
1964	23	8	1988	36	11
1966	28	12	1990	35	11
1968	30	11	1992	39	12
1970	31	13	1994	35	10
1972	34	13	1996	34	9
1974	37	15	1998	35	10

SOURCE: Adapted by the author from National Election Study data presented in Harold W. Stanley and Richard G. Niemi, eds., *Vital Statistics on American Politics, 1999–2000* (Washington, D.C.: Congressional Quarterly Press, 2000), 112.

There was a notable increase among both types of independents between 1964 and 1974. In that span of five elections, the percentage of pure independents almost doubled. Since 1974, the total number of independents has declined slightly, while the number of pure independents has decreased by one-third. This has been accompanied by an increase in the number of partisans (Bartels 2000).

The pattern in Pennsylvania has been very different. The percentage of voters who registered with either the Republican or Democratic Party is listed in Table 2.3. A brief discussion regarding methodology is required. In earlier decades, the number of voters who registered with minor parties was detailed, as was the number of voters who registered independent or nonpartisan. In the last three decades, registration figures were given for more significant third parties (e.g., Libertarian), with the remainder listed under the heading "other parties." For the purposes of this analysis, we will consider anyone not registered as a Republican or a Democrat to be an independent.

For several reasons, this approach seems reasonable. First, in earlier decades, when a distinction was made between third-party registration and independents, the vast majority of voters who did not identify with one of the major parties were independents. For example, in 1925, of those not registered with one of the two major parties, 0.2 percent were registered with the Labor Party, 0.4 percent were registered with the Socialist Party, and 0.8 percent were registered with the Prohibition Party; 8.0 percent were registered as independents. In 1930, only 0.6 percent of the voters

Table 2.3 Republican and Democratic registration as a percentage of total registration, selected years, 1925–1998

Year	Major-party registration as a percentage of total registration
1925	90.5
1930	94.7
1940	98.6
1950	98.8
1960	98.6
1970	97.9
1980	94.7
1990	95.1
1998	90.7

SOURCE: Figures calculated by the author from data in *The Pennsylvania Manual,* selected volumes.

were registered with the Labor, Socialist, or Prohibition Party, while 4.7 percent were registered as independents. Second, independence has always been measured in relation to an identification with the Republican or Democratic Party. Finally, Pennsylvania has always employed a closed primary. The only way a voter could participate in either of the major party primaries was to be registered with one of the parties. Thus, it seems reasonable to assume that voters with even a modicum of partisan feelings would register as having a party affiliation.

There was a temporary increase in the number of non–major party registrants during the 1970s, but the most significant change occurred during the 1990s. By the end of the decade, almost one voter in ten in Pennsylvania was registered as independent, nonpartisan, or with a minor party. The present situation is not unique, however; a similar situation existed during the 1920s. In fact, the magnitude was much greater then. In 1998, at least 10 percent of the registered voters were independents in sixteen counties, while in 1925 that figure was reached in thirty counties. Moreover, in Bucks (39 percent), Franklin (37 percent), Lebanon (37 percent), and Warren (33 percent) Counties, the 1925 proportion was greater than 30 percent. In 1998, the highest incidence of independence was 16 percent; in 1925, seventeen counties exceeded that figure. In 1930, there still were sixteen counties where at least 10 percent of the voters were independents.

Evidence that the Pennsylvania situation during the 1920s was not unique is provided by Kristi Andersen. Using data from some early survey research, she reports high levels of nonvoting and nonpartisanship among young people and new citizens during that decade. During the 1930s these voters disproportionately entered the electorate as Democrats. She argues that the New Deal realignment nationally was due primarily to the mobilization of these new, independent voters (Andersen 1979).

Figures 2.1 and 2.2 display the counties with greater than 10 percent independent voters in 1925 and 1998. In 1925, the counties are dispersed throughout the state. There is a large cluster of counties in the southeastern part of the state as well as several in the northeastern part of the state. In addition, there are six counties in the western half of the state. In 1998, the counties are clustered in the southeastern part of the state and along the eastern border.

Fifteen counties exceeded the threshold margin in both years. They are shown in Figure 2.3. Included are the counties of suburban Philadelphia and the adjacent counties to the north. In the latter group are all the counties (York, Lancaster, Lebanon, Berks, Lehigh, and Northampton) of

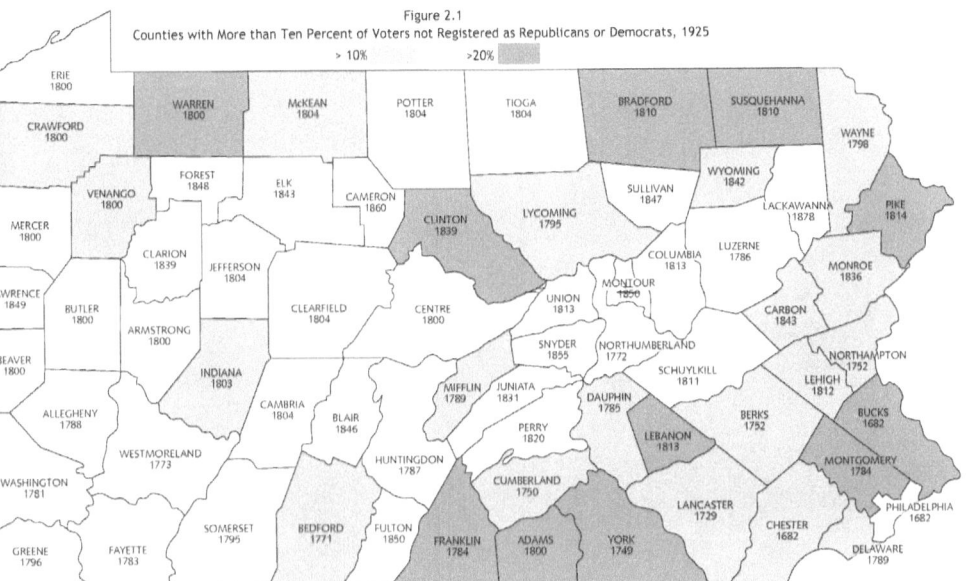

Figure 2.1
Counties with More than Ten Percent of Voters not Registered as Republicans or Democrats, 1925

the Pennsylvania Dutch region of the state. The presence of a significant number of independents does not, however, guarantee competition. For example, the four counties with more than 30 percent independents in 1925 (Bucks, Lebanon, Warren, and Franklin) had a mean percentage vote Republican during the 1920s of 64, 63, 70, and 58 in gubernatorial elections and 72, 79, 80, and 70 in presidential elections.

Previous research suggests a number of factors that relate to political independence, but these factors may not fully explain the high incidence of independence in the fifteen counties under discussion. During the 1920s, support for minor parties was correlated with urbanness and the presence of significant numbers of foreign-born citizens (Alderfer and Luhrs 1946, 51–52). But during that time, only four of the fifteen counties were more than 50 percent urban, and only one, Northampton, had a foreign-born percentage greater than the state mean.

The increase in independence since the 1960s has been attributed to increasing independence among younger voters (Miller and Shanks 1996). During the 1990s, survey data have revealed a relationship between age and independence: younger voters are more likely to be independents. More than half of the respondents between the ages of eighteen and twenty-nine identified themselves as independents (Stanley and Niemi 2000, 115; Flanigan and Zingale 2002, 90). However, according to the 2000

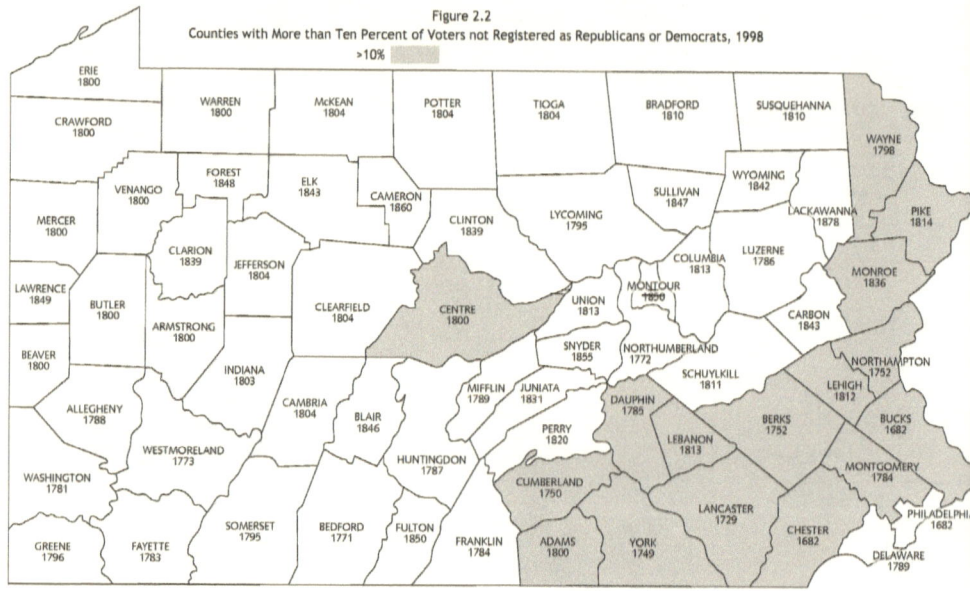

Figure 2.2
Counties with More than Ten Percent of Voters not Registered as Republicans or Democrats, 1998

census, only Cumberland County, among the fifteen counties, has a percentage of voters between the ages of twenty and twenty-four that exceeds the state mean; and only Cumberland and Dauphin Counties have percentages of voters between twenty and thirty-four that exceeds the state mean.

A different approach—such as analyzing voter turnout data—may help make sense of these fifteen counties by indicating whether the independents in these counties "behaved" like pure independent voters. National data show that during the 1990s pure independents had turnout rates that were 15 to 20 points lower than the rates for weak identifiers and independents leaning toward the Republican or Democratic Party, and 30 to 40 points lower than rates for strong identifiers. Therefore, it would not seem unreasonable to expect to find that rates of turnout in counties with large concentrations of independent voters would be below the state mean. That, however, was not the case in either 1926 or 1998. In 1998, nine of the fifteen counties had rates of turnout below the state mean, while in 1926 that was the case in only two of the counties.

A possible explanation for this phenomenon is that the independents in these counties have tended to lean toward one of the two major parties rather than be pure independents. These "leaners" tend to behave like weak partisans; in some cases they even show more partisan loyalty than weak identifiers do (Keith et al. 1992). These counties may have larger concentrations than other counties of voters who identify themselves as independents but who conduct themselves as partisans. However, this does little to explain the propensity of voters in these counties to identify with other than the Republican or Democratic Party.

The explanation that appears to be the most promising in answering this question is political culture. Six of the counties (York, Lancaster, Lebanon, Lehigh, Berks, and Northampton) are the Pennsylvania German counties. Seven of the remaining nine counties border these counties. In the two counties (Wayne, Pike) that do not share a border with one of the Pennsylvania German counties, German ancestry predominates. The current data suggest that there might possibly be a relationship between the "Pennsylvania Dutch" political culture and a propensity to political independence.

The classic formulations of Daniel Elazar (1984) regarding political culture might explain these patterns. Elazar identified three major political subcultures within the United States: individualistic (I), moralistic (M), and traditionalistic (T). States and regions within states were classified as being characterized by one of these three major subcultures, or by some combination of the three. Overall, Pennsylvania is considered to have an individualistic political culture, but the area of the state represented by the fifteen counties under consideration is characterized by IM and MI political cultures. The MI political culture is strongest in the areas covered by Wayne, Pike, and Monroe Counties.

Certain assumptions regarding the political process and citizen participation are associated with each of the subcultures. The immediate concern is the relationship between citizens and political parties. According to Elazar, party regularity is a characteristic of the individualistic political culture. On the other hand, "party regularity is not of prime importance" in the moralistic political culture. Political belief is more important than party loyalty. Thus, it could be hypothesized that higher levels of partisanship would be associated with the individualistic political culture, while higher levels of independence would be associated with the moralistic political culture.

Approximately one hundred studies have employed some form of Elazar's measure of political culture as an independent variable, with varying results (e.g., Sharkansky 1969; Weber and Shaffer 1972; Johnson 1976; Schlitz and Rainey 1978; Joslyn 1980; Lowery and Sigelman 1982; Herzig 1985; Fitzpatrick and Hero 1988; Nardulli 1990; Morgan and Watson 1991;

and Dran, Albritton, and Wyckoff 1991). As part of their study, Schlitz and Rainey specifically examined the relationship between Elazar's political cultures and national and state party identification. They reported that the most notable finding was the lack of variation among the cultures (1988, 412).

Joel Lieske (1993) summarized the major criticisms of Elazar's work and offered a reformulation. He contended that Elazar's formulation of the political cultures was not based on rigorous statistical procedures and pointed out that the original designations had not been updated for more than three decades and that because the boundaries of the subcultures include entire states or large regions within states, there was little empirical precision (889).

To counter these problems, Lieske employed current empirical data to distinguish political subcultures down to the county level. His analysis produced ten distinctive regional subcultures. Lieske then compared the utility of his measure with Elazar's scheme in explaining the variation in several social, political, and policy indicators. Included among his political indicators are three measures of party registration. Lieske reported that Elazar's classification does significantly better in accounting for Democratic and independent registration (906).

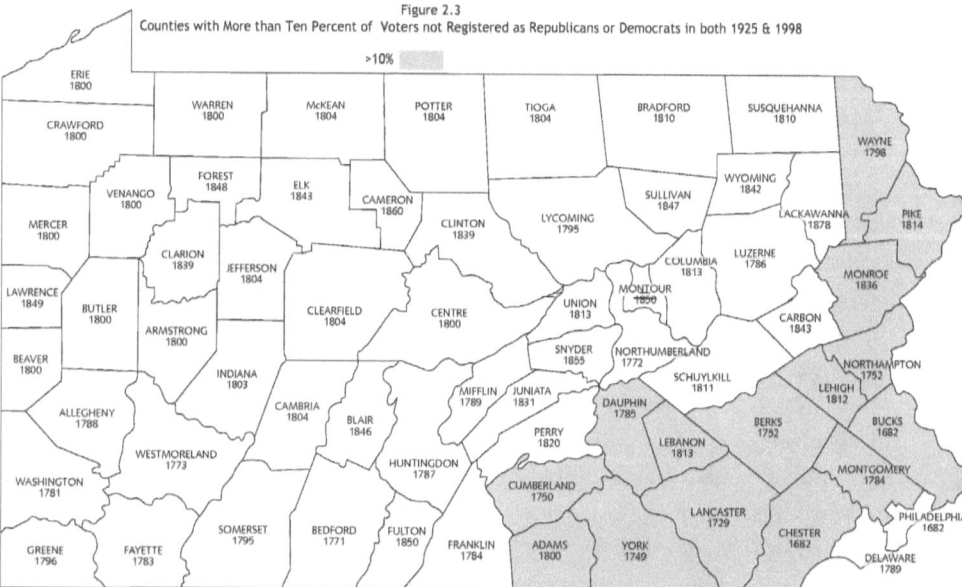

Figure 2.3
Counties with More than Ten Percent of Voters not Registered as Republicans or Democrats in both 1925 & 1998

Additional research is required before more definite conclusions can be offered regarding the relationship between political culture and political independence. For example, in the case of the IM and MI subcultures, what are the relative contributions of the individualistic and moralistic political cultures? Also, is there any association between the Pennsylvania Dutch political culture and Elazar's political subcultures? Finally, given the conflicting results discussed above, exactly how useful are Elazar's political cultures in predicting political behavior? While more research may be needed before a significant relationship can be established, some component of political culture appears to be exerting influence in the present situation. At the very least, the tight geographic clustering of these fifteen counties seems to be more than just a coincidence.

What is noteworthy is that the willingness of voters to adopt an independent stance is not a phenomenon of recent decades. Even during an earlier era characterized by extreme partisanship, a sizable number of voters were not affiliated with either major party.

Registration Versus Vote

The Democrats became the majority party in terms of registered voters in 1960 (see Table 2.4). Their plurality grew to as much as 900,000, but since 1990 it has hovered around 400,000.

Despite this rather sizable advantage, the Democrats have struggled in statewide elections in recent decades, especially in contests for the U.S. Senate (a topic covered in greater detail in Chapter 5). National research shows that party identifiers tend to vote for their party's candidates approximately 75 to 80 percent of the time; this is true in both national and state elections (Stanley and Niemi 2000, 132; Jewell and Olson 1988, 191; Partin 1995). Since partisans tend to vote their identification, the crucial variable could be variations in turnout. Data from the American National Election Study show that Democrats vote less frequently than Republicans do (Beck and Hershey 2001, 160). So, is the inability to prevail consistently with a registration advantage merely a Democratic problem, attributable to its identifiers' lower rates of turnout? The data from the past century suggest that it is not just a Democratic problem, but rather a majority party problem.

The problem facing the majority party in Pennsylvania can be illustrated two ways. Table 2.5 shows the mean percentage vote for each party, for

Table 2.4 Total number of registered Democrats and Republicans, 1925–1998, and registered voters as a percentage of the voting age population (VAP)

Year	Democrats	Republicans	Registered voters as a percentage of VAP
1925	697,180	2,238,084	58.2
1926	657,329	2,279,031	58.3
1928	867,391	2,861,919	74.0
1930	675,584	2,659,850	59.0
1932	833,977	2,911,068	66.2
1934	1,401,005	2,624,386	71.2
1936	2,065,697	2,665,902	83.6
1938	2,209,276	2,372,528	81.0
1940	2,161,307	2,782,890	77.8
1942	1,948,372	2,603,104	71.7
1944	1,854,111	2,645,263	70.8
1946	1,854,080	2,737,279	72.3
1948	1,702,295	2,696,300	69.2
1950	1,930,916	2,772,778	67.2
1952	2,136,511	3,130,078	75.3
1954	2,088,857	2,995,971	72.3
1956	2,450,396	2,897,307	76.4
1958	2,554,007	2,771,613	76.1
1960	2,805,202	2,802,237	79.0
1962	2,896,099	2,700,164	78.8
1964	2,884,396	2,759,565	79.5
1966	2,759,524	2,678,934	76.6
1968	2,715,507	2,775,456	77.3
1970	2,627,130	2,608,411	66.0
1972	2,993,092	2,697,694	71.7
1974	2,884,523	2,479,802	67.8
1976	3,152,450	2,387,197	69.8
1978	3,224,953	2,321,807	69.9
1980	3,072,700	2,374,303	62.3
1982	3,035,523	2,357,448	61.7
1984	3,380,675	2,487,552	67.1
1986	3,128,265	2,422,385	63.5
1988	3,069,234	2,518,282	63.9
1990	2,907,156	2,476,222	59.2
1992	3,043,757	2,567,643	61.7
1994	2,995,594	2,534,087	60.8
1996	3,336,933	2,910,615	67.9
1998	3,514,970	3,072,299	71.6

SOURCE: *The Pennsylvania Manual,* vols. 76–114.

Table 2.5 A comparison of the mean Republican and Democratic vote for selected offices with the mean Republican and Democratic registration statewide, for both majority and minority status, 1925–1998

Registration/Vote	Republican means (%)		Democrat means (%)	
	as majority	as minority	as majority	as minority
Voter registration	62	46	54	38
Vote for president	51 (−11)	49 (+3)	51 (−3)	48 (+10)
Vote for U.S. senator	55 (−7)	55 (+9)	46 (−8)	45 (+7)
Vote for governor	54 (−8)	50 (+4)	50 (−4)	46 (+8)
Vote for U.S. House	55 (−7)	49 (+3)	51 (−3)	45 (+7)
Vote for Pa. House	55 (−7)	49 (+3)	51 (−3)	45 (+7)

SOURCE: Data calculated from the author's research.

both majority and minority status, for several of the offices under examination in this study, in relation to their mean percentage of registered voters.[2] The Republicans were the majority party through the 1950s, while the Democrats have been the majority party since 1960.

Both parties' mean share of the vote was less than their mean share of registered voters for all of the offices when they were the majority party, and more than their mean share of registered voters when they were the minority party. The Republicans' mean percentage of registered voters was significantly greater than the Democrats' mean percentage for both majority and minority status. As the majority party, the Republicans fell further short of their registered voter percentage than the Democrats did; as the minority party, the Democrats exceeded their proportion of registered voters by a larger margin than the Republicans did.

Turnout and loyalty are crucial for a party's electoral success. For a majority party to prevail, unless it enjoys an extraordinary majority, its partisans must turn out in reasonable numbers and support the party's candidates. Tables 2.6 and 2.7 illustrate again that the Pennsylvania Democrats' current dilemma is part of a larger problem facing the majority party.

In these tables, the Turnout-Loyalty Index (TLI) is employed. This index is simply the total votes cast for a particular candidate in a given

---

2. The Republican and Democratic percentages of the vote in this book will be expressed as each party's share of the two-party vote. This will make comparisons among the different categories of elections more meaningful. While minor party candidates are not uncommon for the more visible offices, such as governor or United States senator, they are not very common in other statewide or state legislative races. In addition, our focus is on the Republican and Democratic parties, and not minor parties.

Table 2.6 The turnout–loyalty index for governor, by decade, 1920s–1990s

Decade	Republicans (%)		Democrats (%)	
1920s	48.4	Mean as	55.6	Mean as
1930s	58.9	majority party	99.0	minority party
1940s	59.8	= 57.8	63.7	= 76.4
1950s	64.0		87.3	
1960s	84.3	Mean as	67.3	Mean as
1970s	67.7	minority party	64.8	majority party
1980s	73.4	= 76.2	56.6	= 59.0
1990s	79.4		47.3	

SOURCE: Figures calculated by the author from data in *The Pennsylvania Manual*, selected volumes.

Table 2.7 The turnout–loyalty index for president, by decade, 1920s–1990s

Decade	Republicans (%)		Democrats (%)	
1920s	67.8	Mean as	94.4	Mean as
1930s	56.4	majority party	125.9	minority party
1940s	69.3	= 69.1	102.6	= 103.2
1950s	83.0		90.0	
1960s	74.4	Mean as	94.5	Mean as
1970s	96.8	minority party	67.1	majority party
1980s	96.8	= 83.4	66.8	= 74.6
1990s	65.6		69.9	

SOURCE: Figures calculated by the author from data in *The Pennsylvania Manual*, selected volumes.

election divided by the number of voters registered with that party. The offices examined are governor and president. A mean TLI score has been calculated for each decade. Once again, a comparison will be made between the parties for majority and minority status. To measure partisan turnout and loyalty accurately, survey research would be required. While crude, the index should provide a reasonable approximation of what we are trying to measure.

What is most striking is the similarity between the Republican and Democratic TLI scores when they are the majority and minority party. In the case of the gubernatorial elections, the scores are virtually mirror images. By far the highest TLI score was for the Democrats in presidential elections when they were the minority party.

Over the course of the twentieth century, the parties were equally successful at mobilizing their identifiers. The TLI scores for the majority party have been consistently lower than the corresponding scores for the minority party. The crucial factor is the registration advantage enjoyed by the majority party. The Republicans were much more successful as the majority party than the Democrats have been. But until 1930, almost 80 percent of Pennsylvania voters were registered as Republicans; during their stint as the dominant party, rarely did their percentage of registered voters fall below 59 percent. On the other hand, since they have been the majority party, rarely has the Democratic percentage risen above 54 percent.

The gubernatorial election data dramatically illustrate the different contexts. During the first six decades of the twentieth century, the GOP was mobilizing 60 percent of an electorate that was between 59 and 80 percent Republican; the Democrats were mobilizing 75 percent of a hopeless minority. Since 1960, the Democrats have been mobilizing 60 percent of a party that is favored by only slightly more than half of the voters, while the Republicans are mobilizing 75 percent of an almost equal number of voters. None of this is meant to suggest that the Democrats might not be able to nominate stronger candidates or run better campaigns. Nonetheless, the main factor in distinguishing between the rates of success enjoyed by each party when it was in the majority appears to be the electoral base each party started with.

Recent research by Berwood Yost examines the congruence between voter registration and actual party orientation among Pennsylvania voters. He reports that 21 percent of Pennsylvania voters are misaligned. The percentages are much higher for Democrats (40 percent) and independents (39 percent) than for Republicans (22 percent). When party registration is adjusted to reflect actual party orientation, Republicans actually enjoy a 250,000 voter margin (Yost 2003). Comparable data are not available for previous eras. However, given the TLI scores I have reported, there is no reason to believe that similar phenomena have not occurred during the course of the twentieth century.

It seems reasonable to assume that such misalignment would increase the longer a party has been the majority party. Over time, the loyalty of certain groups in the majority party coalition is reduced. Some groups become disenchanted because the majority party ignores their demands, while the emergence of new issues alters the loyalties of other groups. The change in partisan loyalty would normally be reflected in voting patterns before it is reflected in registration patterns. Some voters probably need time to become comfortable psychologically with their new partisanship before declaring a formal affiliation with what was previously the enemy party; others are probably just too lazy to fill out the forms. Whatever the specific reasons, the result would be that the majority party would receive a share of the vote that was less than its proportion of registered voters, while the minority party would receive a share of the vote that was greater than its proportion of registered voters.

Turnout

Percentage of Voting Age Population

There has been a precipitous decline in voter turnout in Pennsylvania since 1960. However, this more recent pattern is part of a century-long trend. Turnout percentages for presidential and gubernatorial election years are displayed in Table 2.8. It can be noted that gubernatorial elections in Pennsylvania have always been scheduled in nonpresidential election years.

Both patterns of decline can be seen clearly. Over the course of the century, turnout in presidential elections fell from approximately 80 percent of eligible voters to approximately 50 percent; for gubernatorial elections, the decline was from approximately 70 percent to approximately 35 percent. During the past three decades, presidential turnout has declined from approximately 70 percent to approximately 50 percent; gubernatorial turnout fell from approximately 60 percent to approximately 35 percent. By the end of the century, slightly more than half of the eligible electorate was participating in presidential elections, while barely a third bothered to cast ballots in gubernatorial contests.

Turnout in presidential election years has been consistently higher than in gubernatorial election years. The decline in gubernatorial turnout has been more precipitous both over the century and since the 1960s. Presidential turnout has declined 33.3 percent since 1900, and 29.1 percent since 1960. Gubernatorial turnout has fallen 53.0 percent since the turn of the century, and 46.7 percent since 1960. These patterns of decline in Pennsylvania mirror national trends. National turnout in presidential elections has declined 31 percent since 1900, and 22 percent since 1960. However, the decline in Pennsylvania in nonpresidential election years has been much more precipitous: the comparable national declines have 35 percent since 1900, and 24 percent since 1960.

While the trend since 1900 has been for decreased turnout, the decline in Pennsylvania has not been steady. For both presidential and guberna-

Table 2.8 Voter turnout in presidential and gubernatorial elections, as a percentage of voting age population (VAP), 1900–1998

Year	Presidential	Gubernatorial	Year	Presidential	Gubernatorial
1900	75.0		1950		50.6
1902		70.0	1952	65.6	
1904	79.0		1954		53.2
1906		64.3	1956	65.4	
1908	81.0		1958		57.0
1910		55.0	1960	70.5	
1912	67.1		1962		61.7
1914		61.3	1964	67.9	
1916	71.5		1966		57.0
1918		49.9	1968	66.9	
1920	71.6		1970		52.1
1922		28.9	1972	57.9	
1924	42.6		1974		44.1
1926		29.8	1976	58.2	
1928	62.5		1978		47.1
1930		37.2	1980	52.2	
1932	50.5		1982		42.1
1934		52.2	1984	55.4	
1936	73.2		1986		38.8
1938		67.4	1988	51.9	
1940	64.2		1990		33.6
1942		40.1	1992	54.6	
1944	59.7		1994		39.4
1946		48.8	1996	50.0	
1948	58.7		1998		32.9

SOURCE: Figures calculated by the author. The turnout data come from *The Pennsylvania Manual*, vols. 101, 114; data for the voting age population come from the *Statistical Abstract of the United States*, selected volumes.

torial elections, three distinct eras emerge: 1900–1948, 1950–68, and 1970–98 (see Table 2.9). Turnout in both categories fell in the first era, rose in the second, and then declined again in the third. The declines in the first and third eras were greater for the gubernatorial election years.

The admission of women to the Pennsylvania electorate in 1922 had a decided impact on turnout. Turnout in the 1922 gubernatorial election fell 21 points from the 50 percent turnout in the 1918 contest between William C. Sproul and Eugene C. Bonniwell, itself a low-turnout election. Turnout did not improve in 1926, but by 1938 it had rebounded to 67 percent. Turnout in the 1924 presidential election declined almost 30 points from 1920, but then rebounded almost 20 points in 1928. By 1936, presidential turnout had returned to its 1920 level. So, although the addition of

Table 2.9 Percentage increase or decrease in voter turnout for presidential and gubernatorial elections for three eras: 1900–1948, 1950–1968, and 1970–1998

	Percentage increase/decrease per election	
Era	Presidential	Gubernatorial
1900–1948	−1.4	−1.8
1950–1968	+1.6	+1.6
1970–1998	−2.4	−3.0

SOURCE: Figures calculated by the author from data in *The Pennsylvania Manual*, vols. 101, 114.

women to the electorate had an immediate, dramatic effect on turnout levels, the effect was short term.

The impact of young voters was quite the reverse. While their initial impact was not as consequential as that of women, their long-term influence has been monumental. In the first presidential election in which eighteen-year-olds participated (1972), turnout declined by 9 percent; the comparable figure for the first gubernatorial election (1974) was 8 percent. However, unlike the situation with women voters, turnout has not rebounded. In their major work, Miller and Shanks (1996) maintain that young voters are responsible for the post-1960 decline in turnout. While women augmented the size of the electorate by a greater factor than young voters did, the latter group apparently will have a more lasting, if deleterious, effect on rates of turnout.

Percentage of Registered Voters

Turnout can also be expressed as a percentage of registered voters (see Table 2.10). Employing this standard will yield an enhanced perception of electoral participation, since many citizens do not even bother to register. Traditionally, citizens who made the effort to register automatically identified themselves as more politically motivated than their fellow citizens. States with more lenient registration procedures historically have had higher rates of voter registration and turnout (Teixeira 1992, chap. 4; Wolfinger and Rosenstone 1980, 72–78). In fact, getting voters registered has long been considered the crucial step in the process; an overwhelming proportion of registered voters typically vote.

Prior to 1996, approximately 80–85 percent of registered voters regularly turned out for presidential elections. Turnout rates in gubernatorial

Table 2.10 Voter turnout in presidential and gubernatorial elections, as a percentage of registered voters, 1926–1998

Year	Presidential	Gubernatorial	Year	Presidential	Gubernatorial
1926		46.7	1964	84.2	
1928	79.3		1966		73.4
1930		59.8	1968	84.8	
1932	73.1		1970		68.3
1934		70.4	1972	78.2	
1936	84.2		1974		63.3
1938		82.1	1976	80.4	
1940	81.3		1978		64.5
1942		55.2	1980	85.6	
1944	83.2		1982		64.6
1946		67.2	1984	78.2	
1948	83.9		1986		57.9
1950		74.5	1988	77.2	
1952	85.7		1990		53.9
1954		72.2	1992	82.8	
1956	84.4		1994		61.0
1958		73.9	1996	66.1	
1960	88.2		1998		41.7
1962		80.2			

SOURCE: Figures calculated by the author from data in *The Pennsylvania Manual*, vols. 76–114.

elections were much less consistent. The notion that getting citizens registered is the crucial factor in raising turnout rates is being severely tested by the National Voter Registration Act of 1993. Citizens in every state can now register by mail and at a variety of state agencies, including the motor vehicle department. One no longer needs to be a highly motivated citizen to become a registered voter. During the first eight months of the act's operation, more than five million Americans registered to vote. In several states the rate of registration was three times the normal rate, or greater. However, the percentage of registered voters who actually vote has been declining; between 1968 and 1996, the figure fell from 90 percent to 66 percent (U.S. Bureau of the Census 1998a, 297; 1998b).

The impact of the act in Pennsylvania can be seen vividly by examining the last two presidential and gubernatorial elections of the century. Between 1992 and 1996, the percentage of the voting age population who registered to vote in the presidential election increased from 65.9 percent to 74.9 percent; however, the percentage of registered voters who actually cast ballots tumbled from 82.8 percent to 66.1 percent. In 1998, 79.8 percent of the voting age population registered for the gubernatorial election, compared with 64.7 percent four years earlier, while the actual turnout among registered voters plummeted from 61.0 percent to 41.7 percent. In actual numbers, more than 1.5 million Pennsylvanians added their names to the registration rolls between 1994 and 1998, while turnout fell by more than 500,000 voters.

Pennsylvania's experience was not unique. The percentage of registered voters increased between 1992 and 1996 in thirty-nine of the forty-four states covered by the National Voter Registration Act. Overall, the percentage of registered voters increased from 70.6 percent of the voting age population to 76.3 percent. Voter turnout declined in all fifty states between 1992 and 1996, falling from 55.9 percent to 49.8 percent (Federal Election Commission 1997).

The Pennsylvania experience demonstrates that easing registration procedures no longer guarantees increased voter turnout. The new "motor-voter" provisions are enrolling (and making it more difficult to remove from the rolls) a larger number of citizens who have a smaller interest in political activity. The motivational level required to become registered under the simplified procedures is not commensurate with the level required to actually get to the polls and vote. There is compelling evidence that the electorate in coming years will be larger, but less motivated, less informed, and less active.

Split-Ticket Voting

A century ago, it was the rare voter who split his ticket between the parties. Overwhelmingly, voters identified with a party and consistently voted a straight ticket to support that party's candidates. But during the past half-century, especially since the 1960s, ticket-splitting has increased significantly (DeVries and Tarrance 1972; Wattenberg 1994, chaps. 9, 10). Today, according to National Election Studies data, about one voter in five splits a ballot between presidential and congressional candidates, about one in four between U.S. House and Senate candidates, and approximately one in two between state and local candidates.

As was the case with voter independence, to measure the incidence of ticket-splitting over the course of the century would require survey research. Lacking this, I developed two alternative measures. The first is the Partisanship Consistency Index (PCI). I examined the individual elections for president, senator, governor, each statewide office (including lieutenant governor prior to 1970), as well as the total votes cast for each party's U.S. House candidates and each party's Pennsylvania House candidates, for each election year. In each case, I calculated the Republican percentage of the two-party vote. (Again, in the case of the latter two categories of elections, the measure is the Republican share of the two-party vote cast for all members of the Pennsylvania congressional delegation and all members of the Pennsylvania House.) The PCI is simply the difference between the highest Republican percentage and the lowest Republican percentage. For example, if the highest percentage was 60 percent and the lowest was 57 percent, the PCI would be 3.0. (The percentage could refer to the Republican share of the two-party vote for one of the specific offices, or to the Republican share of the statewide vote for all congressional candidates or all state House candidates.) This gives a rough indication of how consistent voters were in supporting their party's candidates. I then calculated a mean PCI score for each decade.[3] A low PCI score suggests that voters tended to vote a straight ticket; a high PCI score suggests that voters tended to split their tickets between the parties.

The second measure is the percentage of split results. This is simply the number of elections won by the minority party in that election expressed as a percentage of the total number of elections. For example, if the Republicans won five of the elections, and the Democrats one, the percentage of split results would be one divided by six (16.7 percent). I used the same elections to calculate the percentage of split results that I used to determine the PCI. A low percentage of split results is another indication that voters consistently supported the candidates from their party. Once again, I calculated a mean percentage for each decade. The results for both measures can be found in Table 2.11.

The PCI scores remain consistently low until the 1960s, with the notable exception of the 1910–18 period. That decade's high score is a consequence of the 1910 and 1914 elections.

In 1910, Democratic candidates received 35.3 percent of the statewide vote for the Pennsylvania House and one-third of the votes for the U.S.

---

3. The mean PCI score for the decade is the mean of the PCI scores for each of the five elections within the decade. In determining the PCI score, one election was omitted from the calculations in each of three decades. This was done because one election in a particular year was so aberrant that it completely distorted the partisan voting pattern for that year and, subsequently, the decade. The elections omitted were the 1912 presidential election, the 1926 United States Senate election, and the 1930 gubernatorial election. The particular factors associated with each of these elections are discussed in the text.

Table 2.11 Mean partisanship consistency index and percentage of split results, by decade, 1900–1998

Measure	1900–1908	1910–1918	1920–1928	1930–1938	1940–1948	1950–1958	1960–1968	1970–1978	1980–1988	1990–1998
PCI	4.3	7.1	4.0	3.1	1.6	3.3	6.9	10.7	12.0	13.1
Split results	3.6%	3.7%	0.0%	0.0%	0.0%	10.3%	17.9%	27.3%	35.7%	28.0%

SOURCE: Data calculated from the author's research.

House of Representatives. On the other hand, the Democratic candidate for governor, Webster Grim, received only 23.8 percent of the two-party vote for governor. His popular vote total (129,395) was the lowest total a Democratic candidate had received since 1838. A third-party candidate, William H. Berry, received 382,127 votes.

Berry had ridden public outrage over the misuse of state funds to a victory in the contest for state treasurer in 1905. Berry and Woodrow Wilson, in the 1912 presidential election, were the only two Democrats to win a statewide contest between 1900 and 1932. Treasurers for some time had been depositing state funds in friendly banks and sometimes using the funds for personal speculation. By 1905, the amount of money involved had grown to $14 million (Klein and Hoogenboom 1973, 421–22). In 1905, the Democrats nominated Berry, a Methodist minister and reform mayor of Chester, as their candidate for treasurer. Also backed by Independent Republicans (the Lincoln Party), Prohibitionists, and Philadelphia's City Party, Berry was victorious. In fact, adherents of these three parties supplied 36 percent of his votes.

Shortly after taking office, Berry uncovered evidence of corruption in the construction of the new state capitol. The old capitol had burned on February 2, 1897, and the legislature had appropriated $4 million for the construction of a new building. It was announced in August 1906 that the new capitol had been completed under budget. Berry soon discovered that the costs of decorating and furnishing the new facility had pushed the actual cost to nearly $13 million. For example, a contractor had agreed to supply a chandelier for $193.50, but then billed the state by the pound; the fixture ended up costing the state $2,500. Berry estimated that the capitol had cost $5 million more than it should have. Eventually, fourteen men were convicted of fraud, including the former state treasurer and former auditor general.

Despite his record, Berry was passed over for the Democratic gubernatorial nomination in 1910. Instead, the nomination went to Grim, a virtually unknown attorney from Doylestown. It turned out that Boies Penrose had bought off the Democratic leadership and controlled the Democratic convention. Independent Republicans and dissident Democrats then formed the Keystone Party and nominated Berry (Beers 1980, 54–55).

In 1914, the high PCI was due to the difference between the Democrat votes for governor and senator. The Democratic candidate for governor, Vance C. McCormick, polled 43.5 percent of the vote in losing to Martin G. Brumbaugh, while fellow Democrat A. Mitchell Palmer garnered only 33.9 percent of the vote while being defeated by Boies Penrose for the U.S. Senate.

The PCI more than doubled in the 1960s. This was followed by significant jumps during the 1970s and 1980s, and a slight increase during the 1990s. Pennsylvania voters were most consistent in their partisanship during the 1940s. The current PCI is four times what it was at the beginning of the century. Contemporary Pennsylvania voters are much less consistent in casting their ballots than were their forebears sixty to a hundred years ago. The 1990 election offers a prime example. That year, the Democratic candidate for governor, Robert P. Casey, received 67.7 percent of the two-party vote, Democratic candidates for the U.S. House of Representatives captured 45.4 percent of the vote, and Democratic candidates for the Pennsylvania House garnered 56.1 percent of the vote.

National Election Studies data reveal a similar pattern at the national level. A dramatic increase in Senate-House and state-local ticket-splitting began in the 1960s and has persisted. Ticket-splitting between presidential and House candidates increased sharply during the 1970s and 1980s, but declined during the 1990s (Stanley and Niemi 2000, 133).

A variation of the PCI is displayed in Table 2.12. For each election year, I calculated the proportion of the elections under examination where the percentage of the two-party vote was within 1, 2, or 3 percentage points. I then derived a mean for each decade. The figures listed below represent the mean percentage of the races under consideration that fell within each of the categories during each of the five election years within each decade.

No particular pattern emerges from the first column. However, the pattern becomes much clearer in the second column, and exceptionally clear in the third column. From 1900 to 1958, with the exception of the 1910–18 period, approximately 85 to 100 percent of the separate elections were within 3 percentage points of each other every two years. During this era, voters were remarkably loyal to their parties. A decline then began in

Table 2.12 Split-ticket voting examined by the incidence of close elections, by decade, 1900–1998

Decade	Percentage of elections within		
	1 percentage point	2 percentage points	3 percentage points
1900–1908	57.1	66.7	85.7
1910–1918	37.0	55.6	67.0
1920–1928	60.0	73.3	83.3
1930–1938	48.3	75.9	93.1
1940–1948	89.3	100.0	100.0
1950–1958	65.5	86.2	96.6
1960–1968	53.6	75.0	75.0
1970–1978	36.4	45.5	45.5
1980–1988	50.0	57.1	60.7
1990–1998	41.7	50.0	58.3

SOURCE: Data calculated from the author's research.

the 1960s that continued, although not consistently, until the end of the century. Once again, the 1940s stand out. Every election year during that decade, an average of 89 percent of the vote percentages fell within one point of each other, and an incredible 100 percent fell within 2 points of each other. During that decade, voters rarely strayed from their parties. These data show clearly how voter loyalty has decreased as the century has progressed.

The pattern just identified is also revealed when the data for split results are examined. The only split results between 1900 and 1948 were the previously discussed victories by William Berry and Woodrow Wilson. Over the next four decades, the percentage of split results increased steadily, before declining during the 1990s. The 1992 election illustrates the recent pattern. While Democratic presidential candidate Bill Clinton (55.5 percent) carried the state, and the Democrats also elected a state treasurer (64.9 percent), the Republicans were electing a U.S. senator (51.5 percent), the attorney general (51.4 percent), and the auditor general (53.1 percent).

Of interest is whether, when voters are not consistent in their partisanship, they tend to desert their party in specific types of elections. Each decade's votes were examined to determine which category (categories) deviated most from the other election results. Presidential elections were the most deviant in seven decades, and senatorial and gubernatorial elections were the most deviant in three decades. This is not surprising. These are the three most visible elections for most voters. Voters are more likely to abandon their party to support such candidates, especially presidential

Table 2.13 The recalculated partisanship consistency index, by decade, 1900–1998

Measure	1900–1908	1910–1918	1920–1928	1930–1938	1940–1948	1950–1958	1960–1968	1970–1978	1980–1988	1990–1998
PCI	3.9 (4.3)	5.3 (7.1)	3.3 (4.0)	2.7 (3.1)	1.2 (1.6)	1.8 (3.3)	2.3 (6.5)	3.9 (9.9)	4.4 (12.0)	9.1 (13.1)

SOURCE: Data calculated from the author's research.

or gubernatorial candidates, than they are to support candidates of the opposing party for the legislature or other, less visible statewide offices.

Presidential, senatorial, and gubernatorial election results were removed from the analysis to see if this had a significant impact on the PCI. The recalculated PCI is displayed in Table 2.13. The original PCI scores are in parentheses. The recalculation results in lower PCI scores, especially so in the last four decades. Moreover, the decline in partisanship now does not appear until the 1990s. But when it occurs, it is dramatic. The impact of presidential, senatorial, and gubernatorial elections on partisan voting is clear from these data. Partisan voting is much more consistent in the other categories of elections; only in the last decade does partisanship begin to wane.

An examination of the PCI and split results reveals that partisan voting has declined over the past century, especially during the past four decades. This breakdown in party loyalty shows up most often in presidential, senatorial, and gubernatorial elections. Voters are more likely to be induced to shed their partisanship to support attractive opposition candidates in such races. National data reveal that voters are most likely to desert their party when they are attracted to a visible candidate from the other party who runs a well-funded campaign, usually an incumbent (Beck et al. 1992; Burden and Kimball 1998).

Summary

This chapter examined several aspects of turnout and voting in Pennsylvania during the past one hundred years. Notable changes have taken place in such areas as registration, the incidence of independence among voters, turnout, and split-ticket voting.

From the 1920s through the 1960s, approximately 70–80 percent of Pennsylvanians were registered to vote. This percentage declined slowly from 1970 to 1994, and then increased significantly in the late 1990s. This latter surge can be attributed to the implementation of the National Voter Registration Act of 1993. By the end of the century, approximately one resident in ten was registered as an independent. While high by recent standards, this percentage is not without historical precedent. Similar proportions of Pennsylvanians were registered as independents during the 1920s. In fact, the magnitude was greater during the earlier decade; in four counties, the incidence of independence exceeded 30 percent.

Much has been made recently regarding the relative lack of electoral success on the part of the Democrats, despite a statewide plurality of approximately 400,000 registered voters. However, the Democrats are turning out the same percentage of their registered voters as the Republicans did when they were the majority party. The difference in their rates of success appears to be the voter base each party began with. When they were the majority party, the Republicans enjoyed a base that was between 59 and 80 percent of registered voters; rarely has the Democratic base been more than 54 percent. In effect, numbers have been working against the Democrats.

There has been a century-long decline in voter turnout, as well as a post-1960 decline. From 1900 to 1998, turnout declined from approximately 80 percent to approximately 50 percent in presidential elections, and from approximately 70 percent to approximately 35 percent in gubernatorial elections. Since 1960, presidential turnout dropped from approximately 70 percent to approximately 50 percent, and gubernatorial turnout fell from approximately 60 percent to approximately 35 percent. Three distinct eras were identified in terms of turnout: 1900–1948, 1950–68, and 1970–98. Turnout declined during the first and third eras, while it increased during the second.

Turnout as a percentage of registered voters took a dramatic downturn during the late 1990s. This was primarily a result of the implementation of the National Voter Registration Act of 1993. The Act has made it much easier for citizens to get registered. Many of these individuals clearly still lack the requisite motivation to actually vote. Between 1994 and 1998, 1.5 million new names were added to the voter registration lists in Pennsylvania, while turnout fell by more than half a million.

Split-ticket voting in the state increased significantly during the last four decades of the twentieth century. The Partisanship Consistency Index (PCI), which was used to measure ticket-splitting, more than doubled during the 1960s. This was followed by significant increases during the next two decades, and a slight increase during the 1990s. The PCI at the end of the century was four times what it was at the beginning of the century. Through the 1950s, with the exception of the 1910–18 period, between approximately 85 percent and 100 percent of the separate elections fell within 3 points of each other every two years. Straight-ticket voting reached its pinnacle during the 1940s: the two-party percentages of the vote in the elections under consideration were within 2 percentage points of each other an amazing 100 percent of the time.

It was discovered that voters were more likely to desert their party in presidential, senatorial, and gubernatorial elections. Apparently, voters can be more easily induced to abandon their party affiliation in these more visible races than in less visible statewide races or legislative races. When the PCI was recalculated without these three categories of elections, the increase in ticket-splitting did not show up until the 1990s. The increase was a sharp one, however: the PCI more than doubled.

Ticket-splitting was also measured by examining the percentage of split results. Split results were virtually unknown between 1900 and 1948. Then steady increases were recorded during the next three decades before the incidence of split results leveled off during the 1990s. It is no longer uncommon for the parties to divide the offices being contested.

LEGISLATIVE ELECTIONS

The decline in competition in congressional elections since the 1960s has been well documented during the past twenty-five years (Mayhew 1974; Cover and Mayhew 1977; Born 1979; Erikson 1971; Cover 1977; Ferejohn 1977; Nelson 1978–79; Parker 1980; Alford and Hibbing 1981). Data presented by these researchers have established that congressional incumbents have sought reelection at higher rates, have won by increasingly larger margins, and have faced less competition. The decline in the number of competitive districts has been dubbed by Mayhew (1974) as "the case of the vanishing marginals."

Some dissent has been offered from the general line of argument. Burnham (1970) and Garand and Gross (1984) argue that the decline in competition is part of a long-term trend that began in the mid-1890s. Garand and Gross show that since 1965 the difference in the percentage of the vote obtained by incumbent and nonincumbent winners has been declining;

they therefore contend that the decline in competition should be more accurately portrayed as a winners' advantage rather than an incumbents' advantage.

Collie (1981) and Jacobson (1987) dispute the notion that the increasing margins of victory are related to decreasing levels of electoral turnover. They both present data indicating that while incumbents are winning by larger margins, they are no safer than they were prior to the 1960s. Erikson (1976) offers similar data.

Beginning in the 1980s, political scientists turned their attention to state legislative elections. A series of studies attempted to ascertain whether a number of the relationships uncovered in the analysis of congressional elections also characterized state legislative elections (Jewell and Breaux 1988; Garand 1991; Weber, Tucker, and Brace 1991; Ray and Havick 1981; Breaux 1990; Jewell 1994; Breaux and Gierzynski 1996; Tidmarch, Lonergan, and Sciortino 1986; Tucker and Weber 1985; Carey, Niemi, and Powell 2000). While considerable interstate variation exists, trends in state legislative elections tend to mirror those in congressional elections.

Jewell (1994) notes a moderate increase in state House and Senate reelection rates between 1968 and 1988. In related works, Jewell and Breaux (1988) and Breaux and Gierzynski (1996) suggest that this modest relationship is primarily due to the fact that at the beginning of the period many of the states' legislators already enjoyed high reelection rates. Likewise, the percentage of legislators seeking reelection has not increased significantly since 1968; once again, the explanation offered is that by the late 1960s many states had such a large number of legislators running for reelection that a dramatic increase was not possible.

It is clear, however, that incumbents are obtaining an increasingly larger portion of the two-party vote (Garand 1991; Jewell and Breaux 1988; Breaux and Gierzynski 1996). However, such a pattern has not been identified in open-seat races; the average winning percentages in these contests in 1988 were virtually unchanged from 1968 (Jewell and Breaux 1988; Breaux and Gierzynski 1996). The authors conclude that since only incumbents are securing a larger percentage of the vote, the trend can be attributed to the increasing power of incumbency rather than to an increase in the number of safe districts.

Garand (1991) argues that while incumbents increased their vote proportions between 1968 and 1986, their rates of reelection did not increase significantly. He divides the incumbents into different categories based on their proportion of the vote in the preceding election. In almost every year the most marginal incumbents have the highest rate of defeat. Overall, marginal incumbents (defined as a previous vote of less than 60 percent) were defeated at much higher rates than safe incumbents. Among House incumbents, those in the marginal category were defeated almost 16 percent of the time, compared to 2 percent for incumbents in the safe category; among Senate incumbents, the figures were 18 percent and 6 percent, respectively. He contends that his findings offer limited support for Jacobson's (1987) argument that this relationship can be attributed to a greater volatility in interelection vote swings in recent decades.

However, he differs from Jacobson regarding another issue. Jacobson argues that the meaning of marginality has varied over time; for example, he finds that an incumbent elected in the 1970s with between 60 and 65 percent of the vote was just as likely to lose in the next election as was an incumbent elected in the 1950s with between 50 and 55 percent of the vote. Garand, on the other hand, maintains that the meaning of marginality did not change during the period he examined. Both studies, however, examined a limited number of elections.

In a study of eight state legislatures, Ray and Havick (1981) report that state legislative competition declined over the years 1892–1972. The level of competition varied from state to state and tended to fluctuate within given states. Their findings support Burnham's (1970) contention that competition tends to increase during periods of party realignment. They found a high proportion of competitive districts during the 1890s. The number of competitive districts declined during the first three decades of the twentieth century, falling below 20 percent in three of the states during the 1920s. This was followed by a sharp increase in competition during the 1930s. After the increases of the 1930s, a gradual decline began which continued until the end of their study in 1972.

Tucker and Weber (1985) examined competition for seats in the lower houses of the legislatures of thirteen states during the 1950–80 period. They found the number of marginal districts declining in six of the states (including Pennsylvania) and remaining stable in the other seven. Weber, Tucker, and Brace (1991) updated the original study through 1986, and added seven states to the data base. They discovered less competition for lower house seats in fifteen of the states included in their study.

Tidmarch, Lonergan, and Sciortino (1986) document a decline in the number of marginal seats in forty-eight state legislatures during the 1970s. The incidence of marginal districts varied among the states and from election to election. In only a few states was the decline uninterrupted.

Also, states tended to display a consistent pattern in both houses; either a high incidence of marginal districts in both or a low incidence in both. A study of forty-nine states presented data showing a decline in the proportion of marginal races between 1968 and 1988. The percentage of competitive races declined from about 40 percent to 28 percent (Van Dunk and Weber 1997). Both studies reported a decline in marginal seats in Pennsylvania.

The percentage of contested seats has declined in most states since the 1950s (Tucker and Weber 1985; Weber, Tucker, and Brace 1991; Tidmarch, Lonergan, and Sciortino 1986; Jewell and Breaux 1988; Breaux and Gierzynski 1996). The decreasing number of contested elections in Pennsylvania was singled out as particularly notable in two of the studies (Jewell and Breaux 1988; Weber, Tucker, and Brace 1991).

Two other studies cite a decline in the percentage of contested legislative races. Almost 80 percent of the races were contested during the 1970s, as opposed to approximately 67 percent during the 1980s and 1990s (Van Dunk and Weber 1997; Squire 1998). During the 1990s there is evidence of fewer contested races in states with more professional legislatures (Squire 1998).

The data presented by Breaux and Gierzynski (1996) indicate that the proportion of races won by a contested incumbent has declined in ten states (Pennsylvania is one of those states); in the remaining states, incumbents were contested at relatively high rates during the periods included in the study. In nine of the ten states (including Pennsylvania) there was no similar decline in the proportion of contested open-seat races. The authors suggest that the decline in the number of contested races is due to the increasing power of incumbency. Moreover, there was only a small increase in the average winning margins of contested incumbents. Breaux and Gierzynski contend that where the average winning percentage of incumbent candidates has increased, it is primarily a result of a larger percentage of uncontested races.

The research conducted during the 1970s, 1980s, and 1990s has increased our understanding of many aspects of congressional and state legislative races. But these initial studies need to be supplemented. In particular, additional historical perspectives are needed. It is crucial to determine whether the trends which have been identified since the late 1960s are unique to the last three decades of the century or are part of a longer-term pattern. If the latter is the case, it is important to ascertain when the trends actually began. Case studies of individual states can provide even greater specificity.

This chapter will examine competition for the Pennsylvania General

Assembly and for Pennsylvania representatives to the U.S. House of Representatives between 1900 and 1998. In particular, we will examine (1) the proportion of incumbents running for reelection; (2) the proportion of incumbents running for reelection who were successful; (3) the proportion of marginal districts; (4) the proportion of contested elections; and (5) the relationship between votes and seats.

Data and Methods

We will examine all Pennsylvania House, Senate, and congressional elections between 1900 and 1998. The election data were obtained from editions of *The Pennsylvania Manual* and its predecessor, *Smull's Legislative Hand Book*. The cutoff figure for marginality is 60 percent. A safe seat is one where the winning candidate obtains at least 60 percent of the major party vote; a marginal seat is one captured with less than 60 percent of the major party vote. Some studies of district marginality have used a cutoff figure of 55 percent. It was felt that the 60 percent cutoff would provide a more stringent test of marginality.

The use of multimember state House districts until the 1966 election presents a problem. Determining the percentage of the vote obtained by the individual candidates—and thus, the proportion of safe seats—is much more difficult when multimember districts are utilized. The method employed here is the one suggested by Niemi, Jackman, and Winsky (1991): the creation of pseudopairs of Republican and Democratic candidates. For example, the Republican with the highest vote would be matched with the Democrat with the lowest vote, and then the second-highest Republican with the Democrat with the second-lowest vote. If the Democrats ran only two candidates in a three-seat district while the Republicans ran a complete slate, the Republican with the highest vote would be considered unopposed.

Primary election results are not reported for much of the period covered by this study. Therefore, the data on the percentage of incumbents running for reelection actually represent the percentage of incumbents seeking reelection who survived the primary.

Nonincumbent winners includes victorious candidates in open-seat races as well as challengers who defeat incumbents. Over this century, a respectable number of challengers have secured at least 60 percent of the vote while defeating incumbents.

The Pennsylvania General Assembly

Incumbents Running for Reelection

The percentage of incumbents running for reelection has increased significantly during the past century (see Table 3.1). During the first decade of the century, 41 percent of House incumbents and 36 percent of Senate incumbents sought reelection; by the 1990s, that figure had grown to almost 90 percent for House members and over 80 percent for senators. For representatives, the percentage running for reelection increases each decade. For senators, the percentage increases through the 1930s, declines slightly during the 1940s, rebounds sharply during the 1950s, and then declines again during the 1960s and 1970s. The proportion of senators seeking reelection during the 1980s was essentially the same as the proportion running for another term during the 1950s. The 1980s witnessed a notable increase in the number of incumbents running for reelection, especially among senators. The increase during the 1990s was greater for senators than it was for representatives. The increase in the number of incumbents running during the twentieth century is certainly due to a variety of factors: the fact that being a legislator has become a full-time, well-paying job, the advantages increasingly enjoyed by incumbents, and the existence of fewer competitive districts.

Reelection Success of Incumbents

As revealed in Table 3.2, the current high rate of reelection success enjoyed by incumbents is nothing new. Eighty-four percent of House incumbents and 92 percent of Senate incumbents running were reelected during the years 1900–1908. The rate of success rarely has dipped below 80 percent in either house. Both House and Senate incumbents suffered significant reversals in their rates of reelection success during the 1910–18 and 1930–38

Table 3.1 Percentage of incumbents running for reelection, by chamber and decade, 1900–1998

Chamber	1900–1908	1910–1918	1920–1928	1930–1938	1940–1948	1950–1958	1960–1968	1970–1978	1980–1988	1990–1998
House	41	52	66	69	77	79	82	83	87	89
Senate	36	48	61	69	66	79	71	73	80	84

SOURCE: Data calculated from the author's research.

Table 3.2 Percentage of incumbents winning reelection, by chamber and decade, 1900–1998

Chamber	1900–1908	1910–1918	1920–1928	1930–1938	1940–1948	1950–1958	1960–1968	1970–1978	1980–1988	1990–1998
House	84	81	86	76	78	88	94	93	98	97
Senate	92	75	96	68	87	88	92	89	96	96

SOURCE: Data calculated from the author's research.

eras. Reelection rates jumped for both representatives and senators during the 1980s.

The rates of success for senators fluctuated wildly from 1900 until the end of the 1940s. Dramatic decreases in the percentage of successful candidates alternated with dramatic increases. Relative stability has existed since then. The patterns for House incumbents have been much more moderate. The current high rate of success enjoyed by Senate incumbents since 1980 only matches the figure for senators seeking reelection during the 1920s. Eighty-eight percent of incumbents in both houses have been reelected since 1900.

The fluctuations in reelection rates among senators is attributable to significant declines during the second and fourth decades of the twentieth century. More specifically, the crucial elections were 1912 and 1936. Sixty-four percent of Senate incumbents were reelected in 1912, and 31 percent were reelected in 1936; the comparable House rates in those years were 77 percent and 79 percent.

In 1912, Republican dissidents led by William Flinn, Alexander P. Moore, and Edwin Van Valkenburg gained control of the state convention and sent a delegation to the 1912 Republican National Convention pledged to Theodore Roosevelt. The supporters of William Howard Taft at the convention routed Roosevelt and the Progressives and nominated Taft for president. Insurgents from Pennsylvania and other states nominated Roosevelt on the Progressive ticket. The Progressives were known as the Washington Party in Pennsylvania (although some candidates still ran as Progressives in the state). The Roosevelt forces carried Pennsylvania by 50,000 votes, but Woodrow Wilson was elected president (Klein and Hoogenboom 1973, 424).

The Republican Party's internecine warfare adversely affected GOP Senate candidates in 1912. Progressive voters were directly responsible for the defeat of all five Republican incumbents who lost. Beyond that, Washington Party votes provided the margin of victory for eleven Republican and three Democratic senators.

The 1936 election represented the high-water mark for Franklin Roosevelt and his New Deal in Pennsylvania. Roosevelt received 58 percent of the two-party vote in 1936, compared with 47 percent in 1932; while he also carried the state in 1940 and 1944, Roosevelt could not match his 1936 share of the vote. The Democrats picked up fifteen Senate seats in 1936, in contrast to the three seats they gained in 1932. Of the thirteen Senate incumbents who were defeated in 1936, twelve were Republicans. Seven of the defeated incumbents had won with less than 60 percent of the vote in 1932.

Most incumbent Republican senators were able survive Roosevelt's initial presidential campaign. By 1936, however, they were no match for the Democratic New Deal coalition. In both 1912 and 1936, Pennsylvania Senate elections were decidedly influenced by national political conflicts; the impact on House elections was not as dramatic. The geographically smaller, more homogeneous House districts would seem to afford representatives more protection from such trends than do the larger, more heterogeneous Senate districts. Tables 3.4 and 3.6 reveal that House districts have consistently been safer than Senate districts.

The rate of reelection success for incumbents has increased as the advantages accruing from incumbency have increased. Two advantages have become especially important. Partisan gerrymandering has significantly reduced the number of districts where challengers have a realistic opportunity to win. This produces a twofold advantage for incumbents: they tend to run in districts where their party has a decided registration advantage; and the bleak electoral outlook for the minority party reduces the likelihood that a formidable challenger can be recruited.

Legislative party leaders also control a significant amount of money that can be funneled to incumbents. Some of the money is directly contributed to the incumbent's campaign. Other funds take the form of WAMs, or walking around money. These funds are given to loyal legislators to fund various pork barrel projects in their districts. The fiscal year 2004 budget contained $50 million worth of WAM funds.

The higher reelection rates have contributed to a reduction in the rate of turnover among members (see Table 3.3). At the beginning of the century, the mean rate of turnover every two years was approximately 60 percent in the House and approximately 35 percent in the Senate. By the 1980s, it was 14 percent and 11 percent. Significant reductions occurred

Table 3.3 Mean rate of membership turnover, by chamber and decade, 1900–1998

Chamber	1900–1908	1910–1918	1920–1928	1930–1938	1940–1948	1950–1958	1960–1968	1970–1978	1980–1988	1990–1998
House	62	58	42	47	40	30	18	22	14	13
Senate	34	32	22	27	22	16	20	16	11	20

SOURCE: Data calculated from the author's research.

during the 1980s. However, the rate of turnover almost doubled in the Senate during the 1990s. This has returned the Senate rate to the levels seen during earlier decades. Whether the recent figures are an aberration remains to be seen.

Incidence of Marginal Districts

The decline in the number of competitive legislative districts since the 1960s has been well established by political scientists. What is less well established is whether these contemporary trends are unique. As mentioned above, Ray and Havick (1981) offered evidence that the pattern of the last three decades of the twentieth century is part of a long-term trend beginning in the 1890s. The present data confirm some of their findings, but differ in other respects.

Table 3.4 documents the trend for the Pennsylvania House. Confirming the results of the previous studies, the number of marginal districts has decreased since the 1960s. However, the relationships are considerably more complicated than that.

During the 1980s and 1990s, more than 80 percent of all House seats were won with at least 60 percent of the vote, as were almost 90 percent of the seats retained by incumbents. As impressive as these figures are, they are only slightly higher than the comparable figures for the 1920s. In fact, nonincumbent winners enjoyed their largest margins of victory during the 1920s. Table 3.5 helps further to put the current percentages into perspective, by comparing the post-1960 figures with the percentages from the first three decades of the century.

The proportion of safe districts between 1900 and 1928 was similar to the proportion since 1960. The percentages of all candidates and incumbents obtaining at least 60 percent of the vote is slightly higher in the recent period. However, the proportion of nonincumbents winning with at least 60 percent of the vote was notably greater during the earlier period.

Table 3.4 Percentage of safe House seats, by decade and category of winner, 1900–1998

Winner	1900–1908	1910–1918	1920–1928	1930–1938	1940–1948	1950–1958	1960–1968	1970–1978	1980–1988	1990–1998
All	53	56	76	45	45	40	50	62	81	83
Incumbent	60	66	82	53	58	44	53	70	87	86
Nonincumbent	49	49	69	35	26	30	40	34	48	59

SOURCE: Data calculated from the author's research.

Table 3.5 A comparison of the percentage of safe House seats, by category of winner, from 1900 to 1928 and from 1960 to 1998

Winner	1900–1928	1960–1998
All	62	69
Incumbent	69	74
Nonincumbent	56	45

SOURCE: Data calculated from the author's research.

The data for state Senate elections reveal similar patterns (see Table 3.6). The proportion of safe Senate districts in the 1990s is very close to the figure for the 1920s. The percentage of incumbents securing reelection by safe margins during the most recent decade is almost identical to the figure for the 1920s. Nonincumbents in Senate races, like their House counterparts, obtained the largest proportion of safe-margin victories during the 1920s.

Table 3.7 contrasts the 1900–1928 and 1960–98 periods for Senate elections. The total proportion of seats being won by safe margins, as well as the proportion being won by incumbents, is slightly higher in the 1960–98 period. As was the case with House elections, Senate nonincumbents during the 1960–98 period did not match the electoral margins they secured during the years 1900–1928.

Data from both House and Senate elections offer limited support for Burnham's (1970) argument that electoral competition increases during periods of partisan realignment. The number of marginal districts increased dramatically during the 1930s. However, the pattern in Pennsylvania differs from those in the states examined by Ray and Havick (1981). In the eight states they studied, a decline in the number of competitive districts began during the 1940s. In Pennsylvania, the trend that began in the 1930s

Table 3.6 Percentage of safe Senate seats, by decade and category of winner, 1900–1998

Winner	1900–1908	1910–1918	1920–1928	1930–1938	1940–1948	1950–1958	1960–1968	1970–1978	1980–1988	1990–1998
All	46	45	71	40	42	34	51	52	73	74
Incumbent	61	56	78	55	46	41	59	64	83	79
Nonincumbent	39	42	70	26	38	23	35	31	50	52

SOURCE: Data calculated from the author's research.

Table 3.7 A comparison of the percentage of safe Senate seats, by category of winner, from 1900 to 1928 and from 1960 to 1998

Winner	1900–1928	1960–1998
All	54	63
Incumbent	65	71
Nonincumbent	50	42

SOURCE: Data calculated from the author's research.

did not run its course until the end of the 1950s. A dramatic increase in the proportion of safe House and Senate seats occurred from 1960 to 1998.

As would be expected, the proportion of incumbents winning by safe margins exceeds that of nonincumbents. However, the gains made by nonincumbents since 1960, especially during the 1980s and 1990s, exceed those made by incumbents. Evidence for such a claim can be extrapolated from the data in Table 3.4 and Table 3.6. Since the end of the 1950s, the proportion of safe House seats has increased by 108 percent; safe seats won by incumbents have increased by 95 percent, while those won by nonincumbents have increased by 97 percent. The most dramatic gains were registered during the 1980s. During the 1980s, the proportion of safe House seats increased by 31 percent; nonincumbent safe seats increased by 41 percent compared with a 24 percent increase by incumbents. This pattern has continued during the 1990s: the percentage of nonincumbent safe seats has grown by 23 percent while the percentage of incumbent safe seats has decreased by one percent.

The story is somewhat different on the Senate side. Nonincumbents, again, have made bigger gains both since 1960 and during the 1980s and 1990s. Since the end of the 1950s, the proportion of safe Senate seats has increased by 118 percent, with a 93 percent increase by incumbents and a

126 percent increase by nonincumbents. The proportion of safe Senate seats jumped by 40 percent during the 1980s; included was a 30 percent increase by incumbents and a 61 percent increase by nonincumbents. During the 1990s, the percentage of incumbent safe seats has declined by 5 percent while nonincumbent safe seats have increased by 4 percent.

Legislative districts in Pennsylvania, not simply those won by incumbents, have become much less competitive since the 1950s. The number of marginal districts has been significantly reduced. During the past two decades, on the basis of election results, only thirty-five to forty House districts and about a dozen Senate districts could be considered marginal. Reapportionment has certainly contributed to this situation. Pennsylvania has long engaged in bipartisan gerrymandering. Ken Gormley, former executive director of the state's reapportionment commission, explains:

> Preservation of jobs is the most powerful driving force behind reapportionment; even more powerful than political rivalries or personal hatreds. The fact is, Democrats and Republicans rally 'round the common goal of preserving each others' political necks first. Only then, after most members' jobs are safe and secure, will the knives be sharpened for occasional raids on the opposing political party, or attacks on hated personalities. (Keefe and Ogul 1997, 80)

Another important factor contributing to the current dearth of marginal districts is the voter registration advantage enjoyed by the dominant party in most districts. Table 3.8 presents these data.

At least 60 percent of the voters are registered with the dominant party in 55 percent of the House districts and 50 percent of the Senate districts. At least 55 percent of the voters are registered with the dominant party in 70 percent of the House districts and 72 percent of the Senate districts. The similarity between the comparable figures in the smaller, more homogeneous House districts and the larger, more diverse Senate districts is noteworthy. Because most voters tend to vote their party affiliation in legislative elections, most legislative districts in Pennsylvania are reasonably safe for one of the parties. Only about one-quarter of the districts in each chamber could be considered competitive, based on party registration. That estimate closely matches the proportion of safe seats won in each house during the 1980s and 1990s.

Table 3.8 Percentage of voters registered with dominant party, by chamber, 1995–1996

Party	0–50%	50–54.9%	55–59.9%	60–100%	Total
		House Districts			
Republican	3.4% (7)	15.3% (31)	9.4% (19)	21.1% (43)	49.2% (100)
Democrat	3.9% (8)	6.9% (14)	6.4% (13)	33.5% (68)	50.8% (103)
Total	7.3% (15)	22.2% (45)	15.8% (32)	54.7% (111)	100.0% (203)
		Senate Districts			
Republican	6.0% (3)	8.0% (4)	18.0% (9)	16.0% (8)	48.0% (24)
Democrat	0.0% (0)	14.0% (7)	4.0% (2)	34.0% (17)	52.0% (26)
Total	6.0% (3)	22.0% (11)	22.0% (11)	50.0% (25)	100.0% (50)

SOURCE: Figures calculated by the author from data in *Guidebook to Pennsylvania Legislators, 1995–1996* (Sacramento, Calif.: STATENET, 1995).

Contested Elections

For most of the twentieth century, it was rare for a legislative candidate in Pennsylvania to run unopposed in the general election. That changed dramatically during the 1980s and 1990s, especially for incumbents (see Table 3.9 and Table 3.10). As more districts become safe for one party or the other, it is understandable that the minority party would have a difficult time finding candidates who were willing to undertake a futile campaign. Among earlier decades, the 1910–38 period stands out as one of relatively less competition in House elections; so too do the 1920s and 1930s for Senate elections. The earlier eras were characterized by virtually total Republican dominance.

The growing margins of victory enjoyed by incumbents since 1968 have been attributed in large part to the increasing number of uncontested races involving incumbents (Jewell and Breaux 1988; Breaux and Gierzynski 1996). The number of uncontested legislative races in Pennsylvania remained insignificant through the 1960s; there was a modest increase during the 1970s, and a dramatic upsurge during the 1980s. The only exceptions to the pattern were in the House from 1910 to 1938 and in the Senate during the 1920s and 1930s, especially among incumbents. Table 3.11 examines the impact of uncontested elections on the incidence of marginality during the 1970s, 1980s, and 1990s. The percentages in parentheses are the proportions of candidates in each category who obtained 60 percent of the vote or more in contested elections. Controlling for competition does not alter

Table 3.9 Percentage of contested House candidates, by type of candidate and decade, 1900–1998

Candidate	1900–1908	1910–1918	1920–1928	1930–1938	1940–1948	1950–1958	1960–1968	1970–1978	1980–1988	1990–1998
All	96	89	89	92	99	99	99	97	82	74
Incumbent	95	89	87	90	98	99	99	96	77	72
Nonincumbent	96	90	91	96	100	99	100	99	95	92

SOURCE: Data calculated from the author's research.

Table 3.10 Percentage of contested Senate candidates, by type of candidate and decade, 1900–1998

Candidate	1900–1908	1910–1918	1920–1928	1930–1938	1940–1948	1950–1958	1960–1968	1970–1978	1980–1988	1990–1998
All	99	99	95	95	98	99	99	97	86	79
Incumbent	99	99	94	93	99	99	98	96	83	76
Nonincumbent	100	100	96	100	99	100	100	97	96	95

SOURCE: Data calculated from the author's research.

Table 3.11 Percentage of safe House and Senate seats, by decade and category of winner, in all (contested) races, 1970–1998

Candidate	1970–1978	1980–1988	1990–1998
House			
All	62 (61)	81 (76)	83 (78)
Incumbent	70 (69)	87 (83)	86 (81)
Nonincumbent	34 (34)	48 (45)	59 (55)
Senate			
All	52 (51)	73 (69)	74 (68)
Incumbent	64 (63)	83 (79)	79 (72)
Nonincumbent	31 (30)	50 (46)	52 (50)

SOURCE: Data calculated from the author's research.

any of the relationships. Even in contested races, winners are garnering larger percentages of the vote than they were thirty years ago.

Electoral Marginality and Incidence of Defeat

Garand (1991) presented data showing that marginal incumbents were more likely to lose than safe incumbents were. The data in Table 3.12 strongly support his findings. The table reports the incidence of defeat for

Table 3.12 The relationship between electoral marginality and incumbent defeat, by chamber and decade, 1900–1998

Previous Vote	1900–1908	1910–1918	1920–1928	1930–1938	1940–1948	1950–1958	1960–1968	1970–1978	1980–1988	1990–1998	Mean
House											
<60%	25%	33%	29%	39%	33%	20%	12%	13%	2%	8%	21%
60%+	10%	5%	9%	14%	8%	1%	1%	3%	1%	1%	5%
Senate											
<60%	16%	41%	14%	39%	18%	17%	13%	13%	7%	12%	20%
60%+	0%	0%	0%	30%	5%	6%	0%	5%	2%	1%	5%

SOURCE: Data calculated from the author's research.

marginal and safe incumbents. Since 1900, marginal incumbents clearly have been more vulnerable. Over the course of the century, the mean rate of defeat for marginal House incumbents is 21 percent, compared with five percent for safe incumbents; among senators, the rates are 20 percent and five percent. Both safe House and Senate incumbents suffered the highest incidence of defeat during the 1930s, an amazing 30 percent among senators. As might be expected, only one of those senators was a Democrat.

Garand (1991) contended that the meanings of marginality and safety did not change much between 1968 and 1986. The present data suggest that they did change significantly, especially for House incumbents, over the course of the last century. Notable differences exist between the first five decades and the last five decades. The incidence of defeat for marginal House incumbents fell from 32 percent to 11 percent; for safe House incumbents, the proportion dropped from 8 percent to 1 percent. Among marginal Senate incumbents, the incidence of defeat declined from 26 percent to 12 percent. It is more difficult to make a definitive statement regarding safe Senate incumbents. While the incidence of defeat fell from 7 percent to 3 percent from the first half of the century to the last half, the 30 percent figure for the 1930s distorts the data. Once again, dramatic changes occurred during the 1980s; in both chambers, all incumbents became less vulnerable. Especially dramatic gains were registered by marginal incumbents, particularly in the house.

Incumbents who won by smaller margins in their previous elections are more likely to face strong, well-funded opponents when they run for reelection. State and legislative party organizations concentrate their resources in the few districts where they have an opportunity to gain a seat. Marginal incumbents could be running in competitive districts. They could also be running in districts where their party has an advantage, but for whatever reason, they displayed vulnerability in the previous election. Either way, unlike safe incumbents, they will not have the luxury of running against an unknown challenger who lacks the financial resources to mount an effective campaign. This increases the possibility that they could be defeated.

Vote Share Versus Seats

One of the ways electoral systems are judged is by their degree of proportionality. This is a measure of how accurately votes are translated into seats. In a system with perfect proportionality, a party's share of seats won would exactly equal its system-wide share of legislative votes received. Systems that employ multimember districts and proportional representation are considered to be the most proportional. Conversely, systems that utilize single-member districts and plurality elections are considered to be the least proportional (Rae 1967; Cox 1997). The latter arrangement is used for most elections in the United States. Multimember districts were employed in Pennsylvania House elections prior to 1966.

While some electoral systems are more proportional than others, they all tend to exaggerate the majority party's share of the vote and minimize that of the minority party. It is not difficult to understand how this happens. In single-member districts, 50 percent of the vote plus one will win 100 percent of the seats (one). In theory (but never in practice), the majority party could carry every legislative district with a margin of one vote and win all of the seats. In multimember districts, the majority party tends to win all, or almost all, of the seats being contested.

The result of all this is that a party that wins 55 to 60 percent of the statewide vote for legislative candidates tends to win approximately 65 to 70 percents of the seats. On the other hand, a party that wins 40 to 45 percent of the statewide vote tends to win one-third or fewer of the seats. This helps to create what has been labeled "manufactured majorities" (Patterson 1996, 164–65).

This phenomenon will be examined from two perspectives. First, Table 3.13 examines the relationship between votes and seats for all Pennsylvania House elections during the twentieth century. The mean percentage of the vote and the mean share of seats are given for each of the vote categories. As can be seen, the majority party's share of the vote is exaggerated in each category, with the distortion increasing as the percentage of the vote increases.

Since multimember districts were used until 1966, the relationship between votes and seats will be examined prior to 1966 and since 1966 to see if district magnitude has a significant impact (see Table 3.14). Reflecting the closer competition between the parties during the latter period, neither party has received more 56 percent of the statewide House vote since 1966. The pre-1966 pattern is very similar to the pattern for the entire century.

The pattern since 1966 is very different. Rather than exaggerate the majority party's share of the vote, the tendency has been to minimize

Table 3.13 The relationship between the majority party's statewide share of the vote for Pennsylvania House candidates and the share of House seats won, 1900–1998

	Percentage of Statewide Vote				
Mean	50–54%	55–59%	60–64%	65–69%	over 70%
Mean	52%	57%	64%	66%	73%
Seats	54	68	80	87	92

SOURCE: Data calculated from the author's research.

Table 3.14 The relationship between the majority party's statewide share of the vote for Pennsylvania House candidates and the share of House seats won, 1900–1964 and 1966–1998

	Percentage of Statewide Vote				
Mean	50–54%	55–59%	60–64%	65–69%	over 70%
			1900–1964		
Vote	52%	57%	63%	67%	73%
Seats	56	72	81	88	92
			1966–1998		
Vote	52%	56%	NA	NA	NA
Seats	51	56	NA	NA	NA

SOURCE: Data calculated from the author's research.

that party's share of the vote. In fact, in seven of the seventeen elections since 1966 the majority party's vote share was greater than the percentage of seats won. It was the case for the Republicans four times and for the Democrats three times. On three occasions (two Republican, one Democrat), the percentage of seats won by the majority party was identical to its percentage of the vote. Thus, in only seven of the seventeen elections since 1966 has the majority party won a percentage of seats greater than its percentage of the vote.

Majorities have most definitely not been "manufactured" since 1966. It has been an era of extremely close statewide competition for the Pennsylvania House. With the exception of three sessions (1991, 1992, 1993), each party has controlled approximately one hundred seats since 1979. In twelve of the seventeen elections since 1966, the majority party has received 52 percent or less of the statewide vote cast for House candidates. Similarly, in twelve of the seventeen elections the percentage of seats won by the majority party has been 52 percent or less. In none of the five elections of the 1980s did the majority party ever capture more than 52 percent of either the statewide vote or seats.

As was documented earlier, however, this close statewide legislative competition does not extend into the individual districts. Very little competition exists at the legislative district level. Especially during the 1980s and 1990s, each party has started with approximately an equal number of safe districts. And the trend has been for the districts to become even safer. Realistically, very few districts are candidates for a shift in partisan control. As a result, even when one party obtains an expanded share of the statewide vote it is not likely to increase its share of seats significantly. Basically, in such instances, each party is simply racking up even larger majorities in districts it already safely controls.

Two examples from the past decade are illustrative. The parties traded landslide gubernatorial victories during the 1990s. Democrat Robert Casey secured 68 percent of the vote in his victory over Barbara Hafer in 1990. Republican Tom Ridge obtained 65 percent of the vote in his 1998 victory over Ivan Itkin. The two winners' coattails did not help their parties' house candidates. Fifty-six percent of the statewide vote for House candidates went to Democrats in 1990, and 54 percent went to Republican candidates in 1998. However, the Democrats only won 53 percent of the seats in 1990, and the Republicans only won 51 percent of the seats in 1998. The Democrats gained only four seats in 1990, and the GOP actually lost a seat in 1998. The traditional relationship between votes and seats seems to have been significantly altered in Pennsylvania during the last three decades.

The traditional relationship between vote share and seats benefits the majority party in the state. It can be argued that since 1966 there has been no majority party in Pennsylvania legislative elections. Between 1966 and 1998, there were seventeen House elections; the Democrats won a majority of the statewide vote eleven times, while the Republicans prevailed six times. However, on five occasions, the Democratic margin was 1 percent or less. Thus, over more than three decades, each party garnered a majority of the statewide vote six times, and five elections were a virtual dead heat. There is no majority party to be advantaged.

Incumbent gerrymandering has played a significant role in creating the safe districts described above. As revealed by Table 3.8, at most there are sixty competitive House districts in Pennsylvania. And those figures greatly exaggerate the number of districts where serious competition actually exists every two years. All of this means that each party obtains approximately 50 percent of the statewide House vote each election and wins roughly half of the seats. A scenario for winning proportionately fewer seats than votes also exists: win more votes in your safe districts than the other party wins in its safe districts, but lose a majority of the limited number of competitive districts.

U.S. House of Representatives

Incumbents Running for Reelection

The pattern for members of the U.S. House of Representatives differs from that for members of the General Assembly (see Table 3.15). First, the proportion of incumbents running for reelection at the beginning of the century is much higher among congressional representatives. Two-thirds of incumbents ran for reelection during the first decade of the century, and that rose to around 80 percent during the next four decades. The percentage of state House incumbents running for reelection did not reach 80 percent until the 1960s; that plateau was not attained among state senators until the 1980s. As was the case with state legislators, there was a significant increase in the percentage of incumbents seeking reelection during the 1980s. However, unlike the pattern in the General Assembly, this was followed by a notable drop among incumbents running for reelection during the 1990s.

The pattern prior to the last two decades of the twentieth century is similar to that among state senators: increases through the 1930s, a decline during the 1940s, a rebound during the 1950s, and then declines during the 1960s and 1970s. More congressional incumbents currently are seeking reelection than were at the beginning of the twentieth century, but the increase is not as dramatic as it was among members of the General Assembly. The same factors that induced an increasing number of state legislators

Table 3.15 Percentage of congressional incumbents running for reelection, by decade, 1900–1998

1900–1908	1910–1918	1920–1928	1930–1938	1940–1948	1950–1958	1960–1968	1970–1978	1980–1988	1990–1998
66	76	77	84	80	92	88	87	96	88

SOURCE: Data calculated from the author's research.

to run for reelection as the century progressed also apply for members of Congress.

Reelection Success of Incumbents

This is another group of incumbents who have really never been endangered. Even during the first three decades of the century, between 80 and 90 percent of congressional incumbents won another term (see Table 3.16). Prior to 1960, 82 percent of incumbents were reelected. After 1960, the reelection rate climbed to 96 percent. These data dispute the notion that incumbents are no safer than they were prior to 1960 (Collie 1981; Jacobson 1987; Erikson 1976). Contemporary congressional incumbents are dramatically safer than their pre-1960 predecessors were. The decade-by-decade success rates for congressional incumbents are remarkably similar to those for state senators (see Table 3.2). Eighty-seven percent of congressional incumbents were reelected during the twentieth century; this is virtually identical to the 88 percent rate for incumbents in both houses of the General Assembly. Like their General Assembly counterparts, congressional incumbents have been advantaged by partisan gerrymandering and increased legislative party money.

Incidence of Marginal Districts

The Pennsylvania data conform to the national pattern of fewer marginal districts since the 1960s, but also support the contention by Burnham (1970) and Garand and Gross (1984) that the decline in competition is part of a century-long trend. By the 1980s and 1990s, approximately three-fourths of the districts were safe. During the first three decades of the century, that was the case in only one-half of the districts (see Table 3.17). As was the case with the General Assembly, the percentages for the 1920s

Table 3.16 Percentage of congressional incumbents winning reelection, by decade, 1900–1998

1900–1908	1910–1918	1920–1928	1930–1938	1940–1948	1950–1958	1960–1968	1970–1978	1980–1988	1990–1998
92	78	89	63	79	90	97	95	95	95

SOURCE: Data calculated from the author's research.

Table 3.17 Percentage of congressional safe seats, by decade and category of winner, 1900–1998

Winner	1900–1908	1910–1918	1920–1928	1930–1938	1940–1948	1950–1958	1960–1968	1970–1978	1980–1988	1990–1998
All	48%	39%	63%	36%	35%	41%	59%	65%	74%	75%
Incumbent	58	55	76	49	49	44	62	74	82	84
Nonincumbent	36	17	30	14	13	27	38	26	0	28

SOURCE: Data calculated from the author's research.

stand out among the earlier decades. Garand and Gross (1984) report similar findings. While the comparison is not as strong as it was with the state House and Senate, the percentages are relatively similar. Once again, what we are seeing in the contemporary period is not without historical precedent. One notable difference from the state legislative data is that fewer safe districts were won by congressional nonincumbent candidates in the last decade of the century than in the first decade.

The data from the 1930s and 1940s further support Burnham's contention that competition increases during periods of realignment. Gerrymandering during recent decades has also contributed to fewer competitive districts.

Significant increases in the proportion of safe districts took place during the 1960s, 1970s, and 1980s. Only slight changes occurred during the 1990s. The one exception was among nonincumbents; however, the increase during the 1990s still left the percentage of safe districts below the figure for the 1960s.

The relative gains made by congressional incumbents and nonincumbents since 1960, and during the past two decades, differs from the pattern observed among Pennsylvania legislators. In the case of the General Assembly, the incidence of safe districts had increased more rapidly for nonincumbents. That is not the case here. From the end of the 1950s through the end of the century, the incidence of safe congressional districts increased by 83 percent. Safe seats won by incumbents increased by 91 percent, compared with only four percent for nonincumbents. During the past four decades, districts won by incumbents have become much less competitive. Districts won by nonincumbents have remained relatively unchanged. During the 1980s and 1990s, the percentage of safe seats increased by 15 percent; the gain was 14 percent among incumbents, compared with 8 percent among nonincumbents.

Contested Elections

Uncontested congressional elections were an unknown phenomenon until the 1970s (see Table 3.18). The most significant decline in electoral competition was registered during the 1990s. The change has occurred solely among incumbents; nonincumbents still uniformly face competition.

Congressional incumbents are more likely to be challenged than their General Assembly counterparts are. But clearly some of the congressional races are viewed as so hopeless that it is not possible for one of the parties to field a candidate.

As was the case with the General Assembly, we want to determine if the decline in marginal districts during the past thirty years can be attributed to the increasing number of uncontested races. The results can be seen in Table 3.19. Once again, the percentages in parentheses are the proportion of candidates in each category who obtained 60 percent of the vote or more in contested elections. The impact of the uncontested races is most evident during the 1990s. But controlling for competition does not alter the basic relationship: all winners, even in contested races, have been getting a larger share of the vote over the last three decades.

Electoral Margin and Incidence of Defeat

Marginal incumbents were much more vulnerable during the twentieth century (see Table 3.20). The mean rate of defeat for marginal incumbents was 19 percent, more than three times the mean rate for safe incumbents. Jacobson (1997, 126) presents national data for the period 1950–94 that reveals that the mean rate of defeat for marginal incumbents was 12 percent; for safe incumbents, the rate was 7 percent. For the period 1950–98, the rates in Pennsylvania were 10 percent and 3 percent. Thus, both

Table 3.18 Percentage of contested congressional candidates, by type of candidate and decade, 1900–1998

Candidate	1900–1908	1910–1918	1920–1928	1930–1938	1940–1948	1950–1958	1960–1968	1970–1978	1980–1988	1990–1998
All	100%	100%	100%	100%	100%	100%	100%	98%	93%	87%
Incumbent	100	100	100	100	100	100	100	98	93	85
Nonincumbent	100	100	100	100	100	100	100	100	100	100

SOURCE: Data calculated from the author's research.

Table 3.19 Percentage of safe congressional seats, by decade and category of winner, in all (contested) races, 1970–1998

Winner	1970–1978	1980–1988	1990–1998
All	65% (62%)	74% (73%)	75% (68%)
Incumbent	74 (72)	82 (81)	84 (77)
Nonincumbent	26 (26)	0 (0)	28 (28)

Source: Data calculated from the author's research.

categories of incumbents in Pennsylvania had lower rates of defeat during that period, especially safe incumbents.

Safe incumbents suffered their highest rates of defeat between 1910 and 1918 and 1930–38. Two distinct patterns emerge again when the century is divided in half. During the first five decades, the mean rate of defeat for marginal candidates was 28 percent, compared with 10 percent during the last five decades. Among safe incumbents, the rate of defeat for the two periods dropped from 9 percent to 3 percent. This further supports the possibility that the meaning of marginality changed over the course of the century. Jacobson (1987) and Garand, Wink, and Vincent (1989) reach similar conclusions.

As was the case with state legislators, marginal congressional incumbents are more likely to attract strong challengers with enough money to run an effective campaign. Some of these challengers will win.

Vote Share Versus Seats

Table 3.21 presents the relationship between the statewide vote for congressional candidates and the percentage of seats won. Once again, mean percentages are given for votes and seats for each of the vote categories. Overall, the expected pattern emerges and is consistent with the pattern for state House candidates from 1900 to 1998.

The aggregate data, however, mask a number of elections that are at variance with the basic trend. In eight of the seventeen elections since 1966, the percentage of seats won by the majority party was less than its share of the vote. Furthermore, on five of these occasions (all Republican) the party that garnered a majority of the vote won fewer than half the seats. It should be pointed out that in each of these instances the Democrats won one more seat than the Republicans. Three of the elections (1992, 1994, 1998) took place during the 1990s.

Table 3.20 The relationship between electoral marginality and congressional incumbent defeat, by decade, 1900–1998

Previous Vote	1900–1908	1910–1918	1920–1928	1930–1938	1940–1948	1950–1958	1960–1968	1970–1978	1980–1988	1990–1998	Mean
<60%	17%	33%	28%	33%	29%	14%	9%	11%	6%	10%	19%
60%+	0	20	1	17	7	3	2	3	5	4	6

SOURCE: Data calculated from the author's research.

Table 3.21 The relationship between the majority party's statewide share of the vote for congressional candidates and the share of congressional seats won, 1900–1998

Mean	Percentage of statewide vote				
	50–54%	55–59%	60–64%	65–69%	70%+
Vote	52%	57%	62%	68%	73%
Seats	57	63	82	88	96

SOURCE: Data calculated from the author's research.

As was the case with Pennsylvania House elections, there does not appear to be a majority party for congressional elections. The Democrats won a majority of the statewide congressional vote ten times between 1966 and 1998, and the Republicans did so seven times. Gerrymandering has also helped to create safer congressional districts.

The data for congressional and state legislative elections since 1966 call into question the assumption that the majority party will regularly have its vote share magnified when the electoral system translates votes into seats. During periods when the statewide vote is closely divided, it seems clear that the party receiving a majority of the statewide vote may capture less than a proportionate share of the seats on a fairly regular basis. This tendency apparently can be facilitated by bipartisan gerrymandering aimed at protecting incumbents.

Summary

This chapter examined legislative competition in Pennsylvania during the years 1900–1998. A primary purpose was to try to put several post-1960 trends identified by previous writers into historical perspective, using Pennsylvania as a case study. The results reported here confirm some of the earlier findings, but modify others. In keeping with the format of the chapter, the findings for state legislative and congressional elections will be summarized separately.

General Assembly

There has been a significant increase in the number of incumbents seeking reelection since 1900. While the rate of success for incumbents seeking reelection has increased since 1960, the present figures do not represent a radical departure from the situation around the turn of the century. Between 1900 and 1908, the reelection rate was 85 percent for House incumbents and 92 percent for Senate incumbents. Rarely has the reelection rate for incumbents in either house dropped below 80 percent. The present reelection rate for senators (96 percent) is identical to the rate for the 1920s. During the twentieth century, incumbents in Pennsylvania have never really been an endangered species.

The proportion of General Assembly seats being won by safe margins has also increased since 1960. But once again, the contemporary trend is not unique. The proportion of safe seats during the period 1960–98 is not dramatically different in either chamber from the proportion of safe seats during the 1900–1928 period. In fact, nonincumbent winners obtained 60 percent or more of the vote more frequently during the earlier era.

The proportion of marginal districts increased in both chambers during the 1930s. This supports Burnham's (1970) argument that electoral competition increases during periods of partisan realignment. This trend toward greater competition continued through the 1950s in Pennsylvania. A likely factor in the recent decline in marginality is that either the Democrats or the Republicans enjoy a decided edge in partisan registration in most districts. The dominant party has enrolled at least 55 percent of the voters in 70 percent of both House and Senate districts. This is an important advantage, since most voters vote their party identification in legislative elections.

Unopposed general election candidates were rare in Pennsylvania until the 1980s. A dramatic increase in the number of contested races, especially those featuring incumbents, occurred during the 1980s. However, controlling for competition does not alter any of the relationships regarding marginality. Even in contested races, House and Senate winners, both incumbents and nonincumbents, are receiving larger percentages of the vote than was the case thirty years ago.

Electoral marginality was found to be related to rates of incumbent defeat. Incumbents who won their previous election by a safe margin had a dramatically lower rate of defeat than marginal candidates. Rates of defeat dropped significantly for both safe and marginal incumbents in both houses during the 1980s. The incidence of defeat for both categories of incumbents in both houses decreased significantly between the first five decades of the century and the second.

As expected, over the course of the century the party winning a majority of the statewide House vote won a share of seats greater than its proportion of the vote. However, that has not tended to be the case since 1966. In seven of the seventeen elections since 1966 the majority party's share of seats was less than its proportion of the vote. In fact, in only seven of the seventeen elections has the majority party won a percentage of seats greater than its share of the vote. In twelve of the seventeen elections the majority party has won 52 percent or less of the statewide vote cast for House candidates; also, in twelve of the seventeen elections the majority party has secured 52 percent or fewer of the House seats. This all suggests that in periods of close competition the assumed relationship between votes and seats may not prevail.

The current dearth of marginal districts is basically a return to the conditions that existed during the first three decades of the century. The proportion of districts won by safe margins during the 1920s would not be matched until the 1980s. The 1930s witnessed a dramatic increase in competition, a trend that would continue through the 1950s. It is this three decade trend that makes the post-1960 decreases in competition appear so dramatic.

As Table 3.22 makes clear, the period covered by this study can be divided into three phases, each spanning approximately one-third of the century. The first phase includes the years 1900–1928. During this phase 62 percent of House seats were won by safe margins, as were 54 percent of Senate seats. The second phase, 1930–58, saw a dramatic increase in marginality; the proportion of safe seats plummeted to 43 percent in the House, and 39 percent in the Senate. During the third phase, 1960–98, the proportion of safe seats rebounded dramatically—to 69 percent in the House and 63 percent in the Senate.

Table 3.22 A comparison of the percentage of safe House and Senate seats, by category of winner, 1900–1928, 1930–1958, and 1960–1998

Winner	1900–1928	1930–1958	1960–1998
House			
All	62%	43%	69%
Incumbent	69	52	74
Nonincumbent	56	30	45
Senate			
All	54%	39%	63%
Incumbent	65	47	71
Nonincunbent	50	28	42

SOURCE: Data calculated from the author's research.

The contemporary decline in marginality is not simply a result of the increased impact of incumbency. Nonincumbent candidates have also increased significantly the proportion of seats they are winning by safe margins. Regardless of the status of the candidates, there simply is not much competition in Pennsylvania legislative elections at present.

U.S. House of Representatives

The percentage of congressional incumbents running for reelection has increased over the past century. The increase was not as dramatic as it was among state legislators, however, because a higher percentage (66 percent) of congressional incumbents were running at the turn of the century. As was the case among state legislators, there was a notable increase in the number of incumbents running during the 1980s. Seventy-six percent of incumbents ran for reelection during the first half of the century, compared with 90 percent during the second half.

Congressional incumbents, like their state legislative counterparts, have never really had to fear for their political lives. Even during the first three decades of the century, the reelection rate was between 80 and 90 percent. During the past three decades, 95 percent of incumbents were successful in their reelection attempts.

Congressional districts have also become much safer since 1900. During the 1900–1928 period approximately one-half of the districts could be considered safe; by the 1980s and 1990s, three-fourths of the districts fell into that category. The 1920s again stand out as a decade characterized by a lack of competition. It would be the 1970s before the level of safe districts recorded during the 1920s would be attained again.

While the patterns are not quite as striking as they were among members of the General Assembly, the century can again be divided into three distinct phases (see Table 2.23). During the first phase, 50 percent of congressional seats were safe. During the second phase, that figure fell to 37 percent. During the four decades of the third phase, the proportion of safe seats increased dramatically to 68 percent.

Uncontested congressional races did not occur in Pennsylvania until the 1970s. The steepest drop in electoral competition occurred during the 1990s. The decline in contested elections has taken place exclusively among incumbents. As was discovered among state legislators, the decline in marginal districts cannot be ascribed to the increasing number of uncontested

Table 3.23 A comparison of the percentage of safe congressional seats, by category of winner, 1900–1928, 1930–1958, and 1960–1998

Winner	1900–1928	1930–1958	1960–1998
All	50%	37%	68%
Incumbent	63	57	76
Nonincumbent	28	18	23

SOURCE: Data calculated from the author's research.

races. Even in contested elections, winners have been receiving a larger percentage of the vote over the last thirty years.

Marginal incumbents were defeated at three times the rate of safe incumbents during the twentieth century. Safe incumbents incurred their highest rates of defeat between 1910 and 1918, and 1930 and 1938. Among both safe and marginal incumbents, the rates of defeat fell by two-thirds between the first half and the second half of the century.

The basic pattern over the course of the century is for the party receiving a majority of the statewide votes cast for congressional candidates to win a percentage of seats that is greater than its proportion of the vote. However, that pattern has not held up since 1966. In eight of the seventeen elections between 1966 and 1998, the majority party won fewer seats than its share of the vote. On five of those occasions, three times during the 1990s, the Republican Party won a majority of the vote and a minority of the seats.

This chapter has helped to put several aspects of legislative elections in Pennsylvania in historical perspective. In particular, it has been shown that high rates of incumbent reelection and low rates of marginal districts are not post-1960 trends. Incumbents have always been safe in Pennsylvania, and the proportion of safe districts was reasonably high at the beginning of the century.

LEGISLATIVE CAREERISM

Congress has been home to professional politicians for decades. In large part, that has been due to the fact that the position of representative or senator has long been a full-time, well-paying job. For most of the twentieth century that was not the case at the state level. State legislatures were part-time institutions populated by part-time legislators. As recently as 1960, only nineteen states held annual sessions, and legislators' salaries were extremely low. At present, forty-four states hold annual legislative sessions, and the past two decades have seen salaries rise significantly. By virtually any measure, state legislatures presently are more professional institutions than were their 1960s' predecessors (Rosenthal 1998; Patterson 1996).

One notable consequence of this increasing professionalism is the significant increase in the proportion of career politicians serving in these bodies. Today, more state lawmakers identify themselves as legislators, define their jobs as full time, and seek a career in the legislature or higher office. While these patterns are not uniform across the states, the trends are unmistakable (Rosenthal 1998). The public generally views these changes unfavorably. Many citizens perceive professional politicians as more concerned with protecting their careers than with serving the public.

Such attitudes help to explain why a majority of citizens favor term limits. Voters in twenty-two states and the District of Columbia approved term limits for members of Congress. These were struck down by the U.S. Supreme Court. Citizens also used the initiative to adopt term limits for state legislators in twenty-one states; in Utah and Louisiana the legislature instituted term limits. State supreme courts in Massachusetts, Washington, Oregon, and Wyoming have overturned term limits. Term limits were repealed by the legislatures in Idaho and Utah. At present, term limits for state legislators are in effect in fifteen states.

The Pennsylvania General Assembly is categorized as a professional legislature. Peverill Squire (1992, 72) ranks Pennsylvania fifth on his index of professionalization. The National Conference of State Legislatures identifies Pennsylvania as one of nine full-time legislatures (Kurtz 1992). Both studies rank states according to legislators' salaries, staff size, and length of session.

There is evidence of a high degree of careerism among current Pennsylvania legislators. Seventy-seven percent of the members report that they are full-time legislators (Gordon 1994, 25). Eighty-four percent of House members define their occupation as legislator, as do 70 percent of senators; the corresponding figures for 1960 were 8 percent and 4 percent (Kennedy 1999, 53). Finally, the rate of turnover for the decade of the 1990s was 13 percent in the House and 20 percent in the Senate; during the 1960s, the rates were 18 percent and 20 percent.

Thus, the preliminary evidence suggests a notable increase in careerism in the General Assembly during the past three decades. The recent trends imply that Pennsylvania voters are sending professional politicians to both the General Assembly and Congress. The significance of these trends can be better assessed by placing them in historical context. This chapter will examine the incidence of careerism among members of the General Assembly and the Pennsylvania congressional delegation during the twentieth century.

Data and Methods

This chapter will first examine the career of every member of the General Assembly and the Pennsylvania congressional delegation initially elected to office between 1900 and 1985. The tenure of these individuals will be calculated through December 1999. Once again, the data were obtained from *The Pennsylvania Manual* and its predecessor, *Smull's Legislative Hand Book*. This analysis will focus on the level of careerism for each decade of this century. Legislators will be grouped according to the decade in which they were first elected to the General Assembly or to Congress. Figures will be presented indicating the percentage of members elected during each decade who served one term or less, five years or more, ten years or more, and fifteen years or more, and the mean number of years served by members during each decade.

After this, a comparison will be made of the political backgrounds of members of the General Assembly serving in 1901 with those serving in 1995. Previous party and elective office experience will be examined.

Careerism Among Members of the General Assembly

The Pennsylvania House of Representatives

Table 4.1 displays the career patterns of House members during the last century. The tenure of current members provides a dramatic contrast with that of representatives elected around the turn of the century. Over half of the individuals elected between 1900 and 1909 served for 2 years or less; among those elected during the 1980s, only 10 percent had a tenure of one term or less. While only 12 percent of the members elected during the first decade of the century served 5 years or more, 85 percent of those elected during the 1980s held office that long; 3 percent of those elected during the 1900–1909 period served 10 years or more, compared with 66 percent of those elected during the 1980s. Only 1 percent of the representatives elected between 1900 and 1909 served for 15 years or more; by the 1980s, that figure had increased to 47 percent The mean tenure increased during the century from 3.3 years to 12.3 years. The figures for the last two decades will increase as nineteen members elected during the 1970s were still in office as of December 1999, as were thirty-one members elected during the 1980s.

Among House members, the past century has witnessed a steady decline in the number of members serving only one term and a concomitant increase in the number of members serving multiple terms. By the end of the 1990s fewer than one representative in ten was serving only one term, while almost nine of ten were serving five years or more and almost seven

Table 4.1 Percentage of members of the Pennsylvania House of Representatives serving selected terms of office, and mean tenure, by decade elected, 1900–1985

Tenure (years)	Decade Elected								
	1900–1909	1910–1919	1920–1929	1930–1939	1940–1949	1950–1959	1960–1969	1970–1979	1980–1985
1–4	52.0%	49.9%	40.5%	40.3%	41.1%	30.7%	23.1%	19.6%	9.5%
5+	12.1	17.6	30.4	29.6	40.4	48.3	61.2	60.8	85.3
10+	2.8	4.6	7.7	12.8	21.6	28.6	30.4	40.4	65.5
15+	1.1	1.6	1.4	4.1	7.8	7.9	12.5	22.9	47.4
Mean	3.3	3.6	4.0	4.6	5.7	6.6	7.9	9.3	12.3

SOURCE: Figures calculated by the author from data in *The Pennsylvania Manual*, selected volumes.

of ten were in office for ten years or more. The mean tenure was more than twelve years with that figure certain to rise much higher by the time all the members elected during the 1980s finally leave office.

The Pennsylvania Senate

Like their House counterparts, state senators in Pennsylvania have dramatically increased their tenure since 1900 (see Table 4.2). Sixty-four percent of senators elected during the first decade of the century served one term or less, compared with 14 percent of those elected during the 1980s. The percentage of senators who served 5 years or more has more than doubled, increasing from 36 percent to 86 percent; the percentage serving 10 years or more has gone from 15 percent to 82 percent. While only 5 percent of senators remained in office for 15 years or more at the beginning of this century, 64 percent did so by the 1980s. The mean tenure increased from 5.9 years during the first decade of the century to 13.2 years during the 1970s and 13.8 years during the decade of the 1980s. The figures for the 1970s and 1980s are significantly understated as nine senators elected during each decade were still in office at the end of 1999.

A Comparison of Pennsylvania House and Senate Careerism Patterns

The foregoing data substantiate the findings of previous research that legislative careerism has increased significantly since the 1960s. At least in Pennsylvania, however, this change is part of a pattern that has been developing since the beginning of the twentieth century. The basic trend in each house over the course of the century was toward greater careerism.

Table 4.2 Percentage of members of the Pennsylvania Senate serving selected terms of office, and mean tenure, by decade elected, 1900–1985

Tenure (years)	Decade Elected								
	1900–1909	1910–1919	1920–1929	1930–1939	1940–1949	1950–1959	1960–1969	1970–1979	1980–1985
1–4	64.0%	61.4%	38.7%	49.3%	39.6%	25.0%	33.3%	18.0%	13.6%
5+	36.0	38.6	61.3	50.7	60.4	75.0	66.7	82.0	86.4
10+	14.6	19.3	25.8	30.7	28.3	47.7	42.1	56.0	81.8
15+	4.5	10.2	8.1	17.3	20.8	18.2	17.5	44.0	63.6
Mean	5.9	6.8	7.6	8.8	9.0	9.8	9.8	13.2	13.8

SOURCE: Figures calculated by the author from data in *The Pennsylvania Manual*, selected volumes.

There has been a dramatic drop in the number of legislators serving only one term and a concomitant increase in the number of members serving two or more terms.

Only one in ten representatives and one in seven senators now serve just one term. On the other hand, almost half of the representatives and almost two-thirds of the senators are now serving fifteen years or more. The mean tenure has also risen significantly. The average member of the General Assembly now has a legislative career that spans more than a dozen years. There are, however, some differences between the patterns in the two chambers.

Careerism has increased at a much more uniform rate in the House. Also, dramatic increases were registered in all of the measures of careerism in the House during the decade of the 1980s. In the case of the Senate, the most crucial recent decade was the 1970s. By the end of the century, senators enjoyed an advantage on every measure of careerism except the percentage of members serving just one term.

Careerism among Pennsylvania Members of the U.S. House of Representatives

The careerism patterns among members of Congress are inconsistent and not what might be expected (see Table 4.3). As expected, the tenure of members of Congress has increased significantly since 1900. Forty-three percent of representatives served one term at the beginning of the century. That percentage dipped to just 5 percent among members elected during the 1970s, before rebounding to 27 percent during the 1980s. Forty-

Table 4.3 Percentage of members of the Pennsylvania congressional delegation serving selected terms of office, and mean tenure, by decade elected, 1900–1985

Tenure (years)	Decade Elected								
	1900–1909	1910–1919	1920–1929	1930–1939	1940–1949	1950–1959	1960–1969	1970–1979	1980–1985
1–4	42.7%	35.7%	34.1%	30.2%	43.1%	27.3%	10.5%	4.5%	27.3%
5+	42.7	42.9	52.3	46.0	46.6	59.1	84.2	59.1	72.7
10+	16.0	28.6	20.5	22.2	29.3	40.9	68.4	45.5	72.7
15+	1.3	19.6	2.3	7.9	17.2	27.3	31.6	27.3	45.5
Mean	5.3	7.1	6.0	6.5	7.9	9.8	14.4	10.6	11.6

SOURCE: Figures calculated by the author from data in *The Pennsylvania Manual*, selected volumes.

three percent of representatives served 5 or more years at the beginning of the century, and 16 percent served 10 or more years; by the end of the century the figure for both categories had increased to 73 percent. Only 1 percent of the members served for 15 years or more during the first decade of the century, compared with 46 percent among members elected during the 1980s. The mean tenure more than doubled, from 5.3 years to 11.6 years. The mean rate for the last two decades will increase as two members elected during the 1970s, and three members elected during the 1980s, were still in office as of December 1999.

The mean tenure increases from 1900–1909 to 1910–19, but then declines during the 1920s and 1930s. The rate then increases over the next three decades, peaking during the 1960s. The 1960s are the crucial decade for members of Congress. The biggest gains in tenure were registered during that decade, and the mean tenure was never higher. By the 1980s, more Pennsylvania representatives were serving for ten years or longer, or fifteen years or longer, than ever before, but the mean tenure had declined by almost three years since the 1960s. The main explanation for the lower overall tenure was the fact that the percentage of members serving just one term had returned to the levels of the 1950s.

A Comparison of Careerism Patterns among Members of the General Assembly and Pennsylvania Members of the U.S. House of Representatives

Contrary to what might be expected, tenure among members of Congress has not been consistently greater than among members of the General

Assembly. Table 4.4 lists the mean rate for all three groups of legislators. Tenure among members of Congress generally has been more extensive than among state representatives, but not as extensive as among state senators.

One obvious factor that could contribute to greater tenure among senators is their longer term of office. Table 4.5 reports the relationship between the mean rates of tenure and the mean rates of incumbent reelection success for all three groups of legislators for the twentieth century.

The evidence points to the importance of the four-year term for members of the Senate. Senators enjoyed longer tenure than representatives at either level with virtually identical reelection rates. The fact that Senate incumbents were reelected at the same rate as House incumbents runs counter to the research conducted by Carey, Niemi, and Powell (2000). They found that the four-year term correlated with a reduced probability of an incumbent winning. The authors also reported that serving in a professional legislature increased an incumbent's chances of winning. According to their measure of legislative professionalism, Pennsylvania ranked behind only California. The General Assembly has long been recognized as a professional legislature. Serving in a professional legislature has apparently given Pennsylvania senators an advantage not enjoyed by their counterparts in most other states. The last time that senators achieved the highest reelection rates was the 1940s. Members of Congress had the highest rates during the 1950s, 1960s, and 1970s, and state representatives recorded the highest rates during the last two decades of the century.

A direct comparison can be made between the two groups of representatives. Despite having essentially the same reelection rates, members of Congress established a mean tenure rate that was 38 percent higher than the rate for state representatives. The level of careerism over the course of the century clearly was higher for members of Congress than for members of the state House.

While differences exist among the groups of lawmakers, the main point remains that more career politicians currently are serving in the three chambers than was the case a hundred years ago.

A Comparison of the Political Backgrounds of Pennsylvania Legislators: 1901 and 1995

For an increasing number of members in many states, service in the state legislature has become a political career (Rosenthal 1998). Such certainly

Table 4.4 A comparison of mean rates of tenure (in years) for members of the General Assembly and members of the Pennsylvania congressional delegation, by decade elected, 1900–1985

Chamber	Decade Elected								
	1900–1909	1910–1919	1920–1929	1930–1939	1940–1949	1950–1959	1960–1969	1970–1979	1980–1985
Pennsylvania House	3.3	3.6	4.0	4.6	5.7	6.6	7.9	9.3	12.3
U.S. House	5.3	7.1	6.0	6.5	7.9	9.8	14.4	10.6	11.6
Pennsylvania Senate	5.9	6.8	7.6	8.8	9.0	9.8	9.8	13.2	13.8

SOURCE: Figures calculated by the author from data in *The Pennsylvania Manual*, selected volumes.

Table 4.5 Mean rates of tenure and mean rates of incumbent reelection success for members of the General Assembly and members of the Pennsylvania congressional delegation, 1900–1998

Office	Mean tenure (years)	Mean reelection rate (%)
Pennsylvania House	6.4	88
U.S. House	8.8	87
Pennsylvania Senate	9.4	88

SOURCE: Data calculated from the author's research.

seems to be the case in Pennsylvania. A number of factors have contributed to an acceleration of this trend during the past thirty years: more states are holding annual sessions of the legislature; legislators' salaries have increased significantly; more staff assistance is available; and the time demands of the job have increased. The result is that, by almost any definition, these individuals are professional politicians. The notion is that these contemporary professionals provide a dramatic contrast to the amateur "citizen-legislators" who populated the statehouses in previous eras.

As the nineteenth century drew to a close, access to the political system was controlled by dominant leaders who headed strong, cohesive political parties. Party officials anointed nominees and then mobilized compliant party identifiers to turn out and support the endorsed candidates. The majority of appointive positions were also controlled by the parties through a politics of patronage. It was an age of dominant parties and strong leadership.

The political environment in Pennsylvania at the dawn of the twentieth century possessed all of the characteristics just described. The post–Civil War years saw the development of strong political parties in Pennsylvania which have persisted to the present day. In Chapter 1, we discussed the domination of the Cameron-Quay-Penrose Republican organization from 1867 to 1921. A prominent historian contends that these leaders could "make" mayors, governors, legislators, congressmen, and even presidents (Smith 1964).

Political parties no longer exert such total control over the political system. The direct primary has removed the parties' monopoly over nominations, and partisan loyalty among voters and legislators has been significantly reduced. These contrasts exist in Pennsylvania, although not to the degree they exist in other states. Political party organizations in

Pennsylvania remain among the strongest in the nation. Pennsylvania is one of only four states where both major party organizations are ranked strong at both the state and local levels (Jewell and Olson 1988, 63–70). Both party organizations recruit and endorse candidates for a variety of offices. Forty percent of all candidates for the General Assembly in 1994 reported that they had been recruited by their political party (Kennedy 1999, 58–61).

While the political environment may not have changed as dramatically in Pennsylvania between 1901 and 1995 as in many other states, the political context certainly has been altered. Perhaps most notably, the direct primary, mandatory since 1913, has removed the stranglehold the parties had on nominations. Even though both parties still recruit and endorse candidates for the legislature, the direct primary offers candidates a viable alternative to obeisance to party leaders. Also, while Pennsylvania parties remain strong compared with those in other states, this must be placed in historical perspective. No one would suggest that even Pennsylvania's strong parties possess anything close to the power wielded by parties a hundred years ago.

Thus, it seems reasonable to expect that the political backgrounds of current legislators would differ from those of lawmakers elected at the beginning of the twentieth century. Reflecting the dominance of earlier parties, it is expected that legislators in 1901 would have held more party offices. In an era when nominations were controlled by party leaders, party service and loyalty were key prerequisites to a political career.

The expectations regarding previous office-holding are not as clear. In this era of professional politicians, it is possible that individuals would hold more local offices as they try to develop name recognition and political credentials in preparation for their assault on the state legislature and, possibly, higher offices. On the other hand, name recognition and perceived political availability are no longer dependent upon prior office-holding. If one can afford to hire first-rate political consultants, one can rather quickly establish name recognition and political credibility. It is much easier today to run for the legislature without previous political experience. Indeed, one could argue that today, in at least some districts, a candidate who could present himself or herself as an outsider—one not tainted by previous office-holding—would be more attractive to voters. Thus, it is possible that a sizable number of individuals might have bypassed the entry-level offices and gone directly to the state legislature.

House of Representatives

Information regarding political backgrounds was obtained for 186 of the 204 House members serving in 1901, and all 203 members of the 1995 House. All of the data refer to positions held prior to the member's initial election to the House. The information will be presented in two formats. Table 4.6 provides more detailed information regarding a variety of partisan and elective positions. The figures in Table 4.6 do not total 100 percent because while some members may have held a number of previous party and/or elective offices, others held no previous positions. Table 4.7 presents the same information in a summary form.

For both sessions, the most common background was an elective position at the local level. However, almost twice as many members held such positions in 1901 as in 1995. As expected, legislators in 1901 had more experience with the state party, but current lawmakers had much more local party activity. County office-holding was virtually identical.

Table 4.6 A comparison of the previous political backgrounds of members of the Pennsylvania House of Representatives, 1901 and 1995

Previous position	Session	
	1901	1995
County office	9.7% (18)	7.9% (16)
Local Elective Position	42.5% (79)	24.1% (49)
Delegate to national convention	3.8% (7)	3.4% (7)
Delegate to state convention or committee	18.3% (34)	3.9% (8)
Member of county committee	12.4% (23)	11.3% (23)
Member of local party committee	6.5% (12)	16.7% (32)

SOURCE: Figures calculated by the author from data in *Smull's Legislative Hand Book, 1901,* and *The Pennsylvania Manual,* vol. 112.

Table 4.7 A summary of the previous political backgrounds of members of the Pennsylvania House of Representatives, 1901 and 1995

Previous position	Session	
	1901	1995
Party	12.4% (23)	18.7% (38)
Elective	33.3% (62)	22.6% (45)
Both party and elective	16.7% (31)	8.4% (17)
No previous political experience	37.6% (70)	50.7% (103)

SOURCE: Figures calculated by the author from data in *Smull's Legislative Hand Book, 1901,* and *The Pennsylvania Manual,* vol. 112.

The summary data reveal that, contrary to our expectations, previous party office-holding is more common among contemporary legislators. On the other hand, members of the 1901 House were more likely to have held previous elective offices, and almost twice as likely to have previously held both party and elective positions. Finally, slightly more than half of the members in 1995 came to office with no previous party or elective experience, compared with 38 percent of those serving in 1901. Members in 1901 entered the legislature with longer political resumes than contemporary lawmakers do.

While the findings regarding representatives are not entirely consistent with our expectations, they can be reconciled with the basic arguments made earlier. It is clear that today it is possible to get elected to the House with no previous party or elective experience. One can establish a career in the legislature without first having held local office. With the aid of political consultants and modern campaign technology, contemporary candidates find it easier to convince voters that their private sector experience has adequately prepared them for legislative office. Moreover, an electorate which professes a preference for "citizen-legislators" and a disdain for professional politicians is less likely to view a lack of a political background as a liability.

Senate

Information regarding political backgrounds was obtained for forty-six of the fifty senators serving in 1901, and all fifty senators serving in 1995. The format is the same as the data for representatives. The data will be presented in detailed form in Table 4.8 and in summary form in Table 4.9. As was the case with representatives, a senator may have held a variety of previous partisan or elective positions, or no previous positions.

As expected, senators had much more extensive party backgrounds in 1901, especially at the state and county levels. The results regarding previous elective offices are mixed. Senators serving at the turn of the century were much more likely to have held county or local office. On the other hand, contemporary senators are more likely to be former representatives: half of the senators in 1995 were former members of the House.

As was predicted, senators in 1901 were more likely to have held party positions. Senators serving in 1995 held more previous elective offices, primarily because half of them had previously served in the House. Four times as many senators had held both party and elective offices in 1901

Table 4.8 A comparison of the previous political backgrounds of members of the Pennsylvania Senate, 1901 and 1995

	Session	
Previous position	1901	1995
House of Representatives	32.6% (15)	50.0% (25)
County office	28.3% (13)	8.0% (4)
Local elective position	32.6% (15)	16.0% (8)
Delegate to national convention	6.5% (3)	2.0% (1)
Delegate to state convention or committee	15.2% (7)	2.0% (1)
Member of county committee	30.4% (14)	12.0% (6)
Member of local committee	4.3% (2)	4.0% (2)

SOURCE: Figures calculated by the author from data in *Smull's Legislative Hand Book, 1901*, and *The Pennsylvania Manual*, vol. 112.

Table 4.9 A summary of the previous political backgrounds of members of the Pennsylvania Senate, 1901 and 1995

	Session	
Previous position	1901	1995
Party	13.0% (6)	8.0% (4)
Elective	32.2% (15)	54.0% (27)
Both party and elective	32.2% (15)	8.0% (4)
No previous political experience	21.7% (10)	30.0% (15)

SOURCE: Figures calculated by the author from data in *Smull's Legislative Hand Book, 1901*, and *The Pennsylvania Manual*, vol. 112.

than in 1995. Thirty percent of the senators serving in 1995 had no previous political experience, compared with 22 percent of their 1901 counterparts. Once again, evidence has been offered to show that today an extensive political background is not a prerequisite to a legislative career.

The notion of what constitutes a successful political career also changed over the course of the twentieth century. In 1900, for many politicians, election to either house of the state legislature would have been considered the culmination of a successful political career. There was plenty of power and action at the state level, especially in Pennsylvania. For some, a seat in the legislature would have been viewed as less desirable than a position in one of the powerful county or city machines. In fact, at midcentury, Sorauf (1963, 83–84) observed that "certainly, within Philadelphia and Allegheny counties, election to the House ranks as only a medium-sized political plum, less desirable than local elective office or many local political patronage jobs." Today, state legislative positions are more likely to be considered stepping-stones to a statewide office or a career in Congress.

Conclusions

The previous political backgrounds of representatives and senators are similar, but not identical. As expected, senators serving in 1901 held more party positions, especially at the county level, than senators serving in 1995 did; contrary to expectations, House members serving in 1995 had more extensive partisan backgrounds, especially at the local level, than their 1901 counterparts did. What is more significant, however, is that in neither era did members of either house have extensive backgrounds as party officeholders. The figures for 1901 were especially surprising. It was expected that more than one in eight legislators would have held party positions.

House members at the turn of the century had more extensive elective backgrounds than members in 1995; the figures for senators are the reverse. The disparities between the two periods for senators can be attributed to the fact that half of the senators in 1995 had served in the House, compared with only a third of the senators serving in 1901. Members of both houses of the General Assembly were more likely to have held both party and elective positions in 1901 than in 1995; likewise, notably fewer members were elected to the legislature with no previous political experience in the earlier period than in the more recent period. State lawmakers a century ago served more extensive political apprenticeships than present-day legislators do.

Reflecting that longer apprenticeship, representatives and senators were elected to the state legislature at a later age a century ago. Table 4.10 presents the mean and median age at which House and Senate members initially were elected to their respective chambers in 1901 and 1995. The mean age for representatives in 1901 was forty-two, compared with thirty-nine in 1995. Senators were forty-six at the time of their initial election in 1901, a figure that had dropped to forty-three by 1995. The same differences are reflected in the median ages of the two groups of lawmakers. Probably one other factor contributes to the reduced age threshold. During recent decades, the mean age of virtually every type of elected official has been declining. Modern campaigning, especially television, has placed a heightened emphasis on appearing vital, energetic, and attractive. During the era of the candidate-centered campaign, the trend has been toward younger candidates.

Table 4.10 The mean and median age of members of the General Assembly at the time of their initial election, 1901 and 1995

Session	Mean age	Median age
	House	
1901	42.0	41.0
1995	38.9	37.0
	Senate	
1901	46.5	47.0
1995	43.2	42.0

SOURCE: Figures calculated by the author from data in *Smull's Legislative Hand Book, 1901*, and *The Pennsylvania Manual*, vol. 112.

Summary

This chapter examined the level of careerism in the General Assembly and among members of the Pennsylvania delegation to the U.S. House of Representatives. The first part of the chapter analyzed the mean number of years served by members who were elected during each decade of the twentieth century. The second part of the chapter compared the political backgrounds of state representatives and senators who served in the 1901 and 1995 sessions of the General Assembly.

The trend for members in all three chambers is for increased careerism over the course of the century. In the contemporary period, compared to the beginning of the century, fewer members are serving only one term, and more members are serving multiple terms. The mean tenure has increased significantly for all three groups. At the state level, the rate of increase was more uniform for House members. The key decade in terms of increased tenure for state representatives was the 1980s. The 1970s was the crucial decade for state senators.

For members of the congressional delegation, the biggest increases occurred during the 1960s; in fact, congressional tenure was at its greatest during that decade. The percentage of members elected during the 1980s serving multiple terms increased significantly, but this was offset by the fact that the percentage of representatives serving only one term returned to the level of the 1950s.

Over the century, tenure was greatest for state senators, followed by members of Congress, and then state representatives. The crucial factor appears to be the four-year term served by senators, as their rate of reelection is virtually identical to the rates for the other two groups of legislators.

The contemporary Pennsylvania legislature is a more professional body than its 1901 predecessor, and the level of careerism among members has increased dramatically. In addition, party organizations have seen their influence greatly reduced. In such an altered political environment, it would be expected that the political backgrounds of members serving in the institution would also undergo a transformation. Indeed, the members serving in 1995 looked different from those holding office in 1901.

Among House members, the most common background in both eras was local elective office, but twice as many representatives had held such positions in 1901. Members serving in 1901 were more likely to have held a previous elective office, and twice as likely to have held both previous party and elective positions. In 1995, more than half the representatives had no previous political experience, compared with 38 percent in 1901.

Among senators, those holding office in 1901 had more extensive party experience than those serving in 1995, especially at the state and county levels. Members of the 1901 Senate were more likely to have held county or local office, while those in office in 1995 were more likely to have been state representatives (50 percent). Those serving at the beginning of the century were also four times more likely to have previously held both a party office and an elective office. Thirty percent had no previous experience in 1995, as contrasted with 22 percent in 1901.

Considerably more members embark upon their legislative careers today with no previous political experience. The availability of political consultants in conjunction with the direct primary has made candidates less dependent upon the party organizations. It seems clear that, even in Pennsylvania, with its long history of strong party organizations, potential candidates no longer have to serve long apprenticeships with the party. Political neophytes can decide to run for the General Assembly. In a number of areas in the state, these individuals must still be acceptable to the party leadership. Apparently, however, acceptance is no longer predicated on extensive party and electoral experience. Increasingly, too, many electoral functions today are being performed by legislative campaign committees responsible to the party caucuses, and not the traditional party organizations.

STATEWIDE ELECTIONS

While hundreds of contests were being fought in individual legislative districts every two years, Pennsylvania voters collectively were deciding a number of important races at the statewide level. The two most important decisions facing the Keystone State's electors were their choices for governor and president. Beginning in 1914, U.S. senators were also popularly elected. Finally, voters had to fill a variety of statewide offices. The auditor general and treasurer were elected throughout the twentieth century; at one time or another, the lieutenant governor (1900–1966), secretary of interior affairs (1900–1966), and attorney general (1980–present) were also selected by the voters.

This chapter will examine the twentieth-century elections for governor, president, U.S. senator, and statewide offices. Detailed analysis will be provided for gubernatorial and presidential elections. For both offices, county voting patterns will be provided for each decade and for the entire century. Data relating to each party's overall rate of success in statewide elections will be presented. One section of the chapter will analyze the Democrats' inability to elect U.S. senators. Overall partisan trends for all of the offices being examined in this chapter will be discussed.

Gubernatorial Elections

1900–1908

Republican candidates won both elections and garnered 55 percent of the two-party vote. However, the 57 percent of the vote obtained by Samuel W. Pennypacker in 1902, and the 53 percent captured by Edwin S. Stuart in 1906 would be dwarfed by the majorities piled-up by Republican candidates in the next two decades. Pennypacker carried thirty-eight of the sixty-seven counties in 1902, and Stuart captured thirty in 1906. Forty-four counties returned Republican majorities for the decade (see Figure 5.1). The Republicans did well in urban areas, with Philadelphia and Allegheny Counties both returning heavy GOP majorities (see Table 5.1). Democratic strength was clustered in the east-central and northeastern counties.

1910–1918

The Republicans won three gubernatorial elections during the decade with an average of 66 percent of the two-party vote, including an incredible 76 percent majority racked up by John K. Tener in his rout of Webster Grim in 1910. Fifty-four counties returned GOP majorities for the decade, including Philadelphia and Allegheny Counties (see Figure 5.2). The 1914 election was an anomaly. While receiving only 44 percent of the two-party vote and losing to Republican Martin C. Brumbaugh, Democratic candidate Vance C. McCormick carried forty-four counties. Tener carried fifty-five counties, as did William C. Sproul in 1918. Democratic strength during the decade basically was concentrated in a group of counties in the east-central part of the state.

1920–1928

The Republican domination of gubernatorial elections reached its peak during the 1920s. For the decade, the GOP averaged 67 percent of the two-party vote, capped-off by the 75 percent received by John S. Fisher in

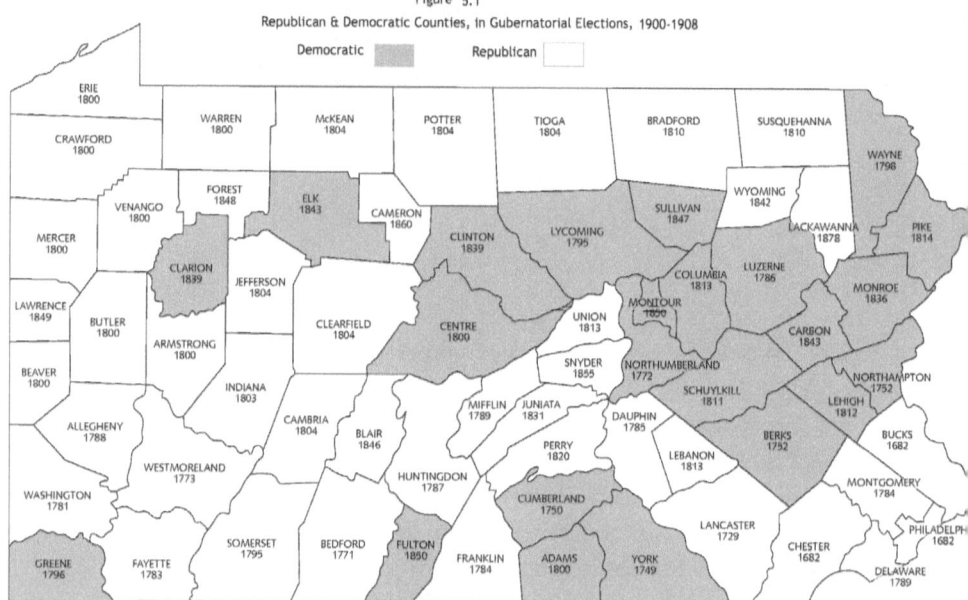

Figure 5.1
Republican & Democratic Counties, in Gubernatorial Elections, 1900-1908

Table 5.1 The ten most Republican and ten least Republican counties in gubernatorial elections, 1900–1908

Most Republican		Least Republican	
County	%	County	%
Allegheny	68.9	Monroe	23.0
Lancaster	66.4	Pike	32.2
Indiana	65.6	Colombia	32.4
Somerset	63.4	Montour	32.5
Philadelphia	63.3	Elk	35.5
Tioga	62.3	Berks	36.4
Lebanon	60.6	Greene	38.6
Delaware	59.5	Clarion	40.3
Forest	59.1	Fulton	40.7
Warren	58.8	Carbon	42.7

SOURCE: Data calculated from the author's research.

1926 as he crushed Philadelphia judge Eugene C. Bonniwell. Fisher's 737,543 vote margin was a record. Bonniwell, the first Pennsylvania Catholic to run for governor, was making his second attempt to capture the office. In his first race in 1918, he had garnered only 36 percent of the two-party vote while losing to William C. Sproul.

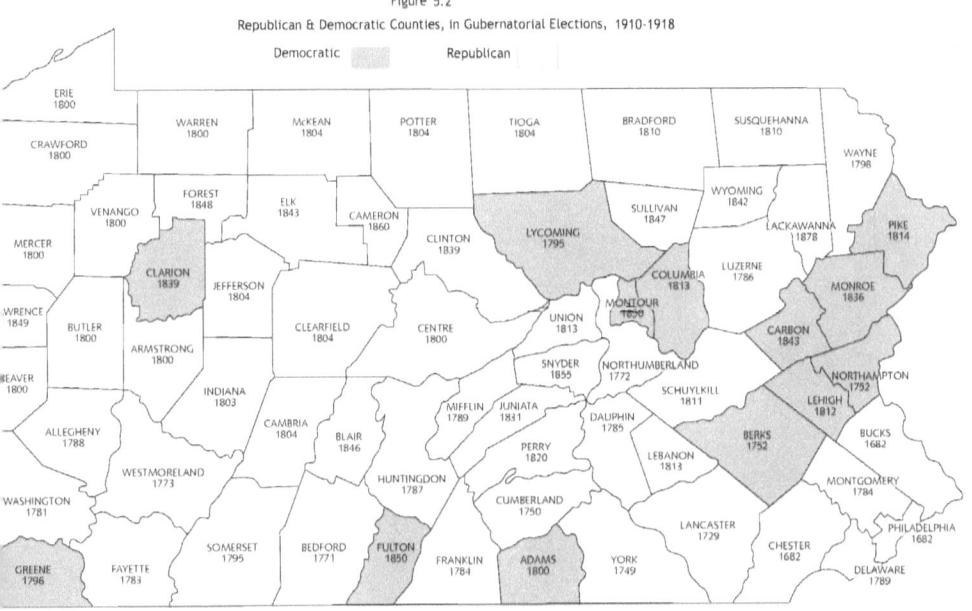

Figure 5.2
Republican & Democratic Counties, in Gubernatorial Elections, 1910-1918

Table 5.2 The ten most Republican and ten least Republican counties in gubernatorial elections, 1910–1918

Most Republican		Least Republican	
County	%	County	%
Delaware	78.7	Monroe	35.6
Philadelphia	78.3	Pike	36.4
Lancaster	75.9	Columbia	39.1
Indiana	74.3	Berks	40.3
Dauphin	73.5	Greene	42.1
Tioga	73.3	Fulton	46.4
Lebanon	72.8	Lehigh	46.8
Lawrence	72.7	Adams	47.6
Huntingdon	72.0	Montour	47.7
Somerset	71.3	Northampton	47.9

SOURCE: Data calculated from the author's research.

In 1926, Bonniwell captured only one county, Monroe, and that by a mere fourteen votes. Gifford Pinchot carried thirty-six counties in winning his first term in 1922. For the decade, only eight counties went Democratic (see Figure 5.3). Four of the Democratic counties were in the east-central part of the state; Greene County once again produced a Democratic

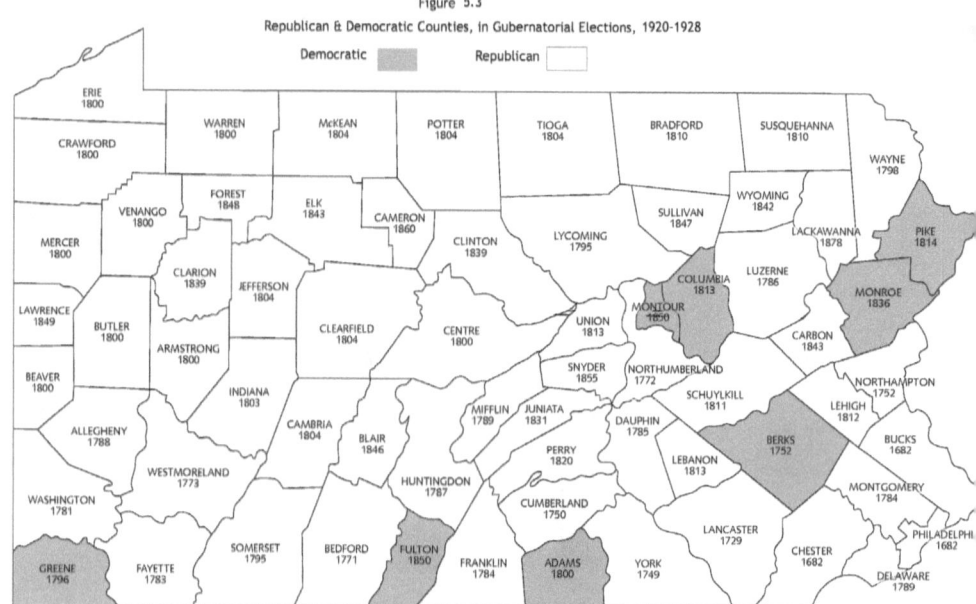

Figure 5.3
Republican & Democratic Counties, in Gubernatorial Elections, 1920-1928

Table 5.3 The ten most Republican and ten least Republican counties in gubernatorial elections, 1920–1928

Most Republican		Least Republican	
County	%	County	%
Philadelphia	80.3	Monroe	40.0
Elk	79.0	Fulton	42.5
Tioga	77.5	Berks	45.7
Delaware	77.3	Greene	46.0
Erie	75.3	Adams	47.4
Bradford	73.1	Columbia	48.3
Cameron	72.9	Montour	48.6
Indiana	75.5	Pike	49.6
Forest	72.4	Northampton	50.0
Somerset	72.3	Carbon	51.1
		Clarion	51.1

SOURCE: Data calculated from the author's research.

majority. Allegheny County was not among the ten most Republican counties during the decade, but its 72 percent figure left it just outside the cutoff number. The Philadelphia County proportion was an impressive 80 percent (see Table 5.3).

1930–1938

It was during this decade that the Democratic Party became competitive in Pennsylvania. The mean Republican percentage for the decade dropped from the approximately two-thirds margin of the previous two decades to only 51 percent. Still, the Democrats won only one of the three elections during the 1930s. That was in 1934, when George H. Earle captured 51 percent of the two-party vote in defeating William A. Schnader, and became the first Democrat elected governor since Robert E. Pattison won by seventeen thousand votes in 1890. Gifford Pinchot won for the second time in 1930, and Arthur H. James was victorious in 1938. Pinchot obtained 51 percent of the two-party vote, and James received 54 percent; Pinchot carried 60 counties and James prevailed in 61.

Fifty-two counties gave Republican candidates a majority of the vote during the decade (see Figure 5.4). Democratic strength persisted in the east-central part of the state. Berks and Monroe Counties went Democratic for the fourth consecutive decade, and Lehigh and Northampton Counties for the third time in four decades. The 1930s witnessed the establishment of prominent electoral patterns that would persist for the remainder of

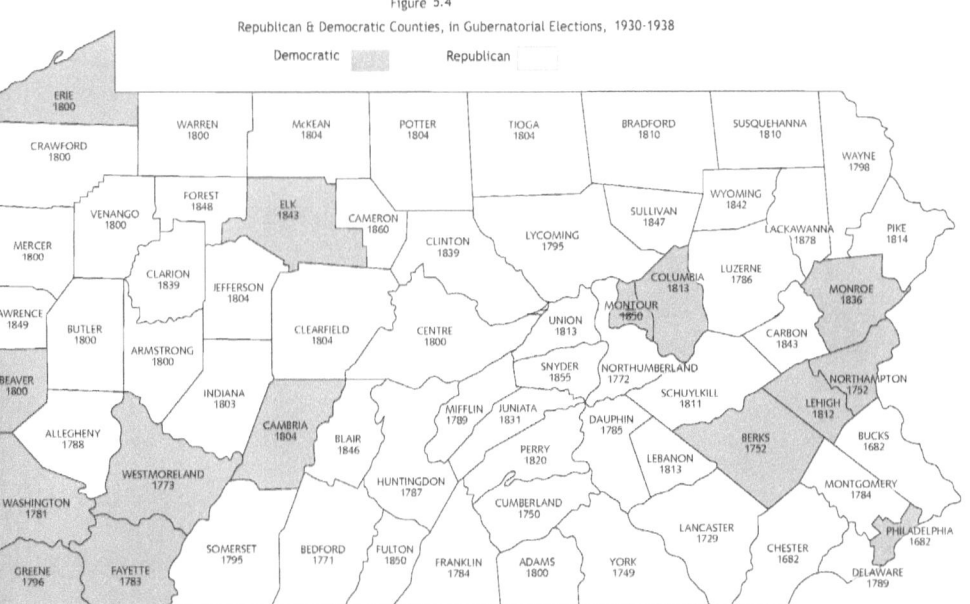

Figure 5.4
Republican & Democratic Counties, in Gubernatorial Elections, 1930-1938

Table 5.4 The ten most Republican and ten least Republican counties in gubernatorial elections, 1930–1938

Most Republican		Least Republican	
County	%	County	%
Tioga	72.1	Philadelphia	42.0
Wayne	71.7	Berks	42.2
Bradford	70.3	Greene	44.8
Snyder	69.6	Fayette	45.7
Huntingdon	69.5	Montour	45.7
Union	68.5	Lehigh	45.8
Venango	67.1	Erie	46.0
Cameron	66.4	Monroe	46.8
Forest	66.2	Elk	47.2
Wyoming	66.1	Cambria	47.8

SOURCE: Data calculated from the author's research.

the century. For the first time, Philadelphia became one of the ten most Democratic counties (see Table 5.4). The southwestern part of the state was established as a Democratic stronghold; Greene County went Democratic for the fourth consecutive decade.

1940–1948

The Republicans won both elections and averaged 57 percent of the two-party vote. Edward Martin got 54 percent of the two-party vote and won 57 counties in 1942; James H. Duff captured 59 percent of the vote and carried sixty counties in 1946. Duff also initiated another interesting pattern: since the end of World War II, the two parties have alternated eight-year reigns in the governor's mansion.

Only nine counties produced Democratic majorities for the decade (see Figure 5.5). Democratic strength was confined basically to the southwestern corner of the state; however, Northampton County again went Democratic.

1950–1958

For the first time during the twentieth century, the Republican Party averaged less than 50 percent of the two-party vote for governor (49 percent) for a decade. Democrats won two of the three elections. Republican John S. Fine captured 51 percent of the two-party vote and fifty-one counties in

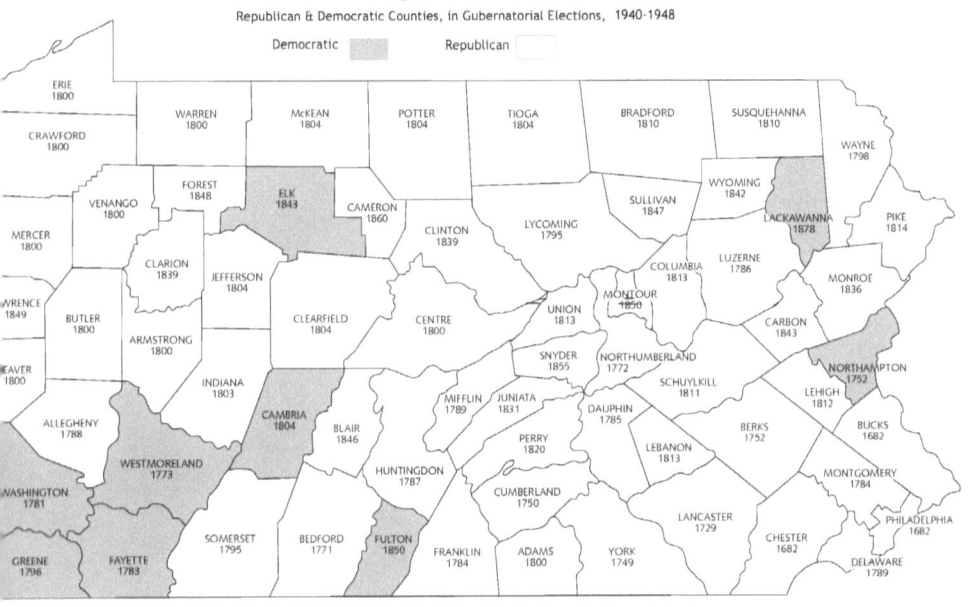

Figure 5.5
Republican & Democratic Counties, in Gubernatorial Elections, 1940-1948

Table 5.5 The ten most Republican and ten least Republican counties in gubernatorial elections, 1940–1948

Most Republican		Least Republican	
County	%	County	%
Tioga	79.0	Greene	45.7
Bradford	75.1	Washington	46.6
Venango	74.5	Fayette	47.3
McKean	74.4	Lackawanna	47.7
Wayne	73.9	Westmoreland	49.0
Union	73.1	Cambria	49.7
Snyder	72.8	Northampton	49.8
Warren	72.5	Elk	49.9
Montgomery	72.5	Fulton	49.9
Lancaster	70.6	Berks	50.0

SOURCE: Data calculated from the author's research.

1950. Democrat George M. Leader received 54 percent of the vote and carried thirty-four counties during his victory in 1954. The Democrats retained control of the governorship when David L. Lawrence garnered 51 percent of the vote and won fifty counties in 1958.

The Democrats had an advantage in twenty-one counties during the 1950s (see Figure 5.6). In the eastern part of the state, the Democratic

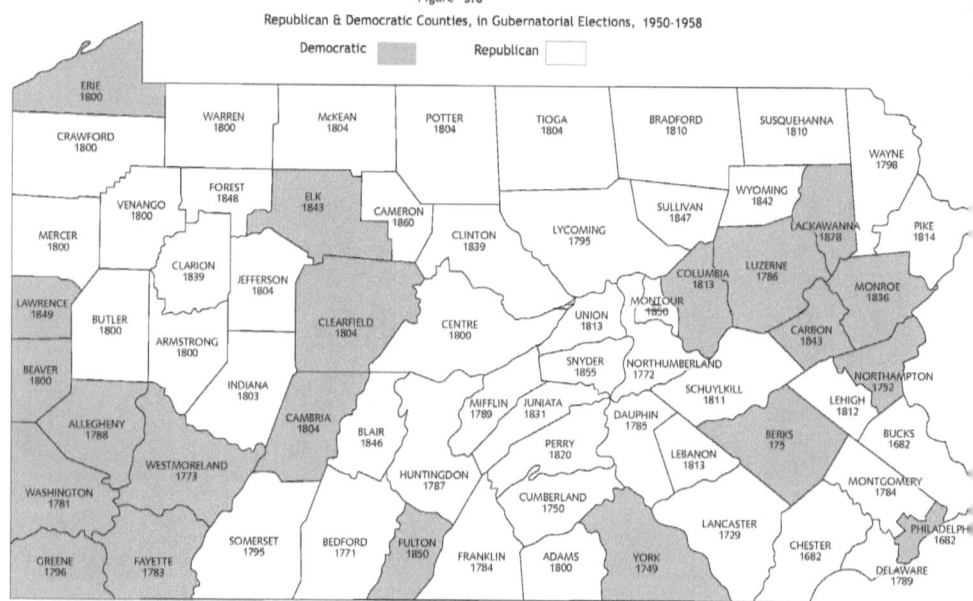

Figure 5.6
Republican & Democratic Counties, in Gubernatorial Elections, 1950-1958

Table 5.6 The ten most Republican and ten least Republican counties in gubernatorial elections, 1950–1958

Most Republican		Least Republican	
County	%	County	%
Union	72.1	Philadelphia	38.3
Snyder	71.3	Cambria	40.2
Tioga	67.3	Fayette	40.3
Wayne	66.5	Lackawanna	41.6
Bradford	65.3	Washington	42.6
Venango	65.1	Beaver	43.1
Lancaster	64.8	Westmoreland	43.2
Wyoming	64.5	Greene	43.8
McKean	63.0	Allegheny	45.5
Montgomery	62.5	York	45.6

SOURCE: Data calculated from the author's research.

counties included Philadelphia, York, and seven counties in the east-central region. Out west, the Democrats controlled the counties in the southwestern corner of the state, plus five other counties, including Erie. This was the first decade that the Democrats won a majority in both Philadelphia and Allegheny Counties, a pattern that would recur with the exception of the 1960s.

1960–1968

The Republicans captured 54 percent of the two-party vote and won both elections. William W. Scranton carried sixty-two counties in 1962, and Raymond P. Shafer prevailed in fifty-five counties in 1966. For the decade, the Democrats received a majority of the vote in only nine counties (see Figure 5.7). The principal area of strength for the Democrats was again the southwestern corner of the state (with the exception of Allegheny County). In the east, they secured a majority in Philadelphia, Northampton, Luzerne, and Lackawanna Counties.

1970–1978

The Democrats garnered 53 percent of the two-party vote while winning two of three elections. Milton J. Shapp, the first Pennsylvania governor eligible to succeed himself, won in 1970 and 1974. Shapp carried thirty-six counties in 1970, but only twenty-six while winning reelection in 1974. Republican Dick Thornburgh replaced Shapp in 1978, receiving 53 percent of the vote and prevailing in fifty counties.

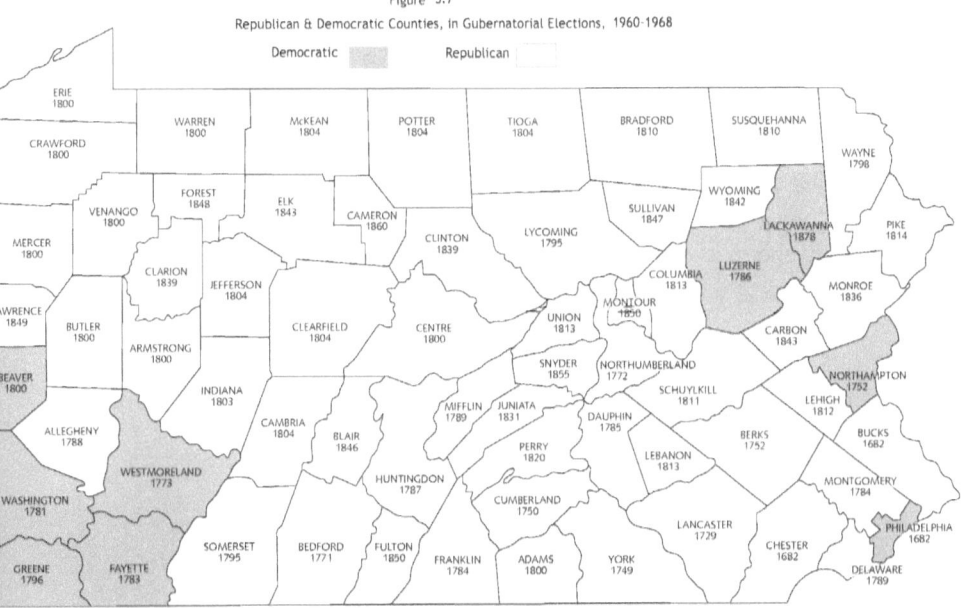

Figure 5.7
Republican & Democratic Counties, in Gubernatorial Elections, 1960-1968

Table 5.7 The ten most Republican and ten least Republican counties in gubernatorial elections, 1960–1968

Most Republican		Least Republican	
County	%	County	%
Union	75.2	Philadelphia	42.9
Snyder	73.9	Fayette	44.3
Wyoming	72.1	Greene	45.2
Lancaster	72.0	Washington	45.4
Wayne	71.3	Westmoreland	47.0
Pike	70.0	Beaver	47.1
Tioga	69.5	Northampton	48.7
Bradford	69.4	Lackawanna	49.6
Chester	67.6	Luzerne	49.9
Lebanon	67.4	Erie	50.2

SOURCE: Data calculated from the author's research.

Twenty-seven counties were in the Democratic column for the decade (see Figure 5.8). The party did especially well in the western part of the state, winning Allegheny County and most others in the southwestern and west-central areas. In the East, the Democrats carried Philadelphia County and eight others, including the traditional strongholds of Berks and Northampton Counties. This would be the last decade that the latter two counties would fall into the Democratic column.

1980–1988

The parties split two elections, swapping 51–49 percent victories. In 1982, Dick Thornburgh carried forty-six counties in winning reelection, while in 1986 Democrat Robert P. Casey won the first of his two terms despite capturing only twenty-four counties. For the decade, the Democrats came out ahead in twenty-four counties (see Figure 5.9). The geographical pattern varied only slightly from the previous decade. As in the 1970s, the Democrats did well in the southwestern and west-central counties. In the east, they once again carried Philadelphia County. In addition, they swapped Berks, Lehigh, and Northampton Counties for several counties in the center of the state.

1990–1998

For the second consecutive decade, the Republicans and Democrats each received 50 percent of the two-party vote. How they did it was highly

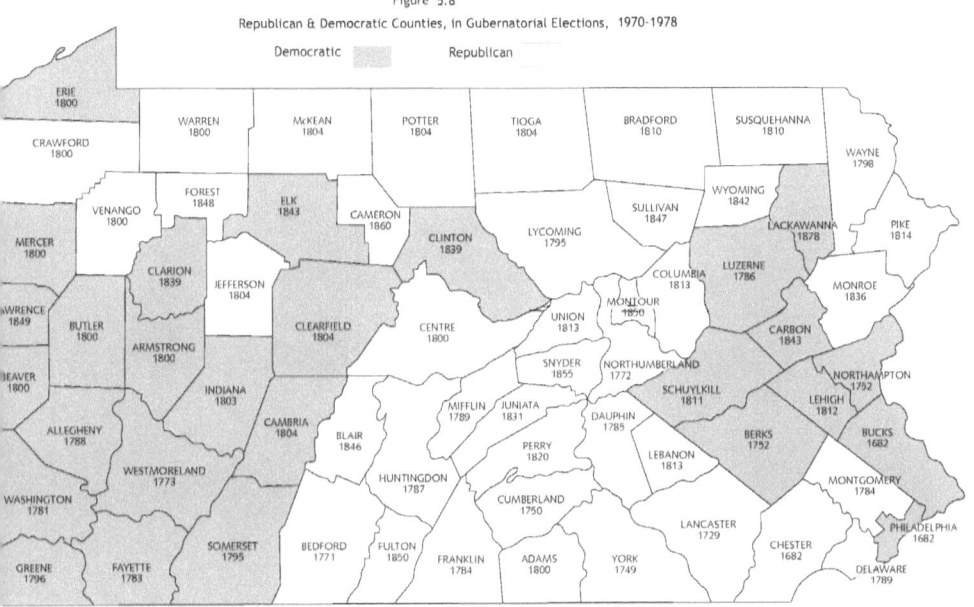

Figure 5.8
Republican & Democratic Counties, in Gubernatorial Elections, 1970-1978

Table 5.8 The ten most Republican and ten least Republican counties in gubernatorial elections, 1970–1978

Most Republican		Least Republican	
County	%	County	%
Wayne	69.7	Beaver	35.5
Union	69.1	Washington	36.3
Snyder	69.0	Westmoreland	36.5
Bradford	67.7	Fayette	37.6
Tioga	67.6	Philadelphia	37.9
Wyoming	67.1	Greene	39.3
Lancaster	66.6	Cambria	40.8
Pike	64.9	Northampton	42.7
Susquehanna	64.4	Allegheny	42.8
McKean	62.3	Lawrence	43.0

SOURCE: Data calculated from the author's research.

unusual. Democrat Robert P. Casey obtained 68 percent of the two-party vote in his successful reelection attempt in 1990; Republican Tom Ridge coasted to reelection in 1998, capturing 65 percent of the vote. Both incumbents won sixty-six of the sixty-seven counties. Sandwiched in between was Ridge's initial victory in 1994. He got 53 percent of the vote and prevailed in fifty-six counties.

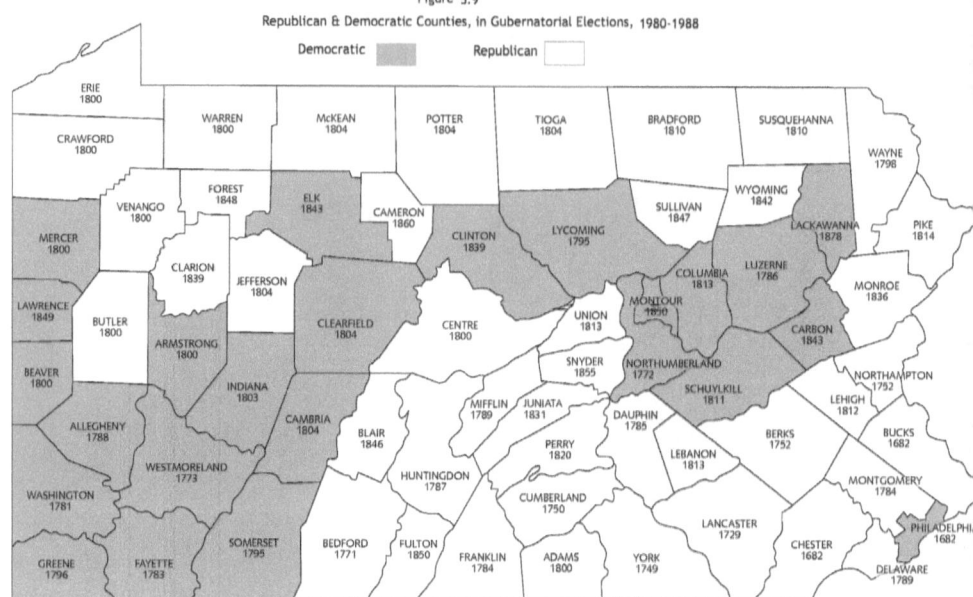

Figure 5.9
Republican & Democratic Counties, in Gubernatorial Elections, 1980-1988

Table 5.9 The ten most Republican and ten least Republican counties in gubernatorial elections, 1980–1988

Most Republican		Least Republican	
County	%	County	%
Lancaster	71.3	Fayette	33.5
Chester	68.0	Beaver	35.7
Montgomery	67.0	Greene	35.7
Snyder	63.8	Philadelphia	36.1
Bradford	63.3	Lackawanna	37.6
Delaware	62.8	Cambria	37.6
McKean	61.7	Luzerne	39.3
Cumberland	61.4	Northumberland	40.3
Bucks	61.0	Washington	40.5
Union	60.4	Lawrence	40.6

SOURCE: Data calculated from the author's research.

The Democrats could lay claim to only sixteen counties for the decade (see Figure 5.10). They once again carried the counties in the southwestern part of the state. In the east, Philadelphia, Luzerne, and Lackawanna Counties went Democratic for the fifth decade in a row; Carbon County went Democratic for the fourth time in five decades.

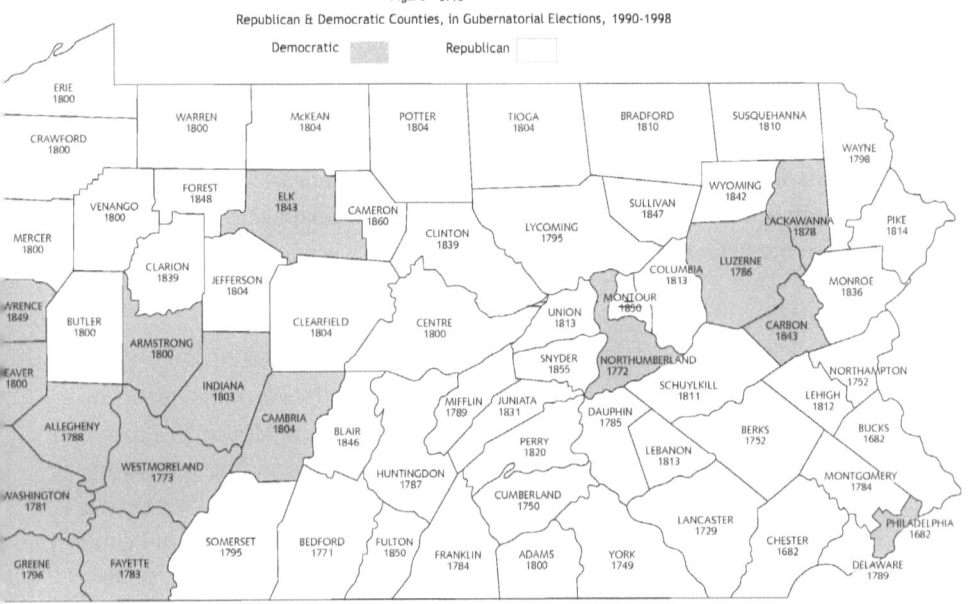

Figure 5.10
Republican & Democratic Counties, in Gubernatorial Elections, 1990-1998

Table 5.10 The ten most Republican and ten least Republican counties in gubernatorial elections, 1990–1998

Most Republican		Least Republican	
County	%	County	%
Bradford	64.7	Philadelphia	31.1
Potter	63.4	Fayette	34.6
Tioga	63.3	Greene	38.1
McKean	62.6	Cambria	38.2
Snyder	62.6	Lackawanna	39.4
Chester	62.6	Beaver	40.8
Crawford	61.7	Washington	41.4
Pike	60.7	Luzerne	43.6
Bedford	60.7	Westmoreland	44.0
Sullivan	60.5	Allegheny	44.4

SOURCE: Data calculated from the author's research.

Presidential Elections

1900–1908

Republican presidential candidates captured 66 percent of the two-party vote in sweeping the first three elections of the twentieth century. Theodore

Roosevelt won 72 percent of the vote and carried sixty-one counties in 1904. William McKinley garnered 63 percent of the vote in 1900, and William Howard Taft received 62 percent in 1908. McKinley won fifty-four counties, and Taft won fifty-six. The Democrats prevailed in only eleven counties during the decade (see Figure 5.11). These counties were located primarily in the eastern part of the state. Both Philadelphia and Allegheny Counties were solidly Republican, giving approximately three-fourths of their vote to GOP candidates (see Table 5.11).

1910–1918

The Democrats bounced back during this decade, thanks to the impact of Theodore Roosevelt on the 1912 election. After William Howard Taft won the Republican nomination, a group of insurgents, including some from Pennsylvania, nominated Roosevelt as the candidate of the Progressive Party. The Progressive Party was known as the Washington Party in Pennsylvania. In fact, of the 444,894 votes Roosevelt won in the state, 350,865 came on the Washington Party line. Roosevelt won the state's electoral votes.

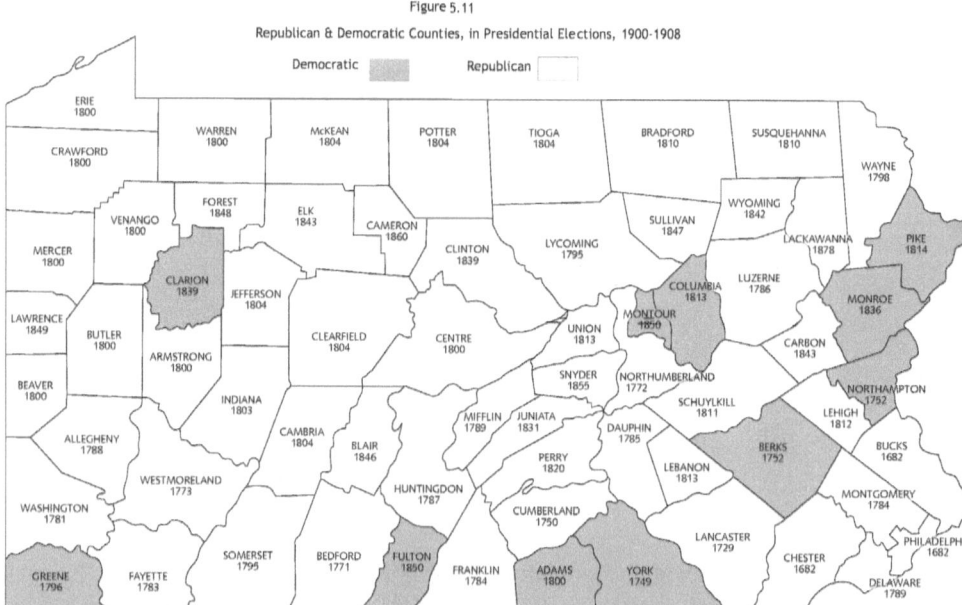

Figure 5.11
Republican & Democratic Counties, in Presidential Elections, 1900-1908

Table 5.11 The ten most Republican and ten least Republican counties in presidential elections, 1900–1908

Most Republican		Least Republican	
County	%	County	%
Indiana	78.2	Monroe	32.6
Tioga	77.2	Pike	35.1
Somerset	76.7	Greene	40.7
Delaware	76.6	Columbia	41.5
Philadelphia	76.1	Berks	45.0
Lancaster	75.2	Montour	45.8
Allegheny	73.6	Fulton	47.3
Warren	72.8	Adams	49.1
Blair	72.8	Northampton	49.3
Huntingdon	72.6	Clarion	49.4

SOURCE: Data calculated from the author's research.

Because Roosevelt siphoned off so many Republican votes, the Democratic candidate, Woodrow Wilson, won 59 percent of the two-party vote. Sixty-one of the state's sixty-seven counties went Democratic. The Republicans rebounded behind Charles Evans Hughes in 1916; he received 58 percent of the vote in Pennsylvania and won forty-three counties.

The Democrats more than quadrupled their success from the previous decade, prevailing in forty-eight counties (see Figure 5.12). However, the Republicans still were dominant in Philadelphia and Allegheny Counties. While 63 percent of the vote in Philadelphia County went for Republican candidates (see Table 5.12), a scant 51 percent of the vote in Allegheny County went to GOP presidential candidates.

1920–1928

The Republican Party came back with a vengeance during the 1920s, capturing 71 percent of the two-party vote. None of the elections was close: Warren G. Harding won 71 percent of the vote and sixty-four counties in 1920; Calvin Coolidge won 77 percent of the vote and sixty-three counties in 1924; Herbert Hoover won 66 percent of the vote and sixty-four counties in 1928. So total was the Republican dominance that the Democrats carried only Greene County for the decade (see Figure 5.13). The Republican percentages of the vote were astounding and would never be duplicated. Among the ten most Republican counties, five had percentages above 81

112 ★ ELECTIONS IN PENNSYLVANIA

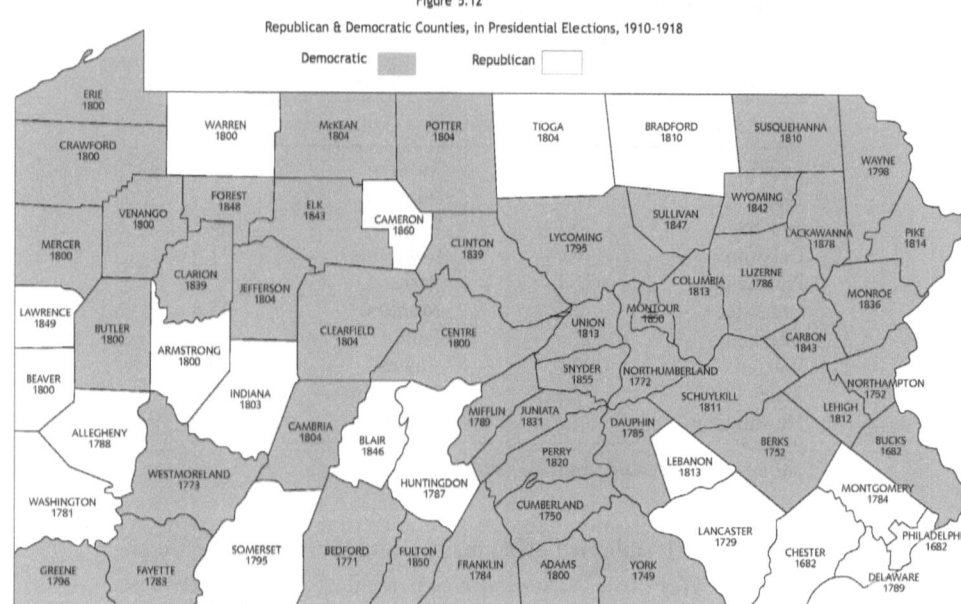

Figure 5.12
Republican & Democratic Counties, in Presidential Elections, 1910-1918

Table 5.12 The ten most Republican and ten least Republican counties in presidential elections, 1910–1918

Most Republican		Least Republican	
County	%	County	%
Lancaster	63.2	Monroe	22.5
Delaware	63.1	Columbia	24.7
Philadelphia	63.1	Greene	25.1
Tioga	59.9	Pike	27.0
Indiana	59.5	Montour	29.0
Cameron	59.1	Fulton	31.4
Lawrence	54.1	Adams	31.9
Somerset	53.3	Clarion	33.5
Lebanon	52.4	Lycoming	34.4
Warren	52.3	York	34.4

SOURCE: Data calculated from the author's research.

percent, and all were at least 79 percent (see Table 5.13). The GOP received at least 60 percent of the vote in six of the ten least Republican counties.

1930–1938

The parties split two elections, with the Democrats winning 53 percent of the two-party vote during the decade. Republican Herbert Hoover received

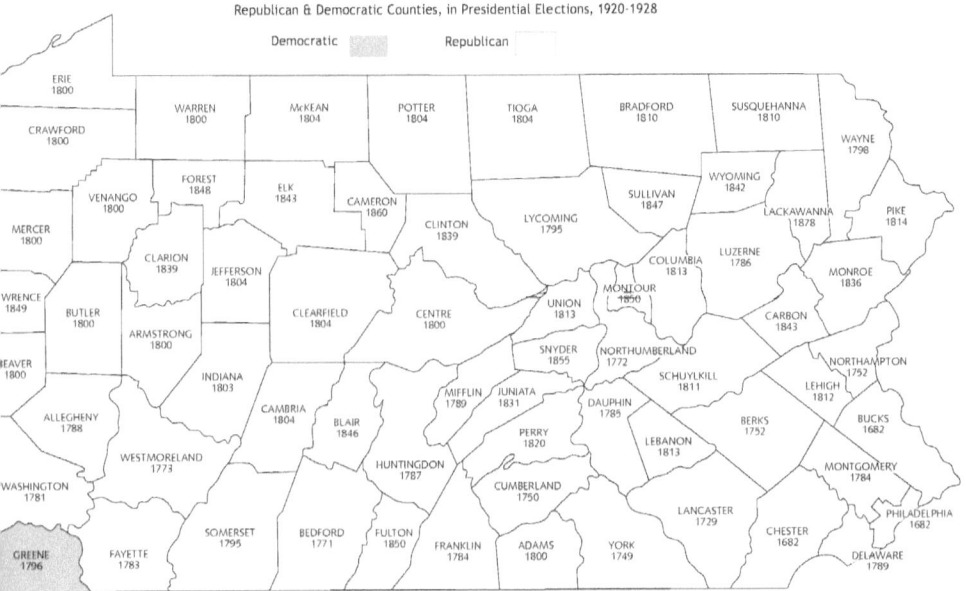

Figure 5.13
Republican & Democratic Counties, in Presidential Elections, 1920-1928

Table 5.13 The ten most Republican and ten least Republican counties in presidential elections, 1920–1928

Most Republican		Least Republican	
County	%	County	%
Tioga	87.6	Greene	47.9
Indiana	81.7	Monroe	55.2
Bradford	81.5	Fulton	55.9
Somerset	81.3	Columbia	56.7
Huntingdon	81.1	Lackawanna	59.4
Lawrence	80.1	Adams	60.0
Venango	79.6	Montour	61.7
Warren	79.6	Fayette	62.6
Delaware	79.6	Berks	62.7
Snyder	79.2	Sullivan	63.3
Union	79.2	Clarion	63.3

SOURCE: Data calculated from the author's research.

53 percent of the vote and carried forty counties during his victory in 1932. Democrat Franklin D. Roosevelt garnered 58 percent of the vote and prevailed in forty-one counties in winning reelection in 1936. Largely on the strength of the 1936 election, the Democrats predominated in thirty-one counties during the 1930s (see Figure 5.14). The counties in the south-

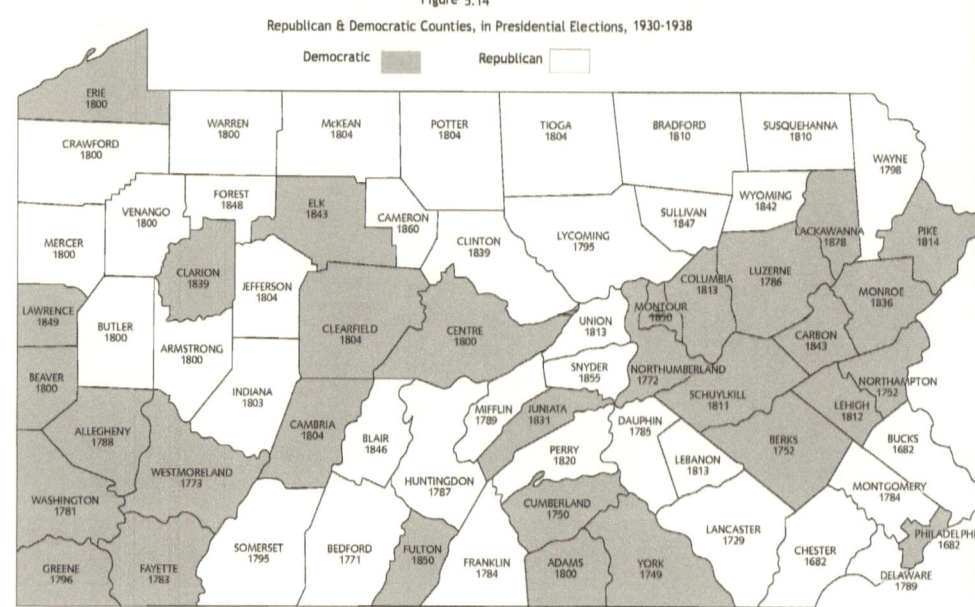

Figure 5.14

Republican & Democratic Counties, in Presidential Elections, 1930-1938

Table 5.14 The ten most Republican and ten least Republican counties in presidential elections, 1930–1938

Most Republican		Least Republican	
County	%	County	%
Tioga	72.9	Fayette	33.9
Bradford	66.6	Greene	34.3
Venango	66.1	Westmoreland	36.5
Union	65.0	Washington	36.6
Wayne	64.3	Allegheny	38.5
Snyder	63.0	Cambria	38.7
Forest	63.0	Berks	39.7
Huntingdon	62.6	Monroe	41.8
Chester	61.7	Northumberland	42.1
Delaware	61.7	Montour	42.2

SOURCE: Data calculated from the author's research.

western corner of the state were established as a Democratic stronghold. The Democrats also carried a large block of counties in the east-central part of the state, and two other blocks in the south-central and central areas of the state. The Democrats also prevailed in Philadelphia and Allegheny Counties for the first time.

1940–1948

During the 1940s, the Democrats won two of three elections and received 51 percent of the two-party vote. Franklin D. Roosevelt got 54 percent of the vote and won forty-two counties in 1940; in 1944 his share of the vote shrunk to 51 percent, but he won fifty-one counties. Republican Thomas E. Dewey captured 52 percent of the vote in 1948 and prevailed in fifty-four counties.

The seventeen counties which gave a majority of their votes for the decade to Democratic candidates was slightly more than half the party's total for the 1930s (see Figure 5.15). Once again, Philadelphia County and the southwestern counties went Democratic. In the eastern part of the state, York County and group of counties in the east-central part of the state again went Democratic. Clinton County and three counties in the west-central area of the state rounded out the Democratic bastions.

1950–1958

Republican Dwight D. Eisenhower carried Pennsylvania in 1952 and 1956 and received an average of 55 percent of the two-party vote. Eisenhower won fifty-seven counties in 1952 and sixty-two counties in 1956. Only seven

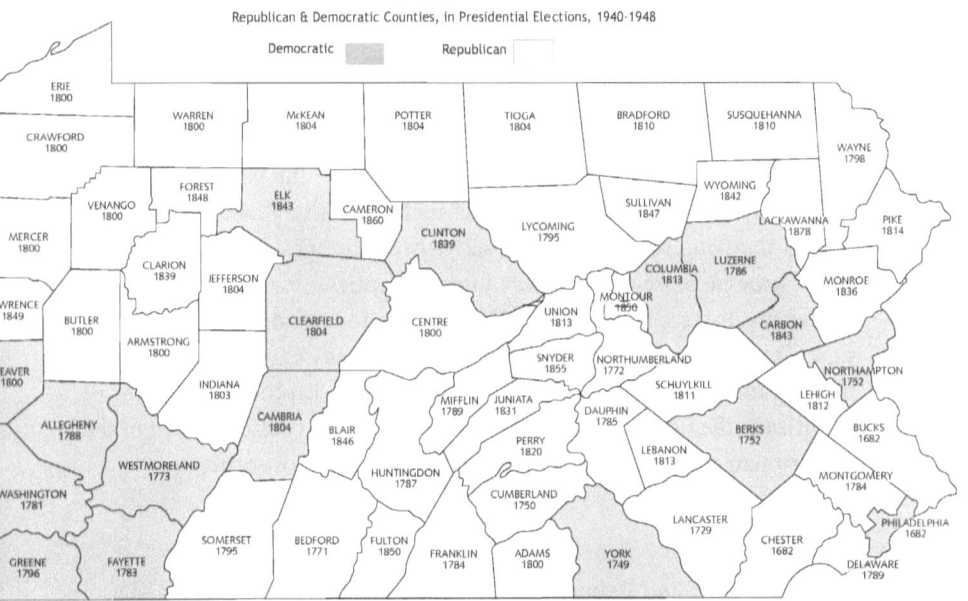

Figure 5.15
Republican & Democratic Counties, in Presidential Elections, 1940-1948

Table 5.15 The ten most Republican and ten least Republican counties in presidential elections, 1940–1948

Most Republican		Least Republican	
County	%	County	%
Union	75.3	Washington	36.7
Tioga	75.2	Fayette	37.2
Wayne	74.8	Greene	39.1
Snyder	74.5	Westmoreland	40.5
Bradford	71.1	Cambria	41.0
Venango	70.6	Berks	42.5
Wyoming	69.8	Allegheny	42.7
Potter	67.9	Beaver	43.1
McKean	67.0	Lackawanna	43.2
Susquehanna	66.8	Philadelphia	43.5

SOURCE: Data calculated from the author's research.

counties went Democratic for the decade (see Figure 5.16). The Democrats won a majority of the two-party vote in Philadelphia County and six counties in the southwestern corner of the state. However, they did not prevail in Allegheny County.

1960–1968

In terms of victories and percentage of the two-party vote, the Democrats enjoyed their best decade during the 1960s. The Democrats won all three elections and garnered 56 percent of the vote. The vote figure was largely attributable to Lyndon Baines Johnson's landslide (65 percent) victory in 1964. John F. Kennedy received only 51 percent of the vote in 1960, and Hubert H. Humphrey fared only slightly better in 1968, securing 52 percent of the vote. Johnson carried sixty-three counties, but Kennedy and Humphrey each prevailed in only fifteen counties.

Twenty-three counties went Democratic for the decade (see Figure 5.17). Once again, both Philadelphia and Allegheny Counties were in the Democratic column. In addition, the Democrats captured a number of counties in the east-central part of the state. The party also did well in the western half of the state, especially in the southwestern corner.

1970–1978

The Democrats and Republicans split two elections, with the GOP getting 54 percent of the two-party vote. The difference was that Richard

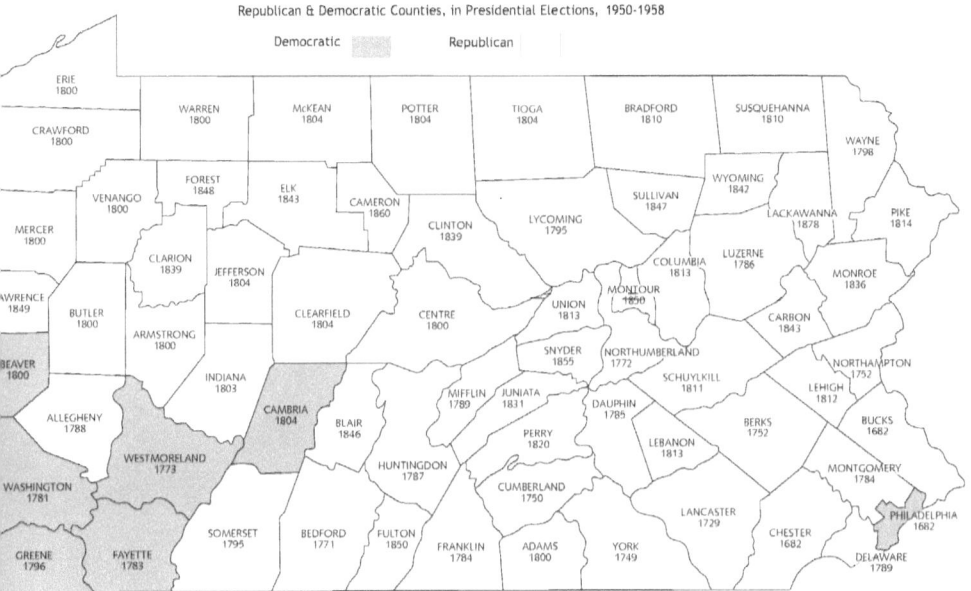

Figure 5.16
Republican & Democratic Counties, in Presidential Elections, 1950-1958

Table 5.16 The ten most Republican and ten least Republican counties in presidential elections, 1950–1958

Most Republican		Least Republican	
County	%	County	%
Union	79.3	Fayette	37.9
Snyder	79.3	Greene	42.1
Tioga	77.8	Washington	42.2
Wayne	77.5	Philadelphia	42.3
Pike	75.4	Westmoreland	45.0
Wyoming	74.9	Cambria	48.1
Venango	74.1	Beaver	48.4
Susquehanna	72.9	Lackawanna	51.2
Warren	72.7	Allegheny	52.1
Cameron	71.9	Northampton	53.8

SOURCE: Data calculated from the author's research.

Nixon defeated George McGovern in a landslide (60 percent) in 1972, while Jimmy Carter eked out a victory (51 percent) over Gerald R. Ford in 1976. Nixon predominated in sixty-six counties, while Carter prevailed in only forty-six.

For the decade, the Democrats obtained a majority of the vote in only five counties (see Figure 5.18). They carried Philadelphia and Lackawanna

Figure 5.17

Republican & Democratic Counties, in Presidential Elections, 1960-1968

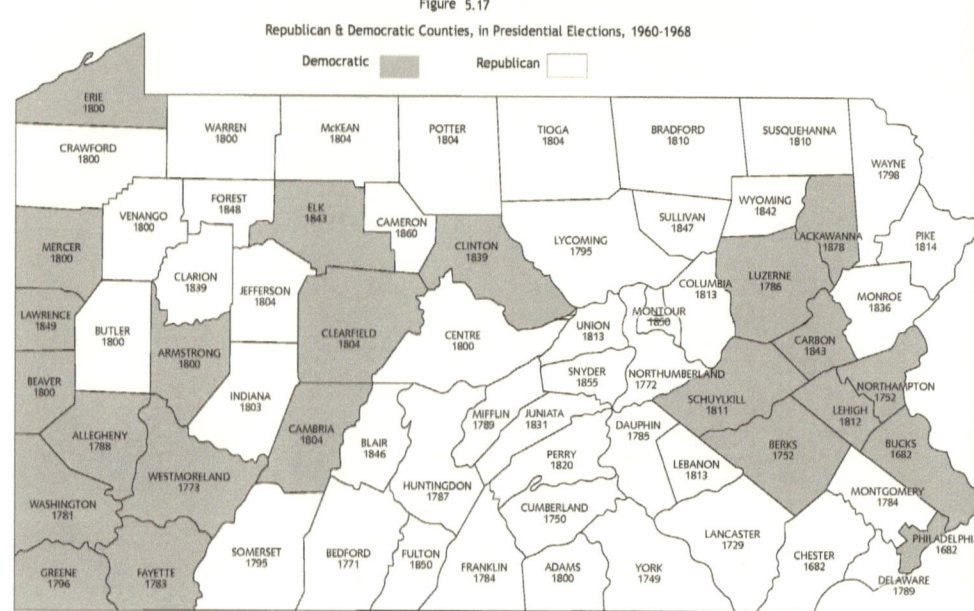

Table 5.17 The ten most Republican and ten least Republican counties in presidential elections, 1960–1968

Most Republican		Least Republican	
County	%	County	%
Snyder	70.9	Philadelphia	30.3
Union	69.1	Fayette	34.1
Tioga	64.9	Lackawanna	34.9
Wayne	64.0	Washington	35.4
Lebanon	63.7	Beaver	36.6
Lancaster	63.3	Westmoreland	37.1
Pike	63.1	Luzerne	37.3
Bradford	62.3	Greene	38.7
Perry	62.2	Cambria	39.5
Wyoming	61.9	Allegheny	39.5

SOURCE: Data calculated from the author's research.

Counties in the east, and Greene, Washington, and Fayette Counties in the west.

1980–1988

The Republican Party received 53 percent of the two-party vote while sweeping all three elections during the 1980s. Ronald Reagan defeated

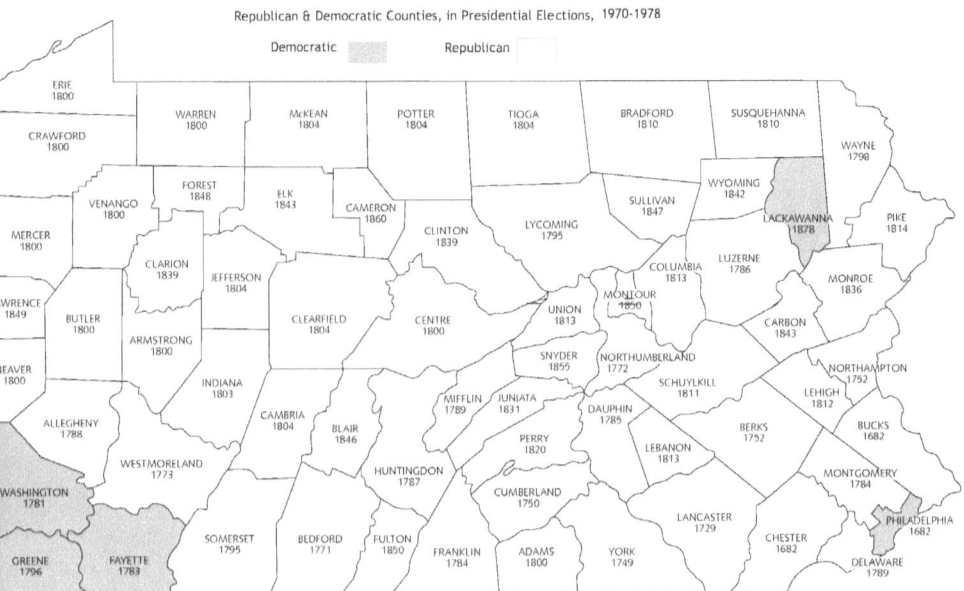

Figure 5.18
Republican & Democratic Counties, in Presidential Elections, 1970-1978

Table 5.18 The ten most Republican and ten least Republican counties in presidential elections, 1970–1978

Most Republican		Least Republican	
County	%	County	%
Snyder	73.9	Philadelphia	38.9
Lancaster	72.0	Fayette	46.6
Lebanon	71.4	Washington	47.5
Wayne	70.7	Greene	48.0
Union	70.1	Lackawanna	49.7
Cumberland	68.9	Northampton	50.0
Blair	68.7	Beaver	50.1
Pike	68.6	Westmoreland	50.2
Perry	68.3	Lawrence	50.9
Wyoming	68.2	Allegheny	52.4

SOURCE: Data calculated from the author's research.

Jimmy Carter in 1980 and Walter F. Mondale in 1984, winning 54 percent of the vote both times; George Bush garnered 51 percent of the vote in his win over Michael S. Dukakis in 1988. Reagan received a majority of the vote in fifty-seven counties in 1980 and fifty-six counties in 1984; despite his smaller margin of victory, Bush carried more counties than Reagan had, winning sixty-two in 1988.

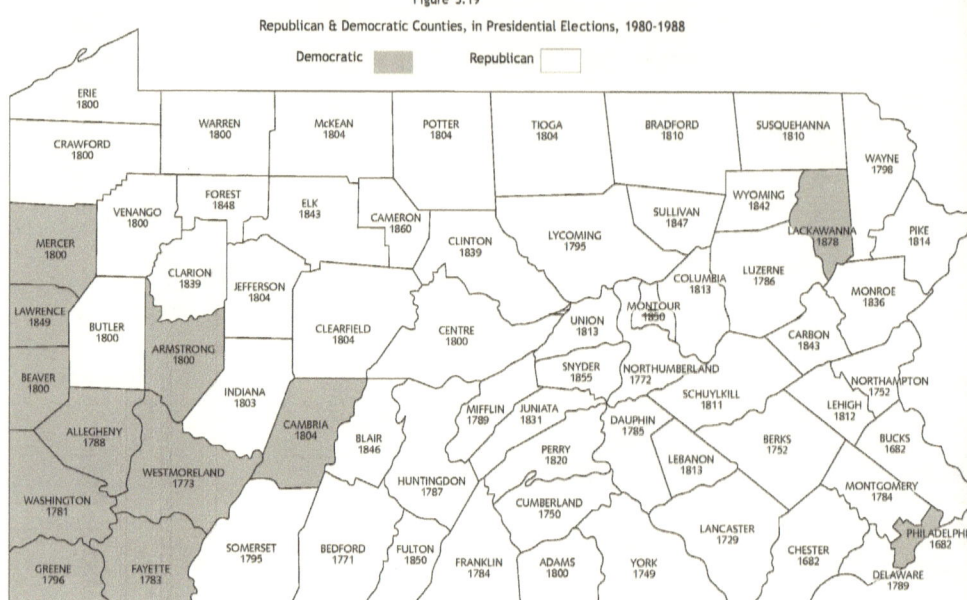

Figure 5.19
Republican & Democratic Counties, in Presidential Elections, 1980-1988

For the decade, the Democrats carried twelve counties. As was the case in the previous decade, the Democrats carried only Philadelphia and Lackawanna Counties in the eastern half of the state. On the other side of the state, they prevailed in the southwestern corner of the state once again, and added several adjacent counties in the west-central region, and Cambria County (see Figure 5.19).

1990–1998

Two victories by Bill Clinton helped the Democrats secure 55 percent of the two-party vote for the decade. Clinton obtained 56 percent of the vote and carried forty counties while defeating George Bush in 1992. He received 55 percent of the vote and won thirty-nine counties while defeating Bob Dole and winning reelection in 1996.

The Democrats prevailed in twenty-six counties during the 1990s (see Figure 5.20). In the east, they won Philadelphia County and a band of counties stretching northward along the eastern border of the state. They also captured a majority of the counties in the western half of the state, including all the counties in the southwestern corner.

Table 5.19 The ten most Republican and ten least Republican counties in presidential elections, 1980–1988

Most Republican		Least Republican	
County	%	County	%
Snyder	77.4	Philadelphia	34.8
Lancaster	73.3	Beaver	37.3
Wayne	73.3	Fayee	37.5
Union	72.3	Greene	38.2
Lebanon	71.3	Washington	40.0
Wyoming	70.9	Allegheny	41.9
Pike	70.4	Cambria	44.2
Bradford	69.1	Lawrence	45.0
Perry	69.6	Westmoreland	46.5
Chester	68.6	Armstrong	48.1
Potter	68.6		
Tioga	68.6		

SOURCE: Data calculated from the author's research.

Patterns of County Partisan Support

Counties Won

What seems most obvious from the data in Table 5.21 is the decided Republican advantage in counties controlled throughout the twentieth century. The Democrats won a majority of the counties only six times in gubernatorial elections (1906, 1914, 1934, 1954, 1970, and 1990), and only three times in presidential elections (1912, 1936, and 1964). Even when the Democrats were winning elections, they frequently were winning only a minority of the counties. Moreover, currently, seven (Berks, Bucks, Chester, Delaware, Lancaster, Montgomery, and York) of the ten largest counties are controlled by the Republicans. Only Allegheny, Philadelphia, and Westmoreland Counties are consistently Democratic. This clearly illustrates why it is necessary for the Democrats to win substantial majorities in Philadelphia and Allegheny Counties.

Most Republican Counties in Gubernatorial Elections

Table 5.22 displays all the counties that were among the ten most Republican, along with the decades they achieved that ranking. Heading the list

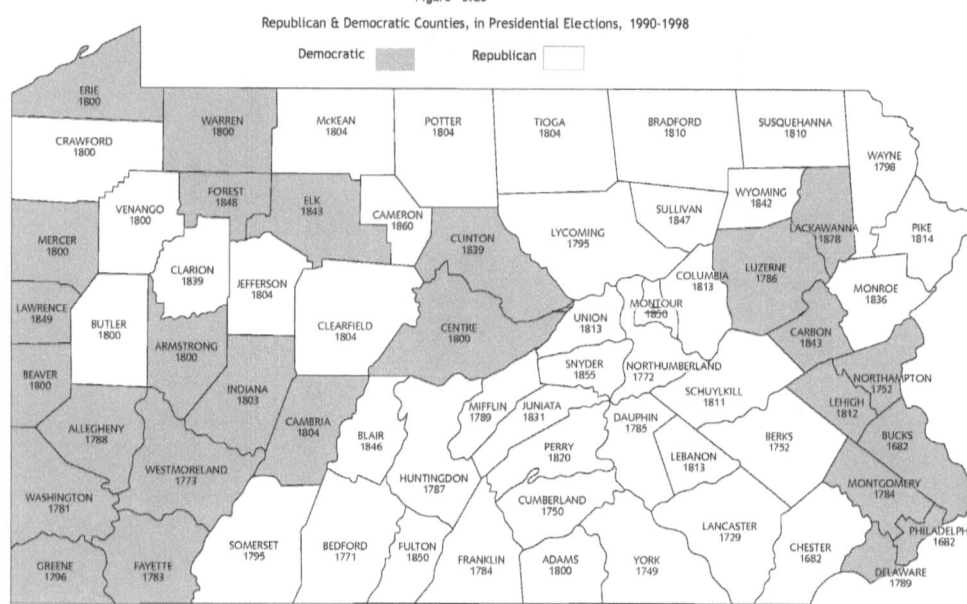

Figure 5.20
Republican & Democratic Counties, in Presidential Elections, 1990-1998

Table 5.20 The ten most Republican and ten least Republican counties in presidential elections, 1990–1998

Most Republican		Least Republican	
County	%	County	%
Snyder	68.3	Philadelphia	20.3
Lancaster	66.1	Greene	31.8
Perry	64.9	Fayette	32.1
Potter	64.0	Beaver	36.0
Union	64.0	Washington	36.4
Franklin	63.2	Cambria	38.9
Lebanon	62.1	Allegheny	39.0
Bedford	62.0	Lawrence	39.0
Fulton	62.0	Lackawanna	39.7
Cumberland	61.3	Erie	41.1

Source: Data calculated from the author's research.

is Tioga County, which achieved that status in nine of the ten decades, followed by Bradford County, with eight inclusions. Lancaster and Snyder Counties were ranked that high seven times. Rounding out the list of counties that were in the top ten in at least five of the decades were Union (6), McKean (5), and Wayne (5) Counties. Snyder and Union Counties are located in the middle of the state. The geography is characterized by forests

Table 5.21 Number of counties won by Republican and Democratic candidates in gubernatorial and presidential elections, 1900–1998

Year	Gubernatorial elections Republican	Gubernatorial elections Democratic	Presidential elections Republican	Presidential elections Democratic	Year	Gubernatorial elections Republican	Gubernatorial elections Democratic	Presidential elections Republican	Presidential elections Democratic
1900			54	13	1950	51	16		
1902	38	29			1952			57	9
1904			61	6	1954	33	34		
1906	30	37			1956			62	5
1908			56	11	1958	50	17		
1910	55	12			1960			52	15
1912			6	61	1962	62	5		
1914	23	44			1964			4	63
1916			43	24	1966	55	12		
1918	55	12			1968			52	15
1920			64	3	1970	31	36		
1922	36	31			1972			66	1
1924			63	4	1974	41	26		
1926	66	1			1976			46	21
1928			64	3	1978	50	17		
1930	60	7			1980			57	10
1932			40	27	1982	46	21		
1934	31	36			1984			56	11
1936			26	41	1986	43	24		
1938	61	6			1988			62	15
1940			42	25	1990	1	66		
1942	57	10			1992			40	27
1944			51	16	1994	56	11		
1946	60	7			1996			39	28
1948			54	13	1998	66	1		

SOURCE: Figures calculated from data in *The Pennsylvania Manual*, selected volumes.

Table 5.22 Counties that ranked among the ten most Republican counties in gubernatorial elections, and the decade(s) they achieved that ranking, 1900–1998

County	1900s	1910s	1920s	1930s	1940s	1950s	1960s	1970s	1980s	1990s
Tioga	1900s	1910s	1920s	1930s	1940s	1950s	1960s	1970s		1990s
Bradford			1920s	1930s	1940s	1950s	1960s	1970s	1980s	1990s
Lancaster	1900s	1910s			1940s	1950s	1960s		1970s	1980s
Snyder				1930s	1940s	1950s	1960s	1970s	1980s	1990s
Union				1930s	1940s	1950s	1960s	1970s	1980s	
McKean					1940s	1950s		1970s	1980s	1990s
Wayne				1930s	1940s	1950s	1960s	1970s		
Delaware	1900s	1910s	1920s						1980s	
Wyoming				1930s		1950s	1960s	1970s		
Indiana	1900s	1910s	1920s							
Philadelphia	1900s	1910s	1920s							
Forest	1900s		1920s	1930s						
Venango				1930s	1940s	1950s				
Montgomery					1940s	1950s			1980s	
Pike							1960s	1970s		1990s
Chester							1960s		1980s	1990s
Allegheny	1900s									
Somerset	1900s		1920s							
Lawrence	1900s	1910s								
Warren	1900s				1940s					
Lebanon	1900s	1910s					1960s			
Huntingdon		1910s		1930s						
Cameron			1920s	1930s						
Dauphin		1910s								
Elk			1920s							
Erie			1920s							
Susquehanna								1970s		
Cumberland									1980s	
Bucks									1980s	
Potter										1990s
Crawford										1990s
Bedford										1990s
Sullivan										1990s

SOURCE: Data calculated from the author's research.

and mountains and rich agricultural valleys. Lancaster County is located in the southeastern part of the state and, while urban, is an important agricultural county. The other four counties are located in the northern tier, and are rural and forested in character.

Included in this list of counties are several that were among the ten most Republican counties earlier in the century, but which have not made the list for a number of decades. Most have remained bastions of Republicanism. Included in this group are Somerset, Indiana, Warren, Forest, Huntingdon, Venango, Dauphin, Erie, and Cameron Counties. While dispersed geographically, they are all located in the western half of the state. Only Venango, Dauphin, and Erie Counties are urban counties. However, some of them underwent partisan transformations. The most dramatic transformations took place in Philadelphia and Allegheny Counties; these two counties have become the keys to Democratic success in the state. Lawrence and Elk Counties also became Democratic counties over the course of the century; both are urban counties in the western half of the state.

Most Republican Counties in Presidential Elections

The counties that were included among the ten most Republican in presidential elections are presented in Table 5.23. Heading the list again is Tioga County, along with Snyder and Union Counties; all achieved that status in eight decades. They are followed by Lancaster (6), Wayne (6), Lebanon (5), Bradford (5), and Wyoming (5) Counties. Lebanon County is a rural county located in the eastern middle section of the state; it is the home of the industrial city of Lebanon. Wyoming County is a rural county in the northeastern section of the state. Rural and forested in nature, it was settled by older American stock from New England and New York.

As was the case with gubernatorial elections, there are a number of counties that were among the ten most Republican earlier in the century, but have not been among that group in recent decades. With three exceptions, they have remained solidly Republican. Included in the group that has remained loyal to the GOP are Indiana, Somerset, Delaware, Warren, Blair, Huntingdon, Cameron, Venango, Forest, McKean, Susquehanna, and Warren Counties. Blair County is located in the southern middle part of the state; Somerset County is one of the southern tier counties. Both are forested and agricultural in nature. Delaware County is an urban county adjacent to Philadelphia County. McKean and Susquehanna Counties are rural counties located in the northern tier; both are rural and forested. Philadelphia, Allegheny, and Lawrence Counties all moved into the Democratic camp during the twentieth century.

Six (Tioga, Bradford, Lancaster, Snyder, Union, and Wayne) of the counties were among the ten most Republican counties in at least five decades for both gubernatorial and presidential elections. There is no particular geographic pattern. Tioga, Bradford, and Wayne Counties are in the northern tier of counties, Union and Snyder Counties are in the center of the state, and Lancaster County is in the bottom tier of counties. All, however, are decidedly rural in nature. The mean percentage urban

Table 5.23 Counties that ranked among the ten most Republican counties in presidential elections, and the decade(s) they achieved that ranking, 1900–1998

County	Decade									
Tioga	1900s	1910s	1920s	1930s	1940s	1950s	1960s		1980s	
Snyder			1920s	1930s	1940s	1950s	1960s	1970s	1980s	1990s
Union			1920s	1930s	1940s	1950s	1960s	1970s	1980s	1990s
Lancaster	1900s	1910s					1960s	1970s	1980s	1990s
Wayne				1930s	1940s	1950s	1960s	1970s	1980s	
Lebanon		1910s					1960s	1970s	1980s	1990s
Bradford			1920s	1930s	1940s		1960s		1980s	
Wyoming					1940s	1950s	1960s	1970s	1980s	
Venango			1920s	1930s	1940s	1950s				
Pike						1950s	1960s	1970s	1980s	
Perry							1960s	1970s	1980s	1990s
Delaware	1900s	1910s	1920s	1930s						
Indiana	1900s	1910s	1920s							
Warren	1900s	1910s	1920s							
Huntingdon	1900s		1920s	1930s						
Potter					1940s				1980s	1990s
Philadelphia	1900s	1910s								
Cameron		1910s				1950s				
Lawrence		1910s	1920s							
Chester				1930s					1980s	
Susquehanna					1940s	1950s				
Cumberland								1970s		1990s
Blair	1900s							1970s		
Forest				1930s						
McKean					1940s					
Warren						1950s				
Franklin										1990s
Bedford										1990s
Fulton										1990s
Allegheny	1900s									

SOURCE: Data calculated from the author's research.

for these six counties in 1990 was 23 percent. The mean percentage African American population was 2.2 percent, and the mean per capita income was $17,458. The three northern counties are heavily forested. Union and Snyder Counties contain forests and mountains as well as rich agricultural valleys, and Lancaster County contains some of the state's best farm land.

Least Republican Counties in Gubernatorial Elections

Listed in Table 5.24 are the counties which were among the ten least Republican counties during the past ten decades. The list is topped by Greene County, which qualified in every decade. Fayette County is second with

Table 5.24 Counties that ranked among the ten least Republican counties in gubernatorial elections, and the decade(s) they achieved that ranking, 1900–1998

County	1900s	1910s	1920s	1930s	1940s	1950s	1960s	1970s	1980s	1990s
Greene	1900s	1910s	1920s	1930s	1940s	1950s	1960s	1970s	1980s	1990s
Fayette				1930s	1940s	1950s	1960s	1970s	1980s	1990s
Philadelphia				1930s		1950s	1960s	1970s	1980s	1990s
Cambria				1930s	1940s	1950s		1970s	1980s	1990s
Washington					1940s	1950s	1960s	1970s	1980s	1990s
Berks	1900s	1910s	1920s	1930s	1940s					
Northampton		1910s	1920s		1940s		1960s	1970s		
Lackawanna					1940s	1950s	1960s		1980s	1990s
Beaver						1950s	1960s	1970s	1980s	1990s
Westmoreland					1940s	1950s	1960s	1970s		1990s
Monroe	1900s	1910s	1920s	1930s						
Columbia	1900s	1910s	1920s		1940s					
Montour	1900s	1910s	1920s	1930s						
Fulton	1900s	1910s	1920s		1940s					
Pike	1900s	1910s	1920s							
Elk	1900s			1930s	1940s					
Allegheny						1950s		1970s		1990s
Luzerne							1960s		1980s	1990s
Clarion	1900s		1920s							
Lehigh		1910s		1930s						
Adams		1910s	1920s							
Erie				1930s			1960s			
Lawrence								1970s	1980s	
Carbon	1900s		1920s							
York						1950s				
Northumberland									1980s	

SOURCE: Data calculated from the author's research.

seven inclusions. Next come three (Philadelphia, Cambria, and Washington) counties that made the list six times, followed by five (Berks, Lackawanna, Northampton, Beaver, and Westmoreland) counties that were included in the group five times. Greene, Fayette, Cambria, Washington, Beaver, and Westmoreland Counties are all located in the southwestern corner of the state. Most of these counties are part of the Pittsburgh metropolitan area. This is the soft coal region; Greene County is the only predominantly agricultural county. Northampton and Berks Counties are both urban counties located in the southeastern corner of the state. They are the homes of Easton and Reading. These are two of the counties that comprise the Pennsylvania Dutch area of Pennsylvania. Lackawanna County is located in the northeastern corner of the state. It is located in the hard coal region and has been the destination of large numbers of immigrants from southeastern and eastern Europe.

A dozen counties were among the ten least Republican counties only in earlier decades. Six (Monroe, Pike, Montour, Berks, Lehigh, and York) of them became Republican during the century; two (Clarion and Adams) others were classified as Republican over the course of the century. Columbia, Fulton, and Carbon Counties were classified as competitive for the century. Only one, Elk County, was classified as Democratic for the century. Lehigh, York, Pike, and Monroe Counties are located in the eastern middle section of the state. These counties are a combination of agricultural areas and industrial centers. Montour, Carbon, and Columbia Counties are also located in the eastern middle part of the state and are part of the hard coal region. Fulton and Adams Counties are located in the southern tier and are a combination of farmland and forests. Clarion County is a combination of forest and agricultural land and is located in the western middle part of the state.

Least Republican Counties in Presidential Elections

As was the case with gubernatorial elections, Greene County was among the ten least Republican counties in every decade. Fayette County was among that group eight times, followed by Washington and Allegheny Counties, which made the list seven times. Included six times were Lackawanna, Westmoreland, Cambria, Beaver, and Philadelphia Counties.

Once again, a dozen counties that were among the ten least Republican counties in earlier decades have not achieved that status for several decades. Of those counties, six (Monroe, Pike, Berks, Fulton, Columbia, and York) became more Republican as the century went on. Six counties (Clarion, Adams, Lycoming, Sullivan, Montour, and Northumberland) were classified as Republican over the course of the century. Thus, none of the twelve remained Democratic or even competitive. Lycoming County is located in the northern middle part of the state; this section of the state contains forests, mountains, and rich agricultural valleys. Sullivan and Northumberland Counties are located in the eastern middle part of the state and are part of the hard coal region.

Greene, Fayette, Washington, Lackawanna, Westmoreland, Cambria, Beaver, and Philadelphia Counties were among the ten least Republican counties at least five times for both gubernatorial and presidential elections. Unlike the situation with gubernatorial elections, there is a definite geographic pattern with these counties. The southwestern corner of the

Table 5.25 Counties that ranked among the ten least Republican counties in presidential elections, and the decade(s) they achieved that ranking, 1900–1998

County	Decade									
	1900s	1910s	1920s	1930s	1940s	1950s	1960s	1970s	1980s	1990s
Greene	1900s	1910s	1920s	1930s	1940s	1950s	1960s	1970s	1980s	1990s
Fayette			1920s	1930s	1940s	1950s	1960s	1970s	1980s	1990s
Washington				1930s	1940s	1950s	1960s	1970s	1980s	1990s
Allegheny				1930s	1940s	1950s	1960s	1970s	1980s	1990s
Lackawanna			1920s		1940s	1950s	1960s	1970s		1990s
Westmoreland				1930s	1940s	1950s	1960s	1970s	1980s	
Cambria				1930s	1940s	1950s	1960s		1980s	1990s
Beaver					1940s	1950s	1960s	1970s	1980s	1990s
Philadelphia					1940s	1950s	1960s	1970s	1980s	1990s
Monroe	1900s	1910s	1920s	1930s						
Berks	1900s		1920s	1930s	1940s					
Montour	1900s	1910s	1920s	1930s						
Fulton	1900s	1910s	1920s							
Adams	1900s	1910s	1920s							
Northampton	1900s					1950s		1970s		
Clarion	1900s	1910s	1920s							
Lawrence								1970s	1980s	1990s
Columbia	1900s	1910s	1920s							
Pike	1900s	1910s								
Lycoming		1910s								
York		1910s								
Sullivan			1920s							
Northumberland				1930s						
Luzerne							1960s			
Armstrong									1980s	
Erie										1990s

SOURCE: Data calculated from the author's research.

state, encompassing much of the Pittsburgh metropolitan area, is a Democratic stronghold. In the east, Philadelphia and Lackawanna Counties are Democratic bastions.

For the most part, these are urban counties; the mean percentage urban in 1990 was 59 percent. The two exceptions are Greene (11 percent) and Fayette (29 percent) Counties. This is in sharp contrast to the 23 percent urban figure registered by the most Republican counties. The mean percentage African American population was 3.3 percent, which is 50 percent larger than the percentage for the most Republican counties. Both of these differences would be expected, given the electoral bases of the parties. What was not expected was that the mean per capita income in the least Republican counties, $17,566, would be higher than the figure for the most Republican counties. The difference is largely attributable to the income levels in Cambria, Lackawanna, Washington, and Westmoreland Counties. Among the most Republican counties, only Lancaster County had a per capita income that exceeded the figures in those four counties.

Democratic Success in Statewide Elections

To this point, findings have been presented in terms of the Republicans' rate of success. This section will analyze how the Democrats have fared in the various categories of statewide elections. One reason for this presentation is to monitor the Democrats' fortunes as they progressed from their status as a hopeless minority party to being the majority party in the state. A second reason is to provide background for an analysis of Democratic fortunes in senatorial elections.

Comparative Democratic Success, 1900–1998

The Democratic Party's rates of success are documented in Table 5.26. Democrats were most successful in presidential elections (40 percent), followed by statewide elections (32 percent), gubernatorial elections (28 percent), and senatorial elections (19 percent). It should be noted that the Democrats won a minority of the elections in every category. The Republican dominance during the first three decades of the twentieth century is again made manifest by the data. Democratic fortunes improved significantly during the 1930s. The best decade overall for Democratic candidates was the 1960s. That was also the best decade for Democratic presidential and statewide candidates. Democratic gubernatorial candidates fared best during the 1950s and 1970s; for Democratic senatorial candidates, the highest rate of success occurred during the 1940s.

U.S. Senate Elections

During the past three decades, both academics and journalists increasingly have commented on the inability of the Democratic Party to elect a U.S. senator. The last Democrat elected to the Senate in a regularly scheduled election was Joe Clark in 1962. The only break in this Republican dominance was Harris Wofford's victory over former governor Dick Thornburgh in a 1991 special election to replace the late John Heinz. This futility has persisted in the face of the previously discussed 400,000 plu-

Table 5.26 Democratic victories in statewide elections, by category and decade, 1900–1998

Decade	Presidential	Gubernatorial	Senatorial	Statewide	Totals
1900–08	0–3	0–2	NA	1–12	1–17
1910–18	1–2	0–3	0–2	0–10	1–17
1920–28	0–3	0–2	0–5	0–10	0–20
1930–38	1–2	1–3	1–4	4–10	7–19
1940–48	2–3	0–2	2–3	4–10	8–18
1950–58	0–2	2–3	1–4	4–10	7–19
1960–68	3–3	0–2	1–3	7–10	11–18
1970–78	1–2	2–3	0–3	4–4	7–12
1980–88	0–3	1–2	0–4	3–9	4–18
1990–98	2–2	1–3	1–4	2–6	6–15
Totals	10–25	7–25	6–32	29–91	52–173
(%)	40%	28%	19%	32%	30%

SOURCE: Figures calculated by the author from data in *The Pennsylvania Manual*, selected volumes.

rality enjoyed by the Democrats in registered voters. What is clear from the previous section, however, is that these more recent events are part of a century-long pattern. The Democratic Party in Pennsylvania was less successful in U.S. Senate elections than in any other category of statewide elections during the twentieth century.

The Democrats' relative inability to elect U.S. senators becomes even more unusual when their rates of success as a minority party and a majority party are compared. Strangely, the Democrats were more successful in electing senators when they were the minority party (see Table 5.27).

In percentage terms, the incidence of Democratic victories at least doubled in every category after 1960, except in senatorial elections; in senatorial elections, their rate of success fell by more than a third. During the Democrats' stint as the minority party, they elected U.S. senators as frequently as they elected officials to other offices. As the majority party, however, their futility in senatorial elections stands out conspicuously. In the case of U.S. Senate elections, being the majority party has proven to be a burden for the Democrats.

Moreover, even when the Democratic senatorial candidates won, they generally just barely won. Their most successful showing occurred in the 1991 special election when Harris Wofford received 55 percent of the vote. In their five victories in regularly scheduled elections, Democratic candidates never received more than 52 percent of the two-party vote. While they were the minority party, the Democrats won Senate seats in 1934 (Joseph F.

Table 5.27 Democratic victories, by category, before and after 1960

Presidential	Gubernatorial	Senatorial	Statewide	Totals
		Before 1960		
4–15	3–15	4–18	13–62	24–110
27%	20%	22%	21%	22%
		After 1960		
6–10	4–10	2–14	16–27	28–61
60%	40%	14%	59%	46%

SOURCE: Figures calculated by the author from data in *The Pennsylvania Manual*, selected volumes.

Guffey), 1940 (Joseph F. Guffey), 1944 (Francis J. Myers), and 1956 (Joseph S. Clark). The respective percentages of the two-party vote obtained by Democratic candidates were 52.2 percent. 52.2 percent, 50.3 percent, and 50.2 percent. In the sole victory as the majority party, Joe Clark garnered 51.1 percent of the vote in 1962. In his two victories in 1956 and 1962, even Joe Clark barely eked out wins over his Republican opponents.

It should be pointed out that since 1960 the Republicans have fielded a string of moderate to liberal senatorial candidates. Included would be GOP victors Hugh Scott (1964, 1970), Richard Schweiker (1968, 1974), Arlen Specter (1980, 1986, 1992, 1998), and John Heinz (1982, 1988). The only consistently conservative winner since 1960 was Rick Santorum (1994). Thus, the ideological differences between the Republican and Democratic senatorial candidates have not always been dramatic.

The much ballyhooed recent lack of Democratic success in U.S. Senate elections is clearly part of a long-term trend. So, while the current situation may be more desperate than in the past, it is not unique. In the next section, a perspective will be offered regarding the Democrats' futility in senatorial elections during the past three decades.

Democratic Strongholds and Democratic Support, 1970–1998

Most election calculations begin with the assumption that a candidate will run strongly in areas dominated by his or her party. This base will then be supplemented by votes garnered in areas less loyal to the party. Conversely, if a candidate fares poorly, it frequently can be traced to his or her inability to carry party strongholds by typical margins. During the past thirty years, Democratic candidates for the U.S. Senate have run exceptionally poorly in areas of party strength.

Table 5.28 Mean Democratic vote for president, governor, and U.S. senator in six counties, by decade, 1970–1998

Office	1970s	1980s	1990s
President	52.8%	61.7%	67.4%
Governor	61.8	62.0	61.6
U.S. Senator	55.4	54.9	53.9

SOURCE: Data calculated from the author's research.

Six counties (Philadelphia, Beaver, Fayette, Greene, Washington, and Allegheny) have ranked among the top ten most Democratic counties in terms of the percentage of the two-party vote Democratic in both presidential and gubernatorial elections during the 1970s, 1980s, and 1990s. Democratic senatorial candidates consistently have polled significantly fewer votes in these counties than have their party brethren running for president and governor. Table 5.28 summarizes the votes received by Democratic candidates for these offices during the last three decades.

This pattern is reinforced by data from the individual counties, especially Philadelphia and Allegheny Counties. Failure to rack up substantial majorities in these two counties virtually dooms a statewide Democratic candidate. Since 1970, Democratic senatorial candidates have run significantly worse than Democratic presidential and gubernatorial candidates in these key areas. In fact, in Allegheny County, Democratic senatorial candidates have received less than half of the two-party vote in each of the last three decades. Thus, recent failures in senatorial elections can be attributed to the party's candidates being rejected by a significant number of the party's most loyal voters.

The Democrats' lack of success in Allegheny County since 1970 is attributable, in part, to the fact that the Republicans have fielded two popular candidates from that county. The late John Heinz was elected three times (1976, 1982, 1988), and Rick Santorum was elected to his first term in 1994. Heinz carried Allegheny County in all three of his campaigns. Santorum did not win Allegheny County, but he did capture 47 percent of the two-party vote.

The fact that the GOP was able to trump the Democrats in Allegheny County by fielding attractive candidates from the Pittsburgh area does not detract from the fact the Democrats enjoy better than a two-to-one registration advantage in Allegheny County and that it remains a Democratic stronghold. It also does not account for the fact that Arlen Specter,

Table 5.29 Mean Democratic vote for president, governor, and U.S. senator in six counties, by county, 1970–1998

County	President	Governor	U.S. Senator
Philadelphia	68.7%	65.0%	60.3%
Beaver	58.9	62.7	54.7
Fayette	61.3	64.8	57.7
Greene	60.7	62.3	55.6
Washington	58.7	60.6	52.4
Allegheny	55.6	55.3	47.6

SOURCE: Data calculated from the author's research.

from Philadelphia County, won Allegheny County in the 1986, 1992, and 1998 senatorial elections. If the Democrats want to win senatorial elections, or any other statewide election, for that matter, they simply must find a way to carry Allegheny County by a sizable margin.

Summary

This chapter examined elections for governor, president, U.S. senator, and statewide offices. The first section analyzed patterns of county support in gubernatorial and presidential elections. The Democrats won a majority of the counties only six times in gubernatorial elections and only three times in presidential elections. Tioga County ranked among the ten most Republican counties in gubernatorial elections in nine decades, followed by Bradford County, which made the list eight times. Tioga County also topped the list for presidential elections, along with Snyder and Union Counties; all three were included in the top ten list in eight decades.

Tioga, Bradford, Lancaster, Snyder, Union, and Wayne Counties were among the ten most Republican counties in at least five decades for both gubernatorial and presidential elections. There is no particular geographic pattern among these counties. However, they are basically rural counties; they had a mean percentage urban of 23 percent in 1990. The mean percentage African American population was 2.2 percent, and the mean per capita income was $17,458.

Greene County was among the ten least Republican counties in gubernatorial elections in all ten decades. Fayette County was next, with seven citations. Greene County was also among the ten least Republican counties in presidential elections in every decade, followed again by Fayette

County with eight inclusions. Greene, Fayette, Washington, Lackawanna, Westmoreland, Cambria, Beaver, and Philadelphia Counties were among the ten least Republican counties in at least five decades for both gubernatorial and presidential elections. A definite geographic pattern exists among these counties. Most of the Pittsburgh metropolitan area is covered by these counties. Philadelphia and Lackawanna Counties are Democratic strongholds in the eastern part of the state. These are also primarily urban counties, with a mean percentage urban of 59 percent in 1990. The mean percentage African American population was 3.3 percent, and the mean per capita income was $17,566.

During the century, the Democrats enjoyed their greatest rate of success in presidential elections (40 percent), followed by statewide elections (32 percent), gubernatorial elections (28 percent), and senatorial elections (19 percent). The Democrats' recent travails in senatorial elections are part of a century-long pattern. The Democrats actually were more successful in senatorial elections when they were the minority party. After the Democrats became the majority party in 1960 their rate of success in other categories of statewide elections at least doubled; however, in senatorial elections, their rate of success fell by one-third. Moreover, when Democratic senatorial candidates won during the twentieth century, they just barely won.

Six counties (Philadelphia, Beaver, Fayette, Greene, Washington, and Allegheny) were among the ten most Democratic counties in both gubernatorial and presidential elections during the 1970s, 1980s, and 1990s. In all these counties, Democratic senatorial candidates received a smaller percentage of the two-party vote than did their party's gubernatorial and presidential candidates in each of the past three decades. In fact, in Allegheny County, Democratic senatorial candidates have received a minority of the vote in all three decades. Thus, Democratic candidates are losing because they are being rejected by some of their party's most loyal voters.

PRIMARY ELECTIONS

Candidates have been nominated in Pennsylvania through the use of the direct primary since 1914. Reformers promoted the primary essentially as an intraparty substitute for a lack of interparty competition in most regions of the nation. In addition, it was viewed as a tool to wrest control of nominations from party leaders. During the early decades of the twentieth century, Pennsylvania was a prime example of the reformers' concerns on both counts. The Republican Party totally dominated the state, and nominations were controlled by party leaders, especially GOP leaders. There is considerable evidence that the influence of party leaders was not completely eclipsed by the advent of the primary. Sorauf (1963) documented that during the 1950s party leaders were still able to manipulate the results of primary elections, particularly in urban areas, through the techniques of candidate recruitment and endorsement. Kennedy (1999) reported similar, although somewhat lessened, levels of influence during the 1990s.

During the last two decades only two endorsed statewide Republican candidates have been defeated in the primary; the Democratic record is not nearly as impressive.

Competition in Primary Elections

As is the case with many other aspects of electoral politics, the initial insights into the correlates of primary competition were offered by V. O. Key. According to Key (1956), competition increases if no incumbent is running, and as the party's chances of winning the general election increase (172–96). In addition, Key reported that competition increased as urbanism increased (176–79). Overall, Key contended that "such factors as urbanism and incumbency may affect the frequency of primary competition through time but that in the long run the incidence of primary competition is a function chiefly of the prospects for victory in the general election" (179). Sorauf (1963) concurs, writing of state House elections, "The basic determinant of primary competition in Pennsylvania remains the prospects of victory in the election" (111).

It is not difficult to explain the influence of incumbency and prospects for victory. Incumbents enjoy numerous advantages, notably, greater name recognition and significantly greater financial resources. Both combine to discourage challengers. The absence of an incumbent, on the other hand, enhances the prospects for other candidates. Increased prospects for victory, especially in the absence of an incumbent, encourage competitors because the nomination is worth pursuing. The party nominee has a realistic opportunity to win the general election. Conversely, if the prospects for victory are bleak, the nomination is not worth seeking, as a general election defeat is virtually preordained.

Both Key and Sorauf documented a sizable fall-off in primary competition in the parties' safest districts, those in which the party's candidate polled more than 60 percent of the vote in the general election. Key states that while no entirely satisfactory explanation exists, ruralism seems to be relevant. In his data, 35 percent of the rural districts were uncontested, compared with only 7 percent of the districts in the most urbanized areas (1956, 179). Regarding these safe districts, Sorauf suggests that "perhaps these are the most homogenous, unified, conforming areas or the ones with the strongest party organizations and the most electoral discipline" (1963, 111).

Sorauf emphasized the impact of political culture on the strength and activities of political parties. He discovered that both the strongest party organizations and the most serious attempts to control primary elections occurred in urban areas. Overt attempts to control the primary by the Republican Party took place in urban areas, regions of Democratic strength, almost as frequently as did Democratic attempts. As Sorauf explains:

> The ethos that encourages or tolerates disciplined organization apparently accepts those tactics necessary to maintain that power. The endorsement of candidates in a primary fight also becomes politically easier in heterogeneous, urban areas. Here, politics can be ruthless because they can be aloof and impersonal. In the tightly knit rural and small-town communities, personal friendships and local ties soften the party resolve. Therefore, the ability of the parties to control the primary—or at least to attempt that control—appears to be a function of both the political culture of the constituency and of the nature of the party organization. (1963, 55)

However, organizational involvement in the nominating process was not necessarily enough to forestall a primary contest. As Sorauf relates:

> The rate of contest is actually higher in the very primaries which are dominated by strong party organizations with a willingness to try, either openly or covertly, to influence their outcome. There is, of course, no way of knowing how many additional primary fights the endorsements of strong party organizations may have prevented, but the fact remains that primary contests take place, not only where expectations of victory are greatest, but also where the party machine is most virile. (1963, 113)

Sorauf's findings differed from Key's with regard to the impact of incumbency. Key's data for state House candidates in Missouri and Ohio revealed that incumbents were less likely to face a challenge than were nonincumbents. On the other hand, Sorauf found that competition was greater in districts featuring an incumbent. Incumbents were present in 57 percent of the contested Democratic primaries, compared with only 28 percent of those without a contest; the comparable figures for the GOP were 68 percent and 48 percent (1963, 112).

For all the categories of elections under examination, the level of competition varied considerably over the course of the last century. This section will examine the factors associated with the varying degrees of competition.

Gubernatorial and Senatorial Primaries

The level of competition varied considerably in these statewide primaries, from unopposed candidates to the 1934 Republican gubernatorial primary, which featured sixteen contestants. Table 6.1 presents the results of all gubernatorial and senatorial primaries from 1926 to 1998.[1] The figure for each year is the percentage of the primary vote received by the winning candidate. The number in parentheses is the number of candidates contesting the primary.

Democratic gubernatorial primaries were more likely to be contested than Republican primaries were (see Table 6.2). The only uncontested Democratic primary was the one in 1930. The data for primaries featuring an incumbent are not very meaningful, since incumbents could not seek reelection until 1974; thus, each party had only two primaries in which an incumbent was present. But nonincumbent Democratic candidates faced challengers more often than their GOP counterparts did. The figures for majority-minority status are interesting. All majority party primaries were contested; this supports the notion that competition increases when the prospects for general election success are greater.

However, notable partisan differences exist regarding minority status— 89 percent of Democratic primaries were contested, compared with 60 percent of Republican primaries. During many of these years, the Democrats were a hopeless minority. It might be expected that the biggest challenge facing party leaders would be to find any viable candidate. A closer examination mitigates the impact of the data. In three of the eight contested primaries when the Democrats were the minority party, the winner received more than 70 percent of the vote, and in a fourth, more than 60 percent. In only three did the winner obtain less than 50 percent of the vote. A contested primary is clearly not the same thing as a seriously competitive one.

Republican winners were more likely to receive more than 60 percent of the vote. The difference was more pronounced when comparing outcomes under the conditions of minority status. Conversely, Democratic

---

1. The Election Bureau in the Secretary of State's Office has primary election voting data back only to 1926.

Table 6.1 The percentage of the vote received by the winning candidate (and the number of contestants) in gubernatorial and senatorial primaries, by party and year, 1926–1998

Year	Republican gubernatorial	Republican senatorial	Democratic gubernatorial	Democratic senatorial
1926	46.1 (4)	41.1 (3)	36.0 (3)	unopposed
1928		81.8* (3)		unopposed
1930	41.2 (4)	48.7 (4)	unopposed	unopposed
1932		62.0* (3)		64.4 (2)
1934	38.8 (16)	50.4 (4)	60.8 (5)	76.2 (3)
1936				
1938	65.6 (4)	62.1* (3)	46.0 (3)	64.6 (3)
1940		71.4 (3)		53.7* (3)
1942	55.2 (2)		49.4 (5)	
1944		unopposed*		unopposed
1946	77.0 (3)	90.4 (2)	72.2 (2)	unopposed*
1948				
1950	54.7 (3)	69.0 (2)	78.9 (3)	unopposed
1952		75.2* (3)		68.9 (2)
1954	74.0 (3)		52.7 (3)	
1956		85.0* (2)		unopposed
1958	53.3 (4)	74.0 (3)	74.4 (3)	74.2 (2)
1960				
1962	78.1 (2)	unopposed	73.1 (3)	unopposed*
1964		89.1* (2)		45.4 (3)
1966	78.0 (3)		48.6 (3)	
1968		unopposed		53.3* (2)
1970	unopposed	unopposed*	57.6 (6)	53.8 (3)
1972				
1974	76.9 (3)	unopposed*	70.4* (3)	47.0 (4)
1976		37.8 (6)		68.8 (2)
1978	34.3 (6)		43.3 (5)	
1980		36.4 (8)		53.3 (8)
1982	unopposed*	unopposed*	57.6 (4)	57.2 (3)
1984				
1986	unopposed	76.2* (2)	56.4 (3)	47.3 (4)
1988		unopposed*		45.4 (4)
1990	54.4 (2)		77.5* (2)	
1992		65.1* (2)		44.8 (5)
1994	34.6 (5)	81.5 (2)	31.2 (7)	unopposed
1996				
1998	unopposed*	67.2* (3)	49.2 (3)	50.0 (3)

SOURCE: Figures calculated by the author from data in *The Pennsylvania Manual*, selected volumes.

*indicates incumbent.

Table 6.2 A summary of gubernatorial primary elections, by party and selected variables, 1926–1998

Democratic		Republican	
Contested primaries			
Total contested			
95% (18)		79% (15)	
Incumbent-nonincumbent			
Incumbent	Nonincumbent	Incumbent	Nonincumbent
100% (2)	94% (16)	0% (2)	88% (15)
Majority-minority status			
Majority	Minority	Majority	Minority
100% (10)	89% (8)	100% (9)	60% (6)
Winners receiving >60%			
42% (8)		53% (10)	
Majority-minority status			
Majority	Minority	Majority	Minority
30% (3)	56% (5)	33% (3)	70% (7)
Winners receiving <50%			
37% (7)		26% (5)	
Majority-minority status			
Majority	Minority	Majority	Minority
40% (4)	33% (3)	33% (3)	20% (2)

SOURCE: Data calculated from the author's research.

winners were more likely to secure the nomination with less than a majority of the vote, during both majority and minority status. Remarkably, since 1926 both Republican and Democratic winners received an average of 58 percent of the vote.

In summary, Democratic gubernatorial primaries were more likely to be contested, with Democratic winners less likely to garner more than 60 percent of the vote, and more likely to win with less than a majority of the vote.

Table 6.3 summarizes the data for senatorial elections.

Unlike the gubernatorial primaries, the Republican senatorial primaries were more likely to be contested. The GOP enjoyed a sizable advantage whether or not an incumbent was running. Both parties had 46 percent of their primaries contested when they were in the minority, while the Republicans had a slight advantage as the majority party. Overall,

Table 6.3 A summary of U.S. Senate primary elections, by party and selected variables, 1926–1998

Democratic		Republican	
Contested primaries			
Total contested			
65% (17)		73% (19)	
Incumbent-nonincumbent			
Incumbent	Nonincumbent	Incumbent	Nonincumbent
50% (2)	68% (15)	64% (9)	83% (10)
Majority-minority status			
Majority	Minority	Majority	Minority
85% (11)	46% (6)	92% (12)	46% (6)
Winners receiving >60%			
58% (15)		81% (21)	
Majority-minority status			
Majority	Minority	Majority	Minority
31% (4)	92% (12)	77% (10)	85% (11)
Winners receiving <50%			
19% (5)		15% (4)	
Majority-minority status			
Majority	Minority	Majority	Minority
38% (5)	0% (0)	15% (2)	15% (2)

SOURCE: Data calculated from the author's research.

Republican winners were much more likely to obtain more than 60 percent of the vote. This is attributable to a lopsided GOP advantage under majority party status; the Democrats enjoyed a slight advantage under minority party status.

Virtually an equal percentage of winners in each party received less than 50 percent of the vote. An interesting difference emerges when the majority-minority status data are examined. All of the Democratic winners who won with less than 50 percent of the vote did so when the party had majority status; similar GOP winners were equally divided between majority and minority status. The last five Democratic primaries have been especially competitive. Three winners obtained less than 50 percent of the vote, and a fourth exactly 50 percent. Over the course of the century, Democratic candidates had a somewhat harder time securing their party's nomination. Republican winners averaged 67 percent of the vote, compared with 57 percent for Democratic winners.

As was the case with gubernatorial primaries, Democratic winners were less likely to receive more than 60 percent of the vote and more likely to win with less than 50 percent of the vote. But unlike the case with the gubernatorial primaries, Republican senatorial primaries were more likely to be contested.

Key's arguments regarding competition in primary elections received support from the present data for gubernatorial and senatorial elections. Competition was greater when no incumbent was present, and competition increased when the party's prospects in the general election were better. Next, we will examine primary elections for the Pennsylvania House and Senate and the U.S. House of Representatives.

Primaries for the Pennsylvania General Assembly and U.S. House of Representatives

This section will examine Pennsylvania General Assembly and congressional primary elections from 1972 to 1998. The intent was to begin the analysis of these elections with the 1970 contest, since the 1970s were the first decade where single-member districts were employed for Pennsylvania House elections for the entire decade. However, the Bureau of Elections in the Office of the Secretary of State could only provide primary results for General Assembly and congressional elections beginning with the 1972 primary.

Congressional primaries have always been more likely to be contested (see Table 6.4). Virtually no differences exist between the rates of opposition in Pennsylvania House and Senate primaries. For all three categories of elections, the rates of contested primaries declined significantly over the three decades. For congressional primaries, the rate fell from 52 percent to 35 percent; for Senate primaries, from 38 percent to 15 percent; and for House primaries, from 34 percent to 20 percent.

The incidence of contested primaries has fallen steadily for each office during the past three decades. By the 1990s, only slightly more than one-third of the congressional candidates, and approximately 20 percent of Senate and House candidates faced opposition. In each decade, congressional primaries were the most likely to feature contests. At present, congressional candidates are almost twice as likely to face opponents as their brethren

Table 6.4 The percentage of contested congressional and Pennsylvania General Assembly primaries, by type of candidate, office, and decade, 1972–1998

Candidate	U.S. House of Representatives		
	1972–1978	1980–1988	1990–1998
All	52% (102)	42% (94)	35% (68)
Incumbents	48% (43)	38% (42)	30% (29)
Nonincumbents	55% (59)	47% (52)	39% (39)

Candidate	Pennsylvania Senate		
	1971–1978	1980–1988	1990–1998
All	38% (76)	23% (53)	15% (33)
Incumbents	39% (34)	24% (26)	13% (14)
Nonincumbents	38% (42)	15% (27)	17% (19)

Candidate	Pennsylvania House of Representatives		
	1972–1978	1980–1988	1990–1998
All	34% (538)	23% (415)	20% (342)
Incumbents	37% (262)	23% (210)	17% (157)
Nonincumbents	32% (276)	23% (205)	23% (185)

SOURCE: Data calculated from the author's research.

in the General Assembly are. The figures for the Senate and House attest to the virtual lack of competition today in most legislative districts.

The data support the findings of both Key and Sorauf regarding the relationship between incumbency and primary competition. The results for all three decades of congressional elections and for General Assembly elections for the 1990s support Key's contention that primary competition occurs less frequently when an incumbent is running. However, the data for General Assembly elections during the 1970s and 1980s substantiate Sorauf's findings that incumbents were present in a larger percentage of contested primaries.

The above data, however, do not speak to the seriousness of the competition. The mere presence of an opponent does not mean that a particular candidate faces a major challenge. The quality of competition is examined in Table 6.5. This shows the percentage of opposed candidates who received at least 60 percent of the vote.

Overall, a majority of the contested candidates for these three offices won the nomination with less than 60 percent of the vote. However, the patterns vary by incumbency status, office, and decade. It is also important to keep in mind that only a small percentage of the candidates had to concern themselves with a primary opponent.

Table 6.5 The percentage of opposed congressional and General Assembly candidates who received at least 60 percent of the primary election vote, by type of candidate, office, and decade, 1972–1998

Candidate	U.S. House of Representatives		
	1972–1978	1980–1988	1990–1998
All	48% (49)	63% (59)	50% (34)
Incumbents	74% (32)	79% (33)	72% (21)
Nonincumbents	29% (17)	50% (26)	33% (13)

Candidate	Pennsylvania Senate		
	1971–1978	1980–1988	1990–1998
All	38% (29)	53% (28)	42% (14)
Incumbents	53% (18)	58% (15)	43% (6)
Nonincumbents	26% (11)	48% (13)	42% (8)

Candidate	Pennsylvania House of Representatives		
	1972–1978	1980–1988	1990–1998
All	45% (245)	45% (187)	49% (168)
Incumbents	63% (168)	58% (122)	66% (103)
Nonincumbents	28% (77)	32% (65)	35% (65)

SOURCE: Data calculated from the author's research.

Congressional candidates, especially incumbents, were the most likely to obtain more than 60 percent of the vote in every decade. Incumbents won safe majorities much more often than nonincumbents did; this pattern was most pronounced in congressional elections. At the other extreme, basically no difference existed between Senate incumbents and nonincumbents during the 1990s. Congressional and Senate winners had their largest margins of victory during the 1980s, while for House winners that was true during the 1990s.

What is most striking, if the congressional and Senate results for the 1980s are removed from the analysis, is the consistency of the percentages over the three decades. In particular, the figures for the 1970s and 1990s are similar. The only percentages that are significantly different are those for Senate incumbents and nonincumbents. Senate incumbents who are opposed are winning with smaller majorities, while nonincumbents with opposition are receiving a significantly larger share of the vote. Combined, the two trends suggest the presence of more viable challengers and open-seat candidates in Senate races.

Two incentives, in particular, could entice stronger challengers to oppose an incumbent in the primary. The first is that the incumbent has

Table 6.6 The relationship between Pennsylvania Senate incumbents who received less than 60 percent of the vote in a primary election and the vote in the previous and subsequent general elections, by decade, 1972–1998

Decade	N	Incumbents receiving less than 60% in previous election	Winners receiving more than 60% in subsequent election
1970s	6	17% (1)	50% (3)
1980s	9	33% (3)	33% (3)
1990s	14	50% (7)	43% (6)
Total	29	38% (11)	41% (12)

SOURCE: Data calculated from the author's research.

evidenced vulnerability. One clear indication of vulnerability is a close race in the previous general election. A second inducement is the strong possibility that the nominee will win the general election easily. The relationship between those two factors and Senate incumbents who received less than 60 percent of the vote in the primary is examined in Table 6.6. This table lists the percentage of such incumbents who received less than 60 percent of the vote in the previous general election, and the percentage of winners of these primaries who received more than 60 percent of the vote in the subsequent general election.

The most obvious trend is that vulnerability increasingly is being revealed in the previous general election. By the 1990s, half of the incumbent senators who received less than 60 percent of the vote in the primary previously had been elected in marginal races. Conversely, a declining percentage of winners has gone on to prevail in the general election by a safe margin. Overall, the impact of the two incentives has been almost identical: 38 percent of the beleaguered incumbents received less than 60 percent of the vote in the previous general election, and 41 percent of the winners went on to garner more than 60 percent of the vote in the following general election.

The impact of these two factors on the fortunes of congressional and House incumbents who received less than 60 percent of the primary vote is reported in Table 6.7.

The most dramatic contrast is between Pennsylvania Senate and House incumbents. The pattern for House incumbents who received less than 60 percent of the vote in the primary is the exact opposite of the pattern for incumbent senators. Over the course of the three decades, the percentage of such incumbents who obtained less than 60 percent of the vote in the previous election tumbled from 35 percent to 21 percent, while the per-

Table 6.7 The relationship between congressional and Pennsylvania House incumbents who received less than 60 percent of the vote in a primary election and the vote in the previous and subsequent general elections, by decade, 1972–1998

Decade	N	Incumbents receiving less than 60% in previous election	Winners receiving more than 60% in subsequent election
U.S. House of Representatives			
1970s	14	36% (5)	64% (9)
1980s	10	40% (4)	60% (6)
1990s	8	37% (3)	75% (6)
Total	32	38% (12)	66% (21)
Pennsylvania House of Representatives			
1970s	100	35% (35)	65% (65)
1980s	83	22% (18)	75% (62)
1990s	39	21% (8)	85% (33)
Total	221	28% (61)	72% (159)

SOURCE: Data calculated from the author's research.

centage of winners who captured more than 60 percent of the vote in the subsequent general election jumped from 65 percent to 85 percent. Overall, 28 percent of these incumbents got less than 60 percent of the vote in the previous election, and 72 percent of the winners garnered more than 60 percent of the vote in the following general election.

The data suggest that, by the end of the century, state senators and representatives incurred serious challengers for different reasons. Senators attracted strong opponents after evidencing electoral weakness in the previous general election. Competitive House primaries, on the other hand, appear to have been associated more with increased prospects of general election success.

The percentage of embattled congressional incumbents who received less than 60 percent in the previous general election held steady at approximately 40 percent over the period. The percentage of winners who went on to receive more than 60 percent of the vote in the general election increased from 64 percent to 75 percent. Overall, 38 percent of the incumbents who received less than 60 percent of the vote in the primary polled less than 60 percent of the vote in the previous election, while 66 percent of the winners went on to tally more than 60 percent of the vote in the following general election. Thus, as was the case with House members, competitive primaries appear to be related increasingly to general election prospects.

Table 6.8 The incidence of primary election defeat for congressional and General Assembly incumbents, by decade, 1972–1998

Office	1972–1978	1980–1988	1990–1998
U.S. House of Representatives	2% (2)	4% (4)	1% (2)
Pennsylvania Senate	3% (3)	6% (7)	1% (1)
Pennsylvania House of Representatives	3% (26)	3% (26)	1% (5)

SOURCE: Data calculated from the author's research.

The incidence of primary defeat for incumbents is detailed in Table 6.8. The highest rate of defeat occurred during the 1980s, especially for state senators. This was followed by a dramatic decline during the 1990s. By the end of the century, only 1 percent of the incumbents in each election category were the victims of primary election upsets.

The Relationship Between Contested Primaries and General Election Vote

The previous section established a relationship between primary challenges to certain incumbents and the vote in the subsequent general election. This section will examine the relationship between competition in all Pennsylvania House primaries between 1972 and 1998 and the vote in the general election. Both Key (1956) and Sorauf (1963) reported increased primary competition when the party's prospects of success in the general election were greater. Both also cited a sizable decline in competition in those districts in which the parties received more than 60 percent of the vote.

The present findings are detailed in Table 6.9. The percentage of contested and uncontested primaries for each party are reported for each decade. The general election vote is presented as the Republican share of the two-party vote. Each district is placed into one of three categories: <40.0%, 40.1–59.9%, >60.0%. This clearly identifies those districts in which the Republican (>60.0%) and Democratic (<40.0%) parties received more than 60 percent of the vote. The middle category (40.1–59.9%) represents the marginal districts.

The data from all House races substantiate the earlier finding that primary competition increases as the party's prospects in the general election improve. As can be seen above, as the Republican share of the general election vote increases competition in the Republican primary increases, while that in the Democratic primary decreases. Conversely, competition

Table 6.9 The relationship between contested and uncontested primaries for the Pennsylvania House of Representatives and the vote in the general election, by party and decade, 1972–1998

	1972–1978		1980–1988		1990–1998	
Republican vote	Contested	Uncontested	Contested	Uncontested	Contested	Uncontested
Democrats						
<40.0%	46%	40%	62%	34%	59%	45%
40.1–59.9%	42%	33%	27%	16%	33%	12%
>60.0%	13%	28%	11%	51%	9%	44%
(N)	(360)	(452)	(275)	(740)	(181)	(934)
Republicans						
Republican vote	Contested	Uncontested	Contested	Uncontested	Contested	Uncontested
<40.0%	18%	41%	18%	45%	20%	46%
40.1–59.9%	54%	32%	43%	15%	41%	12%
>60.0%	28%	28%	39%	40%	39%	42%
(N)	(178)	(634)	(143)	(872)	(157)	(858)

SOURCE: Data calculated from the author's research.

in the Democratic primary increases as the Republican share of the vote decreases, while competition in the Republican primary decreases.

However, the present data do not comport with previous findings of a drop-off in competition in the parties' safest districts. That is the case with the Republican primaries, but not with the Democratic primaries. On the Democratic side, competition increases steadily as the party's share of the general election vote increases. Just as Key and Sorauf found no obvious explanation for the consistent decline in competition in the parties' safest districts, there is no patent explanation for the divergent pattern in the current findings.

Key suggested that ruralism might be a possible explanation for the decline in competition in the safest districts. He reported lower levels of competition in rural districts. The relationship between urbanism and ruralism and primary competition is the focus of the next section.

Urban-Rural Differences in Primary Election Competition

The impact of urban-rural differences on primary competition will be examined using 1990 census data and primary elections for the Pennsylvania House of Representatives during the 1990s. Following the lead of Sorauf (1963, 23) and Kennedy (1999, 62), House districts will be placed in one of three categories. *Cities* (38 districts) includes districts that contain a municipality with a population of more than 100,000 (this category includes the cities of Philadelphia, Pittsburgh, and Allentown). *Urbanized* (99 districts) contains districts where a majority of the population resides in urban places with populations between 2,500 and 100,000. *Rural* (66 districts) is comprised of all districts where a majority of the population lives in places with a population of less than 2,500.

The expected partisan pattern exists among the three categories (see Table 6.10). The proportion of Democratic districts increases as urbanism increases, while the incidence of Republican districts increases as ruralism increases. Ninety-two percent of the districts in the *Cities* category are Democratic, while 65 percent of the districts in the *Rural* category are Republican.

Contrary to previous findings, there was no dramatic difference in the level of primary competition in urban and rural areas (see Table 6.11). In fact, the incidence of contested primaries was virtually identical among the three categories.

The proportion of races in which an incumbent ran was also essentially identical, regardless of the degree of urbanization (see Table 6.12).

Table 6.10 The relationship between partisanship and urban-rural categories among Pennsylvania House of Representatives districts, 1990–1998

	Urban-Rural Classification		
	Cities	Urbanized	Rural
Democratic districts	92%	46%	35%
Republican districts	8%	55%	65%
(N)	(38)	(99)	(66)

SOURCE: Data calculated from the author's research.

Table 6.11 The incidence of contested primaries among urban-rural categories, Pennsylvania House of Representatives, 1990–1998

	Urban-Rural Classification		
	Cities	Urbanized	Rural
	32.8%	34.3%	32.7%
(N)	(190)	(495)	(330)

SOURCE: Data calculated from the author's research.

Table 6.12 The relationship between incumbency and urban-rural categories, Pennsylvania House of Representatives, 1990–1998

	Urban-Rural Classification		
Incumbency	Cities	Urbanized	Rural
Races with incumbent	94% (179)	89% (441)	87% (287)
% incumbents contested	30% (46)	14% (72)	14% (41)
Dem.% incumbents	84% (150)	47% (206)	39% (112)
% incumbents contested	31% (46)	23% (48)	20% (22)
Rep.% incumbents	16% (29)	53% (235)	61% (175)
% incumbents contested	3% (1)	10% (24)	11% (19)
(N)	(190)	(495)	(330)

SOURCE: Data calculated from the author's research.

However, incumbents were considerably more likely to be opposed in the *Cities* category than in the *Urbanized* or *Rural* categories. In fact, the percentage of contested races is more than halved as one moves from the most urbanized to the least urbanized category.

The partisan differences are especially noteworthy. In Philadelphia, Pittsburgh, and Allentown, 84 percent of the incumbents were Democrats, and 31 percent of them were opposed. In the *Rural* category, 61 percent of the incumbents were Republicans, with 11 percent of them opposed. Democratic incumbents were more likely to be opposed in every urban-rural category. They were approximately twice as likely as their GOP counterparts to be opposed in the *Urbanized* and *Rural* categories, and almost eleven times as likely to be opposed in the *Cities* category. Focusing on the most Democratic districts (cities) and the most Republican districts (rural) reveals distinctive partisan differences. In their respective strongholds, Democratic incumbents appeared more frequently, and were almost three times more likely to be opposed.

The relationship between contested primaries in urban and rural districts and the vote in the general election is portrayed in Table 6.13. In each of the three urban-rural categories the percentage of contested and uncontested primaries are listed. As was the case above, the general election vote is presented as the Republican share of the two-party vote.

For each party, the highest incidence of contested primaries occurred in the districts that represented the party's greatest strength. In the case of the Democrats, those were city districts where the Republican vote was less than 40 percent; for the GOP, those were rural districts where the Republican vote was greater than 60 percent. This tendency was most pronounced for the Democrats. The 89 percent figure in the most Democratic districts was almost double the next highest percentage. The pattern for the Democrats was for the most competition to take place in those districts where the vote was most Democratic. This was even the case in rural districts where, overall, the Republicans are much stronger than the Democrats. The picture was somewhat different on the Republican side. Fewer than half (47 percent) of the most Republican districts had a contest in the primary. And with the exception of rural districts, GOP competition was more likely to occur in marginal districts.

This suggests a possible explanation for the divergent partisan patterns regarding competition in each party's safest districts, reported in Table 6.9. The increasing Democratic competition as Democratic vote share increases is primarily attributable to the extraordinary level of competition in the districts in the *Cities* category. On the other hand, while the Republicans have their highest incidence of competition in the safest rural districts, this is not enough to offset the fact that, overall, the highest level of GOP competition occurs in marginal districts in the *Cities* and *Urbanized* categories.

Table 6.13 The relationship between contested and uncontested primaries for the Pennsylvania House of Representatives and the vote in the general election, by party and urban-rural classification, 1990–1998

	Urban-Rural Classification						
	Cities		Urbanized		Rural		
Republican vote	Contested	Uncontested	Contested	Uncontested	Contested	Uncontested
			Democrats			
<40.0%	89%	27%	49%	32%	44%	33%
40.1–59.9%	9%	36%	45%	33%	37%	33%
>60.0%	2%	37%	6%	35%	19%	34%
(N)	(53)	(527)	(80)	(1405)	(48)	(932)
			Republicans			
Republican vote	Contested	Uncontested	Contested	Uncontested	Contested	Uncontested
<40.0%	43%	33%	17%	34%	22%	34%
40.1–59.9%	43%	33%	47%	32%	32%	33%
>60.0%	14%	34%	37%	33%	47%	32%
(N)	(7)	(578)	(90)	(1395)	(60)	(915)

SOURCE: Data calculated from the author's research.

Voter Turnout in Primary Elections

The century-long decline in voter turnout in general elections was documented in Chapter 2. Here we turn our attention to turnout in primary elections. The trend for primaries is presented in Table 6.14. Voter turnout in gubernatorial primaries is examined. As was the case in Chapter 2, turnout is expressed as the percentage of voting age residents. The difference between primary and general election turnout is presented in the second column.

For three-quarters of a century, the trend has been a significant, albeit uneven, decline in primary turnout. Initially, turnout averaged approximately one-third of the eligible electorate, peaking at 48 percent in 1938, when Arthur H. James ended Gifford Pinchot's attempt to become governor a third time by defeating him in the GOP primary. Turnout fell to between one-fifth and one fourth of the electorate in the 1940s, where it remained through the 1970s. The rate fell below 20 percent during the last two decades of the century, bottoming out at 11 percent in 1998, when Tom Ridge was unopposed for reelection in the Republican primary, and the Democratic primary featured three opponents not viewed as viable candidates. Underscoring voter apathy in primary contests is the fact that only once (1966) since 1938 has turnout in the gubernatorial primary exceeded 30 percent.

Comparable data do not exist that would allow a comparison of the century-long trend in Pennsylvania with patterns in other states. However, Jewell and Morehouse (2001) present data that allow some post-1960s comparisons. Primary election turnout has declined in southern states since the mid-1960s. Turnout in the once dominant Democratic Party primary has declined significantly, but has not been matched by a concomitant increase in the primary of the resurgent Republican Party (123–25). The authors also reported that between 1968 and 1998 primary turnout in the two-party states was approximately 51 percent of the turnout in the general election (123). During that same time, primary turnout in Pennsylvania averaged 47 percent of the general election turnout.

With the exception of 1926, primary turnout has lagged behind general election turnout. Over the period being examined, general election turnout has generally been between 20 and 30 percentage points higher. During the past two decades, primary turnout has lagged approximately 20 points behind general election turnout. The events associated with the aberrant 1926 election merit discussion.

Table 6.14 Percentage voter turnout in primaries, and the difference between primary and general election turnout, in gubernatorial primaries, 1926–1998

Year	Primary turnout	Difference	Year	Primary turnout	Difference
1926	31.7%	+1.9%	1966	30.8%	−26.2%
1930	33.0%	−4.2%	1970	22.6%	−29.5%
1934	35.8%	−16.4%	1974	21.9%	−22.2%
1938	47.9%	−19.5%	1978	28.7%	−18.4%
1942	23.6%	−16.5%	1982	15.0%	−27.1%
1946	20.9%	−27.9%	1986	17.3%	−21.5%
1950	28.6%	−22.0%	1990	15.5%	−18.1%
1954	22.0%	−31.2%	1994	23.2%	−16.2%
1958	29.5%	−27.5%	1998	11.1%	−21.8%
1962	26.0%	−35.7%			

SOURCE: Figures calculated by the author. The turnout data came from *The Pennsylvania Manual,* selected volumes; data for the voting age population came from the *Statistical Abstract of the United States,* selected volumes.

The 1926 Republican gubernatorial primary was inextricably tied to that year's GOP senatorial primary. Governor Pinchot, never a favorite of Republican leaders and the party's monied interests, challenged incumbent GOP senator George Wharton Pepper in the primary. Pepper was the organization candidate and also the favorite of the corporate interests and most of the press; Pinchot was the anti-organization candidate. Also jumping into the primary was William S. Vare, the Philadelphia Republican boss. Superimposed on all this was the prohibition issue: Vare was wet, Pinchot was dry, and Pepper's position was not clear. At stake was not only a seat in the U.S. Senate, but also the position of party leader, unclaimed since the death of Boies Penrose (Dunaway 1948, 490).

Pepper's running mate for governor was John S. Fisher, and Vare ran on a slate with Edward E. Beidelman. Vare won the senatorial primary by a vote of 596,502 to 515,502 for Pepper and 329,127 for Pinchot. Vare went on to defeat Democrat William B. Wilson in the general election, but because of excessive expenditures in the primary, the Senate, three years later, refused to seat him.

Initially, Vare's partner Beidelman was deemed to carry the state by 13,325 votes. Then there was a "two-day countout" in Allegheny County, and Fisher emerged with an 18,423 vote statewide victory. It was alleged that ballot boxes were tossed in the river; however, Vare worked similar magic in Philadelphia, where he carried forty-seven of forty-eight wards. In Beidelman's hometown of Harrisburg, Fisher was completely shut out in one ward. Beidelman complained that he had instructed that at least one vote was to have gone to Fisher, to which his ward leader responded, "Yes, boss, but the folks up there love you so" (Beers 1980, 91).

The scandal in Pittsburgh grew and eventually led to an investigation of ballot-box stuffing. In 1931 and 1932, almost 150 residents of the city were convicted of such charges. Later, in his autobiography, Pepper reflected on his experience and advised future candidates: "The universal experience of senators is that they dare not get their candidacies mixed with the candidacies of state office seekers. If they do, they thereby multiply their political liabilities and divide their political assets" (Beers 1980, 91).

Summary

This chapter examined competition and voter turnout in primary elections. Included in the analysis were primaries for governor, U.S. Senate, U.S. House of Representatives, and the Pennsylvania General Assembly.

Democratic gubernatorial primaries were more likely to be contested. Democratic winners were less likely to receive 60 percent of the vote and more likely to win with less than 50 percent of the vote. Republican senatorial primaries were more likely to be contested. Once again, however, Democratic winners were less likely to garner 60 percent of the vote, and more likely to win with less than a majority.

Congressional primaries were more likely to be contested than primaries for the Pennsylvania legislature were. Virtually no difference existed in the incidence of competition between state House and Senate primaries. For all three categories of elections, competition has decreased since the 1970s. By the 1990s, only slightly more than one-third of the congressional primaries and about one-fifth of the General Assembly primaries were contested.

The data for all three decades of congressional primaries, and for General Assembly primaries during the 1990s, support Key's contention that less competition exists when an incumbent is present. The data for General Assembly primaries during the 1970s and 1980s support Sorauf's finding that incumbents were more likely to be present in contested primaries.

Of those candidates who were opposed in congressional and General Assembly primaries, more than half won with less than 60 percent of the vote. Congressional candidates, especially incumbents, were more likely to receive more than 60 percent of the vote. Different patterns existed for candidates who received less than 60 percent of the primary vote. State senators seemed to be challenged because they evidenced weakness in the previous general election. On the other hand, state representatives and congressional candidates seemed to attract more serious competition when the prospects of general election success were greater. By the end of the century, only 1 percent of state legislative and congressional candidates were being defeated in the primary.

Among Democratic candidates for the state House, competition increased steadily as the prospects for general election success increased. Among Republican candidates, however, there was a drop-off in competition in the safest districts. A potential explanation seems to be an extraordinary level of competition (89 percent) in the Democratic primaries in the safest Democratic urban districts. On the other hand, while the Republicans have their highest incidence of competition (47 percent) in their safest rural districts, this is not enough to offset the fact that the highest overall level of Republican competition occurs in marginal districts in more urban areas.

Each of the General Assembly districts was assigned to one of three categories on an urban-rural continuum. As expected, increasing urbanism was associated with an increasing incidence of Democratic districts. Virtually no difference existed in the incidence of competition among the three categories. Incumbents were most likely to be challenged in the most urban districts. In the most urban districts, 84 percent of the incumbents were Democrats, and 31 percent were opposed; in the least urban districts, 62 percent of the incumbents were Republican, and 11 percent were opposed.

Voter turnout in gubernatorial primary elections has declined over the course of the century. With the exception of the aberrant 1926 election, turnout in the primary has always lagged behind general election turnout. At present, approximately 20 percent more voters turn out for the general election than for the primary.

PATTERNS OF PARTISANSHIP

In previous chapters, twentieth-century legislative and statewide elections were analyzed in detail. Numerous trends were identified regarding state legislative, congressional, gubernatorial, presidential, and statewide office elections. In this chapter, the focus will shift to an analysis of partisan patterns over the course of the century. Several specific patterns will be examined.

First, an attempt will be made to pinpoint when the New Deal realignment occurred in Pennsylvania. Second, the relationship between the Republican vote and the degree of urbanization and ethnic and racial diversity in each county will be examined. This will allow us to develop profiles of typical Republican and Democratic counties prior to, and after, the New Deal realignment. Third, all sixty-seven counties will be categorized according to their level of competition in gubernatorial and presidential elections during the twentieth century. Next, profiles will be presented of contemporary Republican and Democratic state legislative districts. Finally, a summary will be presented of the home counties of successful gubernatorial, senatorial, and statewide officeholders.

Partisan Realignment in Pennsylvania

The Concept of Partisan Realignment

V. O. Key Jr. was the first political scientist to discuss the issue of partisan realignment. His initial foray was a 1955 article in which he introduced the concept of "critical elections." These are elections "in which the depth and intensity of electoral involvement are high, in which more or less profound readjustments occur in the relations of power within the community, and in which new and durable electoral groupings are formed" (Key 1955, 4). His argument emerged from a study of election results in several New England towns between 1916 and 1952. He identified 1928 as a critical election.

Four years later, Key significantly modified his original argument. He stated that partisanship may not change as dramatically as he originally contended. He now suggested that such realignments may take place over a period of years. He labeled such occurrences secular realignments and defined a secular realignment as "a movement of the members of a population category from party to party that extends over several presidential elections and appears to be independent of the peculiar factors influencing the vote at individual elections" (Key 1959, 199).

Walter Dean Burnham attempted to develop a theory of realignment in *Critical Elections and the Mainsprings of American Politics* (1970). He was concerned with "critical realignments," as distinguished from stable alignment periods, secular realignments, and deviating elections. The "ideal-typical" critical realignment differs from the other phenomena in several important ways.

> To recapitulate, then, eras of critical realignment are marked by short, sharp reorganizations of the mass coalitional bases of the major parties which occur at periodic intervals on the national level; often are preceded by major third-party revolts which reveal the incapacity of "politics as usual" to integrate, much less aggregate, emergent political demand; are closely associated with

abnormal stress in the socioeconomic system; are marked by ideological polarizations and issue-distances between the major parties which are exceptionally large by normal standards; and have durable consequences as constituent acts which determine the outer boundaries of policy in general, though not necessarily of politics in detail. (10)

Burnham argues that such realignments occur approximately every thirty to thirty-eight years. He identified four realignment eras, with the midpoint years 1854, 1874, 1894, and 1930.

Realignments can vary considerably in their impact on the party system. The party system may not appear perceptibly different following the realignment; on the other hand, the party system may be dramatically transformed, including the disappearance of existing parties and the emergence of new parties (Sundquist 1983). The realignment of the 1850s saw the disappearance of the Whig Party and the emergence of the Republican Party; the realignment of the 1890s witnessed the strengthening of the majority Republican Party; the realignment of the 1930s featured the replacement of the Republicans by the Democrats as the majority party.

The 1890s Realignment

The realignment of 1893–96, precipitated by the 1893 depression, created the political environment that prevailed until the 1930s. The ultimate result was to transform Pennsylvania into a one-party state. For the first three decades of the twentieth century the Democratic Party was, at best, an afterthought to most Pennsylvania voters. What little competition existed, existed within the Republican primary.

As the last decade of the nineteenth century dawned, Pennsylvania was a state that normally went Republican, but by narrow margins. Philadelphia and Allegheny Counties were crucial to GOP statewide success, while the Democrats generally did best in rural areas. The 1893–96 realignment affected almost all sixty-seven counties uniformly; thus, few changed their relative position in relation to other counties (Burnham 1970, 39).

While most counties became more Republican, the shift to the GOP was more pronounced in the more urban counties, especially Philadelphia and Allegheny Counties. The Democrats also suffered significant declines in support in those rural counties that had supported the party since the Civil War. The most Republican area was in the southeastern corner of the state, including Philadelphia County and the adjacent counties. The Democratic strongholds were in rural and semirural counties remote from the major metropolitan centers. The more Republican counties also contained more Pennsylvania Germans and newer immigrant groups (Burnham 1970, 42–44).

African American citizens had obtained the right to vote in Pennsylvania in 1874. The Constitution of 1838 had limited suffrage to white citizens. The Constitution of 1874 dropped the term "free white citizen" from the suffrage requirements. While possessing some political power, they were usually not crucial to the success of the Republican machine. However, most African American voters were exceedingly loyal to the GOP.

Thus, as the twentieth century began, Pennsylvania was a solidly Republican state. The GOP strength was in urban areas, especially Philadelphia and Pittsburgh. The party also did well among immigrants and African Americans. The Democrats were a hapless minority party whose minimal support was located in rural areas.

The New Deal Realignment

Two major topics will be addressed in this section. The first is the timing of the New Deal realignment in Pennsylvania. An attempt will be made to identify the election or elections that were crucial in shaping the realignment. Second, we will examine whether the realignment occurred at the same time for different categories of elections. Previous analyses of realignments typically focused on a particular category of elections, usually presidential elections. We will analyze gubernatorial, presidential, Pennsylvania House, and U.S. congressional elections. Of concern is whether the partisan realignments took place during the same (or comparable) election years for the different categories of elections. Both categories of legislative elections are held every even-numbered year. Gubernatorial and presidential elections are held in alternating even-numbered years. Therefore, if gubernatorial and presidential realignments occurred within two years of each other, those would constitute comparable election years.

Burnham (1970) identified the ten-election sequence between 1922 and 1940, with the midpoint year 1931, as a realigning cycle in Pennsylvania. His basic measure was the mean Democratic percentage of the total vote for all elections in which the state was the elective unit. According to Burnham, 1932 was a "bridge" election: the 1932 percentage is more closely correlated with the two subsequent elections than with previous elections, but it displays a moderately high correlation with all elections between 1916 and 1940 (56–58). He also states that the "whole period from 1924 on reveals heavy *within-state* reshuffling of voting behavior" (58).

Burnham also contends that the coalitions formed during the 1930s have continued to persist:

> The Republican electoral base has remained in the familiar pattern established the 1930s: native-stock elements living in rural areas, small towns, and suburbs: people with advantages of wealth and education; and people of "obsolescent" social strata, particularly those of traditionalist socioreligious perspectives who tend to resist changes which seem to threaten their traditions. The Democratic electoral base has included disproportionate support among the electorally active poor, Negroes, Jews, Catholics, trade-unionists, and residents of the central city in metropolitan areas. (59)

Several measures will be employed to compare the present data with Burnham's findings. The first will compare the mean Republican percentage of the vote in each election year with the mean Republican percentage of the vote in the four previous elections for each of the categories of election being examined. The results for gubernatorial and presidential elections are presented in Table 7.1. The percentage Republican of the two-party vote (%Rep), the mean percentage Republican of the two-party vote for the previous four elections (Previous), and the difference (Dif) between the Republican vote in the current year and the previous four elections are given.

Both sets of data suggest that a secular realignment occurred in Pennsylvania during the 1930s and early 1940s. Among gubernatorial elections, 1930 and 1934 stand out. The 1936 election, sandwiched by the significant 1932 and 1940 elections, is most conspicuous among the presidential contests. Individual county results were examined in an attempt to determine which gubernatorial and presidential election was the most crucial.

The county-by-county results point to 1932 and 1934 being the crucial elections. In the 1934 gubernatorial election, the Republican percentage of the two-party vote declined by 10 percentage points or more from the previous election in forty-five counties; that was the case in thirty-one counties in 1930. The change in 1934 was 20 percentage points or more in sixteen counties. Three counties (Lehigh, +13; Montgomery, +13; Philadelphia,

Table 7.1 A comparison of the mean Republican share of the vote in given elections with the mean Republican share of the vote in the four previous elections, for gubernatorial and presidential elections, 1900–1998

	Governor				President		
Year	%Rep.	Previous	Dif.	Year	%Rep.	Previous	Dif.
1902	57%	55%	+2%	1900	63%	56%	+7%
1906	53%	56%	−3%	1904	72%	58%	+14%
1910	76%	57%	+19%	1908	62%	62%	0
1914	57%	61%	−4%	1912	41%	65%	−24%
1918	64%	61%	+3%	1916	58%	58%	0
1922	59%	62%	−3%	1920	71%	58%	+13%
1926	75%	64%	+11%	1924	77%	58%	+19%
1930	51%	64%	−13%	1928	66%	62%	+4%
1934	49%	62%	−13%	1932	53%	68%	−13%
1938	54%	59%	−5%	1936	42%	67%	−25%
1942	54%	58%	−4%	1940	47%	60%	−13%
1946	59%	52%	+7%	1944	49%	52%	−3%
1950	51%	54%	−3%	1948	52%	48%	+4%
1954	46%	55%	−9%	1952	53%	48%	+5%
1958	49%	53%	−4%	1956	57%	50%	+7%
1962	56%	51%	+5%	1960	49%	53%	−4%
1966	53%	51%	+2%	1964	35%	53%	−18%
1970	43%	51%	−8%	1968	48%	49%	−1%
1974	46%	50%	−4%	1972	60%	51%	+9%
1978	53%	50%	+3%	1976	49%	48%	+1%
1982	51%	49%	+2%	1980	54%	48%	+6%
1986	49%	48%	+1%	1984	54%	53%	+1%
1990	32%	50%	−18%	1988	51%	54%	−3%
1994	53%	46%	+7%	1992	45%	52%	−7%
1998	65%	46%	+19%	1996	45%	51%	−6%

SOURCE: Data calculated from the author's research.

+28) saw the Republican share of the vote increase by 10 percentage points or more. In each case, this increase followed a dramatic decline in the Republican share of the two-party vote in 1930 (Lehigh, −27; Montgomery, −34; Philadelphia, −58).

While the 1934 election results in these three counties seem contrary to expectations, particularly in Philadelphia County, they are a consequence of the unusual nature of the 1930 election. The Republican candidate again was Gifford Pinchot, seeking a second term. Pinchot was caught in the middle of a Republican civil war between the followers of Joseph R. Grundy, Republican financier and founder and president of the Pennsylvania Association of Manufacturers, and Philadelphia boss William S. Vare. Vare was still angry with Pinchot for his role in the 1926 senatorial rebuke. Vare's animosity was so great that he backed Pinchot's Democratic opponent, John M. Hemphill; Grundy, however, supported Pinchot. Much GOP money, especially the liquor money, went with Hemphill, who was also supported by the *Philadelphia Inquirer* and the *Pittsburgh Post-Gazette*.

The key issue in the campaign was prohibition. Hemphill was opposed to prohibition, and Pinchot was an ardent dry. Wet Republicans supported Hemphill, and dry Democrats fled to Pinchot. Followers of Vare, businessmen associated with utilities and railroads, both attacked by Pinchot, and wets deserted the GOP and created the Liberal Party, endorsing the candidacy of Hemphill (Klein and Hoogenboom 1973, 451–52), and providing him with 36 percent of his total vote.

Pinchot won by 58,670 votes, but he trailed other Republican candidates on the ticket by approximately 400,000 votes. He obtained approximately 200,000 Democratic votes statewide. Vare took some revenge by orchestrating a 245,518 margin of victory for Hemphill in Philadelphia. Hemphill captured forty-seven of the city's forty-eight wards (Beers 1980, 94). Pinchot did better among those who favored prohibition and in rural areas.

Thus, in many respects, the 1930 election was an aberration. Overall, Republican support in Lehigh, Montgomery, and Philadelphia Counties fell between 1926 and 1934. The GOP percentage of the two-party vote fell 11 points in Lehigh County, 21 points in Montgomery County, and 30 points in Philadelphia County.

The 1932 presidential election is the most dramatic in either set of data. The Republican share of the two-party vote declined by 10 percentage points or more in fifty-nine counties. The Republican share did not increase in a single county. In 1936, the GOP share of the vote declined by 10 percentage points or more in only nineteen counties. Even more dramatically, no county registered a decline in the Republican share of the vote in the 1940 election; moreover, in only six counties that year was the GOP gain 10 percentage points or more. Further attesting to the dramatic changes that transpired in 1932, the decline in the Republican share of the vote was 20 percentage points or more in thirty-one counties, and 30 percentage points or more in three counties (Franklin, –30; Juniata, –33; York, –34).

The significance of individual gubernatorial elections during the 1930s realignment is examined from another perspective in Table 7.2. This presents the correlation between the Republican share of the two-party vote for governor for the elections between 1922 and 1942. For each election,

Table 7.2 Coefficients of correlation between Republican voting in gubernatorial elections, 1922–1942

	1922	1926	1930	1934	1938	1942
1922		.67	.08	.36	.30	.33
1926	.67		.43	.43	.38	.44
1930	.08	.43		.54	.40	.47
1934	.36	.43	.54		.78	.80
1938	.30	.38	.40	.78		.92
1942	.33	.44	.47	.80	.92	

SOURCE: H. F. Alderfer and Fannette H. Luhrs, *Gubernatorial Elections in Pennsylvania, 1922–1942* (State College, Pa.: The Pennsylvania Municipal Publications Service, 1946), 55.

counties are ranked according to the Republican percentage of the vote; these ranks are then correlated with each other.

These data reinforce the importance of the 1934 election. The 1934, 1938, and 1942 elections are strongly correlated with each other. The Republican voting patterns are almost identical. The 1922 election is very similar to the 1926 election; however, it shows little similarity to the 1930 election. This is interesting, because the same Republican candidate, Gifford Pinchot, ran in both years. By the end of the 1920s, as was discussed above, the wet-dry issue had become important, and a rift had developed between Pinchot and the Republican organization (Alderfer and Luhrs 1946, 55). While the 1930 election is not similar to the 1922 election, it is similar to all the others.

Table 7.3 displays similar data for the presidential elections between 1920 and 1940. The results support Burnham's contention that 1932 was a "bridge" election. The 1932 election is highly correlated with every other election. The 1920 election is most similar to the 1924 election. The 1924 and 1932 elections are very similar. The 1932, 1936, and 1940 elections are extremely similar.

Realignment patterns for elections to the Pennsylvania House and U.S. House of Representatives are displayed in Table 7.4. The format is identical to the one used in Table 6.1.

In both sets of legislative elections, the years 1932, 1934, and 1936 stand out. In each of those elections, the Republican share of the two-party vote was dramatically lower than the average for the previous four elections. The Democrats gained forty-three state House seats in 1932, fifty-two in 1934, and thirty-seven in 1936, increasing their membership from 22 to 188. At the congressional level, the Democrats picked up eight seats

Table 7.3 Coefficients of correlation between Republican voting in presidential elections, 1920–1940

	1920	1924	1928	1932	1936	1940
1920		.81	.34	.69	.48	.51
1924	.81		.51	.86	.33	.37
1928	.34	.51		.72	.57	.57
1932	.69	.86	.72		.81	.74
1936	.48	.33	.57	.81		.94
1940	.51	.37	.57	.74	.94	

SOURCE: Data calculated from the author's research.

in 1932, twelve seats in 1934, and four seats in 1936, expanding the number of seats held from three to twenty-seven.

In both the executive and legislative elections, the data suggest that a secular realignment occurred in Pennsylvania during the 1930s and early 1940s. The timing of the realignment was remarkably similar in all four categories of elections. The key gubernatorial election was 1934, and the crucial presidential election was 1932; the 1932, 1934, and 1936 elections to the Pennsylvania House and the U.S. House of Representatives appear to have been of equal importance.

The New Deal realignment, however, did not immediately usher two-party competition into Pennsylvania. The Republican comeback began in 1938. Arthur H. James recaptured the Governor's Mansion for the GOP, and the Republicans picked up seventy-five seats in the Pennsylvania House, and twelve seats in the U.S. House of Representatives. The Democrats temporarily rebounded in 1940 behind FDR, gaining forty-seven Pennsylvania House seats and three congressional seats. However, the Republicans quickly reasserted their dominance. Between 1943 and 1954, the GOP controlled the governorship and both houses of the state legislature. Dewey carried the state in the 1948 presidential election, and Eisenhower won the state in 1952 and 1956. Real interparty competition would not exist in Pennsylvania until the end of the 1950s.

The Relationship Between the Republican Vote and Urbanization, Ethnicity, and Racial Diversity

As I have described, in Pennsylvania at the beginning of the twentieth century, the Republicans were the urban party and the Democrats were the rural party. In addition, the GOP did better among foreign-born and

Table 7.4 A comparison of the mean Republican share of the vote in given elections with the mean Republican share of the vote in the four previous elections, for the Pennsylvania and U.S. Houses of Representatives, 1900–1998

	Pennsylvania House			U.S. House		
Year	%Rep.	Previous	Dif.	%Rep.	Previous	Dif.
1900	59	NA	NA	63	NA	NA
1902	57	NA	NA	64	NA	NA
1904	68	NA	NA	72	NA	NA
1906	58	NA	NA	62	NA	NA
1908	63	61	+2	61	65	−4
1910	65	62	+3	68	65	+3
1912	55	64	−9	54	66	−12
1914	63	60	+3	61	61	0
1916	59	62	−3	59	61	−2
1918	68	61	+7	68	61	+7
1920	70	61	+9	68	61	+7
1922	64	65	−1	61	64	−3
1924	74	65	+9	77	64	+13
1926	76	69	+7	72	69	+3
1928	66	71	−5	66	70	−4
1930	71	70	+1	71	69	+2
1932	55	72	−17	55	71	−16
1934	49	67	−18	50	66	−16
1936	44	61	−17	43	60	−17
1938	53	56	−3	58	55	+3
1940	48	51	−3	48	51	−3
1942	53	49	+4	54	50	+4
1944	50	49	+1	49	51	−2
1946	58	51	+7	58	52	+6
1948	52	52	0	53	52	+1
1950	52	53	−1	52	53	−1
1952	51	53	−2	52	53	−1
1954	49	53	−4	49	53	−4
1956	54	51	+3	53	51	+2
1958	51	52	−1	50	52	−2
1960	50	51	−1	50	51	−1
1962	53	51	+2	50	51	−1
1964	45	52	−7	44	51	−7
1966	52	50	+2	51	49	+2
1968	49	50	−1	48	49	−1
1970	48	50	−2	47	48	−1
1972	52	49	+3	52	48	+4
1974	45	50	−5	41	50	−9
1976	44	49	−5	42	47	−5
1978	50	47	+3	49	46	+3
1980	51	48	+3	51	46	+5
1982	48	48	0	47	46	+1
1984	48	48	0	46	47	−1

Table 7.4 A comparison of the mean Republican share of the vote in given elections with the mean Republican share of the vote in the four previous elections, for the Pennsylvania and U.S. Houses of Representatives, 1900–1998 *(continued)*

	Pennsylvania House			U.S. House		
Year	%Rep.	Previous	Dif.	%Rep.	Previous	Dif.
1986	50	49	+1	46	48	−2
1988	50	49	+1	49	48	+1
1990	44	49	−5	55	47	+8
1992	48	48	0	52	49	+3
1994	53	48	+5	51	51	0
1996	51	49	+2	49	52	−3
1998	54	49	+5	51	52	−1

SOURCE: Data calculated from the author's research.

African American voters. This pattern began to reverse in the 1930s as a result of the New Deal realignment. The Republicans became the party of rural and suburban areas, supported predominantly by native-born and white voters, while the Democrats became the party of metropolitan areas, drawing heavily from foreign-born and African American voters.

To illustrate the nature of these changes, I have presented profiles of Republican and Democratic counties, by decade, for gubernatorial and presidential elections, in Tables 7.5 and 7.6. The tables report the mean urban, foreign-born, and African American percentages of the vote for all counties that cast a majority of their votes for the decade for the GOP or Democratic candidates for the two offices.

Tables 7.5 and 7.6 show clearly the significant changes that resulted from the New Deal realignment. During the first three decades of the century the Republican counties were more urbanized and housed higher percentages of foreign-born and African American residents. (Data for presidential elections during the 1920s are not included, since Greene County was the only county that cast a majority of its votes for Democratic presidential candidates during that decade.) Those patterns were swiftly and permanently reversed during the 1930s. During that and subsequent decades, the more urbanized counties, the counties with higher percentages of foreign-born and African American citizens, were Democratic.

The transformation of the Democrats into the urban party was swift and stunning. Beginning during the 1930s, and extending through the 1950s, decades of voting history were cast aside. Counties that had been

Table 7.5 Mean percentages urban, foreign born, and African American for all Republican and all Democratic counties, by decade, for gubernatorial elections, 1900–1998

	Republican counties			Democratic counties		
Decade	Urban	Foreign born	African American	Urban	Foreign born	African American
1900–1908	27.8	9.9	3.0	30.3	9.0	0.6
1910–1918	34.9	12.3	2.7	33.3	7.8	0.6
1920–1928	39.7	10.7	1.5	27.2	4.7	0.6
1930–1938	36.9	6.4	1.5	55.0	11.4	2.0
1940–1948	39.5	5.3	1.4	44.0	9.5	1.7
1950–1958	37.8	4.3	1.3	54.4	6.9	3.3
1960–1968	39.3	2.8	1.4	61.7	6.4	5.1
1970–1978	33.8	1.7	0.1	54.0	3.7	0.4
1980–1988	34.8	2.0	1.7	49.6	2.2	3.3

SOURCE: Data calculated from the author's research.

Table 7.6 Mean percentages urban, foreign born, and African American for all Republican and all Democratic counties, by decade, for presidential elections, 1900–1998

	Republican counties			Democratic counties		
Decade	Urban	Foreign born	African American	Urban	Foreign born	African American
1900–1908	28.1	10.4	2.7	24.6	4.7	0.8
1910–1918	40.8	14.2	4.0	33.0	3.1	0.9
1920–1928	Only Greene County went Democratic.					
1930–1938	34.8	5.8	1.0	48.2	9.6	1.7
1940–1948	34.4	4.2	1.1	55.7	9.4	2.3
1950–1958	41.8	4.0	1.4	52.9	7.9	6.6
1960–1968	29.6	2.1	1.3	59.7	5.2	3.1
1970–1978	40.8	2.4	0.1	55.7	3.9	4.7
1980–1988	36.3	1.9	1.4	56.4	2.7	6.2
1990–1998	29.5	1.4	1.2	56.8	2.3	3.9

SOURCE: Data calculated from the author's research.

overwhelmingly Republican suddenly became solid Democratic enclaves. The most dramatic reversal occurred in Philadelphia County. During the first three decades of the century, the mean Republican share of the two-party vote for governor was 78 percent, and for president 71 percent; those figures tumbled to 42 percent and 47 percent during the 1930s. During the past seven decades, GOP candidates garnered only 41 percent of the vote in gubernatorial elections and only 37 percent of the vote in presidential elections. In fact, by the 1990s, the figures had plummeted to 31 percent in gubernatorial elections, and 20 percent in presidential elections. Similar, but less dramatic, changes took place in other urban counties, including Allegheny (Pittsburgh), Lackawanna (Scranton), and Luzerne (Wilkes-Barre).

The initial key to the Democratic success in urban areas was the New Deal economic program, which appealed to less prosperous voters, including immigrants and African Americans. In subsequent decades, especially since the 1960s, the Democrats have solidified their relationship with African American voters by becoming the party that championed civil rights. African American voters have become the most loyal voters in the Democratic coalition.

A detailed analysis of the relationship between urbanization and Republican voting, by decade, will be presented below. Because of anomalies in the data, similar analyses of ethnic and racial diversity will not be undertaken. During the first decade of the century, 16 percent of the state's population was foreign born. In only ten counties was the percentage 1 percent or less. By 2000 the percentage foreign born had declined to only 4 percent. During the last decade, the percentage foreign born was 1 percent or less in forty-two counties. The dramatic decline in the percentage of foreign-born citizens during the last half of the twentieth century makes it virtually impossible to establish a meaningful relationship between ethnicity and partisanship. Percentage foreign born would be a reasonable variable for the first half of the century, but not for the second.

The problem with race as a variable was alluded to in Chapter 1. Philadelphia County has never had less than 40 percent of the statewide African American population, and for the last fifty years the percentage has been approximately 60 percent. Philadelphia and Allegheny Counties currently contain 67 percent of the state's African American population; 77 percent of African American citizens presently reside in only six counties. Thus, race has never been a particularly good variable for distinguishing among counties in terms of partisanship.

The relationship between urbanization and Republican voting for governor and president, by decade, is displayed in Tables 7.7 and 7.8. For each decade, the counties are placed in one of four categories according to their percentage urban. Within each category, the mean percentage Republican of the two-party vote has been calculated. The figures in parentheses are the number of counties in each category.

Table 7.7 The relationship between county urbanization and Republican vote for governor, by decade, 1900–1998

	Percentage urban			
Decade	0–24%	25–49%	50–74%	75–100%
1900–1908	54.7 (32)	52.8 (21)	50.3 (11)	66.2 (3)
1910–1918	59.0 (23)	61.2 (26)	56.7 (15)	70.2 (3)
1920–1928	60.8 (20)	62.0 (26)	62.4 (18)	71.8 (3)
1930–1938	60.2 (20)	56.9 (24)	53.7 (18)	49.5 (5)
1940–1948	62.7 (20)	61.7 (24)	60.2 (19)	52.2 (4)
1950–1958	58.0 (17)	54.1 (24)	51.5 (18)	49.8 (8)
1960–1968	63.9 (20)	61.5 (21)	56.7 (17)	54.5 (9)
1970–1978	57.7 (18)	52.7 (24)	50.1 (14)	48.2 (11)
1980–1988	54.2 (25)	51.4 (16)	51.3 (18)	50.5 (8)
1990–1998	56.9 (27)	53.4 (15)	53.0 (16)	48.6 (9)

SOURCE: Data calculated from the author's research.

Table 7.8 The relationship between county urbanization and Republican vote for president, by decade, 1900–1998

	Percentage urban			
Decade	0–24%	25–49%	50–74%	75–100%
1900–1908	61.6 (32)	60.3 (21)	58.9 (11)	69.3 (3)
1910–1918	42.3 (23)	45.9 (26)	39.0 (15)	50.9 (3)
1920–1928	70.6 (20)	72.3 (26)	70.4 (18)	69.4 (3)
1930–1938	54.1 (20)	51.0 (24)	49.9 (18)	43.7 (5)
1940–1948	61.7 (20)	56.0 (24)	53.2 (19)	44.5 (4)
1950–1958	64.5 (17)	61.7 (24)	60.4 (18)	56.6 (8)
1960–1968	58.1 (20)	53.5 (21)	47.5 (17)	43.4 (9)
1970–1978	63.9 (18)	60.5 (24)	58.8 (14)	55.3 (11)
1980–1988	63.5 (25)	60.1 (16)	57.8 (18)	51.2 (8)
1990–1998	55.0 (27)	52.7 (15)	49.9 (16)	42.1 (9)

SOURCE: Data calculated from the author's research.

Through the 1920s, the GOP strength in the most urbanized counties is clear, with the pattern being most pronounced in gubernatorial elections. The only notable exception is the 1920s for presidential elections when the Republicans dominated everywhere. A dramatic drop-off takes place in the 1930s in both categories of elections. From 1930 on, the relationship between urbanization and Republican strength is striking: for both gubernatorial and presidential elections, as urbanization increases, the mean Republican share of the two-party vote steadily declines. Over the course of the last century, Pennsylvania's most urbanized counties were transformed from bastions of Republicanism into Democratic citadels.

Profiles of County Interparty Competition in Gubernatorial and Presidential Elections, 1900–1998

In this section, all sixty-seven counties will be categorized according to their level of interparty competition in both gubernatorial and presidential elections over the course of the twentieth century. This will allow a comparison of partisanship among the counties, as well as the identification of regional patterns.

Competition Index

For each election category, a Competition Index (CI) will be computed for each county. The CI is based on two percentages: (1) the mean Republican percentage of the two-party vote for all twenty-five elections (gubernatorial or presidential) during the century; (2) the percentage of all twenty-five elections in which the Republican candidate won a majority of the two-party vote. The CI is the mean of these two percentages, carried to four decimal places. Potentially, the CI can range from .0000 (absolute Democratic domination) to 1.000 (absolute Republican domination). A CI of .5000 would suggest a competitive environment. A higher score indicates that Republican candidates have won most of the elections, usually obtaining a significant share of the vote.

On the basis of the CI score, the counties were placed into one of seven categories. The categories employed are strongly Republican, moderately Republican, became more Republican, competitive, became more Democratic, moderately Democratic, and strongly Democratic. The "became more Republican" and "became more Democratic" categories require elaboration. Assigned to these categories are counties that began the century (for at least the first three decades) as strongholds for one party and subsequently became (for at least the last three decades) strongholds for the other party. Allegheny and Philadelphia Counties are classic examples of this pattern, having gone from overwhelmingly Republican to overwhelmingly Democratic.

Reflecting the different dynamics of gubernatorial and presidential elections, the cutoff points for each of the categories varies between the two types of elections. The CI scores are the least meaningful for the "became more Republican" and "became more Democratic" categories. Because counties in these categories underwent dramatic shifts in partisanship, and because the counties' attachments to their original and subsequent parties were of varying lengths, the CI scores can vary considerably. Index scores matter less than historical patterns for counties assigned to these categories.

Gubernatorial Elections

In Table 7.9, each county is placed in the appropriate competitive category based upon results in gubernatorial elections between 1902 and 1998. Listed next to each county is its CI score. A detailed summary for each county, including raw vote totals for gubernatorial and presidential elections, and the Republican share of the two-party vote for each election, can be found in the Appendix.

The data in Table 7.9 manifest clearly the extent of Republican dominance during the last century. Twenty-seven counties were classified as strongly Republican, seventeen as moderately Republican, and six as "became more Republican." Thus, fully fifty of the state's sixty-seven counties, to some degree, were controlled by the GOP. Only Greene County was classified as strongly Democratic, and only Elk and Northampton Counties were classified as moderately Democratic; an additional ten counties became more Democratic. Carbon, Columbia, Fulton, and Northumberland Counties were the only counties classified as competitive over the course of the century.

Lancaster County, with a CI score of .8150, ranked as the most Republican county during the twentieth century. The mean Republican vote was 67 percent, and the GOP carried the county in twenty-four of twenty-five gubernatorial elections. Tioga (69 percent, 23–25) and Delaware (64 percent, 24–25) Counties also had CI scores above .8000. The least Republican county was Greene County (.2865). The mean Republican percentage was 41 percent, and the Democrats carried the county in twenty-one of the twenty-five elections.

The secular realignment that began transforming Pennsylvania politics in the 1930s would not fully run its course for several decades. That becomes clear when the counties that became more Republican or more Democratic are examined. Table 7.10 lists the decade in which the change in partisanship was completed for both categories of counties. This is not necessarily the decade in which the previous minority party first obtained a majority of the vote over the course of a decade; rather, it is the decade in which the partisan transformation became permanent.

The transformations were completed as early as the 1930s, and as late as the 1970s. Four each occurred during the 1930s and 1940s, five during the

Table 7.9 Pennsylvania counties, categorized by level of competition in gubernatorial elections, 1902–1998

Strongly Republican				Strongly Democratic			
Lancaster	.8150	McKean	.7550	Greene	.2865		
Tioga	.8065	Dauphin	.7465				
Delaware	.8020	Wayne	.7405				
Lebanon	.7865	Indiana	.7400				
Chester	.7779	Blair	.7385				
Venango	.7750	Wyoming	.7360				
Huntingdon	.7750	Montgomery	.7305				
Snyder	.7775	Crawford	.7185				
Bradford	.7735	Jefferson	.7175				
Warren	.7735	Perry	.7165				
Union	.7725	Somerset	.7155				
Cameron	.7710	Potter	.6985				
Susquehanna	.7695	Franklin	.6890				
Forest	.7685						
Moderately Republican				**Moderately Democratic**			
Butler	.6660	Mercer	.6160	Elk	.4500		
Bucks	.6645	Lycoming	.6145	Northampton	.4170		
Erie	.6585	Juniata	.6140				
Bedford	.6585	Adams	.6105				
Centre	.6575	Clarion	.6050				
Sullivan	.6575	Clinton	.5835				
Cumberland	.6460	Clearfield	.5815				
Mifflin	.6260	Schuylkill	.5810				
Armstrong	.6255						
Became More Republican				**Became More Democratic**			
Pike	.6150	York	.5015	Lawrence	.5530	Philadelphia	.4735
Montour	.5510	Monroe	.4955	Luzerne	.5335	Westmoreland	.4470
Lehigh	.5180	Berks	.4345	Allegheny	.5120	Lackawanna	.4380
				Beaver	.4885	Fayette	.4125
				Cambria	.4805	Washington	.4060
Competitive							
Northumberland	.5350	Carbon	.4620				
Fulton	.5075	Columbia	.4590				

SOURCE: Data calculated from the author's research.

1950s, two during the 1960s, and one during the 1970s. Half of the counties that became more Republican did so during the 1940s, while half of the counties that became more Democratic did so during the 1950s. Philadelphia and Allegheny Counties entered the Democratic column for good during the 1950s. It is interesting to note that Fayette, Washington, and Westmoreland Counties, key components of the Pittsburgh metropolitan area, preceded Allegheny County as Democratic strongholds by two decades.

Table 7.10 Decades in which the change in partisanship became permanent for counties that became more Republican or more Democratic in gubernatorial elections, 1900–1998

Became More Republican		Became More Democratic	
County	Decade	County	Decade
Berks	1960s	Allegheny	1950s
Lehigh	1940s	Beaver	1950s
Monroe	1940s	Cambria	1950s
Montour	1940s	Fayette	1930s
Pike	1930s	Lackawanna	1940s
York	1960s	Lawrence	1970s
		Luzerne	1950s
		Philadelphia	1950s
		Washington	1930s
		Westmoreland	1930s

SOURCE: Data calculated from the author's research.

Several patterns emerge among the counties that were transformed earlier or later during the realignment period. The level of urbanization is especially crucial. The conversion to Republicanism was completed last in Berks and York Counties. Both of these counties became more urban between 1930 and 1960, and both had high percentages of independent voters in 1925, 12 percent in Berks County and 29 percent in York County. Monroe and Montour Counties became less urban during this period, and Pike County never had any urban population. These patterns support the inverse relationship described between urbanism and Republican support after 1930. In addition, Monroe and Montour Counties had low percentages of independent voters in 1925. Twenty-four percent of the registered voters in Pike County were independents in 1925, but it was also the home county of Gifford Pinchot.

Lehigh County is an anomaly. While the county became more Republican during the 1940s, it mirrors Berks and York Counties in terms of the key variables: the county became more urban between 1930 and 1960, and the percentage of independent voters in 1925 was high (10 percent). Despite Lehigh County's becoming more Republican in gubernatorial elections (and being moderately Republican in presidential elections), the Democrats have had a registration advantage there since 1960, and control of county government has been divided during the past four decades. Data from the 2000 census reveal a county with an eclectic demographic profile: income and educational levels above the state mean, but a sizable nonwhite population (13 percent) and 20 percent of the workforce employed in manufacturing jobs.

Urbanism is also central to an understanding of the timing of the movement of counties into the Democratic column. The three counties that became Democratic during the 1930s, Fayette, Washington, and Westmoreland, were all rural. Presumably, such counties could be transformed more quickly than was the case in the more urbanized counties, which were dominated by powerful Republican machines. That would have been the case particularly in Philadelphia, Allegheny, and Luzerne Counties. GOP machines, under various leaders, had controlled Philadelphia and Allegheny Counties for decades. John S. Fine became Luzerne County's GOP chairman in 1922, at the age of twenty-nine. He presided as boss for the next thirty-three years, also serving as governor from 1951 to 1954.

Luzerne, Lackawanna, Fayette, Westmoreland, Washington, Cambria, and Allegheny Counties were also leading coal-mining counties. At midcentury, Luzerne and Lackawanna Counties, along with Schuylkill County, accounted for about 84 percent of the state's anthracite coal production. More than half of the state's bituminous coal output came from Fayette, Westmoreland, and Washington Counties (Dunaway 1948, 612–20). The Democrats polled significant majorities in mining areas during the New Deal realignment.

Catholicism also seems to be related to change. With the exception of Fayette and Philadelphia Counties, all of the counties that became more Democratic in both gubernatorial and presidential elections rank among the top fifteen counties in terms of Catholic adherents. In fact, as of 2000, Cambria, Lackawanna, and Allegheny Counties rank second, third, and fourth in rates of adherence per 1000 population. None of the counties that became more Republican in either gubernatorial or presidential elections rank among the top fifteen counties in that category.

The county classifications are displayed in Figure 7.1. With the exception of Erie County, the entire northern tier of counties was strongly Republican. This was also true of numerous counties in the central part of the state, as well as the counties that comprise the Philadelphia suburban area. The moderately Republican counties generally cluster in the central part of the state. The counties that became more Republican are found in the eastern part of the state; four of the counties (Berks, Lehigh, Monroe, and Pike) are found in a band along the eastern border, bisected by Carbon and Northampton Counties.

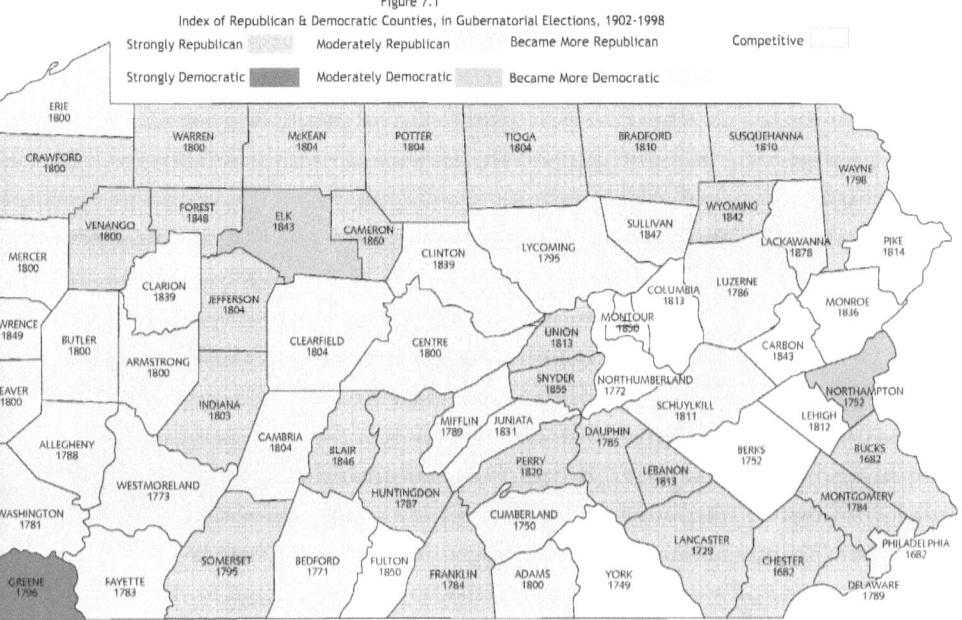

Figure 7.1
Index of Republican & Democratic Counties, in Gubernatorial Elections, 1902-1998

The southwestern corner of the state was clearly a Democratic stronghold during the twentieth century. The only strongly Democratic county, Greene County, is found there. Greene County is surrounded by seven of the ten counties that became more Democratic. The remaining three counties in that category are Philadelphia County, located in the other corner of the state, and Lackawanna and Luzerne Counties, located in the northeastern part of the state. Three of the four competitive counties (Northumberland, Carbon, and Columbia) are located in the east-central part of the state. The fourth, Fulton County, is found in the south-central part of the state.

Presidential Elections

The county classifications and CI scores for presidential elections from 1900 to 1996 are listed in Table 7.11. The format is the same as that used for gubernatorial elections.

The Republican dominance was even more pronounced in presidential elections. More than half of the state's counties, thirty-five, were categorized as strongly Republican. When the moderately Republican (eleven) and "became more Republican" counties (six) are added, a remarkable

Table 7.11 Pennsylvania counties, categorized by level of competition in presidential elections, 1900–1996

Strongly Republican				Strongly Democratic	
Snyder	.8320	Venango	.7560	Greene	.2350
Union	.8225	Blair	.7545		
Lancaster	.8205	Delaware	.7505		
Tioga	.8155	Butler	.7500		
Wayne	.8110	Perry	.7495		
Cameron	.7995	Dauphin	.7465		
Bradford	.7915	Franklin	.7400		
Huntingdon	.7860	Forest	.7320		
Potter	.7855	Warren	.7315		
Lebanon	.7855	Crawford	.7295		
McKean	.7800	Montgomery	.7235		
Wyoming	.7790	Indiana	.7200		
Chester	.7785	Mifflin	.7100		
Susquehanna	.7735	Lycoming	.7085		
Somerset	.7670	Cumberland	.6950		
Jefferson	.7660	Bucks	.6865		
Bedford	.7600	Sullivan	.6810		
		Centre	.6785		

Moderately Republican				Moderately Democratic	
Juniata	.6620	Montour	.6070	Northampton	.4400
Clarion	.6560	Schuylkill	.6060		
Northumberland	.6480	Clearfield	.6050		
Adams	.6400	Mercer	.5860		
Armstrong	.6175	Clinton	.5850		
		Lehigh	.5820		

Became More Republican				Became More Democratic			
Pike	.6265	Monroe	.5280	Lawrence	.5705	Philadelphia	.4155
Fulton	.5870	Berks	.5270	Allegheny	.4300	Lackawanna	.4130
York	.5665	Columbia	.4680	Beaver	.4235	Westmoreland	.3975
				Cambria	.4155	Washington	.3900
						Fayette	.3510

Competitive			
Carbon	.5715	Elk	.5145
Erie	.5445	Luzerne	.5110

SOURCE: Data calculated from the author's research.

fifty-two counties were found on the GOP side of the ledger for the century. Only Greene County was categorized as strongly Democratic, and only Northampton County was classified as moderately Democratic; an additional nine counties became more Democratic. The only competitive counties in presidential elections were Carbon, Elk, Erie, and Luzerne Counties.

Over the course of the twentieth century, Snyder County, with a CI score of .8320, ranked as the most Republican county. The GOP candidates received an average of 70 percent of the vote, and won the county in twenty-four of the twenty-five elections. Also with CI scores above .8000 were Union (69 percent, 24–25), Lancaster (68 percent, 24–25), Tioga (71 percent, 23–25), and Wayne (66 percent, 24–25) Counties. As was the case with gubernatorial elections, Greene County was the least Republican county. The mean Republican percentage was 39 percent, and the Democrats won the county in twenty-three of the twenty-five elections.

Table 7.12 presents the information on counties that changed partisanship. Once again, the decade listed is the decade in which the change in partisanship became permanent.

Half of the counties that became more Republican completed the transformation during the 1940s, and half did so during the 1950s. Eight of the nine counties that became more Democratic were transformed during the 1930s. For gubernatorial elections, the switch to Democratic control was more likely to occur during the 1950s. The inauguration of

Table 7.12 Decades in which the change in partisanship became permanent for counties that became more Republican or more Democratic in presidential elections, 1900–1998

County	Decade
Became More Republican	
Berks	1950s
Columbia	1950s
Fulton	1940s
Monroe	1940s
Pike	1940s
York	1950s
Became More Democratic	
Allegheny	1930s
Beaver	1930s
Cambria	1930s
Fayette	1930s
Lackawanna	1930s
Lawrence	1960s
Philadelphia	1930s
Washington	1930s
Westmoreland	1930s

SOURCE: Data calculated from the author's research.

the New Deal during the 1930s had its most substantial impact among the counties in this classification.

The only counties changing partisanship in presidential elections that did not appear on the gubernatorial listings are Columbia and Fulton Counties, which became more Republican. Fulton County has no urban places. This further supports the tendency of rural areas to become more Republican after the 1930s. The situation in rural Columbia County is more complicated.

Since 1948, Columbia County has gone Republican in ten of thirteen presidential elections. However, the Democrats enjoyed a registration advantage during the entire twentieth century. The county was also classified as competitive in gubernatorial elections. The 2000 census data do not offer a profile of a county where Republicans would find success. The population is 98 percent white and older and less educated than the state average. The median family and per capita incomes are significantly below the state figures, and the percentage of persons living below the poverty line exceeds the state mean. Finally, one-quarter of the workforce is employed in manufacturing. The conservative message espoused by GOP presidential candidates apparently resonates with these voters in a way that cannot be matched by its gubernatorial candidates.

A map of the county classifications appears in Figure 7.2. As was the case with the gubernatorial elections, the northern tier of counties, with the exception of Erie County, was strongly Republican, as were most of the counties in the central part of the state, and those surrounding Philadelphia. The moderately Republican counties still cluster predominantly in the center of the state, but they are more dispersed than was the case with the gubernatorial elections. The counties that became more Republican are again found in the eastern half of the state.

Greene County and seven neighboring counties again comprise the core of Democratic strength in the state. Philadelphia County is the lone pocket of Democratic strength in the southeastern corner of the state. Lackawanna and Northampton Counties are the only other Democratic bastions in the eastern half of Pennsylvania. The initial Democratic strength in Lackawanna County came from the mining areas. In more recent decades, the political organization established by former governor Robert P. Casey and his sons has been crucial. For most of the twentieth century, more than half of the workforce in Northampton County was employed in manufacturing. Thus, there has been a solid base of support for the Democratic Party. However, the county has gone Republican in four of

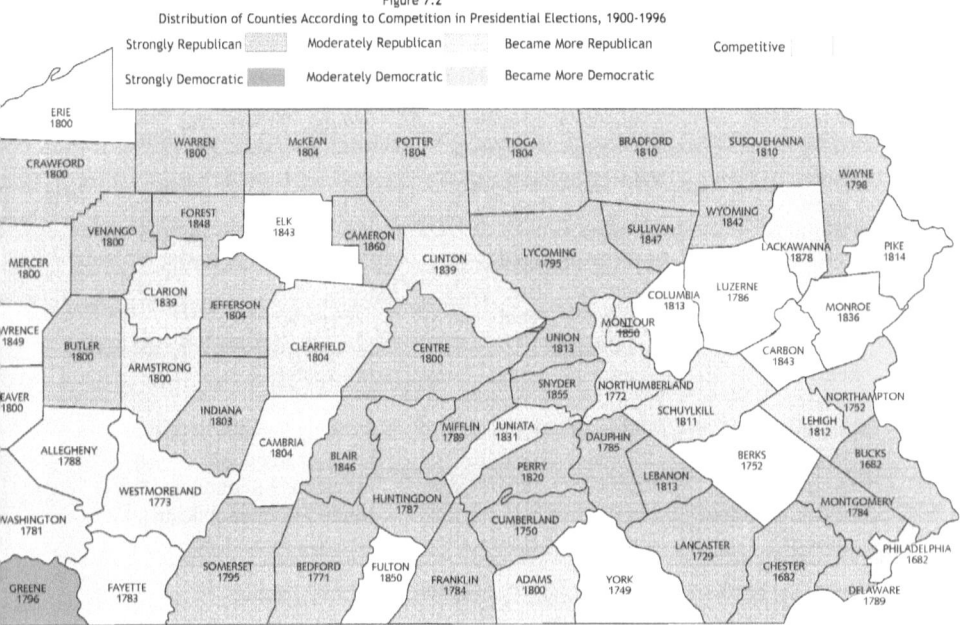

Figure 7.2
Distribution of Counties According to Competition in Presidential Elections, 1900-1996

the last six gubernatorial elections, and in four of the last seven presidential contests. Also, both Lackawanna (50 percent) and Northampton (36 percent) Counties have high percentages of Catholic identifiers. Two of the competitive counties (Luzerne and Carbon) are located in the eastern part of the state, while the other two (Elk and Erie) are located in the western part of the state.

A Comparison of County Classifications in Gubernatorial and Presidential Elections

Even a cursory examination of the two maps suggests a strong relationship between the county voting patterns in gubernatorial and presidential elections. That is indeed the case. The correlation between county rankings on the two Competition Indexes is an extraordinary .92. Not much deviation exists in voting patterns among the counties in the two categories of elections. In fact, only sixteen counties were classified differently in gubernatorial and presidential elections. Those counties, and their respective classifications, are presented in Table 7.13.

With the exception of Erie County, all of the counties with different classifications were more Republican in presidential elections. Eight of

Table 7.13 Counties with different classifications in gubernatorial and presidential elections, 1900–1998

County	Gubernatorial classification	Presidential classification
Bedford	Moderately Republican	Strongly Republican
Bucks	Moderately Republican	Strongly Republican
Butler	Moderately Republican	Strongly Republican
Centre	Moderately Republican	Strongly Republican
Columbia	Competitive	Became more Republican
Cumberland	Moderately Republican	Strongly Republican
Elk	Moderately Democratic	Competitive
Erie	Moderately Republican	Competitive
Fulton	Competitive	Became moderately Republican
Lehigh	Became more Republican	Moderately Republican
Luzerne	Became more Republican	Competitive
Lycoming	Moderately Republican	Strongly Republican
Mifflin	Moderately Republican	Strongly Republican
Montour	Became more Republican	Moderately Republican
Northumberland	Competitive	Moderately Republican
Sullivan	Moderately Republican	Strongly Republican

SOURCE: Data calculated from the author's research.

the counties were moderately Republican in gubernatorial elections and strongly Republican in presidential elections. This fits the general pattern among all counties. Forty-three counties had higher CI scores for presidential elections. The mean CI score was also higher for presidential elections: .6447, compared with .6157 for gubernatorial elections. The mean scores fall in the moderately Republican classification for both categories of elections.

One definite geographic pattern emerges among the sixteen counties. Seven (Northumberland, Montour, Columbia, Luzerne, Bucks, Sullivan, and Lycoming) of them are contiguous counties in the east central part of the state. However, five different patterns of classification differences exist among the counties.

A Profile of Republican and Democratic General Assembly Districts

Nationally, since the New Deal realignment, the two parties have tended to represent distinct demographic groups. A couple of broad distinctions can be drawn. Generally, the Republicans have done better among higher-status groups, while the Democrats have done better among lower-status groups. The Democrats have received high levels of support from minorities, especially African Americans, while the GOP has not received much support from such groups. In this section, general profiles of each party's legislative districts will be presented. House and Senate districts will be discussed separately. The profiles represent the images of the parties just prior to the 1996 elections. At that time, the Republicans held a 29–21 advantage in the Senate, and a 102–101 edge in the House.

House Districts

The profiles of House districts are detailed in Table 7.14. The districts represented by each party are divided into four categories, based on party registration: greater than 60 percent, 55.0–59.9 percent, 50.0–54.9 percent, and less than 50 percent. For each category, means were calculated for each of the variables. Number refers to the number of districts in each category. Thus, Democrats represented sixty-seven House districts where the Democratic share of registered voters was greater than 60 percent, and fifteen districts where the Democratic share of registered voters was less than 50 percent. Income is the mean household income. College is

Table 7.14 A profile of Republican and Democratic House districts, with selected variables, 1996

Registration	Number	Annual income	College-educated (%)	African American (%)	Hispanic (%)
		Democrats			
>60%	67	$32,517	19.7	21.3	2.7
55.0–59.9%	11	33,425	21.5	7.3	3.3
50.0–54.9	8	30,171	17.3	2.6	1.0
<50%	15	36,040	24.1	6.0	1.9
Total	101	32,953	20.4	16.0	2.5
PA	203	36,662	23.0	9.0	1.0
		Republicans			
>60%	42	$45,726	28.5	1.2	1.2
55.0–59.9%	18	39,218	22.9	2.1	1.0
50.0–54.9%	24	41,627	23.0	2.3	1.0
<50.0%	18	38,964	23.8	1.4	2.1
Total	102	42,420	254	1.6	1.3
PA	203	36,662	23.0	9.0	1.0

SOURCE: Figures calculated by the author from data in William Lilley III, Laurence J. De Franco, and William M. Diefenderfer III, *The Almanac of American State Legislatures* (Washington, D.C.: Congressional Quarterly Press, 1994).

the percentage of the population twenty-five and older with at least an associates degree.

Total is the mean percentage for all House and Senate districts for each party, and "PA" is the state mean for each of the variables. Data for all of the variables were obtained from Lilley, DeFranco, and Diefenderfer 1994.

Republican and Democratic legislators do indeed represent different constituencies. The profiles conform to the accepted stereotypes. The typical GOP district is characterized by wealthier and better-educated constituents, and fewer African American and Hispanic residents. Democratic districts, on the other hand, typically have less prosperous constituents, with lower levels of education, and higher percentages of African American and Hispanic citizens.

The most dramatic differences exist between the two most partisan categories. The average household income in the districts with greater than 60 percent Republican registration is more than $13,000 greater than the figure for districts with greater than 60 percent Democratic registration. Similarly, the mean percentage of residents with college degrees is 5 percentage points higher. Conversely, Democratic districts have dramatically greater racial diversity: 21 percent of the residents in Democratic districts are African American, compared with only 1 percent in Republican districts. The Hispanic percentage is also twice as high in the Democratic districts, although neither figure is that large.

With the exception of the percentage of the population who are African American, the partisan differences among the districts with less than 50 percent Republican or Democratic registration are slight. It appears to be useful to distinguish among the districts according to partisan registration. While the basic distinctions between the parties persist, they clearly intensify with increasing partisanship in the districts.

Senate Districts

The corresponding data for Senate districts are reported in Table 7.15. The format is identical to Table 7.14.

As was the case with House districts, the typical party districts are distinctive and in line with expectations. Once again, the most notable differences exist among the districts with greater than 60 percent Republican or Democratic registration. The average household income is almost $19,000 higher in Republican districts, and the percentage of residents with a college degree is 12 percentage points higher. These differences are

Table 7.15 A profile of Republican and Democratic Senate districts, with selected variables, 1996

Registration	Number	Annual income	College-educated (%)	African American (%)	Hispanic (%)
		Democrats			
>60%	17	$30,733	20.2%	20.2%	2.6
55.0–59.9%	2	30,910	19.0	3.5	0.5
50.0–54.9	2	35,673	20.5	3.5	6.5
<50%	0	NA	NA	NA	NA
Total	21	31,220	20.1	17.0	2.7
PA	50	36,662	23.0	9.0	1.0
		Republicans			
>60%	8	49,051	32.3	5.9	1.4
55.0–59.9%	8	37,527	18.9	3.4	1.8
50.0–54.9%	5	35,662	22.0	1.0	1.0
<50.0%	8	38,624	23.8	2.6	1.5
Total	29	40,687	24.5	3.4	1.4
PA	50	36,662	23.0	9.0	1.0

SOURCE: Figures calculated by the author from data in William Lilley III, Laurence J. De Franco, and William M. Diefenderfer III, *The Almanac of American State Legislatures* (Washington, D.C.: Congressional Quarterly Press, 1994).

more significant than was the case with House districts. Racial and ethnic diversity is greater in the Democratic districts, although the differences are not as great as was seen among the House districts.

Home Counties of Officeholders

The dominant role played by Philadelphia (Philadelphia) and Allegheny (Pittsburgh) Counties in Pennsylvania politics during the twentieth century has been made clear. Whether bastions of Republicanism or Democracy, the state's two largest counties regularly have determined the outcomes of statewide elections. Given the political influence exerted by these two counties and their major cities, it could reasonably be assumed that they would also produce a significant proportion of the successful candidates in statewide elections. As will be shown below, that is indeed the case.

In this section, we will examine the home counties of all governors, U.S. senators, and statewide officeholders during the twentieth century. The home county of a particular officeholder will only be counted once for each office, regardless of how many terms the individual served in that office. However, when an individual held more than one office, his or her home county will be counted once for each different office. Also, for each of the three categories of offices examined, the number of officeholders from the Philadelphia and Pittsburgh metropolitan areas will be presented. While the dominance of Philadelphia and Allegheny Counties in statewide politics is unquestioned, the significance of the larger metropolitan areas of which they are a part cannot be gainsaid.

Governor

Twenty men served as the state's chief executive during the twentieth century. The home counties (and the number of individuals from each county) are listed in Table 7.16. Three each came from Philadelphia and Allegheny Counties, and eleven came from the Philadelphia or Pittsburgh metropolitan areas.

U.S. Senator

Nowhere is the significance of the two major cities and their respective metropolitan areas more graphically displayed than in the elections for this office (see Table 7.17). Philadelphia and Allegheny Counties were each the home county for seven senators, and all seventeen called either

Table 7.16 Home counties or areas of Pennsylvania governors, 1900–1998

Home	Number of individuals
Philadelphia County	3
Allegheny County	3
Washington County	2
Montgomery County	2
Luzerne County	2
Lackawanna County	2
Delaware County	1
Pike County	1
Indiana County	1
York County	1
Crawford County	1
Erie County	1
Philadelphia Metropolitan Area	6
Pittsburgh Metropolitan Area	5

SOURCE: *The Pennsylvania Manual*, selected volumes.

Table 7.17 Home counties or areas of
U.S. senators from Pennsylvania, 1914–1998

Home	Number of individuals
Philadelphia County	7
Allegheny County	7
Montgomery County	2
Washington County	1
Philadelphia Metropolitan Area	9
Pittsburgh Metropolitan Area	8

SOURCE: *The Pennsylvania Manual*, selected volumes.

the Philadelphia or Pittsburgh metropolitan areas home. This is quite a testament to the electoral dominance of the state's two major cities and their surrounding suburbs.

Statewide Office

Once again, the two major counties led the way (see Table 7.18). Eleven of the statewide officials were from Philadelphia or Allegheny Counties, and almost half came from the Philadelphia or Pittsburgh metropolitan areas.

Composite

Table 7.19 summarizes the home counties of all individuals who have served as governor, U.S. senator, or a statewide official during the twentieth century. The preeminence of Philadelphia and Allegheny Counties is reinforced by these data. Thirty-one of the eighty-six individuals who held these positions came from the two counties. Moreover, fifty of the 86 came from the Philadelphia or Pittsburgh metropolitan areas.

The relative fortunes of Philadelphia and Allegheny County candidates diverged significantly during the second half of the twentieth century. Eleven Philadelphia County candidates were elected between 1900 and 1950, but only four between 1952 and 1998. The rates of success for Allegheny County candidates actually increased slightly during the last five decades of the century: seven were elected between 1900 and 1950, and nine between 1952 and 1998. The anti-Philadelphia bias, present for most of the state's history, intensified during the course of the twentieth century and certainly affected the fortunes of at least some Philadelphia County candidates.

What also is quite evident is how few counties are on the list. Only twenty-nine of the state's sixty-seven counties were home to one of these

Table 7.18 Home counties or areas of Pennsylvania statewide officials, 1900–1998

Home	Number of individuals
Allegheny County	6
Philadelphia County	5
Delaware County	4
Erie County	4
Lackawanna County	3
Tioga County	2
Washington County	2
Dauphin County	2
Crawford County	2
Clarion County	2
Somerset County	1
Lebanon County	1
Carbon County	1
Clearfield County	1
Lancaster County	1
Fayette County	1
Schuylkill County	1
York County	1
Butler County	1
Luzerne County	1
Montgomery County	1
Cambria County	1
Wayne County	1
Chester County	1
Potter County	1
Northampton County	1
Westmoreland County	1
Philadelphia Metropolitan Area	11
Pittsburgh Metropolitan Area	11

SOURCE: *The Pennsylvania Manual,* selected volumes.

officials. Moreover, only thirteen had more than one of their residents elected to one of the positions. The reality is that candidates from most Pennsylvania counties have no chance of winning a statewide contest.

Summary

This chapter examined a number of partisan patterns that occurred during the twentieth century. Topics included were the timing of the New Deal realignment in Pennsylvania, profiles of typical Republican and

Table 7.19 Home counties or areas of Pennsylvania governors, U.S. senators from Pennsylvania, and Pennsylvania statewide officials, 1900–1998

Home	Number of individuals
Allegheny County	16
Philadelphia County	15
Lackawanna County	5
Delaware County	5
Montgomery County	5
Erie County	5
Washington County	5
Tioga County	2
Luzerne County	5
Crawford County	3
Dauphin County	2
Clarion County	2
Tioga County	2
York County	2
Pike County	1
Somerset County	1
Lebanon County	1
Carbon County	1
Clearfield County	1
Lancaster County	1
Fayette County	1
Schuylkill County	1
Butler County	1
Cambria County	1
Wayne County	1
Chester County	1
Potter County	1
Northampton County	1
Westmoreland County	1
Philadelphia Metropolitan Area	26
Pittsburgh Metropolitan Area	24

SOURCE: *The Pennsylvania Manual*, selected volumes.

Democratic counties before and after the New Deal realignment, categorizations of counties in terms of their competitiveness in gubernatorial and presidential elections, profiles of typical Republican and Democratic General Assembly districts, and a summary of the home counties of twentieth-century governors, U.S. senators, and statewide officeholders.

After the 1890s partisan realignment, Pennsylvania was a one-party state, dominated by the Republicans. The GOP strength was concentrated in urban areas and among immigrants and African American voters. The Democratic strength was found in rural areas. Of concern was when the New Deal realignment transformed Pennsylvania politics.

The key gubernatorial election was 1934. The Republican share of the vote declined by 10 percentage points or more in forty-five counties, and by 20 points or more in sixteen counties. The 1932 election was the key presidential election. The GOP share of the vote declined by 10 or more percentage points in fifty-nine counties. The 1934, 1938, and 1942 gubernatorial elections were highly correlated. The 1932 presidential election, as suggested by Burnham, was a "bridge election," significantly correlated with all other elections between 1920 and 1940. The 1932, 1936, and 1940 presidential elections were highly correlated.

The New Deal realignment was evident in the 1932, 1934, and 1936 elections for the General Assembly and the U.S. House of Representatives. In each case, the Republican share of the vote was significantly lower than was the case in the previous four elections.

The data suggest that a realignment took place in the state during the 1930s and early 1940s. The impact of the realignment was felt at comparable times in all of the elections studied. Real competition, however, did not exist in Pennsylvania until the late 1950s.

The bases of party support were dramatically transformed during the New Deal realignment. The Democrats became the urban party and the party favored by African Americans and foreign-born citizens. The GOP became a rural party. The changes were especially dramatic in the most urbanized counties, particularly Philadelphia County.

In an attempt to classify the sixty-seven counties in terms of their level of competition in gubernatorial and presidential elections over the century, I developed a Competition Index (CI). This was simply the mean of the Republican percentage of the two-party vote in the twenty-five elections held during the century and the percentage of the twenty-five elections won by the Republican candidate, carried to four decimal places. On the basis of the CI score, each county was put in one of seven categories for both gubernatorial and presidential elections.

For gubernatorial elections, twenty-seven counties were classified as strongly Republican, seventeen as moderately Republican, and six as "became more Republican." This meant that fifty of the counties were on the GOP side of the ledger. Lancaster County was the most Republican county, and Greene County was the least Republican county. Those counties that changed partisanship did so from the 1930s through the 1970s:

half of those that became more Republican were transformed during the 1940s; half of those that became more Democratic changed during the 1950s. The most Republican counties were in the northern and central parts of the state, while the most Democratic counties were in the southwestern corner of the state.

In presidential elections, thirty-five counties were classified as strongly Republican, eleven as moderately Republican, and six as "became more Republican." Thus, fifty-two of the sixty-seven counties were in the GOP column. Snyder County was the most Republican county, and Greene County again was the least Republican county. Counties that became more Republican were equally divided between the 1940s and 1950s; eight of the nine counties that became more Democratic were transformed during the 1930s. The geographical distribution of the Republican and Democratic counties was essentially similar to the pattern for gubernatorial counties. The correlation between county CI scores for the two categories of elections was a very strong .92. Forty-three counties had higher CI scores in presidential elections.

In an attempt to develop partisan profiles of contemporary General Assembly districts, all House and Senate districts were placed in one of four categories based on party registration in the district. The profiles were based on data regarding income, education, percentage African American, and percentage Hispanic. As expected, for both houses, Republican districts scored higher on the income and education variables, and Democratic districts scored higher on the measures of racial and ethnic diversity. The differences were most pronounced in the most partisan districts.

The political importance of Philadelphia and Allegheny Counties is graphically demonstrated by an examination of the home counties of the individuals who served as governors, U.S. senators, and statewide office-holders during the twentieth century. Overall, thirty-one of the eighty-six individuals were from the two counties, and fifty of the eighty-six were from the Philadelphia or Pittsburgh metropolitan areas. However, candidates from Philadelphia County were decidedly less successful during the last half of the twentieth century. Only twenty-nine of the state's sixty-seven counties were represented on the list of home counties, and only thirteen were the home of more than one individual. Quite clearly, residents of most Pennsylvania counties have no chance of being elected in a statewide contest.

IN PERSPECTIVE

The purpose of this book was to place contemporary Pennsylvania politics in historical perspective by examining twentieth-century elections in Pennsylvania. Previous researchers have identified a number of post-1960 electoral patterns which they believe constitute marked departures from the past. A particular concern of this study was to attempt to determine which of those patterns represent real breaks with the past, and which are actually continuations of longer-term trends, or a return to conditions previously extant. It was discovered that contemporary politics in the Keystone State is a mixture of century-long trends, recent returns to previous patterns, and recent departures from previous patterns.

The purpose of this chapter is to summarize the major findings reported in the previous chapters. In keeping with the primary objective of developing a historical perspective, each of the major findings will be categorized as representing a link with the past, or as representing a break from the past.

The Past Continued, or the Past Revisited

1. The significant incidence of independence among registered voters during the 1990s is merely a return to a condition that existed during the 1920s.

While almost 10 percent of registered voters were independents in 1998, a similar situation existed during the 1920s. It could be argued, in fact, that the magnitude was greater during the 1920s. At least 10 percent of the registered voters in 1998 were independents in sixteen counties, while that was the case in thirty counties in 1925. In fact, the 1925 proportion of independents was greater than 30 percent in four counties (Bucks, Franklin, Lebanon, and Warren). The highest incidence of independence in 1998 was 16 percent; seventeen counties exceeded that percentage in 1925. In 1930, there still were sixteen counties where at least 10 percent of the voters were independents.

According to Kristi Andersen (1979), the high incidence of independents during the 1920s was due to young voters and new voters. She argues that these voters were instrumental in forging the New Deal realignment. During the contemporary era, the increase in independence since the 1960s has been attributed to increasing independence among young voters (Miller and Shanks 1996). However, an examination of the present data found that only two (Cumberland and Dauphin) of the fifteen counties that had more than 10 percent independent voters in both 1926 and 1998 had percentages of voters between the ages of twenty and thirty-four that were above the state mean.

Voter turnout in these fifteen counties was also examined to see if it was less than the state mean, as might be expected. However, in 1998, only nine of the fifteen counties had rates of turnout below the state mean, while in 1926 that was the case in only two of the counties. It was suggested that perhaps the independents in these counties are "leaners" rather than pure independents. Such individuals profess to be independents but act more like weak partisans.

2. Both parties' mean share of the vote was less than their mean share of registered voters when they were the majority party, and more than their mean share of registered voters when they were the minority party.

Much has been made recently about the Democrats' inability to dominate statewide elections despite having a 400,000 advantage among registered voters. In reality, the Democrats are just as successful in mobilizing their electoral base as the Republicans were when they were the majority party. The crucial factor is the size of the electoral base. Mobilization was measured with the Turnout-Loyalty Index (TLI). This index is the total number of votes cast for a given candidate in a specific election divided by the number of voters registered with that party. A mean TLI score was calculated for each decade for gubernatorial and presidential elections.

The Republican and Democratic TLI scores were strikingly similar when they were the majority and minority party; in fact, the gubernatorial scores were almost identical. The parties were equally successful at mobilizing their identifiers during the twentieth century. However, the Republicans were much more successful as the majority party than the Democrats were. The crucial factor was the larger registration advantage enjoyed by the GOP. Until 1930, almost 80 percent of Pennsylvania voters were registered as Republicans; rarely did that percentage dip below 59 percent. Conversely, since they became the majority party in 1960, rarely has the Democratic figure exceeded 54 percent.

The overriding importance of the size of the electoral base is displayed graphically by data from gubernatorial elections. Prior to 1960, the Republicans were mobilizing 60 percent of an electorate that was between 59 and 80 percent Republican; the Democrats were mobilizing 75 percent of a hopeless minority. Since 1960, the Democrats have been mobilizing 60 percent of an electorate that is just barely a Democratic majority, while the GOP has been mobilizing 75 percent of an almost equal number of voters.

Berwood Yost (2003) has presented data arguing that approximately one of five Pennsylvania voters is misaligned—party registration does not match voting behavior. While comparable data are not available for previous eras, there is no reason to believe that similar phenomena have not occurred during the course of the twentieth century.

It seems reasonable to assume that such misalignment would increase the longer a party has been the majority party. For a variety of reasons, groups begin to desert the majority party. The change in partisan loyalty would normally be reflected in voting patterns before it is reflected in registration patterns. If such misalignment exists, the result would be that the majority party would receive a share of the vote that was less than its proportion of registered voters, while the minority party would receive a share of the vote that was greater than its proportion of registered voters.

3. While General Assembly and congressional incumbents are safer now than they were prior to 1960, they have always been safe.

Members of the General Assembly have always enjoyed high rates of reelection success. During the first decade of the century, 84 percent of House incumbents and 92 percent of Senate incumbents running were reelected. Rarely has the rate of success dipped below 80 percent in either house. The rates for senators fluctuated wildly from 1900 until the end of the 1940s; since that time, they have been relatively stable. The reelection rates enjoyed by Senate incumbents since 1980 only matches the figure for the 1920s. The patterns among House incumbents have been much more moderate. Since 1900, 88 percent of incumbents in both houses have been reelected.

The data for congressional incumbents reveal a similar pattern. During the first three decades of the century, between 80 and 90 percent of congressional incumbents running won another term. The decade-by-decade success rates for congressional incumbents mirror those for state senators. Since 1900, 87 percent of congressional incumbents have been reelected.

The rate of reelection success for incumbents has increased as the advantages accruing from incumbency have increased. Two advantages have become especially important: partisan gerrymandering and legislative party money. Partisan gerrymandering has reduced the number of districts where challengers have a realistic opportunity to win. This means that incumbents tend to run in districts where their party has a decided registration advantage against weak, underfunded opponents. Legislative party leaders also control a significant amount of money that they can channel to incumbents. Some of the money is given in the form of direct contributions. Other money takes the form of WAMs, or walking around money. WAMs are used to fund pork barrel projects in the districts of legislators.

Congressional incumbents also benefit from partisan redistricting and legislative party money.

4. While the incidence of marginal General Assembly and congressional districts has declined significantly since the 1960s, the current pattern does not differ dramatically from the pattern during the first three decades of the century.

For members of both houses of the General Assembly, the high percentage of seats won by safe margins during the 1980s and 1990s are only slightly higher than the comparable figures for the 1920s. In fact, nonincumbent winners in both houses enjoyed their largest margins of victory during the 1920s. The contemporary pattern can be put into historical perspective by comparing the percentages of safe House and Senate seats between 1960 and 1998 with the percentages from the 1900–1920 era. The percentages are similar, especially for representatives. For both houses, the percentages of all candidates and incumbents garnering at least 60 percent of the vote is slightly higher in the contemporary period; however, the percentage of nonincumbents winning with at least 60 percent of the vote in both houses was higher during the earlier period.

In terms of district marginality, the twentieth century can be divided into three phases: 1900–1928, 1930–58, and 1960–98. As described, the current dearth of marginal districts is basically a return to conditions that existed during the first three decades of the century. The 1930–58 phase was characterized by a dramatic increase in the number of marginal districts. It is this three-decade trend that makes the post-1960 decline in marginality appear so dramatic.

The pattern is similar, but not quite as dramatic, for congressional districts. The 1920s again stand out among the earlier decades. The percentages for the 1920s are similar to the current percentages, but the differences are greater than was the case with the General Assembly. One important difference is that fewer safe districts were won by congressional nonincumbent candidates in the last decade of the century than in the first decade.

Once again, the century can be divided into three phases. As was the case with the state House and Senate, although the relationships are not as dramatic, the percentages are most similar during the first and third phases. It is the second phase that stands out because of the high incidence of marginal seats. Mirroring the pattern for the General Assembly, this is what makes the post-1960 decline in marginality seem so significant.

The high incidence of marginal General Assembly and congressional seats during the second phase supports Burnham's (1970) argument that competition increases during periods of realignment. The Democrats became more competitive in Pennsylvania as a result of the New Deal realignment that began in the 1930s. The state finally became competitive by the end of the 1950s—exactly the decades covered by the second phase. During the first phase, the GOP was so dominant that Democratic candidates were rarely competitive. The third phase encompasses the years during which incumbency advantages increased significantly, including incumbent gerrymandering. Today, there simply are few competitive state legislative or congressional districts.

5. While the meaning of marginality has changed over the course of the century, marginal General Assembly and congressional incumbents have always been more likely to lose than safe incumbents have been.

State legislative and congressional incumbents who won the previous election with less than 60 percent of the vote have always been more vulnerable than those who won by a safe margin. During the twentieth century, the mean rate of defeat for marginal state House incumbents was 21 percent, compared with 5 percent for safe incumbents; among state senators, the rates were 20 percent for marginal incumbents and 5 percent for safe incumbents. The rates of defeat for congressional incumbents were almost identical: 19 percent for marginal incumbents, and 6 percent for safe incumbents.

Incumbents who won by smaller margins in their previous elections are more likely to be opposed by strong, well-funded opponents when they run for reelection. State and legislative party organizations allocate their resources to the limited number of "opportunity" races that exist each election. Incumbents who appear vulnerable are likely to be targeted by the opposition party. A marginal incumbent running against a strong challenger with enough money to mount an effective campaign faces a greater chance of being defeated.

6. During the twentieth century, a disproportionate share of individuals who served as governors, U.S. senators, or statewide officials were from Philadelphia or Allegheny Counties, or the Philadelphia or Pittsburgh metropolitan areas.

Located in the opposite corners of the state and housing the state's two major cities, Philadelphia and Allegheny Counties have long been crucial battlegrounds in Pennsylvania politics. They have also been the home county for a significant percentage of successful candidates in statewide elections. But a similar level of influence also attaches to the metropolitan areas of which they are the center.

Of the twenty men who served as governor, three each had Philadelphia or Allegheny Counties as their home, and eleven came from the Philadelphia or Pittsburgh metropolitan areas. The dominance of the two major cities and their respective metropolitan areas is manifested most clearly in U.S. Senate elections. Seven senators each came from Philadelphia and Allegheny Counties, and all seventeen individuals elected during the century resided in the Philadelphia or Pittsburgh metropolitan areas.

Candidates from Philadelphia and Pittsburgh enjoy a decided advantage in statewide elections because of the disproportionate influence exerted by voters in the state's two major cities. In order to prevail, candidates who do not call either of those cities home need some other political attributes to achieve the name recognition required to attract large blocks of voters. As described above, only half as many governors as senators came from Philadelphia or Pittsburgh. Most of the governors who did not reside in Philadelphia or Pittsburgh, however, possessed such attributes.

Arthur H. James and Raymond P. Shafer both previously served as lieutenant governor. Robert P. Casey and Edward Martin both previously held the post of auditor general; moreover, Martin probably was elected to more political offices than any other Pennsylvanian. John K. Tener and William C. Sproul were both candidates put forth by Boise Penrose. John S. Fisher was a state senator who was a disciple of both Penrose and Matthew Quay; in addition, Fisher chaired the committee investigating the capitol graft scandal in 1907. Gifford Pinchot had previously been the state's Forestry Commissioner and had a national reputation as a forester. While the governorship was the only office he ever held, George H. Earle was, by his own admission, swept into office in 1934 as part of the New Deal tidal wave. John S. Fine was the GOP boss in Luzerne County, and Tom Ridge had served as congressman for a decade and had established a solid reputation. Milton J. Shapp and George M. Leader were really the only two virtual unknowns who captured the statehouse.

Eleven of the forty-nine individuals who were elected to a statewide office during the twentieth century were from Philadelphia or Allegheny Counties, and twenty-two came from the Philadelphia or Pittsburgh metropolitan areas. Overall, eighty-six individuals were elected to the governorship, the U.S. Senate, or a statewide office during the twentieth century. Thirty-one of the eighty-six came from Philadelphia or Allegheny Counties, and fifty of the eighty-six came from the Philadelphia or Pittsburgh metropolitan areas.

The relative fortunes of candidates from Philadelphia and Allegheny Counties diverged significantly during the second half of the twentieth century. Eleven Philadelphia County candidates were elected between 1900 and 1950, but only four were victorious between 1952 and 1998. Candidates from Allegheny County were actually slightly more successful during the second half of the twentieth century: seven were elected between 1900 and 1950, and nine were victorious between 1952 and 1998. The state's historic anti-Philadelphia bias intensified during the century and certainly affected the fortunes of at least some Philadelphia County candidates.

Candidates from most counties have no chance of winning a statewide election. Only twenty-nine of the state's sixty-seven counties were home to the winner of a statewide election, and only thirteen had more than one of their residents elected to one of the offices under examination. This graphically displays the overwhelming importance of the state's two major cities and their surrounding suburbs.

7. Despite the dramatic political transformations that occurred in Pennsylvania during the twentieth century, the state has always retained a Republican bias.

In 1900, the Democrats were not a factor in Pennsylvania politics. Republicans held all statewide offices, and most mayor's offices. They also had a 164–84 advantage in the General Assembly and controlled twenty-six of the thirty congressional seats. Forty-two of the sixty-seven counties were controlled by the GOP. Between 1900 and 1932, only two of sixty-three Democratic candidates running statewide were victorious. The Democrats became more competitive during the 1930s; real two-party competition, however, dates from the late 1950s. By 1999, the Republicans held a 133–120 advantage in the General Assembly and an 11–10 edge in congressional seats. Moreover, forty-seven of the sixty-seven counties still were controlled by the GOP.

The century-long underlying Republican advantage at the county level is also shown clearly when the counties are classified according to their level of competition in gubernatorial and presidential elections over the course of the twentieth century. For gubernatorial elections, twenty-seven counties were classified as strongly Republican, seventeen as moderately Republican, and six as "became more Republican"; thus, fifty of the sixty-seven counties were in the GOP column. In presidential elections, thirty-five counties were classified as strongly Republican, eleven as moderately Republican and six as "became more Republican"—only fifteen counties fell on the Democratic side of the ledger.

While the Democrats have made significant inroads in major urban areas since the advent of the New Deal, particularly in Philadelphia and

Pittsburgh, the GOP has remained the party of choice in most areas of the state.

The Past Revised

1. General election turnout among eligible voters has declined significantly since 1900.

During the twentieth century, turnout in presidential elections fell from approximately 80 percent of eligible voters to approximately 50 percent; the decline in gubernatorial elections was from approximately 70 percent to approximately 35 percent. Presidential turnout has declined 33 percent since 1900, and gubernatorial turnout 53 percent. The decline has really accelerated during the past three decades. During that time, presidential turnout has declined from approximately 70 percent to approximately 50 percent, and gubernatorial turnout fell from approximately 60 percent to approximately 35 percent. Those figures represent a 29 percent decline in presidential turnout and a 47 percent decline in gubernatorial turnout.

Three distinct eras exist for both presidential and gubernatorial elections: 1900–1948, 1950–68, and 1970–98. Turnout fell in the first era, rose in the second, and then fell again in the third.

The impact of two significant groups admitted to the electorate during the twentieth century, women and young voters, were decidedly different. Women were admitted to the Pennsylvania electorate in 1922. The initial impact was to reduce turnout dramatically in both presidential (30 points) and gubernatorial (21 points) elections. However, by the late 1930s the turnout rate had been restored to its previous levels. Such was not the case with young voters. Eighteen-year-olds first voted in the state in 1972; the result was a notable drop in both presidential (9 points) and gubernatorial (8 points) turnout. However, unlike the situation with women voters, turnout has not rebounded.

2. General election turnout among registered voters declined precipitously during the 1990s.

It had long been assumed that getting citizens registered was the crucial step in getting them to the polls—the vast majority of registered voters voted. The advent of the National Voter Registration Act of 1993 appears to have seriously challenged that assumption. The act greatly simplified registration procedures and led to the enrollment of millions of new voters across the nation. However, many of these individuals did not subsequently vote. Such was the case in Pennsylvania.

In Pennsylvania, between 1992 and 1996, the percentage of the voting age population who registered to vote in presidential elections increased from 66 percent to 75 percent; however, the percentage of registered voters who actually voted declined from 83 percent to 66 percent. Between 1994 and 1998, the percentage of the voting age population registered for the gubernatorial election increased from 65 percent to 80 percent, while actual turnout fell from 61 percent to 42 percent. In real numbers, more than 1.5 million Pennsylvanians were added to the registration rolls between 1994 and 1998, while turnout declined by more than 500,000 voters. Clearly, there is a significant gap between the motivational level required to get registered under the new procedures and the level required to actually show up at the polls on election day.

3. Split-ticket voting has increased significantly since 1960.

At the beginning of the century, most voters consistently voted a straight party ticket. Indeed, this partisan loyalty persisted for more than five decades. Since then, especially since the 1960s, split-ticket voting has increased significantly. Split-ticket voting was measured by the Partisanship Consistency Index (PCI) and the percentage of split results among the various categories of elections.

The PCI more than doubled during the 1960s; it has increased each subsequent decade. The current PCI is four times what it was at the beginning of the century. A similar pattern exists for split results. The only split results during the first five decades of the century were victories by Democrats William Berry and Woodrow Wilson. The percentage of split results increased steadily during the next four decades, before leveling off during the 1990s.

Not unexpectedly, voters were most likely to desert their party in presidential, senatorial, or gubernatorial elections. These are the most visible elections for voters and more information is likely to be available, including more information about the opposing party's candidates. In such elections, partisans may be enticed by attractive candidates from the other party. Voters are most likely to defect from their party because they are attracted to a visible candidate from the other party, usually an incumbent, who is running a well-funded campaign (Beck, Baum, Clausen, and Smith 1992; Burden and Kimball 1998).

4. The percentage of General Assembly and congressional incumbents running for reelection increased during the twentieth century.

Contemporary legislative incumbents are much more likely to seek reelection than their counterparts a century ago were. This trend is most prominent among General Assembly incumbents. Between 1900 and 1910, 41 percent of House incumbents and 36 percent of Senate incumbents sought reelection; by the end of the century, the figures were almost 90 percent for House members and over 80 percent for senators. For representatives, the percentage running for reelection increased every decade. For senators, the rate of increase was much less consistent: the percentage increased through the 1930s, declined slightly during the 1940s, rebounded sharply during the 1950s, declined during the 1960s and 1970s, and increased during the 1980s and 1990s. Among both representatives and senators, a notable increase in the percentage of incumbents running for reelection took place during the 1980s.

The proportion of congressional incumbents seeking reelection increased during the century, but the increase was not as dramatic as was the case with members of the General Assembly. At the beginning of the century, 66 percent of congressional incumbents sought reelection; that figure had increased to 88 percent by the end of the century. Once again, there was a significant increase in the percentage of incumbents seeking reelection during the 1980s. However, contrary to the pattern in the General Assembly, this was followed by a notable drop among incumbents running for reelection during the 1990s.

More incumbents are running for reelection to the General Assembly and Congress because the job of legislator has become full-time and well-paying. Also, the advantages of incumbency have increased, and fewer districts are competitive.

5. The percentage of General Assembly and congressional candidates who are unopposed in the general election increased dramatically during the 1980s and 1990s.

Until the 1970s, it was rare for a General Assembly or congressional candidate to run unopposed in the general election. The number of opposed candidates, especially incumbents, declined precipitously during the 1980s and 1990s. The dramatic increase in the number of safe districts has made it difficult for one party or the other to induce candidates to undertake what, in effect, are hopeless races.

6. In both Pennsylvania House and congressional elections, the relationship between vote share and seats won has not exaggerated the majority party's share of the vote since 1966.

Over the course of the twentieth century the relationship between vote share and seats won is what was expected: the majority party had its share of the vote exaggerated. However, since 1966 this has not been the case. In fact, the tendency has been to minimize the majority party's share of the vote. In seven of the seventeen House elections since 1966, the majority party's vote share was greater than the percentage of seats won. The Republicans were the victims four times, and the Democrats three times. On three other occasions, the majority party's percentage of the vote and percentage of seats won were identical. In only seven of the seventeen elections since 1966 has the majority party won a percentage of seats greater than its percentage of the vote.

The period since 1966 has been one of extremely close statewide competition for the Pennsylvania House. In twelve of the seventeen elections since 1966, the majority party has received 52 percent or less of the statewide vote cast for House candidates. In an identical number of elections, the percentage of seats won by the majority party has been 52 percent or less.

The findings regarding congressional elections are almost identical. Since 1900, the majority party has had its share of the vote translated into a larger percentage of seats. But once again, the pattern is decidedly different since 1966. In eight of the seventeen elections since that date, the majority party has won a smaller percentage of seats than its share of the vote. On five of these occasions, the party that received a majority of the vote won fewer than half of the seats.

These data for state legislative and congressional elections in Pennsylvania since 1966 call into question the assumption that the majority party will regularly have its vote share magnified when the electoral system translates votes into seats. Apparently, during an era when the statewide vote is closely divided, the party receiving a majority of the statewide vote may regularly win less than a proportionate share of seats.

The traditional relationship between vote share and seats benefits the majority party in the state. It can be argued that since 1966 there has been no majority party in Pennsylvania House or congressional elections. Between 1966 and 1998, there were seventeen House elections; the Democrats won a majority of the statewide vote eleven times, while the Republicans prevailed six times. However, on five occasions, the Democratic margin was 1 percentage point or less. Thus, over more than three decades, each party garnered a majority of the statewide vote six times, and five elections were a virtual dead heat. The results of the congressional elections were similar: the Democrats won a majority of the statewide vote ten times, and the Republicans won a majority of the statewide vote seven times. There is no majority party to be advantaged.

Incumbent gerrymandering has also played a significant role in creating safe districts. There are, at most, sixty competitive House districts in Pennsylvania. And those figures greatly exaggerate the number of districts where serious competition exists every two years. Thus, each party obtains approximately 50 percent of the statewide House vote each election and wins roughly half of the seats. Likewise, fewer than a handful of congressional districts are competitive.

These factors create a plausible scenario for winning proportionally fewer seats than votes: win more votes in your safe districts than the other party wins in its safe districts, but lose a majority of the limited number of competitive districts.

7. Careerism among members of the General Assembly and the Pennsylvania congressional delegation has increased significantly since 1900.

Legislative careerism is much more extensive now than it was a hundred years ago. Tenure has increased dramatically. Fifty-two percent of the members of the Pennsylvania House elected during the first decade of the century served for two years or less; among those elected between 1980 and 1985, only 10 percent served one term or less. At the other extreme, only 1 percent of the members elected during the first decade of the century served fifteen years or more; by the 1980s, that figure had increased to 47 percent. The mean tenure during the century increased from 3.3 years to 12.3 years.

The data for state senators are similar. Sixty-four percent of the senators elected during the first decade of the century served one term or less; that figure had plummeted to 14 percent by the 1980s. Only 5 percent of the senators elected during the first decade of the century served fifteen years or more, compared with 64 percent during the 1980s. The mean tenure increased from 5.9 years to 13.8 years.

While they are not as consistent, the patterns among members of the state's congressional delegation basically confirm the patterns established by the state legislators. Forty-three percent of the members of Congress elected during the first decade of the century served two years or less, compared with 27 percent elected during the 1980s. Only 1 percent of the members of Congress elected during the first decade of the century served fifteen years or longer, a figure that had increased to 46 percent by the 1980s. The mean tenure increased from 5.3 years to 11.6 years. However, among members of Congress, the mean tenure was highest during the 1960s (14.4 years). By the 1980s, more Pennsylvania representatives were serving ten years or longer, or fifteen years or longer, than ever before, but the percentage of members serving one term or less had returned to the levels of the 1950s, thus dragging down mean tenure.

8. Members of the General Assembly elected at the end of the century were more likely to enter office with no previous party or elective experience than were their counterparts elected at the beginning of the century.

Members of both houses were more likely to have held both party and elective positions in 1901 than in 1995. Moreover, fewer members were elected to the legislature with no previous political experience at the beginning of the century than at the end of the century. State legislators a century ago served more extensive political apprenticeships than contemporary legislators do. Among House members, 17 percent had both party and elective experience in 1901, contrasted with 8 percent in 1995; 38 percent had no previous political experience in 1901, compared with 51 percent in 1995. Thirty-two percent of senators had both party and elective experience in 1901, while only 8 percent did in 1995; 22 percent had no previous political experience in 1901, compared with 30 percent in 1995.

9. During the twentieth century, the state's most urbanized counties were transformed from Republican strongholds into Democratic strongholds.

During the first three decades of the century, the Republicans were clearly the urban party in gubernatorial and presidential elections. The GOP vote was greatest in the most urbanized counties; indeed, Philadelphia

(Philadelphia County) and Pittsburgh (Allegheny County) were home to Republican machines. All that changed during the 1930s. Since 1930, in both gubernatorial and presidential elections, as the county level of urbanization has increased, the Republican share of the vote has decreased.

This transformation was manifested most graphically in Philadelphia and Allegheny Counties. In 1900, they were overwhelmingly Republican; by the end of the century, they held the key to Democratic success in statewide elections. Both counties became consistently Democratic in presidential elections during the 1930s, and in gubernatorial elections during the 1950s.

10. Primary election turnout has declined significantly since 1900.

During the century, primary turnout in gubernatorial elections declined from approximately one-third of the voting age population to less than one-fifth of the voting age population. The high-water mark occurred in 1938 when 48 percent of the voting age public went to the polls. Attesting to the tremendous lack of interest in the nominating contests is the fact that only once (1966) since 1938 has turnout in the gubernatorial primary exceeded 30 percent. Primary election turnout has typically lagged between 20 and 30 percentage points behind general election turnout.

A Final Note

The political environment in Pennsylvania is markedly different today than it was a hundred years ago. For example, the competitive balance between the parties, the degree of partisanship, and the level of citizen involvement have all been significantly altered. Still, a time traveler from 1900 would not find himself or herself in a totally alien political universe. There are definitely aspects from his or her political world that, while somewhat changed, would be recognizable. That is the most important lesson to be learned from the present data.

It is hoped that the previous chapters have demonstrated the importance of placing current political trends into historical perspective. In examining trends, the selection of a base year (or decade) is the most critical decision. Many of the current trends are presented as significant changes that have occurred since the 1960s. While they are that, the present data have suggested that they may be more: namely, a return to conditions that existed earlier in the century. A longer time line may be needed to ascertain whether current patterns are unique. Our study of twentieth-century politics in Pennsylvania has shown that while some current trends are new, others most definitely are not.

A crucial remaining research question is whether the present findings are unique to Pennsylvania, or typical of patterns in other states. Similar studies of other states are needed to answer that question. Such studies would help us to better understand historical patterns that are unique to individual states as well as those that are shared. Such information could only enhance our understanding of contemporary state politics.

POSTSCRIPT

The previous chapters analyzed various aspects of electoral behavior and election outcomes in Pennsylvania during the twentieth century. The data in those chapters were aggregated by decade. The purpose of this brief chapter is to update several of the trends through the 2000 and 2002 elections. This will allow an early assessment of whether the patterns from the last century are being sustained or reversed during the first decade of the twenty-first century.

Registration

Percentage Registered

The percentage of voting age residents who are registered continues to increase; by 2002, 83.7 percent were registered. The 1998 figure was 79.8 percent.

Independents

The trend of increasing independence described during the 1990s has continued unabated. Between 1998 and 2002 the percentage of voters registered with the two major parties had declined from 90.7 percent to 89.4 percent. In 2002, there were twenty-eight counties where at least 10 percent of the voters were not registered with the two major parties. That is up from sixteen counties in 1998, and almost as high as the thirty counties where that was the situation in 1925. All sixteen counties from 1998 remained on the list in 2002; moreover, the percentage of independent voters increased in all sixteen counties. The twelve counties that did not previously meet the 10 percent threshold in 1998 were Blair, Bradford, Butler, Carbon, Columbia, Delaware, Franklin, Indiana, Montour, Perry, Union, and Warren. The highest proportion of voters not registered with the Republican or Democratic Party in 2002 were in Monroe (17.9 percent) and Pike (17.6 percent) Counties.

Six (Bradford, Carbon, Delaware, Franklin, Indiana, and Warren) of the counties where more than 10 percent of the voters were registered with nonmajor parties in 2002 also exceeded that threshold in 1925. An argument in Chapter 2 suggested that political culture was a possible explanation for the higher incidence of independence among voters in counties that exceeded the 10 percent threshold in both 1925 and 1998. Some additional support for that argument is offered by the 2002 data. Carbon, Delaware, and Franklin Counties fit the geographic pattern reported in Chapter 2. However, Bradford, Indiana, and Warren Counties do not; they are dispersed across the state.

Turnout

Percentage of Voting Age Population

Voter turnout in the 2000 presidential election was 53.7 percent, an increase from the 50.0 percent figure in 1996. Turnout in the 2002 gubernatorial election was 38.3 percent, up from 32.9 percent in 1998. Both contests were predicted to be close, encouraging voters to turn out and cast their ballots.

Percentage of Registered Voters

Continuing the pattern established during the 1990s, voter turnout as a percentage of registered voters declined in the 2000 presidential election, falling to 63.1 percent from the 66.1 percent figure in 1996. However, the pattern was reversed in the 2002 gubernatorial election: turnout increased from 41.7 percent in 1998 to 45.7 percent. Another pattern identified in Chapter 2 continues to hold: the National Voter Registration Act of 1993 is encouraging citizens to register, but many of them are not motivated enough to vote.

Split-Ticket Voting

As the twenty-first century gets under way, a significant percentage of Pennsylvania voters continue to split their ballots. The PCI was 14.3 in 2000 and 12.5 in 2002. The mean for the first two elections of the decade was 13.4, higher than the 13.1 score for the 1990s. The percentage of split results was 42.9 percent in 2000 and 33.3 percent in 2002. The mean of 38.1 percent is higher than the figures for either the 1990s (28.0 percent) or the 1980s (35.7 percent).

Removing the presidential, senatorial, and gubernatorial results from the PCI score produces mixed results. The 2000 PCI remains the same, as the largest differences in the Republican share of the two-party vote occurred in the contests for attorney general (55.6 percent) and auditor general (41.3 percent). However, removing Republican gubernatorial candidate Mike Fisher's percentage (45.4 percent) from the 2002 analysis dramatically lowers the PCI from 12.5 to 3.1. The mean of 7.8 for the recalculated PCI is lower than the 9.1 figure for the 1990s.

Pennsylvania General Assembly

Incumbents Running for Reelection

As the Pennsylvania General Assembly increasingly becomes more professional, the percentage of incumbents seeking reelection continues to rise. (To maintain methodological consistency, the percentage of incumbents seeking reelection will once again be the percentage of incumbents running for reelection who survived the primary.) Ninety-two percent of House members sought reelection in 2000, and 90 percent decided to run again in 2002. The mean of 91 percent exceeds the mean of 89 percent for the 1990s. On the Senate side, 92 percent of incumbents sought reelection in 2000, as did 88 percent in 2002. The mean of 90 percent is greater than the 84 percent figure for the 1990s.

Reelection Success of Incumbents

The advantages of incumbency continue to virtually guarantee electoral success for those incumbents who run again. Ninety-nine percent of House incumbents who ran were reelected in 2000, as were 98 percent in 2002. The mean of 98 percent is slightly higher than the 97 percent figure for the 1990s. On the Senate side, 91 percent of incumbents won in 2000; in 2002 the figure was a perfect 100 percent. The mean of 95 percent was just slightly lower than the 96 percent mean for the 1990s.

Incidence of Marginal Districts

Not only are incumbents winning more often, but also they are winning by increasingly larger margins. The incidence of marginal districts continues to decline. Eighty-nine percent of House seats were won with at least 60 percent of the vote in 2000; the figure for 2002 was an almost identical 88 percent. The mean of 88 percent is a significant increase over the mean of 83 percent for the 1990s.

The significant early twenty-first century increase in safe districts can also be seen in Senate elections. Seventy-two percent of Senate districts were won by safe margins in 2000; that figure jumped to 88 percent in 2002. The mean of 80 percent is notably higher than the mean of 74 percent for the 1990s.

Contested Elections

The dramatic drop in the percentage of contested elections continues into the new century. Only 62 percent of House elections were contested in 2000, and only 63 percent were contested in 2002. The mean of 62 percent is a precipitous decline from the 74 percent figure for the 1990s.

A similar pattern is present in Senate elections, but with dramatically different results in the two elections. Only 64 percent of the Senate elections were contested in 2000; however, that figure jumped to 84 percent in 2002. The mean of 74 percent is a significant decline from the 79 percent mean for the 1990s.

Vote Share Versus Seats

The post-1966 pattern of the majority party winning a smaller proportion of seats than its proportion of the vote continued in the 2000 and 2002

House elections. The GOP secured 53 percent of the vote in 2000, but only 51 percent of the seats; the figures for 2002 were 58 percent and 54 percent.

U.S. House of Representatives

Incumbents Running for Reelection

The decline in the percentage of incumbents running for reelection between the 1980s and 1990s continued during the first two elections of the new century. Ninety percent of incumbents ran for reelection in 2000, as did 86 percent in 2002. The mean of 88 percent is identical to the figure for the 1990s. In part, the recent figures are a result of the small number of incumbents involved. The past two general elections saw nineteen and eighteen of a possible twenty-one incumbents running; that hardly represents a wholesale rejection of the office.

Reelection Success of Incumbents

As was the case with members of the General Assembly, congressional incumbents continue to enjoy increasingly greater rates of reelection success. The rates of success were 100 percent in 2000 and 94 percent in 2002. The mean of 97 percent represents an increase over the mean of 95 percent for the 1990s.

The lower percentage for 2002 was a direct result of reapportionment. The Republicans controlled the reapportionment process and drew new boundary lines that enabled them to increase their congressional seat advantage from 11–10 to 12–7. The GOP plan was intended to insure that the two seats the state lost during reapportionment would both be Democratic seats. One of the redrawn districts pitted two Democrats against each other in the primary. The other crucial district featured a general election contested by two incumbents. One of the incumbents was longtime GOP congressman George Gekas; the other was Democratic incumbent Tim Holden. The district had a Republican registration advantage, and it was assumed that Gekas would be able to dispatch Holden. Holden, however, won. Gekas had not faced a serious contender for years and simply ran a poor campaign. Holden, whose relatively conservative ideology played well in the district, ran an energetic, effective campaign. Gekas was the only incumbent to lose in the general election.

Incidence of Marginal Districts

Eighty-one percent of the congressional districts were won by a safe margin in 2000, and 68 percent were won by a safe margin in 2002. The mean of 74 percent virtually matches the means for the last two decades of the twentieth century.

Contested Elections

Contrary to the situation with General Assembly elections, the incidence of contested congressional elections has gone up since the beginning of the new century. Ninety percent of congressional elections were contested in 2000, and that figure increased to 95 percent in 2002. The mean of 92 percent represents an increase over the mean of 87 percent for the 1990s. A couple of points need to be made. First, four of the contested elections were open seat contests; open seat races are virtually guaranteed to be contested. Second, seven of the contested elections featured minor party candidates, usually from either the Green Party or the Libertarian Party. Thus, almost one in five of the elections were not contested by one of the major parties.

Vote Share Versus Seats

In dramatic contrast to the General Assembly data, the 2000 and 2002 congressional election results represent a return to the pre-1966 election pattern of "manufactured majorities." The Republicans garnered 49 percent of the vote in 2000 and obtained 52 percent of the seats; in 2002, the GOP obtained 58 percent of the vote and won 63 percent of the seats. Perhaps there once again is a majority party in congressional elections.

2000 Presidential Election

Democratic presidential candidate Al Gore won Pennsylvania, securing 52 percent of the two-party vote. He carried eighteen counties. The 2000 election results were another testament to the significance of Philadelphia and Allegheny Counties to success in statewide elections, especially for Democrats. Gore carried Philadelphia County by a margin of 449,182 to 100,959 over GOP candidate George W. Bush; the margin in Allegheny

County was 329,963 to 235,361. The combined margin of victory was 422,825, more than twice Gore's statewide margin of 204,840. Gore's totals in the two counties represented 31 percent of his statewide total.

2002 Gubernatorial Election

Democrat Ed Rendell defeated Republican Attorney General Mike Fisher in the contest for the governorship, garnering 55 percent of the two-party vote. Rendell carried eighteen counties. The key to the election was the success of the popular former Philadelphia mayor's success in Philadelphia and its suburbs. Rendell won the five-county Philadelphia metropolitan area by a margin of 847,817 to 332,376 over Fisher. His 515,441 vote margin of victory exceeded his statewide margin of 323,827. The Philadelphia metropolitan area provided 44 percent of Rendell's statewide vote total.

The Primary Elections for the Pennsylvania General Assembly and U.S. House of Representatives Elections

The trends that have developed since the 1970s intensified in the 2000 and 2002 primary elections. Eighteen percent of the congressional primaries were contested in 2000, while 26 percent were contested in 2002. The mean of 22 percent represents a dramatic drop from the mean of 35 percent during the 1990s. Ten percent of the Senate primaries were contested in 2000, and 9 percent were contested in 2002. The mean of 9 percent is a significant decline from the mean of 15 percent during the 1990s. Eleven percent of the House primaries were contested in 2000 and 2002. The mean of 11 percent is almost a fifty percent drop from the mean of 20 percent during the 1990s.

Congressional primaries are still the most likely to be contested. Once again, there is no dramatic difference between the rates of opposition in Pennsylvania House and Senate primaries. The most notable feature of the early twenty-first-century primaries is the precipitous decline in competition.

It was noted in Chapter 6 that a majority of the contested candidates won the nomination with less than 60 percent of the vote; that pattern was modified in 2000 and 2002. Forty-three percent of the contested congressional candidates obtained at least 60 percent of the vote in 2000, and 62 percent did so in 2002. The mean of 52 percent is slightly higher than the 50 percent mean for the 1990s. Twenty-five percent of the contested Senate candidates received 60 percent or more of the vote in 2000; that figure doubled to 50 percent in 2002. The mean of 37 percent is a slight decline from the mean of 42 percent for the 1990s. The figures for contested House candidates in 2000 and 2002 were 54 percent and 52 percent. The mean of 53 percent was an increase from the mean of 49 percent for the 1990s.

The results of the 2000 and 2002 Pennsylvania House primaries provided the most dramatic contrast with the patterns established between 1972 and 1998. Many fewer House candidates are facing primary competition, but those who do are more likely to win with at least 60 percent of the vote. There is, however, a definite pattern to the closely contested primaries. Such primaries are most likely to occur among challengers to an incumbent or in open seat districts. Only 22 percent of the time in 2000 and 2002 did a contested primary won with less than 60 percent of the vote feature an incumbent. It remains the case that incumbents are unlikely to face primary competition; and if they do, they are likely to win by a safe margin.

Appendix
Summary of Gubernatorial and Presidential Election Results for all Pennsylvania Counties, 1900–1998

The appendix presents voting data for all sixty-seven Pennsylvania counties for all twenty-five gubernatorial and presidential elections held during the twentieth century. The following is the key for each table.

- Year = the gubernatorial or presidential election year.
- Rep. = the actual number of votes cast for the Republican candidate.
- Dem. = the actual number of votes cast for the Democratic candidate.
- % Rep. = the percentage of the two-party vote received by the Republican candidate.
- Mean = the mean percentage Republican of the two-party vote for all twenty-five elections.
- Classification = the competitive category for each county based on the results of all twenty-five gubernatorial or presidential elections.

Table A.1 Adams County

Gubernatorial elections				Presidential elections			
Year	Rep.	Dem.	% Rep.	Year	Rep.	Dem.	% Rep.
1902	3096	4123	42.9	1900	3718	3967	48.4
1906	2668	3511	43.2	1904	4017	3809	51.3
1910	2017	2221	47.6	1908	3685	4034	47.7
1914	3722	6239	40.3	1912	819	3682	18.2
1918	3187	2630	54.8	1916	3290	3967	45.6
1922	3210	5540	36.7	1920	5323	3852	58.0
1926	4628	3324	58.2	1924	5778	4840	54.4
1930	6074	4637	56.7	1928	9656	4635	67.5
1934	6603	7366	47.3	1932	6084	7185	45.8
1938	9146	6991	56.7	1936	8336	8313	50.1
1942	6241	4149	60.1	1940	8609	7354	53.9
1946	6876	5876	53.9	1944	8787	5881	59.9
1950	7354	5414	57.6	1948	7988	5409	59.6
1954	7139	7227	49.7	1952	11,016	5691	65.9
1958	9860	7735	56.0	1956	12,250	6281	66.1
1962	11,569	7307	61.3	1960	12,933	7895	62.1
1966	10,470	6054	63.4	1964	8617	11,148	43.6
1970	8207	7028	53.9	1968	11,303	5993	65.4
1974	8682	7247	54.5	1972	13,593	5529	71.1
1978	10,386	6034	63.3	1976	12,133	8771	58.0
1982	11,346	7217	61.1	1980	13,760	7266	65.4
1986	10,511	7277	59.1	1984	16,786	7289	69.7
1990	5680	13,890	29.0	1988	15,650	8299	65.3
1994	12,146	6977	63.5	1992	13,552	9576	58.6
1998	14,810	3682	80.1	1996	15,338	10,774	58.7
Mean			54.0	Mean			56.0
Classification: Moderately Republican				Classification: Moderately Republican			

Table A.2 Allegheny County

Gubernatorial elections				Presidential elections			
Year	Rep.	Dem.	% Rep.	Year	Rep.	Dem.	% Rep.
1902	80,191	31,600	71.7	1900	71,780	27,311	72.4
1906	58,362	29,815	66.2	1904	90,594	21,420	80.9
1910	47,817	4350	91.7	1908	74,080	35,655	67.5
1914	120,791	45,913	72.4	1912	23,822	31,417	43.1
1918	50,922	29,147	63.5	1916	77,483	52,833	59.7
1922	79,418	43,584	64.6	1920	138,908	40,278	77.5
1926	125,063	31,875	79.7	1924	149,296	21,984	87.2
1930	145,285	71741	66.9	1928	215,626	160,733	57.3
1934	148,291	222,178	40.0	1932	152,326	189,839	44.5
1938	241,102	272,555	46.9	1936	176,224	366,593	32.5
1942	171,839	194,600	46.9	1940	263,285	367,926	41.7
1946	271,348	227,354	54.4	1944	261,218	350,690	42.7
1950	246,892	270,577	47.7	1948	253,272	326,303	43.7
1954	236,734	325,018	42.1	1952	359,224	370,945	49.2
1958	269,293	322,063	45.5	1956	384,939	315,989	54.9
1962	348,253	294,488	54.2	1960	320,970	428,455	42.8
1966	274,577	310,449	46.9	1964	241,707	475,207	33.7
1970	182,312	308,770	37.1	1968	264,790	364,906	42.1
1974	204,045	268,636	43.2	1972	371,737	282,496	56.8
1978	241,111	258,981	48.2	1976	303,127	328,343	48.0
1982	250,836	244,391	50.7	1980	271,850	297,467	47.8
1986	181,562	242,296	42.8	1984	284,692	372,576	43.3
1990	109,895	281,883	28.1	1988	231,137	348,814	39.8
1994	180,260	193,459	48.2	1992	183,035	324,004	36.1
1998	169,316	127,994	56.9	1996	204,067	284,480	41.8
Mean			54.4	Mean			50.7
Classification: Became more Democratic				Classification: Became more Democratic			

Table A.3 Armstrong County

Gubernatorial elections				Presidential elections			
Year	Rep.	Dem.	% Rep.	Year	Rep.	Dem.	% Rep.
1902	4308	3263	56.9	1900	6443	3438	65.2
1906	4925	3235	60.3	1904	5798	2260	71.9
1910	3673	550	87.0	1908	6110	3212	65.5
1914	3761	4180	47.4	1912	1904	3027	38.6
1918	4137	1442	74.1	1916	6024	3596	62.6
1922	5082	3905	56.5	1920	8995	3262	73.4
1926	7865	1626	82.9	1924	11,192	2931	79.2
1930	11,679	3791	75.5	1928	17,625	4824	78.5
1934	9734	9343	51.0	1932	10,884	9230	54.1
1938	15,002	9930	60.2	1936	14,195	15,955	47.1
1942	8922	5435	62.1	1940	14,524	12,144	54.5
1946	10,962	5915	65.0	1944	13,656	10,202	57.2
1950	12,039	9794	55.1	1948	11,712	9900	54.2
1954	11,771	12,753	48.0	1952	16,955	13,221	56.2
1958	16,499	12,920	56.1	1956	20,055	12,671	61.3
1962	18,799	12,668	59.7	1960	19,883	14,799	57.3
1966	14,663	12,497	54.0	1964	10,618	21,098	33.5
1970	9375	14,186	39.8	1968	14,132	13,921	50.3
1974	12,372	12,566	49.6	1972	17,557	10,490	62.6
1978	9665	14,263	40.4	1976	13,378	15,179	46.8
1982	11,010	12,563	46.7	1980	12,955	12,718	50.5
1986	9376	11,635	44.6	1984	13,709	14,525	48.6
1990	6192	14,077	30.5	1988	11,509	13,892	45.3
1994	8821	7944	52.6	1992	9122	12,995	41.2
1998	8641	4900	63.8	1996	11,052	11,130	49.8
Mean			57.1	Mean			54.2
Classification: Moderately Republican				Classification: Moderately Republican			

Table A.4 Beaver County

	Gubernatorial elections				Presidential elections		
Year	Rep.	Dem.	% Rep.	Year	Rep.	Dem.	% Rep.
1902	5145	3607	58.8	1900	6759	4076	62.4
1906	3886	3529	52.4	1904	7122	2333	75.3
1910	3510	447	88.7	1908	7008	4200	62.5
1914	4905	5087	49.1	1912	2759	3037	47.6
1918	4863	2448	66.5	1916	6864	5805	54.2
1922	7040	5012	58.4	1920	11,691	4771	71.0
1926	11,641	2988	79.6	1924	16,768	3220	83.9
1930	14,038	10,150	58.0	1928	27,949	11,865	70.2
1934	14,815	25,203	37.0	1932	19,751	19,895	49.8
1938	25,570	24,787	50.8	1936	20,223	35,205	36.5
1942	15,323	14,600	51.2	1940	24,324	33,609	42.0
1946	22,369	18,501	54.7	1944	23,555	32,743	41.8
1950	23,321	24,751	48.5	1948	22,324	26,629	45.6
1954	21,882	35,131	38.4	1952	31,700	38,136	45.4
1958	27,231	35,917	43.1	1956	38,263	36,373	51.3
1962	37,820	36,229	51.1	1960	36,796	47,182	43.8
1966	29,737	39,298	43.1	1964	23,174	60,492	27.7
1970	20,591	43,442	32.2	1968	28,264	45,396	38.4
1974	25,095	36,152	41.0	1972	43,637	31,570	58.0
1978	21,887	44,094	33.2	1976	33,593	46,117	42.1
1982	28,473	45,408	38.5	1980	30,496	43,955	41.0
1986	19,232	39,216	32.9	1984	32,052	54,756	36.9
1990	13,577	43,350	23.8	1988	25,764	50,327	33.9
1994	20,201	26,965	42.8	1992	21,361	44,877	32.2
1998	24,993	19,879	55.7	1996	26,048	39,578	39.7
Mean			49.7	Mean			47.9
Classification: Became more Democratic				Classification: Became more Democratic			

Table A.5 Bedford County

	Gubernatorial elections				Presidential elections		
Year	Rep.	Dem.	% Rep.	Year	Rep.	Dem.	% Rep.
1902	4021	3661	52.3	1900	4790	3445	58.2
1906	3570	3732	48.9	1904	5364	3040	63.8
1910	2355	902	72.3	1908	4784	3196	60.0
1914	2707	3397	44.3	1912	1140	2694	31.4
1918	3587	4555	44.0	1916	3729	3263	53.3
1922	3991	4495	47.0	1920	5800	2594	69.1
1926	3943	1444	73.2	1924	6154	2315	72.7
1930	6569	2929	69.2	1928	9602	1966	83.0
1934	6710	7175	48.3	1932	6597	5075	56.5
1938	9285	8069	53.5	1936	9014	8937	50.2
1942	6031	4497	57.2	1940	8864	7388	54.5
1946	6493	3755	63.3	1944	8703	5115	63.0
1950	6501	5122	55.9	1948	6028	3851	61.0
1954	6989	7291	48.9	1952	9419	5255	64.2
1958	8940	6879	56.3	1956	11,423	6038	65.4
1962	11,660	6596	63.9	1960	12,542	6030	67.5
1966	10,079	5796	63.5	1964	7968	9165	46.5
1970	7796	5966	56.6	1968	10,482	4725	68.9
1974	7928	5136	60.7	1972	11,243	3836	74.6
1978	8147	5690	58.9	1976	9355	6652	58.4
1982	8034	6200	56.4	1980	10,930	4950	68.8
1986	8180	6874	54.3	1984	13,085	5424	70.7
1990	4876	7709	38.7	1988	11,123	5754	65.9
1994	8689	4588	65.4	1992	9216	5840	61.2
1998	8232	2322	78.0	1996	10,064	5954	62.8
Mean			57.4	Mean			58.9
Classification: Moderately Republican				Classification: Strongly Republican			

Table A.6 Berks County

	Gubernatorial elections				Presidential elections		
Year	Rep.	Dem.	% Rep.	Year	Rep.	Dem.	% Rep.
1902	9657	16,646	36.7	1900	13,952	19,013	42.3
1906	7696	13,365	36.1	1904	15,539	16,325	48.8
1910	5354	7997	40.1	1908	13,642	17,381	44.0
1914	8884	13,613	39.5	1912	3032	16,433	15.6
1918	8563	12,161	41.3	1916	11,937	19,267	38.2
1922	13,766	22,793	37.6	1920	22,221	18,361	54.7
1926	17,161	14,671	53.9	1924	28,186	17,220	62.1
1930	12,592	25,533	33.0	1928	47,073	18,960	71.3
1934	19,604	26,709	42.3	1932	27,073	29,763	47.6
1938	35,320	33,377	51.4	1936	26,699	56,907	31.9
1942	20,446	23,479	46.5	1940	32,111	53,301	37.6
1946	31,599	27,333	53.6	1944	35,274	43,889	44.5
1950	32,750	38,291	46.1	1948	35,608	43,075	45.3
1954	31,027	50,957	37.8	1952	51,720	45,874	53.0
1958	42,456	45,118	48.5	1956	57,258	42,349	57.5
1962	52,360	42,688	55.1	1960	61,743	50,572	55.0
1966	47,303	42,838	52.5	1964	36,726	73,444	33.3
1970	30,351	49,239	38.1	1968	50,623	49,877	50.4
1974	34,788	47,359	42.3	1972	66,172	36,563	64.4
1978	43,286	36,252	54.4	1976	54,452	50,994	51.6
1982	46,830	36,930	55.9	1980	60,576	36,449	62.4
1986	43,849	36,147	54.8	1984	74,605	37,849	66.3
1990	29,600	47,887	38.2	1988	70,153	41,040	63.1
1994	48,847	30,740	61.4	1992	52,939	46,031	53.5
1998	49,716	21,336	70.0	1996	56,289	49,887	53.0
Mean			46.9	Mean			49.4
Classification: Became More Republican				Classification: Became More Republican			

Table A.7 Blair County

Gubernatorial elections				Presidential elections			
Year	Rep.	Dem.	% Rep.	Year	Rep.	Dem.	% Rep.
1902	6524	5063	56.3	1900	9749	4528	68.3
1906	6428	4983	56.3	1904	12,482	3662	77.3
1910	4290	1074	80.0	1908	10,583	3981	72.7
1914	8328	6229	57.2	1912	3138	4108	43.3
1918	7627	4148	64.8	1916	9893	7009	58.5
1922	9612	8523	53.0	1920	15,035	5668	72.6
1926	13,640	4879	76.6	1924	20,313	4244	82.7
1930	14,418	12,600	53.4	1928	34,356	12,104	73.9
1934	15,458	16,852	47.8	1932	19,553	13,709	58.8
1938	29,505	20,990	58.4	1936	24,711	27,038	47.7
1942	18,022	10,282	63.7	1940	26,639	21,573	55.2
1946	20,172	8831	69.5	1944	24,925	18,003	58.1
1950	22,334	13,715	61.9	1948	22,382	14,050	61.4
1954	21,352	20,407	51.1	1952	32,113	16,851	65.6
1958	26,256	18,472	58.7	1956	33,623	17,503	65.8
1962	32,352	16,267	66.5	1960	35,297	19,445	64.5
1966	24,817	15,855	61.0	1964	24,301	26,157	48.2
1970	17,125	18,317	48.3	1968	28,780	15,803	64.6
1974	23,216	16,045	59.1	1972	33,126	10,023	76.8
1978	20,976	18,675	52.9	1976	28,290	18,397	60.6
1982	23,180	17,033	57.6	1980	28,931	15,014	65.8
1986	17,509	15,135	53.6	1984	30,104	15,651	65.8
1990	9608	20,713	31.7	1988	25,623	15,588	62.2
1994	17,734	9830	64.3	1992	21,447	14,857	59.1
1998	19,025	4410	81.2	1996	21,282	15,036	58.6
Mean			59.7	Mean			62.9
Classification: Strongly Republican				Classification: Strongly Republican			

Table A.8 Bradford County

Gubernatorial elections				Presidential elections			
Year	Rep.	Dem.	% Rep.	Year	Rep.	Dem.	% Rep.
1902	4875	3644	57.2	1900	8625	4211	67.2
1906	4371	5559	44.0	1904	8303	2858	74.4
1910	3205	536	85.7	1908	7997	3758	68.0
1914	3719	5068	42.3	1912	2034	2960	40.7
1918	4970	1423	77.7	1916	6178	3653	62.8
1922	7384	4316	63.1	1920	11,947	2825	80.9
1926	8107	1647	83.1	1924	11,620	2307	83.4
1930	11,077	3884	74.0	1928	17,251	4281	80.1
1934	11,619	5542	67.7	1932	11,521	5970	65.9
1938	15,609	6962	69.1	1936	16,643	8078	67.3
1942	8708	3126	73.6	1940	14,826	6605	69.2
1946	10,281	3120	76.7	1944	13,472	5523	71.3
1950	10,693	5170	67.4	1948	11,783	4421	72.7
1954	9141	5957	60.5	1952	15,894	4959	76.2
1958	12,206	6480	65.3	1956	15,399	5502	52.9
1962	13,944	6435	68.4	1960	16,252	6920	70.1
1966	11,868	5007	70.3	1964	10,434	10,714	49.3
1970	9946	5580	64.1	1968	13,308	6373	67.6
1974	9815	5457	64.3	1972	15,050	5204	74.3
1978	10,637	3629	74.6	1976	12,851	7913	61.9
1982	10,029	5489	64.4	1980	13,139	6439	67.1
1986	9100	5547	62.1	1984	14,808	5474	73.0
1990	5663	7063	44.5	1988	13,568	6635	67.2
1994	10,538	4700	69.2	1992	10,221	6903	59.7
1998	12,534	3041	80.5	1996	10,393	7736	57.3
Mean			66.7	Mean			66.3
Classification: Strongly Republican				Classification: Strongly Republican			

Table A.9 Bucks County

Gubernatorial elections				Presidential elections			
Year	Rep.	Dem.	% Rep.	Year	Rep.	Dem.	% Rep.
1902	7468	8378	47.1	1900	9263	7287	52.8
1906	7146	7637	48.3	1904	9572	6706	58.8
1910	6254	6404	49.4	1908	9409	7233	56.5
1914	7971	7264	52.3	1912	5452	6773	44.6
1918	7782	4671	62.5	1916	9269	7491	55.3
1922	9612	7537	55.9	1920	14,130	6867	67.3
1926	12,125	4671	72.2	1924	17,460	6582	72.6
1930	13,779	10,625	56.5	1928	28,421	8446	77.1
1934	19,992	17,571	53.2	1932	22,331	14,135	61.2
1938	26,663	16,488	61.8	1936	23,860	24,159	49.7
1942	18,655	10,704	63.5	1940	25,169	20,586	55.0
1946	25,173	12,723	66.4	1944	25,634	17,823	59.0
1950	24,970	19,418	56.2	1948	29,411	16,655	63.8
1954	32,339	31,005	51.0	1952	40,753	24,301	62.6
1958	46,742	41,199	53.2	1956	59,862	38,541	60.8
1962	64,018	42,743	60.0	1960	67,501	57,177	54.1
1966	57,525	42,063	57.8	1964	50,243	78,287	39.1
1970	46,202	58,580	44.1	1968	69,646	57,634	54.7
1974	51,740	63,768	44.8	1972	99,684	56,784	63.7
1978	74,446	53,394	58.2	1976	85,628	79,838	51.7
1982	93,023	57,019	62.0	1980	100,536	59,120	63.0
1986	83,492	55,729	60.0	1984	130,119	74,568	63.6
1990	57,783	81,715	41.4	1988	127,563	82,472	60.7
1994	87,327	55,180	61.3	1992	94,584	97,702	49.2
1998	93,697	39,210	70.5	1996	94,899	103,313	47.9
Mean			56.9	Mean			57.3
Classification: Moderately Republican				Classification: Strongly Republican			

Table A.10 Butler County

	Gubernatorial elections				Presidential elections		
Year	Rep.	Dem.	% Rep.	Year	Rep.	Dem.	% Rep.
1902	5645	5068	52.7	1900	6303	4465	58.5
1906	3893	3171	55.1	1904	6596	3183	67.4
1910	2726	813	74.2	1908	6584	4698	58.3
1914	3660	4779	43.4	1912	1273	4022	24.0
1918	4219	2053	40.2	1916	5458	4544	54.6
1922	6351	4955	56.2	1920	10,467	3829	73.2
1926	7467	2196	77.3	1924	13,113	3462	79.1
1930	10,720	5318	66.8	1928	19,880	6283	76.0
1934	10,954	12,074	47.6	1932	11,543	8717	57.0
1938	17,669	10,797	62.1	1936	16,772	16,008	51.2
1942	12,583	7210	63.6	1940	19,450	13,875	58.4
1946	16,368	7271	69.2	1944	19,341	12,377	61.0
1950	16,225	9442	63.2	1948	17,449	9815	64.0
1954	16,162	14,564	52.6	1952	25,243	15,295	62.3
1958	20,489	14,345	58.8	1956	26,238	13,672	65.7
1962	25,432	14,469	63.7	1960	28,348	17,805	61.4
1966	21,784	15,281	58.8	1964	17,360	27,267	38.9
1970	13,670	19,299	41.5	1968	21,618	19,415	52.7
1974	19,117	16,577	53.6	1972	29,665	14,695	66.9
1978	17,003	23,027	42.5	1976	26,366	22,611	53.8
1982	24,489	21,029	53.8	1980	28,821	19,711	59.4
1986	19,750	17,697	52.7	1984	31,676	24,735	56.2
1990	12,715	25,329	33.4	1988	27,777	22,341	55.4
1994	21,746	13,514	61.7	1992	23,656	22,303	51.5
1998	22,839	10,593	68.3	1996	32,038	21,990	59.3
Mean			57.2	Mean			58.0
Classification: Moderately Republican				Classification: Strongly Republican			

Table A.11 Cambria County

Gubernatorial elections				Presidential elections			
Year	Rep.	Dem.	% Rep.	Year	Rep.	Dem.	% Rep.
1902	8909	8492	51.2	1900	10,476	7168	59.4
1906	8129	6948	53.9	1904	13,109	7223	64.5
1910	5829	1259	82.3	1908	12,325	7979	60.7
1914	9182	9912	48.1	1912	3252	7282	30.9
1918	8343	6054	57.9	1916	10,688	9416	53.2
1922	15,175	11,804	56.2	1920	19,629	6961	73.8
1926	17,169	11,812	59.2	1924	24,728	13,563	64.6
1930	20,592	16,835	55.0	1928	29,494	27,024	52.2
1934	20,140	32.337	38.4	1932	21,351	28,197	43.1
1938	36,834	36,644	50.1	1936	24,378	46,687	34.3
1942	22,120	23,127	48.9	1940	30,306	42,894	41.4
1946	28,265	27,737	50.5	1944	28,203	39,676	41.5
1950	34,245	40,532	45.8	1948	27,725	41,533	40.0
1954	29,477	49,551	37.3	1952	39,294	50,774	43.6
1958	31,329	46,613	40.2	1956	46,373	41,753	52.6
1962	44,204	36,802	54.6	1960	37,062	52,409	41.4
1966	36,847	34,318	51.8	1964	26,281	55,183	32.3
1970	26,184	37,889	40.9	1968	33,280	41,225	44.7
1974	26,946	34,017	44.2	1972	43,825	27,950	61.1
1978	22,427	37,771	37.3	1976	32,469	38,797	45.6
1982	27,539	33,992	44.8	1980	33,072	36,121	47.8
1986	17,158	39,239	30.4	1984	32,173	39,865	44.7
1990	10,104	40,331	20.0	1988	25,626	38,517	40.0
1994	13,944	31,043	31.0	1992	20,770	34,334	37.7
1998	22,266	12,675	63.7	1996	20,341	30,391	40.1
Mean			48.1	Mean			47.1
Classification:				Classification:			
Became More Democratic				Became More Democratic			

Table A.12 Cameron County

Gubernatorial elections				Presidential elections			
Year	Rep.	Dem.	% Rep.	Year	Rep.	Dem.	% Rep.
1902	802	718	52.8	1900	971	514	65.4
1906	822	692	54.3	1904	1228	404	75.2
1910	576	148	79.5	1908	1110	533	67.5
1914	670	472	58.7	1912	388	291	57.1
1918	621	238	72.3	1916	713	452	61.2
1922	967	564	63.2	1920	1364	497	73.3
1926	1175	248	82.6	1924	1366	260	84.0
1930	1144	354	76.4	1928	1564	501	75.7
1934	1493	941	61.3	1932	1438	748	65.8
1938	1994	1007	66.4	1936	1801	1538	53.9
1942	1078	558	65.9	1940	1793	1450	55.3
1946	1528	567	72.9	1944	1729	1115	60.8
1950	1422	879	61.8	1948	1596	858	65.0
1954	1433	1120	56.1	1952	2307	1020	69.3
1958	1748	1097	61.4	1956	2462	841	74.5
1962	2133	1140	65.2	1960	2129	1353	61.7
1966	1695	988	63.2	1964	1376	1904	42.0
1970	1216	1228	49.8	1968	1822	1104	62.3
1974	1447	983	59.5	1972	1935	828	70.0
1978	1377	982	58.4	1976	1616	1319	55.1
1982	1353	1239	52.2	1980	1795	1112	61.7
1986	1245	1109	59.9	1984	2031	990	67.2
1990	721	1314	35.4	1988	1731	901	65.8
1994	748	550	57.6	1992	1173	824	58.7
1998	688	266	72.1	1996	1113	822	57.5
Mean			62.2	Mean			63.9
Classification: Strongly Republican				Classification: Strongly Republican			

Table A.13 Carbon County

	Gubernatorial elections				Presidential elections		
Year	Rep.	Dem.	% Rep.	Year	Rep.	Dem.	% Rep.
1902	2741	3406	44.6	1900	4222	4149	50.4
1906	2288	4168	40.9	1904	4505	2994	60.1
1910	2036	2004	50.4	1908	4486	3890	53.5
1914	3438	3977	46.4	1912	1246	3652	25.4
1918	3126	3203	49.4	1916	4275	4099	51.0
1922	5621	7576	42.6	1920	7900	5030	63.8
1926	8443	5721	59.9	1924	10,236	5150	66.5
1930	9015	7477	54.7	1928	15,047	8010	65.3
1934	7983	10,464	43.2	1932	9918	9874	50.1
1938	13,278	10,980	54.7	1936	11,298	14,179	44.3
1942	7694	7235	51.5	1940	10,618	12,777	45.4
1946	9260	8225	52.9	1944	9837	11,060	47.1
1950	9043	9949	47.6	1948	9744	9438	50.8
1954	9283	10,644	46.6	1952	12,283	10,571	53.7
1958	10,583	11,281	48.4	1956	13,150	9722	57.5
1962	12,317	10,269	54.5	1960	12,856	12,391	50.9
1966	10,404	9416	52.5	1964	7309	15,416	32.2
1970	7797	10,475	42.7	1968	9954	10,634	48.3
1974	7408	9038	45.0	1972	11,639	7774	60.0
1978	8862	7180	55.2	1976	8883	10,791	45.2
1982	7107	9816	42.0	1980	10,042	8009	55.6
1986	6617	8839	42.8	1984	10,701	8836	54.8
1990	4169	9773	29.9	1988	10,232	9104	52.9
1994	7533	6626	53.2	1992	7243	9072	44.4
1998	7503	5246	58.9	1996	7193	9457	43.2
Mean			48.4	Mean			50.3
Classification: Competitive				Classification: Competitive			

Table A.14 Centre County

	Gubernatorial elections				Presidential elections		
Year	Rep.	Dem.	% Rep.	Year	Rep.	Dem.	% Rep.
1902	4181	4574	47.8	1900	4684	4339	51.9
1906	3569	3755	48.7	1904	5291	4015	56.9
1910	2199	911	70.7	1908	4927	3998	55.2
1914	3569	3810	48.4	1912	1507	3445	30.4
1918	3998	2302	63.5	1916	4392	4120	51.6
1922	5180	5945	46.6	1920	7615	4783	61.4
1926	6647	2547	72.3	1924	7723	4443	63.5
1930	8310	5085	62.0	1928	12,005	3431	77.8
1934	8319	9221	47.4	1932	8264	7053	54.0
1938	11,943	9547	55.6	1936	9869	11,734	45.7
1942	7767	5808	57.2	1940	10,665	9869	51.9
1946	8635	5634	60.5	1944	10,048	8064	55.5
1950	6705	4453	60.1	1948	10,416	6515	61.5
1954	9442	9164	50.7	1952	14,700	7391	66.5
1958	11,493	8815	56.6	1956	15,412	7483	67.3
1962	16,698	8086	67.4	1960	18,357	8601	68.1
1966	14,289	9176	60.9	1964	9481	16,556	36.4
1970	11,448	11,762	49.3	1968	15,865	11,163	58.7
1974	12,950	12,891	50.1	1972	20,683	13,194	61.1
1978	18,529	11,343	62.0	1976	21,177	17,867	54.2
1982	19,117	12,610	60.3	1980	20,605	15,987	56.3
1986	17,294	13,029	57.0	1984	27,802	16,194	63.2
1990	11,925	17,442	40.6	1988	23,875	18,357	56.5
1994	17,087	12,569	57.6	1992	20,478	21,177	49.2
1998	20,175	7295	73.4	1996	20,935	21,145	49.8
Mean			57.2	Mean			55.7
Classification: Moderately Republican				Classification: Strongly Republican			

Table A.15 Chester County

Gubernatorial elections				Presidential elections			
Year	Rep.	Dem.	% Rep.	Year	Rep.	Dem.	% Rep.
1902	8591	7205	54.4	1900	13,809	6214	69.0
1906	8067	8420	48.9	1904	14,200	4330	76.6
1910	5498	1449	79.1	1908	13,118	6555	66.7
1914	8704	7669	53.2	1912	5708	6901	45.3
1918	9279	2971	75.7	1916	11,845	8514	58.2
1922	12,351	10,738	53.5	1920	18,129	7004	72.1
1926	17,426	3749	82.3	1924	22,333	5946	78.9
1930	18,820	12,767	59.6	1928	36,659	7689	82.7
1934	25,000	17,878	58.3	1932	29,425	12,040	71.0
1938	31,547	18,181	63.4	1936	29,340	26,676	52.4
1942	20,847	9849	67.9	1940	28,222	22,473	55.7
1946	25,292	9565	72.5	1944	26,655	18,548	59.0
1950	27,247	16,508	62.3	1948	29,258	14,670	66.6
1954	29,960	19,900	60.1	1952	39,961	21,490	65.0
1958	38,017	23,763	61.5	1956	47,225	19,957	70.3
1962	50,804	24,412	67.5	1960	53,059	30,167	63.8
1966	49,920	23,919	67.6	1964	40,280	47,940	45.7
1970	39,723	35,282	53.0	1968	56,073	32,606	63.2
1974	42,948	35,835	54.5	1972	72,726	31,118	70.0
1978	58,481	25,935	69.3	1976	67,686	42,712	61.3
1982	61,616	28,111	68.7	1980	73,046	34,307	68.0
1986	58,518	28,572	67.2	1984	92,221	38,870	70.3
1990	44,262	48,935	47.5	1988	93,522	44,853	67.6
1994	61,890	34,652	64.1	1992	74,002	59,643	55.4
1998	68,572	21,337	76.3	1996	77,029	64,783	54.3
Mean			63.8	Mean			63.7
Classification: Strongly Republican				Classification: Strongly Republican			

Table A.16 Clarion County

	Gubernatorial elections				Presidential elections		
Year	Rep.	Dem.	% Rep.	Year	Rep.	Dem.	% Rep.
1902	2149	3268	39.7	1900	3002	3472	46.4
1906	1740	2506	41.0	1904	2978	2463	54.7
1910	1183	1174	50.2	1908	2915	3291	47.0
1914	1944	3159	38.1	1912	916	3079	22.9
1918	2041	1565	56.6	1916	2595	3269	44.2
1922	2865	4350	39.7	1920	4615	3487	57.0
1926	4541	2723	62.5	1924	5913	3642	61.9
1930	6178	4107	60.1	1928	9183	3746	71.0
1934	5925	7247	45.0	1932	5991	6651	47.4
1938	8915	6303	58.6	1936	8477	8412	50.2
1942	5487	4029	57.7	1940	9035	6564	57.9
1946	6372	3688	63.3	1944	7708	5253	59.5
1950	6224	5578	52.7	1948	6866	4984	57.9
1954	6051	6041	50.0	1952	9340	5212	64.2
1958	8420	5081	62.4	1956	10,048	4955	67.0
1962	9768	5464	64.1	1960	10,307	5506	65.2
1966	7851	5321	59.6	1964	6143	9235	39.9
1970	5579	6006	48.2	1968	8077	5341	60.2
1974	6792	5303	56.2	1972	10,073	4509	69.1
1978	5677	6833	45.4	1976	8360	6585	55.9
1982	6515	6119	51.6	1980	8812	5472	61.7
1986	6464	6022	51.8	1984	9836	5407	64.5
1990	3811	7235	34.5	1988	8026	5616	58.8
1994	6724	4029	62.5	1992	6477	5584	53.7
1998	5861	2112	73.5	1996	6916	5954	53.7
Mean			53.0	Mean			55.2
Classification: Moderately Republican				Classification: Moderately Republican			

Table A.17 Clearfield County

Gubernatorial elections				Presidential elections			
Year	Rep.	Dem.	% Rep.	Year	Rep.	Dem.	% Rep.
1902	6418	5891	52.1	1900	7955	6066	56.7
1906	4983	5911	45.7	1904	9541	4280	69.0
1910	2755	1043	72.5	1908	7726	4954	60.9
1914	4330	6316	40.7	1912	1523	4670	24.6
1918	5128	3617	58.6	1916	5676	6180	47.9
1922	7348	6911	51.5	1920	9615	5987	61.6
1926	10,001	3802	72.4	1924	13,745	5027	73.2
1930	12,808	5907	68.4	1928	16,719	7870	68.0
1934	11,776	15,203	43.6	1932	10,500	11,209	48.4
1938	17,962	16,981	51.4	1936	14,531	20,799	41.1
1942	10,330	9722	51.5	1940	15,407	17,705	46.5
1946	11,651	9702	54.6	1944	13,986	13,617	50.7
1950	11,969	11,964	50.0	1948	11,810	11,347	51.0
1954	11,570	14,485	44.4	1952	16,045	13,376	54.5
1958	14,900	13,757	52.0	1956	17,519	12,852	57.7
1962	17,740	12,745	58.2	1960	18,911	14,212	57.1
1966	114,984	12,309	54.9	1964	11,338	19,211	37.1
1970	10,666	13,502	44.1	1968	14,471	12,369	53.9
1974	11,297	11,301	50.0	1972	16,780	9246	64.5
1978	10,989	12,619	46.5	1976	13,626	13,714	49.8
1982	10,983	12,517	46.7	1980	15,299	11,647	56.8
1986	10,030	13,316	43.0	1984	18,653	11,963	60.9
1990	5793	16,464	26.0	1988	14,296	12,235	53.9
1994	11,713	8432	58.1	1992	11,553	12,247	48.5
1998	11,437	5598	67.1	1996	12,987	11,991	52.0
Mean			52.3	Mean			53.0
Classification: Moderately Republican				Classification: Moderately Republican			

Table A.18 Clinton County

Gubernatorial elections				Presidential elections			
Year	Rep.	Dem.	% Rep.	Year	Rep.	Dem.	% Rep.
1902	2602	3077	45.8	1900	3157	2879	52.3
1906	2541	2979	46.0	1904	3575	1941	64.8
1910	1201	656	64.7	1908	3477	2547	57.7
1914	2646	2531	51.1	1912	1214	2200	35.5
1918	2392	1494	61.5	1916	2794	2967	48.5
1922	2753	3268	45.7	1920	4303	2976	59.1
1926	4019	1902	67.9	1924	5129	1939	72.6
1930	4547	3567	56.0	1928	8120	2849	74.0
1934	5443	5427	50.1	1932	4851	3741	56.4
1938	8118	6472	55.6	1936	6479	8351	43.7
1942	4729	3709	56.0	1940	6291	7419	45.9
1946	5652	3580	61.2	1944	5915	5703	50.9
1950	5607	5143	52.1	1948	5618	5013	52.8
1954	5222	6062	46.3	1952	8125	5758	58.5
1958	6284	5664	52.6	1956	8250	5411	60.4
1962	8157	5607	59.3	1960	9184	5965	60.6
1966	6565	5022	56.7	1964	4298	10,038	30.0
1970	4349	6534	40.0	1968	6563	6301	51.0
1974	4350	5554	43.9	1972	8205	4772	63.2
1978	5563	3703	60.0	1976	5858	6532	47.3
1982	4227	5629	42.9	1980	6288	4842	56.5
1986	4196	4373	49.0	1984	6678	4525	59.6
1990	2832	6796	29.4	1988	5735	5759	49.9
1994	4895	4084	54.5	1992	4471	5397	45.3
1998	5348	2656	66.8	1996	4293	5658	43.1
Mean			52.7	Mean			53.0
Classification: Moderately Republican				Classification: Moderately Republican			

Table A.19 Columbia County

Gubernatorial elections				Presidential elections			
Year	Rep.	Dem.	% Rep.	Year	Rep.	Dem.	% Rep.
1902	2133	4858	30.5	1900	2954	4982	37.2
1906	2826	5401	34.3	1904	3635	4194	46.4
1910	1353	1513	47.2	1908	3718	5373	40.9
1914	1994	5426	26.9	1912	889	4905	15.3
1918	2879	3772	43.3	1916	3013	5785	34.2
1922	3813	6531	36.9	1920	6238	6965	47.2
1926	5997	4022	59.8	1924	7336	7390	49.8
1930	8309	6652	55.5	1928	14,362	5304	73.0
1934	7685	12,003	39.0	1932	8791	10,640	45.2
1938	11,617	10,566	52.4	1936	9674	14,141	40.6
1942	6477	7312	47.0	1940	9518	12,523	43.2
1946	8063	7298	52.5	1944	9336	9647	49.2
1950	8736	9629	47.6	1948	9417	9367	50.1
1954	7998	10,823	42.5	1952	13,008	9467	57.9
1958	10,637	10,126	51.2	1956	13,382	9024	59.7
1962	13,891	9221	60.1	1960	15,310	9322	62.2
1966	11,654	7941	59.5	1964	8982	13,885	39.3
1970	8976	7983	52.9	1968	12,202	8187	59.8
1974	8615	8846	49.3	1972	14,187	7222	66.3
1978	10,907	8122	57.3	1976	11,508	12,051	48.8
1982	9108	10,164	47.3	1980	12,426	9449	56.8
1986	7709	9069	45.9	1984	14,402	8254	63.6
1990	4436	9447	32.0	1988	12,114	7767	60.9
1994	8274	5980	58.0	1992	9742	8261	54.1
1998	8720	4175	67.6	1996	8234	8379	49.6
Mean			47.8	Mean			49.6
Classification: Competitive				Classification: Became More Republican			

Table A.20 Crawford County

	Gubernatorial elections				Presidential elections		
Year	Rep.	Dem.	% Rep.	Year	Rep.	Dem.	% Rep.
1902	6468	6153	51.2	1900	7705	7000	52.4
1906	5459	3583	60.4	1904	7450	3639	67.2
1910	4500	1229	78.6	1908	7679	5668	57.5
1914	4126	5241	44.0	1912	2497	3968	38.6
1918	4592	2843	61.8	1916	5487	5814	48.5
1922	5953	6204	49.0	1920	10,032	4175	70.6
1926	5931	2165	73.2	1924	10,918	2969	78.6
1930	9896	5959	62.4	1928	17,072	6718	71.8
1934	10,616	9377	53.1	1932	10,918	9382	53.8
1938	14,847	8749	65.7	1936	14,463	12,788	53.1
1942	9638	4703	67.2	1940	15,891	10,197	60.9
1946	12,794	5321	70.6	1944	15,205	9216	62.3
1950	13,165	9140	59.0	1948	14,161	9174	60.7
1954	12,322	10,536	53.9	1952	19,079	9874	65.9
1958	13,655	10,749	56.0	1956	18,887	9346	66.9
1962	16,449	9669	63.0	1960	18,754	12,050	60.9
1966	15,671	9703	61.8	1964	10,664	18,212	36.9
1970	10,043	11,885	45.8	1968	14,991	11,345	56.9
1974	12,830	8701	59.6	1972	18,393	9371	66.2
1978	13,214	10,185	56.5	1976	15,301	14,712	51.0
1982	14,654	11,511	56.0	1980	16,552	11,778	58.4
1986	12,546	10,859	53.6	1984	20,181	12,792	61.2
1990	8056	16,154	33.3	1988	17,249	13,021	57.0
1994	19,508	5689	77.4	1992	14,112	12,813	52.4
1998	13,875	4786	74.4	1996	14,659	12,943	53.1
Mean			59.7	Mean			57.9
Classification: Strongly Republican				Classification: Strongly Republican			

Table A.21 Cumberland County

| \multicolumn{4}{c}{Gubernatorial elections} | \multicolumn{4}{c}{Presidential elections} |

Year	Rep.	Dem.	% Rep.	Year	Rep.	Dem.	% Rep.
1902	4783	5885	44.8	1900	5587	5428	50.7
1906	4605	4905	48.4	1904	7138	5033	58.6
1910	3658	1096	76.9	1908	6261	5403	53.7
1914	5468	5695	49.0	1912	2566	5023	33.8
1918	1076	2783	27.9	1916	5296	6432	45.1
1922	6944	11,421	38.0	1920	8579	6455	57.1
1926	9699	4102	70.3	1924	10,196	7643	57.2
1930	16,289	8149	66.7	1928	19,170	5189	78.7
1934	14,099	15,850	47.1	1932	13,098	12,086	52.0
1938	16,769	15,273	52.3	1936	14,912	18,850	44.2
1942	12,750	8178	60.9	1940	15,297	15,758	49.2
1946	15,404	9541	61.7	1944	17,782	12,068	59.6
1950	16,271	13,173	55.3	1948	18,028	11,421	61.1
1954	17,836	16,242	52.3	1952	26,302	12,762	67.3
1958	23,078	16,891	57.7	1956	29,468	13,651	68.3
1962	31,052	15,516	66.7	1960	35,636	15,968	69.1
1966	28,396	13,796	67.3	1964	23,685	26,663	47.6
1970	22,970	18,778	55.0	1968	32,908	15,467	68.0
1974	24,047	20,863	53.5	1972	42,099	14,562	74.3
1978	35,311	14,798	70.5	1976	39,950	23,008	63.5
1982	32,743	21,931	59.9	1980	41,152	19,789	67.5
1986	33,285	19,591	62.9	1984	49,282	21,374	69.7
1990	16,692	32,487	33.9	1988	47,292	24,613	65.8
1994	32,903	19,003	63.4	1992	43,447	26,635	62.0
1998	37,801	8610	81.4	1996	43,943	28,749	60.5
Mean			57.2	Mean			59.0

Classification: Moderately Republican

Classification: Strongly Republican

Table A.22 Dauphin County

	Gubernatorial elections				Presidential elections		
Year	Rep.	Dem.	% Rep.	Year	Rep.	Dem.	% Rep.
1902	10,219	8448	54.7	1900	14,673	7390	66.5
1906	10,652	9295	53.4	1904	16,508	5026	76.7
1910	9197	1110	89.2	1908	15,637	7546	67.4
1914	14,519	10,243	58.6	1912	6012	7470	44.6
1918	13,746	5175	72.6	1916	13,954	11,483	54.8
1922	17,958	17,221	51.0	1920	26,094	11,990	68.5
1926	25632	6260	80.4	1924	27,838	9004	75.6
1930	36,362	10,679	77.3	1928	49,108	9115	84.3
1934	40,121	26,056	60.6	1932	36,278	22,412	61.8
1938	46,815	36,941	55.9	1936	39,598	43,256	47.8
1942	37,206	18,614	66.7	1940	42,394	38,305	52.5
1946	43,498	20,986	67.4	1944	44,725	30,684	59.3
1950	44,247	26,826	62.2	1948	46,861	27,729	62.8
1954	42,705	31,822	57.3	1952	58,385	30,985	65.3
1958	46,647	33,483	58.2	1956	61,342	29,226	67.7
1962	56,702	29,420	65.8	1960	61,726	33,962	64.5
1966	49,406	22,953	68.3	1964	42,718	46,119	48.1
1970	35,515	27,021	56.8	1968	48,394	25,480	65.5
1974	30,337	31,885	48.8	1972	54,307	22,587	70.6
1978	42,546	21,426	66.5	1976	46,819	34,342	57.7
1982	32,796	37,538	46.6	1980	44,039	27,252	61.8
1986	37,641	29,116	56.4	1984	54,330	33,576	61.8
1990	16,833	43,063	28.1	1988	48,917	35,079	58.2
1994	34,689	27,844	55.5	1992	45,479	36,990	55.1
1998	39,914	13,203	75.1	1996	44,417	40,936	52.0
Mean			61.3	Mean			61.3
Classification: Strongly Republican				Classification: Strongly Republican			

Table A.23 Delaware County

Gubernatorial elections				Presidential elections			
Year	Rep.	Dem.	% Rep.	Year	Rep.	Dem.	% Rep.
1902	9539	5435	63.7	1900	13,794	4249	76.4
1906	9111	7357	55.3	1904	15,032	3562	80.8
1910	7158	993	87.8	1908	15,184	5727	72.6
1914	14,110	5876	70.6	1912	8416	6001	58.4
1918	14,721	4196	77.8	1916	16,315	7742	67.8
1922	19,214	7248	72.6	1920	34,126	9602	78.0
1926	27,555	6036	82.0	1924	41,998	6368	86.8
1930	39,133	37,680	52.3	1928	83,092	29,378	73.9
1934	61,576	43,130	58.8	1932	75,291	32,412	69.9
1938	85,727	40,091	68.1	1936	74,898	65,117	53.5
1942	56,547	26,592	68.0	1940	80,158	60,225	57.1
1946	81,930	31,748	72.1	1944	78,533	64,021	55.1
1950	87,255	59,506	59.4	1948	93,412	57,156	62.0
1954	98,569	68,215	59.1	1952	129,743	80,316	61.8
1958	116,227	78,568	59.7	1956	143,663	82,024	63.4
1962	142,262	84,221	62.8	1960	135,672	124,629	52.1
1966	140,225	74,418	65.3	1964	111,189	147,189	43.0
1970	111,079	95,419	53.8	1968	133,777	106,695	55.6
1974	104,860	103,276	50.4	1972	175,414	94,144	65.1
1978	125,744	80,468	61.0	1976	148,679	117,252	55.9
1982	127,584	67,874	65.3	1980	143,282	88,314	61.9
1986	113,628	75,218	60.2	1984	161,754	98,207	62.2
1990	76,531	92,865	45.2	1988	147,656	96,144	60.6
1994	91,589	64,065	58.8	1992	108,587	111,210	49.4
1998	97,746	42,283	69.8	1996	92,628	115,946	44.4
Mean			64.4	Mean			62.1
Classification: Strongly Republican				Classification: Strongly Republican			

Table A.24 Elk County

Gubernatorial elections				Presidential elections			
Year	Rep.	Dem.	% Rep.	Year	Rep.	Dem.	% Rep.
1902	1741	3800	31.4	1900	3254	3105	51.2
1906	2569	3921	39.6	1904	3820	2854	57.2
1910	1096	1717	39.0	1908	2991	2531	54.2
1914	3320	1625	67.1	1912	603	2057	22.7
1918	1559	1579	49.7	1916	2829	2186	56.4
1922	4271	1497	74.0	1920	5267	2003	72.4
1926	5308	1011	84.0	1924	6626	1370	82.9
1930	5692	5089	52.8	1928	5234	7705	40.4
1934	5246	8625	37.8	1932	5797	6461	47.3
1938	6805	6506	51.1	1936	5489	9035	37.8
1942	3858	4609	45.6	1940	6949	6920	50.1
1946	5288	4459	54.2	1944	5645	6097	48.1
1950	4886	5575	46.7	1948	5148	5363	48.7
1954	5268	6709	44.0	1952	7702	6448	54.4
1958	6503	6733	49.1	1956	8947	5498	61.9
1962	7858	5695	58.0	1960	7155	8398	46.0
1966	6016	6296	48.9	1964	4354	10,455	29.4
1970	3938	6995	36.0	1968	6193	6886	47.4
1974	5444	4794	53.2	1972	7900	4710	62.6
1978	4781	6893	41.0	1976	6159	6713	47.8
1982	5564	5917	48.5	1980	7175	5898	54.9
1986	4818	7523	39.0	1984	8470	5486	60.7
1990	2575	8757	22.7	1988	6737	5879	53.4
1994	4784	3229	59.7	1992	4908	5016	49.5
1998	4520	2500	64.4	1996	4889	5749	46.0
Mean			50.0	Mean			50.9
Classification: Moderately Democratic				Classification: Competitive			

Table A.25 Erie County

Gubernatorial elections				Presidential elections			
Year	Rep.	Dem.	% Rep.	Year	Rep.	Dem.	% Rep.
1902	8116	6316	56.2	1900	11,816	7281	61.9
1906	6376	4935	56.4	1904	11,951	5103	70.1
1910	5823	2515	69.8	1908	10,828	6173	63.7
1914	7173	7073	50.2	1912	4958	5637	46.8
1918	6784	5314	56.1	1916	8933	9641	48.1
1922	12,977	6132	67.9	1920	19,465	6311	75.5
1926	12,476	2612	82.7	1924	19,480	3502	84.8
1930	12,975	18,919	40.7	1928	30,542	19,278	61.3
1934	17,368	23,761	42.2	1932	18,371	19,592	48.4
1938	34,701	28,438	55.0	1936	25,607	33,042	43.7
1942	19,110	12,771	59.9	1940	36,608	31,735	53.6
1946	27,713	16,978	62.0	1944	35,247	32,912	51.7
1950	31,981	29,772	51.8	1948	33,806	28,159	54.5
1954	30,755	37,417	45.1	1952	48,836	36,619	57.1
1958	39,449	37,837	51.0	1956	54,430	33,802	61.7
1962	48,066	42,766	52.9	1960	51,525	53,723	49.0
1966	41,273	45,598	47.5	1964	31,393	72,944	30.1
1970	32,046	45,977	41.1	1968	43,134	51,604	45.5
1974	38,833	34,576	52.9	1972	61,542	42,022	59.4
1978	41,670	35,899	53.7	1976	49,641	55,385	47.3
1982	45,830	41,439	52.5	1980	48,918	45,946	51.6
1986	37,583	35,727	51.3	1984	55,860	52,471	51.6
1990	20,424	52,265	28.1	1988	48,306	53,913	47.3
1994	65,181	21,422	75.3	1992	39,283	56,381	41.1
1998	49,027	16,783	74.5	1996	39,884	57,508	41.0
Mean			55.7	Mean			53.1
Classification: Moderately Republican				Classification: Competitive			

Table A.26 Fayette County

	Gubernatorial elections				Presidential elections		
Year	Rep.	Dem.	% Rep.	Year	Rep.	Dem.	% Rep.
1902	8758	8296	51.4	1900	9637	7650	55.7
1906	8038	5435	59.7	1904	11,486	6779	62.9
1910	7042	2092	77.1	1908	10,012	8220	54.9
1914	9818	8056	54.9	1912	4168	7363	36.1
1918	9298	5610	62.4	1916	9838	10,416	48.6
1922	11,922	10,978	52.1	1920	20,186	13,358	60.2
1926	14,105	4772	74.7	1924	19,064	8855	68.3
1930	15,875	13,105	54.8	1928	27,693	19,063	59.2
1934	20,401	32,528	38.5	1932	15,903	27,662	36.5
1938	26,245	33,844	43.7	1936	21,984	48,291	31.3
1942	16,714	18,806	47.0	1940	23,908	41,960	36.3
1946	21,356	23,389	47.7	1944	21,945	35,093	38.5
1950	20,986	28,400	42.5	1948	20,401	34,971	36.8
1954	19,408	39,181	33.1	1952	27,348	43,921	38.4
1958	23,053	34,204	40.3	1956	21,857	38,312	36.3
1962	27,577	31,464	46.7	1960	27,120	41,560	39.5
1966	21,809	30,190	41.9	1964	16,127	43,155	27.2
1970	16,109	29,234	35.5	1968	18,921	34,340	35.5
1974	118,084	22,604	44.4	1972	27,288	22,475	54.8
1978	13,843	28,225	32.9	1976	20,021	32,232	38.3
1982	15,791	27,739	36.3	1980	19,252	27,963	40.8
1986	11,704	26,540	30.6	1984	21,314	35,098	37.8
1990	5882	28,719	17.0	1988	16,915	33,098	33.8
1994	12,710	22,497	36.1	1992	12,820	30,577	29.5
1998	13,215	12,863	50.7	1996	14,019	26,359	34.7
Mean			46.5	Mean			42.2
Classification:				Classification:			
Became More Democratic				Became More Democratic			

Table A.27 Forest County

Gubernatorial elections				Presidential elections			
Year	Rep.	Dem.	% Rep.	Year	Rep.	Dem.	% Rep.
1902	1043	807	56.3	1900	1309	714	64.7
1906	1037	633	62.0	1904	1328	410	76.4
1910	511	194	72.5	1908	1119	512	68.6
1914	478	576	45.3	1912	240	373	39.2
1918	530	236	69.2	1916	617	463	57.1
1922	804	496	61.8	1920	993	389	71.8
1926	647	132	83.0	1924	1130	280	80.1
1930	1135	300	79.1	1928	1707	289	85.5
1934	1368	1020	57.3	1932	1090	569	65.7
1938	1819	1104	62.2	1936	1757	1157	60.3
1942	1103	664	62.4	1940	1811	919	66.3
1946	1203	607	66.5	1944	1344	673	66.6
1950	1188	723	62.2	1948	1209	687	63.8
1954	1004	834	54.6	1952	1511	627	70.7
1958	1348	814	62.3	1956	1535	622	71.2
1962	1420	852	62.5	1960	1497	828	64.4
1966	1136	607	65.2	1964	900	1249	41.9
1970	880	728	54.7	1968	1172	669	63.7
1974	979	755	56.5	1972	1374	509	73.0
1978	974	972	50.1	1976	1135	1017	52.7
1982	1050	810	56.5	1980	1209	819	59.6
1986	966	813	54.3	1984	1468	839	63.6
1990	595	1104	35.0	1988	1159	895	56.4
1994	1197	480	71.4	1992	801	890	47.4
1998	987	375	72.5	1996	902	964	48.3
Mean			61.7	Mean			62.4
Classification: Strongly Republican				Classification: Strongly Republican			

Table A.28 Franklin County

Gubernatorial elections				Presidential elections			
Year	Rep.	Dem.	% Rep.	Year	Rep.	Dem.	% Rep.
1902	5757	5441	51.4	1900	6483	4500	59.0
1906	4411	5088	46.4	1904	7062	4110	63.2
1910	3373	1239	73.1	1908	6938	4682	59.7
1914	4334	5324	44.9	1912	2710	4505	37.6
1918	4662	2697	63.3	1916	5674	5336	51.5
1922	5618	7522	42.7	1920	8376	5020	62.5
1926	7113	2524	73.8	1924	9791	5770	62.9
1930	10,671	5329	66.7	1928	16,345	3027	84.4
1934	10,255	10,614	49.1	1932	10,992	9338	54.1
1938	14,189	12,155	53.9	1936	13,616	15,632	46.5
1942	9411	5831	61.7	1940	13,084	12,713	50.7
1946	10,702	6664	61.6	1944	13,380	8807	60.3
1950	11,267	7682	59.4	1948	12,151	7352	62.3
1954	10,956	9804	52.8	1952	16,474	8808	65.2
1958	15,150	12,910	54.0	1956	19,121	11,060	63.4
1962	18,640	11,581	61.7	1960	22,010	12,088	64.5
1966	17,566	11,024	61.4	1964	13,525	19,332	41.2
1970	12,986	11,972	52.0	1968	19,146	11,451	62.6
1974	12,377	12,261	50.2	1972	24,093	9456	71.8
1978	17,323	9014	65.8	1976	20,009	14,643	57.7
1982	16,552	11,496	59.0	1980	22,716	12,061	65.3
1986	14,750	9429	61.0	1984	27,243	11,480	70.4
1990	8461	15,126	35.9	1988	27,086	12,368	68.6
1994	20,001	10,016	66.6	1992	23,387	13,440	63.5
1998	21,793	6527	77.0	1996	25,392	14,980	62.9
Mean			57.8	Mean			60.0
Classification: Strongly Republican				Classification: Strongly Republican			

Table A.29 Fulton County

	Gubernatorial elections				Presidential elections		
Year	Rep.	Dem.	% Rep.	Year	Rep.	Dem.	% Rep.
1902	806	1117	41.9	1900	1029	1224	45.7
1906	683	1043	39.7	1904	1100	1136	49.2
1910	622	606	50.7	1908	974	1098	47.0
1914	703	1141	38.1	1912	317	1080	22.7
1918	789	775	50.4	1916	802	1196	40.1
1922	933	2068	31.1	1920	1292	1231	51.2
1926	1301	1113	53.9	1924	1160	1207	49.0
1930	2018	1318	60.5	1928	2179	1054	67.5
1934	1924	2147	47.3	1932	1410	1921	42.3
1938	2372	2091	53.1	1936	2085	2431	46.2
1942	1560	1488	51.2	1940	2108	1982	51.5
1946	1742	1838	48.6	1944	2083	1758	54.2
1950	1623	1894	46.1	1948	1760	1684	51.5
1954	1458	2132	40.6	1952	2127	1718	55.3
1958	2038	2144	48.7	1956	2370	1819	56.6
1962	2478	1845	57.3	1960	2698	1672	61.7
1966	2958	1755	54.0	1964	1747	2180	44.5
1970	1783	1825	49.4	1968	2200	1174	58.3
1974	1576	1603	49.6	1972	2515	1192	67.8
1978	1827	1458	55.6	1976	2219	1737	56.1
1982	1794	1753	50.6	1980	2740	1342	67.1
1986	1794	1618	52.5	1984	3254	1309	71.3
1990	1173	1939	37.7	1988	3086	1532	66.8
1994	2319	1316	63.8	1992	2558	1588	61.7
1998	2210	885	71.4	1996	2665	1620	62.2
Mean			49.5	Mean			53.4
Classification:				Classification:			
Competitive				Became More Republican			

Table A.30 Greene County

Gubernatorial elections				Presidential elections			
Year	Rep.	Dem.	% Rep.	Year	Rep.	Dem.	% Rep.
1902	1859	3562	34.3	1900	2427	3674	39.8
1906	2111	2804	42.9	1904	2442	3197	43.3
1910	1401	1320	51.5	1908	2438	3793	39.1
1914	1549	3334	31.7	1912	1150	3551	24.5
1918	2021	2682	43.0	1916	2096	3936	34.7
1922	2457	4907	33.4	1920	4253	5592	43.2
1926	3598	2535	58.7	1924	4590	5874	43.9
1930	4800	4563	51.3	1928	6900	5293	56.7
1934	5186	9257	35.9	1932	4808	9326	34.0
1938	7586	8533	47.1	1936	6359	12,006	34.6
1942	5094	5673	47.3	1940	6726	10,214	39.7
1946	4540	5742	44.1	1944	5747	8392	40.6
1950	4503	7516	37.5	1948	4717	8015	37.0
1954	4662	10,896	30.0	1952	6964	10,125	40.7
1958	6496	8338	43.8	1956	7562	9827	43.5
1962	7615	8719	46.6	1960	7498	9645	43.7
1966	5731	7350	43.8	1964	3896	11,412	34.1
1970	3496	7228	32.6	1968	5099	8198	38.3
1974	5448	5588	49.4	1972	7790	5562	58.3
1978	4029	7215	35.8	1976	5293	8769	37.6
1982	4557	7463	37.9	1980	5336	8193	39.4
1986	3748	7476	33.4	1984	6376	9365	40.5
1990	2157	7998	21.2	1988	4879	9126	34.8
1994	4314	6167	41.2	1992	3482	8438	29.2
1998	4211	3900	51.9	1996	4002	7620	34.4
Mean			41.3	Mean			39.0
Classification: Strongly Democratic				Classification: Strongly Democratic			

Table A.31 Huntingdon County

Gubernatorial elections				Presidential elections			
Year	Rep.	Dem.	% Rep.	Year	Rep.	Dem.	% Rep.
1902	3577	2394	59.9	1900	4645	1989	70.0
1906	2769	2211	55.6	1904	4587	1318	77.7
1910	1598	290	84.6	1908	4503	1917	70.1
1914	3085	2576	54.5	1912	903	1538	37.0
1918	3371	1006	77.0	1916	3806	2181	63.6
1922	3176	3542	47.3	1920	5233	1784	74.6
1926	4598	1041	81.5	1924	6567	1488	81.5
1930	7573	1802	80.8	1928	9920	1470	87.1
1934	7792	4546	63.1	1932	7371	3426	68.3
1938	10,416	5409	65.8	1936	9815	7429	56.9
1942	5855	3035	65.9	1940	9141	5631	61.9
1946	6320	2781	69.4	1944	8106	4131	66.2
1950	6898	4087	62.8	1948	6943	3304	67.7
1954	6654	5583	54.4	1952	9580	4318	68.9
1958	7688	5226	59.5	1956	9698	4618	67.7
1962	9675	5096	65.5	1960	11,116	4710	70.2
1966	7521	4248	63.9	1964	6571	7435	46.9
1970	6036	4810	55.7	1968	8276	4128	66.7
1974	6338	4448	58.8	1972	9606	3394	73.9
1978	6781	4224	61.6	1976	7843	5410	59.2
1982	7287	4659	61.0	1980	8140	5094	61.5
1986	6348	4974	56.1	1984	10,220	4430	69.8
1990	3490	6656	34.4	1988	8800	4752	64.9
1994	6530	3636	64.2	1992	7249	5153	58.5
1998	6253	1936	76.4	1996	7324	5285	58.1
Mean			63.0	Mean			65.2
Classification: Strongly Republican				Classification: Strongly Republican			

Table A.32 Indiana County

	Gubernatorial elections				Presidential elections		
Year	Rep.	Dem.	% Rep.	Year	Rep.	Dem.	% Rep.
1902	4244	2582	62.2	1900	5687	1767	76.3
1906	3800	1706	69.0	1904	6878	1544	81.7
1910	2719	407	87.0	1908	6416	1965	76.5
1914	3467	2840	55.0	1912	1720	1593	51.9
1918	4334	1021	80.9	1916	4887	2398	67.1
1922	4985	3963	55.7	1920	8616	1936	81.6
1926	9100	1084	89.3	1924	12,748	2067	86.0
1930	13,906	3793	78.6	1928	16,706	4810	77.6
1934	10,949	9730	52.9	1932	12,727	8606	59.6
1938	16,401	11,048	59.8	1936	16,530	15,353	51.8
1942	10,080	6756	59.9	1940	15,547	12,035	56.4
1946	11,494	6042	65.5	1944	14,388	8863	61.9
1950	13,022	10,140	56.2	1948	12,640	8543	59.7
1954	12,267	11,818	50.9	1952	16,673	11,620	58.9
1958	15,876	12,234	56.5	1956	18,593	11,268	62.3
1962	18,763	11,870	61.3	1960	18,756	13,174	58.7
1966	15,063	10,411	59.1	1964	11,706	17,568	40.0
1970	10,941	12,598	46.5	1968	14,899	12,175	55.1
1974	12,473	11,990	51.0	1972	18,122	10,833	62.6
1978	11,986	11,911	50.2	1976	15,786	14,650	51.9
1982	14,191	12,761	52.7	1980	15,607	13,828	53.0
1986	10,911	13,369	44.9	1984	18,845	15,791	54.4
1990	6622	15,692	29.7	1988	14,983	16,514	47.6
1994	11,087	10,368	51.7	1992	10,966	15,194	41.9
1998	11,733	6910	62.9	1996	12,874	13,868	48.1
Mean			60.0	Mean			60.0
Classification: Strongly Republican				Classification: Strongly Republican			

Table A.33 Jefferson County

	Gubernatorial elections				Presidential elections		
Year	Rep.	Dem.	% Rep.	Year	Rep.	Dem.	% Rep.
1902	3981	3413	53.8	1900	5950	2663	69.1
1906	3862	3066	55.7	1904	5860	2076	73.8
1910	2814	562	83.4	1908	5652	2986	65.4
1914	3042	4191	42.0	1912	1608	2510	39.0
1918	3578	1385	72.1	1916	4332	3253	57.1
1922	5139	4561	53.0	1920	7970	3000	72.6
1926	8217	2256	78.4	1924	10,673	2664	80.0
1930	10,141	3549	74.1	1928	13,233	4325	75.4
1934	8196	8753	48.3	1932	8246	6570	55.6
1938	12,697	8313	60.4	1936	11,943	11,080	51.9
1942	7571	4520	62.6	1940	12,081	8559	58.5
1946	9149	4135	68.9	1944	10,970	6425	63.1
1950	8603	5471	61.1	1948	9395	5632	62.5
1954	8711	6983	55.5	1952	11,833	6365	65.0
1958	11,329	7637	59.7	1956	13,051	6629	66.3
1962	12,948	7524	63.2	1960	13,845	7811	63.9
1966	10,099	6484	60.9	1964	8373	10,851	43.6
1970	7564	7192	51.3	1968	10,214	6839	59.9
1974	8320	6145	57.5	1972	11,631	5024	69.8
1978	6896	7289	48.6	1976	9437	7456	55.9
1982	7435	6037	55.2	1980	9628	6296	60.5
1986	7171	6947	50.8	1984	11,334	5950	65.6
1990	3918	8117	32.6	1988	9743	6235	61.0
1994	7151	4063	63.8	1992	7271	5998	54.8
1998	6493	2473	72.4	1996	8156	5846	58.2
Mean			59.5	Mean			61.2
Classification: Strongly Republican				Classification: Strongly Republican			

Table A.34 Juniata County

Gubernatorial elections				Presidential elections			
Year	Rep.	Dem.	% Rep.	Year	Rep.	Dem.	% Rep.
1902	1557	1671	48.2	1900	1805	1621	52.7
1906	1290	1506	46.1	1904	1985	1201	62.3
1910	656	209	75.8	1908	1765	1414	55.5
1914	1036	1450	41.7	1912	374	1148	24.6
1918	1364	791	63.3	1916	1254	1497	45.6
1922	1308	2099	38.4	1920	2112	1443	59.4
1926	2400	920	72.3	1924	2177	1420	60.5
1930	3388	1050	76.3	1928	4396	919	82.7
1934	3098	3246	48.8	1932	2752	2805	49.5
1938	3977	3677	52.0	1936	3576	3782	48.6
1942	2928	2643	52.5	1940	3507	3579	49.5
1946	3021	2446	55.2	1944	3512	2666	56.8
1950	2952	2705	52.2	1948	3121	2299	57.6
1954	3060	3533	46.4	1952	3863	2705	58.8
1958	3694	3187	53.7	1956	4258	2779	60.5
1962	4458	3224	58.0	1960	4805	2615	64.8
1966	4037	2630	60.6	1964	3087	4138	42.7
1970	3256	2861	53.2	1968	4039	2321	63.5
1974	2978	3112	48.9	1972	4412	2156	67.2
1978	3814	2389	61.5	1976	3991	3105	56.2
1982	3221	3172	50.4	1980	4139	2696	60.6
1986	3683	2952	55.5	1984	5059	2624	65.8
1990	1637	4617	26.2	1988	4881	2834	63.3
1994	3548	2133	62.5	1992	3980	2601	60.5
1998	3947	1266	75.7	1996	4128	2896	58.8
Mean			54.8	Mean			56.4
Classification: Moderately Republican				Classification: Moderately Republican			

Table A.35 Lackawanna County

Gubernatorial elections				Presidential elections			
Year	Rep.	Dem.	% Rep.	Year	Rep.	Dem.	% Rep.
1902	10,670	16,289	39.6	1900	16,763	14,728	53.2
1906	11,596	17,607	39.7	1904	19,923	10,066	66.4
1910	11,020	5390	67.1	1908	18,590	15,451	54.6
1914	14,006	13,876	50.2	1912	3799	12,423	23.4
1918	11,745	10,949	51.7	1916	17,658	15,727	52.9
1922	25,328	19,667	56.3	1920	40,593	24,581	62.3
1926	31,673	13,634	70.0	1924	37,708	16,859	69.1
1930	34,211	30,472	52.9	1928	46,510	52,665	46.9
1934	42,542	36,800	53.6	1932	34,632	40,793	45.9
1938	60,752	66,885	47.6	1936	51,186	80,585	38.8
1942	35,050	43,472	44.6	1940	54,931	71,343	43.5
1946	47,610	46,089	50.8	1944	47,261	59,190	44.4
1950	50,167	58,414	46.2	1948	46,283	64,495	41.8
1954	47,392	63,029	42.9	1952	61,644	64,926	48.7
1958	44,213	62,172	41.6	1956	64,386	55,741	53.6
1962	61,120	62,166	49.6	1960	49,636	80,098	38.3
1966	52,581	53,497	49.6	1964	31,272	88,131	26.2
1970	42,404	50,493	45.6	1968	44,388	66,297	40.1
1974	35,666	47,212	43.0	1972	58,838	45,465	56.4
1978	43,558	35,411	55.2	1976	43,354	57,685	42.9
1982	31,529	42,270	42.7	1980	44,242	45,257	49.4
1986	26,775	55,979	32.4	1984	48,132	45,851	51.2
1990	10,941	49,282	18.2	1988	42,083	45,591	48.0
1994	26,053	36,014	42.0	1992	33,443	45,054	42.6
1998	35,039	25,297	58.1	1996	26,930	46,377	36.7
Mean			47.6	Mean			46.6
Classification: Became More Democratic				Classification: Became More Democratic			

Table A.36 Lancaster County

Gubernatorial elections				Presidential elections			
Year	Rep.	Dem.	% Rep.	Year	Rep.	Dem.	% Rep.
1902	17,930	7689	70.0	1900	22,230	8427	72.5
1906	18,776	11,057	62.9	1904	26,083	7047	78.7
1910	12,874	2132	85.8	1908	23,523	8109	74.4
1914	17,307	10,304	62.7	1912	12,668	8574	59.6
1918	17,538	4642	79.1	1916	20,292	10,016	66.9
1922	33,577	28,167	54.4	1920	29,549	9521	75.6
1926	30,240	10,718	73.8	1924	42,757	12,091	78.0
1930	24,896	18,205	58.0	1928	55,530	12,146	82.0
1934	33,257	25,580	56.5	1932	34,502	24,406	58.6
1938	47,244	26,581	64.0	1936	42,272	38,454	52.4
1942	31,725	13,802	69.7	1940	44,939	32,210	58.2
1946	38,324	15,237	71.5	1944	44,888	27,353	62.1
1950	40,242	20,617	66.1	1948	46,306	21,308	68.5
1954	41,948	30,046	58.3	1952	64,193	28,146	69.5
1958	52,254	28,378	64.8	1956	69,026	26,538	72.2
1962	67,006	27,089	71.2	1960	78,390	33,233	70.2
1966	62,458	23,494	72.7	1964	52,243	53,041	49.6
1970	48,749	28,918	62.8	1968	69,953	29,870	70.1
1974	49,871	28,474	63.7	1972	81,036	24,223	77.0
1978	59,416	21,768	73.2	1976	72,106	35,533	67.0
1982	63,637	25,939	71.0	1980	79,963	30,026	72.7
1986	68,736	27,247	71.6	1984	99,090	31,308	76.0
1990	24,565	66,069	27.1	1988	96,979	38,982	71.3
1994	66,295	27,376	70.8	1992	88,447	44,255	66.7
1998	72,198	15,891	82.0	1996	92,875	49,120	65.4
Mean			67.0	Mean			68.1
Classification: Strongly Republican				Classification: Strongly Republican			

Table A.37 Lawrence County

	Gubernatorial elections				Presidential elections		
Year	Rep.	Dem.	% Rep.	Year	Rep.	Dem.	% Rep.
1902	4026	2153	65.1	1900	6343	2754	69.7
1906	2997	3253	47.9	1904	7624	1888	80.1
1910	2357	243	90.6	1908	5350	2656	66.8
1914	3755	3155	54.3	1912	2128	1976	51.8
1918	3609	1313	73.3	1916	5134	3966	56.4
1922	5685	4156	57.7	1920	9448	2720	77.6
1926	8497	2325	78.5	1924	12,533	1880	87.0
1930	9900	5347	64.9	1928	20,012	6417	75.7
1934	10,279	13,672	42.9	1932	13,064	9390	58.2
1938	18,581	16,683	52.7	1936	15,458	21,994	41.3
1942	13,076	8589	60.3	1940	19,361	18,814	50.7
1946	17,395	9350	65.0	1944	18,886	17,331	52.1
1950	17,723	14,418	55.1	1948	17,186	14,632	54.0
1954	16,769	19,817	45.8	1952	23,319	21,164	52.4
1958	18,339	20,575	47.1	1956	25,037	19,923	55.7
1962	23,023	17,868	56.3	1960	23,646	24,309	49.3
1966	19,650	17,135	53.4	1964	15,998	29,092	35.6
1970	14,142	18,497	43.3	1968	18,360	21,027	46.6
1974	15,655	15,838	49.7	1972	23,712	17,595	57.4
1978	11,874	21,051	36.1	1976	18,546	23,337	44.3
1982	15,345	20,967	42.3	1980	18,404	19,506	48.5
1986	12,189	19,235	38.8	1984	19,277	23,981	42.0
1990	7282	19,563	27.1	1988	15,829	21,884	42.0
1994	13,102	13,355	49,5	1992	12,359	20,830	37.2
1998	13,115	9259	58.6	1996	13,088	18,993	40.8
Mean			54.6	Mean			54.1
Classification: Became More Democratic				Classification: Became More Democratic			

Table A.38 Lebanon County

	Gubernatorial elections				Presidential elections		
Year	Rep.	Dem.	% Rep.	Year	Rep.	Dem.	% Rep.
1902	4623	2736	62.8	1900	7089	3050	69.9
1906	4583	3263	58.4	1904	6928	2446	73.9
1910	3503	386	90.2	1908	6874	2858	70.6
1914	4815	4093	54.0	1912	2378	2972	44.4
1918	4952	1719	74.2	1916	5876	3821	60.5
1922	4673	4408	51.4	1920	8778	3016	74.4
1926	5562	1849	75.0	1924	9494	2464	79.4
1930	7454	4845	60.6	1928	16,841	3278	83.7
1934	9008	7713	53.9	1932	10,487	5924	63.9
1938	14,484	10,586	57.8	1936	13,213	13,800	48.9
1942	10,080	6821	59.6	1940	13,449	13,315	50.2
1946	14,233	8195	63.5	1944	15,206	11,818	56.2
1950	14,099	9525	59.7	1948	15,553	9418	62.3
1954	14,187	12,014	54.1	1952	20,726	11,611	64.1
1958	17,062	11,090	60.6	1956	22,556	10,406	68.4
1962	20,495	9320	68.7	1960	25,525	11,761	68.4
1966	18,402	9467	66.0	1964	17,891	15,882	53.0
1970	13,515	11,520	54.0	1968	21,832	9529	69.6
1974	13,233	11,198	54.2	1972	25,008	6683	78.9
1978	16,652	9066	64.7	1976	20,880	11,785	63.9
1982	16,107	12,442	56.4	1980	24,495	8281	74.7
1986	15,815	12,154	56.5	1984	27,008	10,520	72.0
1990	8055	18,776	30.0	1988	24,415	11,912	67.2
1994	16,780	9320	64.3	1992	21,512	12,350	63.5
1998	20,263	4775	80.9	1996	21,885	14,187	60.7
Mean			61.3	Mean			65.1
Classification: Strongly Republican				Classification: Strongly Republican			

Table A.39 Lehigh County

	Gubernatorial elections				Presidential elections		
Year	Rep.	Dem.	% Rep.	Year	Rep.	Dem.	% Rep.
1902	8381	10,364	44.7	1900	9775	10,428	48.4
1906	8027	9648	45.4	1904	11,826	10,134	53.8
1910	5883	6844	46.2	1908	11,593	11,285	50.7
1914	8171	9393	46.5	1912	2722	10,834	25.1
1918	7410	8150	47.6	1916	10,588	11,920	47.0
1922	11,817	12,618	48.4	1920	18,032	10,863	62.4
1926	14,938	10,563	58.6	1924	20,826	10,415	66.7
1930	12,312	25,909	32.2	1928	40,291	13,463	74.9
1934	20,198	21,669	48.2	1932	21,169	21,939	49.1
1938	33,051	24,922	57.0	1936	25,841	35,325	42.2
1942	21,782	15,381	58.7	1940	29,584	33,007	47.3
1946	27,014	18,668	59.1	1944	31,584	29,134	52.0
1950	28,009	25,110	52.7	1948	32,202	26,826	54.5
1954	28,766	31,595	47.6	1952	45,143	33,033	57.7
1958	35,635	34,199	51.0	1956	50,564	29,067	63.5
1962	46,445	32,905	58.5	1960	54,278	39,640	57.8
1966	43,292	33,565	56.3	1964	32,245	60,377	34.8
1970	26,910	43,582	38.2	1968	47,255	44,033	51.8
1974	29,753	38,150	43.8	1972	58,023	33,325	63.5
1978	40,509	28,516	58.7	1976	46,895	46,620	50.1
1982	42,137	31,413	57.3	1980	50,782	34,827	59.3
1986	38,984	31,174	55.6	1984	61,799	41,084	60.1
1990	24,519	42,592	36.5	1988	56,363	42,801	56.8
1994	41,767	27,970	59.9	1992	42,631	46,711	47.7
1998	50,526	22,472	69.2	1996	45,103	48,568	48.2
Mean			51.6	Mean			52.4
Classification:				Classification:			
Became More Republican				Moderately Republican			

Table A.40 Luzerne County

Gubernatorial elections				Presidential elections			
Year	Rep.	Dem.	% Rep.	Year	Rep.	Dem.	% Rep.
1902	13,178	16,816	43.9	1900	21,793	16,470	57.0
1906	14,191	19,685	41.9	1904	27,869	13,497	67.4
1910	12,389	3444	78.2	1908	24,594	17,379	58.6
1914	17,856	16,753	51.6	1912	4970	13,461	27.0
1918	16,546	15,408	51.8	1916	25,348	19,999	55.9
1922	32,709	30,719	51.6	1920	49,419	23,473	67.8
1926	46,862	18,018	72.2	1924	46,475	20,472	69.4
1930	62,012	31,637	66.2	1928	67,872	73,319	48.1
1934	63,523	53,362	54.3	1932	52,672	60,975	46.3
1938	97,373	96,985	50.1	1936	81,572	105,008	43.7
1942	57,019	45,874	55.4	1940	79,685	101,577	44.0
1946	66,138	46,099	58.9	1944	67,984	73,674	48.0
1950	76,661	65,837	53.8	1948	71,674	61,869	53.7
1954	64,501	73,512	46.7	1952	88,967	72,579	55.1
1958	67,314	76,636	46.8	1956	92,458	65,155	58.7
1962	77,533	75,079	50.8	1960	70,711	102,998	40.7
1966	62,145	64,850	48.9	1964	43,895	106,397	29.2
1970	47,225	69,199	40.6	1968	57,044	79,040	41.9
1974	47,015	59,733	44.0	1972	81,358	51,128	61.4
1978	56,054	52,513	51.6	1976	60,058	74,655	44.6
1982	47,021	63,327	42.6	1980	67,822	59,976	53.1
1986	37,572	66,790	36.0	1984	69,169	58,482	54.2
1990	14,487	60,043	19.4	1988	59,059	58,553	50.2
1994	38,233	43,786	46.6	1992	49,285	56,623	46.5
1998	44,030	23,827	64.9	1996	43,577	60,174	42.0
Mean			50.7	Mean			50.2
Classification:				Classification:			
Became More Democratic				Competitive			

Table A.41 Lycoming County

Gubernatorial elections					Presidential elections			
Year	Rep.	Dem.	% Rep.		Year	Rep.	Dem.	% Rep.
1902	5862	7451	44.0		1900	7750	7427	51.1
1906	5014	6633	43.0		1904	8928	6414	58.2
1910	3237	2775	53.8		1908	8708	7144	54.9
1914	4121	6587	38.5		1912	1631	6039	21.3
1918	5261	4111	56.1		1916	6016	6646	47.5
1922	6050	7919	43.3		1920	10,570	5853	64.4
1926	10,082	3754	72.9		1924	14,039	6857	67.2
1930	14,343	8890	61.7		1928	28,720	7132	80.1
1934	13,487	14,743	47.8		1932	16,212	11,499	58.5
1938	22,716	15,580	59.3		1936	18,315	19,376	48.6
1942	13,342	8707	60.5		1940	21,423	18,363	53.8
1946	16,600	9097	64.6		1944	19,886	15,658	55.9
1950	16,016	15,909	50.2		1948	19,118	13,692	58.3
1954	14,700	17,458	45.7		1952	25,753	15,870	61.9
1958	20,696	15,919	56.5		1956	27,030	13,490	66.7
1962	26,505	14,991	63.9		1960	30,083	18,351	62.1
1966	20,934	14,256	59.5		1964	19,011	25,879	42.4
1970	16,743	16,344	50.6		1968	23,830	16,888	58.5
1974	18,794	13,106	58.9		1972	28,913	11,999	70.7
1978	19,371	11,815	62.1		1976	22,648	18,635	54.9
1982	115,578	18,009	46.4		1980	23,415	14,609	61.6
1986	15,080	13,505	52.8		1984	28,498	13,147	68.4
1990	8628	17,238	33.4		1988	24,792	13,528	64.7
1994	19,334	9134	67.9		1992	20,536	13,315	60.7
1998	20,511	6058	77.2		1996	21,535	13,516	61.4
Mean			54.9		Mean			57.7
Classification: Moderately Republican					Classification: Strongly Republican			

Table A.42 McKean County

Gubernatorial elections				Presidential elections			
Year	Rep.	Dem.	% Rep.	Year	Rep.	Dem.	% Rep.
1902	3908	3586	52.1	1900	6319	3427	64.8
1906	2304	4437	34.2	1904	5719	1625	77.9
1910	1986	459	81.2	1908	5073	2867	63.9
1914	2208	3440	39.1	1912	1345	2362	36.3
1918	3328	1587	67.6	1916	4300	3161	57.6
1922	5057	2551	66.5	1920	7830	2505	75.8
1926	5467	1803	75.2	1924	9072	2376	79.2
1930	6432	3677	63.6	1928	14,012	4964	73.8
1934	6388	5326	54.5	1932	9970	4661	68.1
1938	14,970	6602	69.4	1936	11,837	9733	54.9
1942	7572	2704	73.7	1940	14,822	6991	68.0
1946	8776	2887	75.2	1944	11,988	6492	64.9
1950	9908	4591	68.3	1948	10,218	4785	68.1
1954	10,045	5041	66.6	1952	15,256	5373	73.9
1958	10,360	6086	63.0	1956	14,725	5152	74.1
1962	11,382	6142	65.0	1960	13,699	7767	63.8
1966	9027	5144	63.7	1964	7948	10,950	42.1
1970	7297	5284	58.0	1968	10,506	6326	62.4
1974	7883	4774	62.3	1972	11,958	4513	72.6
1978	7106	3586	66.5	1976	10,305	6424	61.6
1982	7352	4335	62.9	1980	9229	5064	64.6
1986	6976	4579	60.4	1984	10,963	4818	69.5
1990	3893	5151	43.0	1988	9323	5300	63.8
1994	6359	2925	68.5	1992	6965	5331	56.6
1998	6742	2086	76.4	1996	6838	5509	55.4
Mean			63.0	Mean			64.0
Classification: Strongly Republican				Classification: Strongly Republican			

Table A.43 Mercer County

Gubernatorial elections				Presidential elections			
Year	Rep.	Dem.	% Rep.	Year	Rep.	Dem.	% Rep.
1902	5374	4926	52.2	1900	6950	4916	58.6
1906	4496	3777	54.3	1904	8574	3839	69.1
1910	3301	804	80.4	1908	6497	5473	54.3
1914	4198	5321	44.1	1912	1873	4039	31.7
1918	4918	2721	64.4	1916	5866	6390	47.9
1922	7052	6200	52.8	1920	11,575	4823	70.6
1926	9856	2245	81.4	1924	14,639	3688	79.9
1930	11,433	7266	61.1	1928	22,599	8204	73.4
1934	12,318	13,807	47.1	1932	14,057	10,961	56.2
1938	19,357	15,264	55.9	1936	18,493	20,879	47.0
1942	13,052	8970	59.3	1940	21,058	16,968	55.4
1946	16,756	9211	64.5	1944	19,606	16,589	54.2
1950	19,413	15,089	56.3	1948	18,916	16,108	54.0
1954	17,812	19,442	47.8	1952	26,424	20,770	56.0
1958	21,195	20,582	50.7	1956	28,785	19,769	59.3
1962	24,841	18,118	57.8	1960	29,109	24,243	54.6
1966	21,630	19,448	52.7	1964	18,153	32,199	36.1
1970	15,740	21,601	42.2	1968	23,131	22,814	50.3
1974	18,808	17,518	51.8	1972	27,961	18,087	60.7
1978	17,052	17,119	49.9	1976	22,469	25,041	47.3
1982	18,217	20,043	47.6	1980	22,372	19,716	53.2
1986	15,577	19,406	44.5	1984	24,211	24,658	49.5
1990	10,479	24,078	30.3	1988	21,301	24,278	46.7
1994	19,617	12,294	61.5	1992	16,081	23,264	40.9
1998	15,958	10,394	60.7	1996	17,213	23,003	42.8
Mean			55.2	Mean			53.2
Classification: Moderately Republican				Classification: Moderately Republican			

Table A.44 Mifflin County

Gubernatorial elections				Presidential elections			
Year	Rep.	Dem.	% Rep.	Year	Rep.	Dem.	% Rep.
1902	1943	1985	49.5	1900	2594	1842	58.5
1906	1532	1686	47.6	1904	3054	1374	69.0
1910	871	426	67.2	1908	2902	1799	61.7
1914	1761	1807	49.3	1912	654	1400	31.8
1918	2170	891	70.9	1916	2105	1965	51.7
1922	1957	2351	45.4	1920	3872	2400	61.7
1926	3364	992	77.2	1924	4780	1999	70.5
1930	6247	1818	77.4	1928	8932	1270	87.5
1934	4978	5021	49.8	1932	5525	3654	60.2
1938	7839	6573	54.4	1936	6867	9581	41.7
1942	4227	3159	57.2	1940	6352	6993	47.6
1946	5028	3211	61.0	1944	6205	5694	52.1
1950	5889	5089	53.6	1948	5666	4762	54.3
1954	5406	5689	48.7	1952	8620	5889	59.4
1958	6960	4775	59.3	1956	8638	5078	63.0
1962	8465	4808	63.8	1960	10,315	4816	68.2
1966	7595	4847	61.0	1964	6006	8811	40.5
1970	5909	5250	53.0	1968	8133	5681	58.9
1974	4793	6023	44.3	1972	9989	3667	73.1
1978	6266	4406	58.7	1976	7698	6210	55.3
1982	6391	4948	56.4	1980	7541	5226	59.1
1986	5788	4683	55.3	1984	9106	5178	63.7
1990	2781	6472	30.1	1988	8170	4790	63.0
1994	6140	4068	60.1	1992	6300	4946	56.0
1998	6914	2010	77.5	1996	6888	5327	56.4
Mean			57.2	Mean			58.0
Classification: Moderately Republican				Classification: Strongly Republican			

Table A.45 Monroe County

Gubernatorial elections				Presidential elections			
Year	Rep.	Dem.	% Rep.	Year	Rep.	Dem.	% Rep.
1902	871	3071	22.1	1900	1264	3054	29.3
1906	729	2320	23.9	1904	1446	2587	35.8
1910	628	1511	29.3	1908	1454	3004	32.6
1914	1076	2618	29.1	1912	536	3107	14.7
1918	1283	1361	48.5	1916	1456	3348	30.3
1922	2126	4939	30.1	1920	3278	3396	49.1
1926	2655	2669	49.9	1924	3462	3901	47.0
1930	3730	4469	45.5	1928	7469	3266	69.6
1934	3853	5758	40.1	1932	4659	6357	42.3
1938	6183	5073	54.9	1936	5778	8212	41.3
1942	3831	3517	52.1	1940	6001	6670	47.4
1946	5204	4006	56.5	1944	6202	5490	53.0
1950	5884	5864	50.1	1948	6674	5913	53.0
1954	5458	6699	44.9	1952	9502	5760	62.2
1958	7443	6690	52.7	1956	10,081	5506	64.6
1962	9202	6018	60.5	1960	11,299	6312	64.2
1966	8667	6111	58.6	1964	6281	10,622	37.2
1970	6384	7266	46.8	1968	9465	6946	57.7
1974	6761	6520	50.9	1972	12,701	5619	69.3
1978	9100	6398	58.7	1976	10,228	9544	51.7
1982	9947	7905	55.7	1980	12,357	7551	62.1
1986	9272	7800	54.3	1984	16,109	8193	66.3
1990	6761	12,243	35.6	1988	17,185	9859	63.5
1994	14,409	10,137	58.7	1992	14,557	13,468	51.9
1998	17,243	7160	70.7	1996	17,326	16,547	51.1
Mean			47.1	Mean			49.6
Classification:				Classification:			
Became More Republican				Became More Republican			

Table A.46 Montgomery County

	Gubernatorial elections				Presidential elections		
Year	Rep.	Dem.	% Rep.	Year	Rep.	Dem.	% Rep.
1902	12,988	13,800	48.5	1900	17,051	11,208	60.3
1906	12,889	13,176	49.4	1904	18,833	10,401	64.4
1910	8843	5399	62.1	1908	19,088	11,809	61.8
1914	16,683	11,704	58.8	1912	8978	11,894	43.0
1918	15,915	7359	68.4	1916	20,431	13,658	59.9
1922	22,205	12,094	64.7	1920	31,963	12,239	72.3
1926	28,888	8041	78.2	1924	45,407	11,094	80.4
1930	28,641	36,000	44.3	1928	76,680	23,026	76.9
1934	50,832	37,833	57.3	1932	64,619	32,971	66.2
1938	72,538	33,194	68.6	1936	66,442	57,870	53.4
1942	52,898	23,088	69.6	1940	73,250	49,409	59.7
1946	76,943	24,949	75.5	1944	78,260	47,815	62.1
1950	75,290	48,018	61.0	1948	85,576	41,112	67.5
1954	88,102	54,119	61.9	1952	115,899	57,701	66.8
1958	103,506	62,194	62.5	1956	133,270	59,095	69.3
1962	135,785	68,615	66.4	1960	142,796	92,212	60.8
1966	131,746	67,597	66.1	1964	102,714	135,657	43.1
1970	95,399	100,940	48.6	1968	141,621	102,464	58.0
1974	103,625	101,433	50.5	1972	173,662	91,959	65.4
1978	135,304	70,272	65.8	1976	155,480	112,644	58.0
1982	134,685	63,644	67.9	1980	156,996	84,289	65.1
1986	129,771	66,823	66.0	1984	181,426	99,741	64.5
1990	90,051	89,465	50.2	1988	170,294	109,834	60.8
1994	110,319	85,077	56.5	1992	125,704	136,572	47.9
1998	129,376	62,734	67.3	1996	121,047	143,664	45.7
Mean			62.1	Mean			60.7
Classification: Strongly Republican				Classification: Strongly Republican			

Table A.47 Montour County

Gubernatorial elections				Presidential elections			
Year	Rep.	Dem.	% Rep.	Year	Rep.	Dem.	% Rep.
1902	943	2078	31.2	1900	1292	1875	40.8
1906	906	1772	33.8	1904	1518	1352	52.9
1910	415	499	45.4	1908	1164	1490	43.8
1914	1117	1282	46.6	1912	308	1492	17.1
1918	963	920	51.1	1916	1068	1536	41.0
1922	1494	2146	41.0	1920	2296	1872	55.1
1926	1808	1411	56.2	1924	2499	1799	58.1
1930	2048	2344	46.6	1928	3692	1445	71.9
1934	2013	3045	39.8	1932	2159	2677	44.6
1938	2901	2826	50.7	1936	2350	3534	39.9
1942	2151	1864	53.6	1940	2723	3080	46.9
1946	2385	1665	58.9	1944	2727	2212	55.2
1950	2551	2394	51.6	1948	2690	1964	57.8
1954	2476	2862	46.4	1952	3725	2264	62.2
1958	3154	2416	56.6	1956	3976	2072	65.7
1962	3713	2533	59.4	1960	4154	2629	61.2
1966	3239	2124	60.4	1964	2527	3683	40.7
1970	2902	2614	52.6	1968	3289	2239	59.5
1974	2655	2345	53.1	1972	4386	1755	71.4
1978	2870	1782	61.7	1976	3259	2727	54.4
1982	2537	2496	50.4	1980	3399	2272	59.9
1986	2171	2429	47.2	1984	4174	2055	67.0
1990	1201	2666	31.1	1988	3617	2031	64.0
1994	2809	1640	63.1	1992	3096	2150	59.0
1998	2700	1012	72.7	1996	2785	2183	56.1
Mean			50.2	Mean			53.4
Classification: Became More Republican				Classification: Moderately Republican			

Table A.48 Northampton County

	Gubernatorial elections				Presidential elections		
Year	Rep.	Dem.	% Rep.	Year	Rep.	Dem.	% Rep.
1902	6527	9439	40.9	1900	9849	11,412	46.3
1906	7005	9849	41.6	1904	11,039	9902	52.7
1910	5328	5648	48.5	1908	10,857	11,365	48.8
1914	7925	8520	48.2	1912	3893	10,325	27.4
1918	6464	7297	47.0	1916	9610	11,000	46.6
1922	10,244	12,893	44.3	1920	14,227	9086	61.0
1926	15,202	12,041	55.8	1924	20,459	11,459	64.1
1930	10,961	20,725	52.9	1928	37,403	14,768	71.7
1934	17,274	25,276	40.6	1932	20,779	24,009	46.4
1938	27,062	23,900	53.1	1936	22,827	36,871	38.2
1942	17,308	16,922	50.6	1940	25,385	33,304	43.2
1946	23,770	24,617	49.1	1944	26,643	32,584	45.0
1950	24,720	29,447	45.6	1948	27,030	33,209	44.9
1954	23,343	37,157	38.6	1952	39,131	36,993	51.4
1958	29,204	34,658	45.7	1956	43,375	33,749	56.2
1962	34,369	33,590	50.6	1960	40,683	41,552	49.5
1966	31,203	35,649	46.7	1964	21,048	58,818	26.4
1970	19,017	39,390	32.6	1968	32,033	42,554	42.9
1974	21,690	32,622	39.9	1972	41,822	32,335	56.4
1978	31,024	24,909	55.5	1976	32,926	42,514	43.6
1982	31,252	29,038	51.8	1980	35,787	31,920	52.9
1986	27,723	29,482	48.5	1984	44,648	37,979	54.0
1990	18,153	38,872	31.8	1988	42,748	39,264	52.1
1994	33,704	26,641	55.9	1992	34,429	42,203	44.9
1998	42,352	20,461	67.4	1996	35,726	43,959	44.8
Mean			47.4	Mean			48.0
Classification: Moderately Democratic				Classification: Moderately Democratic			

Table A.49 Northumberland County

Gubernatorial elections				Presidential elections			
Year	Rep.	Dem.	% Rep.	Year	Rep.	Dem.	% Rep.
1902	6043	7395	45.0	1900	8366	7989	51.2
1906	5882	7552	43.8	1904	11,219	5921	65.4
1910	3150	2048	60.0	1908	10,439	8590	54.8
1914	6966	8744	44.3	1912	2371	6802	25.8
1918	6026	6011	50.1	1916	8722	9333	48.3
1922	9601	11,848	44.8	1920	17,288	9854	63.7
1926	12,815	8423	60.3	1924	17,516	7571	69.8
1930	118,097	13,170	57.9	1928	30,949	19,249	61.7
1934	119,064	19,962	48.8	1932	17,982	23,114	43.7
1938	26,440	22,168	54.4	1936	21,758	31,849	40.6
1942	15,628	14,886	51.2	1940	22,914	26,315	46.5
1946	18,746	15,592	54.6	1944	21,995	20,333	52.0
1950	22,230	17,879	55.4	1948	23,535	16,478	58.8
1954	19,085	20,154	48.6	1952	28,861	17,789	61.9
1958	23,650	18,772	55.7	1956	28,583	17,141	62.5
1962	27,215	18,568	59.4	1960	27,568	22,233	55.4
1966	23,432	15,947	59.5	1964	17,046	28,082	37.8
1970	17,132	17,994	48.8	1968	22,366	17,013	56.8
1974	16,757	17,075	49.5	1972	25,912	13,885	65.1
1978	18,264	12,513	59.3	1976	19,283	18,939	50.5
1982	11,562	19,890	36.8	1980	20,608	13,750	60.0
1986	12,660	16,337	43.7	1984	22,109	13,748	61.7
1990	6388	17,948	26.2	1988	20,207	14,255	58.6
1994	12,785	10,633	54.6	1992	15,057	12,814	54.0
1998	13,468	7051	65.6	1996	13,551	13,418	50.2
Mean			51.0	Mean			53.6
Classification: Competitive				Classification: Moderately Republican			

Table A.50 Perry County

Gubernatorial elections				Presidential elections			
Year	Rep.	Dem.	% Rep.	Year	Rep.	Dem.	% Rep.
1902	2759	2461	52.8	1900	3400	2440	58.2
1906	2171	2310	48.4	1904	3433	2094	62.1
1910	1524	705	68.5	1908	3269	2184	59.9
1914	2202	2314	48.8	1912	1140	1941	37.0
1918	2469	1354	66.3	1916	2575	2348	52.3
1922	2859	4138	40.9	1920	3787	2314	62.1
1926	4285	1885	69.4	1924	4185	2710	60.7
1930	5718	1747	76.6	1928	6469	1807	78.2
1934	5191	4538	53.4	1932	4402	3733	54.1
1938	6466	4837	57.2	1936	5759	5780	49.9
1942	4565	2795	62.0	1940	5877	4601	56.1
1946	5133	2602	66.4	1944	5722	3265	63.4
1950	4998	3303	60.2	1948	5444	2596	67.7
1954	5078	4263	54.4	1952	6733	3042	68.9
1958	6031	4261	58.6	1956	7511	3576	67.7
1962	7523	4080	64.8	1960	8134	3413	70.4
1966	6536	3586	64.6	1964	5364	6054	47.0
1970	5038	3897	56.4	1968	6655	2944	69.3
1974	5008	4521	52.6	1972	8082	2731	74.7
1978	7120	3200	69.0	1976	7454	4605	61.8
1982	5942	4978	54.4	1980	8028	3681	68.6
1986	6005	3819	61.1	1984	9365	3692	71.7
1990	3242	6205	34.3	1988	8545	3910	68.6
1994	5522	3094	64.1	1992	7871	4086	65.8
1998	7023	1487	82.5	1996	8156	4611	63.9
Mean			59.3	Mean			61.9
Classification: Strongly Republican				Classification: Strongly Republican			

Table A.51 Philadelphia County

Gubernatorial elections				Presidential elections			
Year	Rep.	Dem.	% Rep.	Year	Rep.	Dem.	% Rep.
1902	170,686	79,636	70.7	1900	173,657	58,179	74.9
1906	126,639	95,803	56.9	1904	227,709	48,875	82.3
1910	130,465	16,474	88.8	1908	185,263	75,310	71.1
1914	182,185	63,380	74.2	1912	91,944	66,308	58.1
1918	152,538	59,327	72.0	1916	194,163	90,800	68.1
1922	245,312	65,711	78.9	1920	307,826	90,151	77.3
1926	312,492	69,294	81.8	1924	347,457	54,213	86.5
1930	111,158	356,676	23.8	1928	420,320	276,573	60.3
1934	343,979	324,143	51.5	1932	331,092	260,276	56.0
1938	417,050	407,361	50.6	1936	329,881	539,757	37.9
1942	317,962	317,805	50.0	1940	354,878	532,149	40.0
1946	440,286	334,165	56.8	1944	346,380	496,367	41.0
1950	374,977	452,055	45.3	1948	425,962	432,699	49.6
1954	320,623	436,896	42.3	1952	396,874	557,352	41.6
1958	290,320	468,318	38.3	1956	383,414	507,289	43.0
1962	339,790	446,528	43.2	1960	291,000	622,544	31.9
1966	309,840	419,656	42.5	1964	239,733	670,645	26.3
1970	233,261	413,742	36.1	1968	254,153	525,768	32.6
1974	168,532	391,272	30.1	1972	344,096	431,736	44.4
1978	336,771	371,646	47.5	1976	239,000	494,579	32.6
1982	196,998	347,129	36.2	1980	244,108	421,253	36.7
1986	172,718	307,233	36.0	1984	267,178	501,369	34.8
1990	114,390	276,390	29.3	1988	219,053	449,566	32.8
1994	100,592	270,380	27.1	1992	133,328	434,904	23.5
1998	107,731	183,066	37.0	1996	85,345	412,988	17.1
Mean			50.7	Mean			47.1
Classification:				Classification:			
Became More Democratic				Became More Democratic			

Table A.52 Pike County

	Gubernatorial elections				Presidential elections		
Year	Rep.	Dem.	% Rep.	Year	Rep.	Dem.	% Rep.
1902	389	862	31.1	1900	694	1236	26.4
1906	462	926	33.3	1904	592	939	38.7
1910	495	683	42.0	1908	715	1069	40.1
1914	325	952	25.4	1912	191	995	16.1
1918	371	514	41.9	1916	598	976	38.0
1922	1260	1400	47.4	1920	1319	880	60.0
1926	1252	1162	51.9	1924	1581	993	61.4
1930	1817	1311	58.1	1928	2354	1024	69.7
1934	1807	1993	47.5	1932	1649	1844	47.2
1938	2368	2082	53.2	1936	2304	2396	49.0
1942	1873	1516	55.3	1940	2596	1818	58.8
1946	2363	1084	68.5	1944	2674	1408	65.5
1950	2741	1704	61.7	1948	2893	1208	70.5
1954	2836	1704	62.5	1952	3810	1383	73.4
1958	3080	1827	62.8	1956	4160	1219	77.3
1962	3526	1667	67.9	1960	4000	1676	70.5
1966	3533	1364	72.1	1964	2651	2753	49.1
1970	3041	1563	66.1	1968	3719	1617	69.7
1974	2898	1756	62.3	1972	4568	1385	76.7
1978	3516	1789	66.3	1976	4241	2775	60.4
1982	3325	2385	58.2	1980	5249	2132	71.1
1986	3529	2304	60.5	1984	6343	2503	71.7
1990	2529	3122	44.8	1988	6659	3097	68.3
1994	5583	2907	65.8	1992	6084	4382	58.1
1998	6843	2726	71.5	1996	6697	5509	54.9
Mean			55.0	Mean			57.3
Classification:				Classification:			
Became More Republican				Became More Republican			

Table A.53 Potter County

Gubernatorial elections				Presidential elections			
Year	Rep.	Dem.	% Rep.	Year	Rep.	Dem.	% Rep.
1902	2942	2172	57.5	1900	3224	2147	60.0
1906	1941	1949	49.9	1904	3976	1074	78.7
1910	1112	392	42.5	1908	3603	1932	65.1
1914	1364	2064	39.8	1912	850	1445	37.0
1918	1809	736	71.1	1916	2386	1733	57.9
1922	1956	2983	39.6	1920	4036	1106	78.5
1926	2127	708	75.0	1924	4087	1161	77.9
1930	3866	1981	66.1	1928	5653	1416	80.0
1934	3209	2856	52.9	1932	3847	2271	62.9
1938	5381	3167	63.0	1936	5172	3553	59.3
1942	3151	1678	65.2	1940	5205	2731	65.6
1946	3484	1234	73.8	1944	4474	1894	70.2
1950	3824	2396	61.5	1948	3672	1729	68.0
1954	3680	3004	55.0	1952	5117	1974	72.2
1958	4222	2908	59.2	1956	5181	2257	69.7
1962	4618	2440	65.4	1960	5099	2715	65.3
1966	3936	1949	66.9	1964	3232	3652	46.9
1970	2937	2176	57.4	1968	4019	1860	68.4
1974	2792	2200	55.9	1972	4422	1710	72.1
1978	3391	1904	64.0	1976	3828	2983	56.2
1982	2929	1890	60.8	1980	4073	2299	63.9
1986	2683	2297	53.9	1984	5164	1789	74.3
1990	1766	2398	42.4	1988	4432	2119	67.7
1994	3434	1377	71.4	1992	3452	1892	64.6
1998	3121	963	76.4	1996	3714	2146	63.4
Mean			59.7	Mean			65.1
Classification: Strongly Republican				Classification: Strongly Republican			

Table A.54 Schuylkill County

Gubernatorial elections				Presidential elections			
Year	Rep.	Dem.	% Rep.	Year	Rep.	Dem.	% Rep.
1902	10,769	15,107	41.7	1900	15,227	14,496	51.2
1906	11,650	14,388	44.7	1904	21,046	10,108	67.5
1910	6880	5563	55.3	1908	18,758	15,481	54.8
1914	16,123	13,103	55.2	1912	3557	11,812	23.1
1918	12,525	11,487	52.2	1916	17,806	13,396	57.1
1922	21,237	21,944	49.2	1920	30,259	18,746	61.7
1926	24,944	16,919	59.6	1924	34,578	10,111	77.4
1930	30,865	21,646	58.8	1928	46,023	40,424	53.2
1934	32,930	35,268	48.3	1932	32,492	35,023	48.1
1938	54,211	46,994	53.6	1936	44,353	55,183	44.5
1942	31,668	25,818	55.1	1940	43,505	48,739	47.2
1946	41,056	23,485	63.6	1944	40,671	35,852	53.1
1950	44,118	34,233	56.3	1948	44,176	28,194	61.0
1954	40,002	34,371	53.8	1952	51,437	34,987	59.5
1958	40,445	35,841	53.0	1956	51,670	31,645	62.0
1962	45,241	34,522	56.7	1960	44,187	44,430	49.9
1966	40,966	30,672	57.2	1964	26,386	50,560	34.3
1970	26,925	36,496	42.5	1968	37,194	34,982	51.5
1974	26,606	30,174	46.9	1972	44,071	26,077	62.8
1978	33,407	24,183	58.0	1976	31,944	33,905	48.5
1982	22,527	32,706	40.8	1980	36,273	24,968	59.2
1986	23,824	25,854	48.0	1984	37,330	25,758	59.2
1990	12,590	29,832	29.7	1988	32,666	24,797	56.8
1994	24,714	18,148	57.6	1992	25,780	23,679	52.1
1998	27,992	12,108	69.8	1996	22,920	24,860	48.0
Mean			52.2	Mean			53.2
Classification: Moderately Republican				Classification: Moderately Republican			

Table A.55 Snyder County

Gubernatorial elections				Presidential elections			
Year	Rep.	Dem.	% Rep.	Year	Rep.	Dem.	% Rep.
1902	1795	1245	59.0	1900	2517	1319	65.6
1906	1415	1254	53.0	1904	2538	971	72.3
1910	1020	215	82.6	1908	2401	1081	69.0
1914	1286	1399	47.9	1912	626	991	38.7
1918	1758	625	73.8	1916	1797	1247	59.0
1922	1822	2055	47.0	1920	2751	964	74.0
1926	1997	468	81.0	1924	3055	970	75.9
1930	4041	1148	77.9	1928	5693	805	87.6
1934	3970	2525	61.1	1932	3423	2176	61.1
1938	6181	2694	69.9	1936	5550	2999	64.9
1942	4059	1643	71.2	1940	5722	2478	69.8
1946	4599	1585	74.4	1944	5696	1795	76.0
1950	4794	2042	70.1	1948	5181	1490	77.7
1954	5075	2837	64.1	1952	6836	1686	80.2
1958	6246	2510	71.3	1956	7102	1959	78.4
1962	7129	2478	74.2	1960	8103	1998	80.2
1966	6014	2156	73.6	1964	5195	4199	55.3
1970	5112	2564	66.6	1968	6784	1993	77.3
1974	5053	2739	64.8	1972	7308	1834	79.9
1978	6324	2039	75.6	1976	6557	3097	67.9
1982	5675	3483	62.0	1980	7634	2418	75.9
1986	6000	3150	65.6	1984	8968	2383	79.0
1990	2697	4777	36.1	1988	9054	2658	77.3
1994	6007	2332	72.0	1992	6934	2952	70.1
1998	5565	1405	79.8	1996	6742	3405	66.4
Mean			66.8	Mean			70.4
Classification:				Classification:			
Strongly Republican				Strongly Republican			

Table A.56 Somerset County

	Gubernatorial elections				Presidential elections		
Year	Rep.	Dem.	% Rep.	Year	Rep.	Dem.	% Rep.
1902	4701	2095	69.2	1900	6677	2151	75.6
1906	3990	2923	57.7	1904	6772	1681	80.1
1910	2783	504	84.7	1908	6478	2246	74.3
1914	3730	3714	50.1	1912	1428	2164	39.7
1918	6146	1630	79.0	1916	6008	2957	67.0
1922	5661	3526	61.6	1920	12,436	2912	81.0
1926	6255	1270	83.1	1924	12,389	2315	84.3
1930	9859	4091	70.7	1928	16,404	4489	78.5
1934	11,853	10,686	52.6	1932	11,857	7919	59.9
1938	19,078	13,105	59.3	1936	17,375	16,184	51.8
1942	11,840	7594	60.9	1940	17,369	14,085	55.2
1946	12,770	6720	65.5	1944	16,039	10,287	60.9
1950	14,401	11,634	55.3	1948	13,910	8727	61.4
1954	14,355	15,252	48.5	1952	18,589	13,167	58.5
1958	16,356	14,620	52.8	1956	20,568	13,163	61.0
1962	20,341	12,734	61.5	1960	20,554	14,739	58.2
1966	17,112	11,507	59.8	1964	14,817	17,938	45.2
1970	12,848	12,503	50.7	1968	17,511	11,515	60.3
1974	13,319	10,880	55.0	1972	19,739	8743	69.3
1978	10,578	14,720	41.8	1976	15,960	13,452	54.3
1982	13,195	13,052	50.3	1980	17,729	11,695	60.3
1986	11,471	14,297	44.5	1984	19,502	13,900	58.4
1990	6937	17,610	28.3	1988	16,809	13,815	54.9
1994	11,724	11,383	50.7	1992	13,858	12,493	52.6
1998	14,829	5676	72.3	1996	14,735	12,719	53.7
Mean			59.1	Mean			61.4
Classification: Strongly Republican				Classification: Strongly Republican			

Table A.57 Sullivan County

Gubernatorial elections				Presidential elections			
Year	Rep.	Dem.	% Rep.	Year	Rep.	Dem.	% Rep.
1902	1098	1350	44.8	1900	1266	1376	47.9
1906	813	1131	41.8	1904	1429	1185	54.7
1910	629	468	57.3	1908	1119	1076	51.0
1914	742	1010	42.3	1912	547	912	37.5
1918	785	629	55.5	1916	888	1037	46.1
1922	1412	1463	49.1	1920	1620	1061	60.4
1926	1061	432	71.1	1924	1668	913	64.6
1930	1531	825	65.0	1928	2044	1101	65.0
1934	1632	1520	51.8	1932	1457	1602	47.6
1938	2292	1461	61.1	1936	2121	1740	54.9
1942	1486	1253	54.2	1940	2059	1626	55.9
1946	1605	1116	59.0	1944	1858	1329	58.3
1950	1685	1369	55.2	1948	1752	1084	61.8
1954	1358	1546	46.8	1952	2011	1239	61.9
1958	1684	1366	55.2	1956	2007	1286	60.9
1962	1838	1349	57.7	1960	1808	1471	55.1
1966	1670	1077	60.8	1964	1344	1690	44.3
1970	1466	1009	59.2	1968	1629	1035	61.1
1974	1546	1085	58.8	1972	1886	885	68.1
1978	1482	936	61.3	1976	1584	1347	54.0
1982	1332	1187	52.9	1980	1676	1074	60.9
1986	1263	1194	51.4	1984	1926	962	66.7
1990	835	1207	40.9	1988	1808	1091	62.4
1994	1480	787	65.3	1992	1340	1030	56.5
1998	1609	524	75.4	1996	1352	1071	55.8
Mean			55.5	Mean			56.2
Classification: Moderately Republican				Classification: Strongly Republican			

Table A.58 Susquehanna County

Gubernatorial elections				Presidential elections			
Year	Rep.	Dem.	% Rep.	Year	Rep.	Dem.	% Rep.
1902	3792	3590	51.4	1900	5019	3527	58.7
1906	3267	2773	54.0	1904	4988	2562	66.1
1910	2228	603	78.7	1908	4999	3230	60.7
1914	2608	3193	44.9	1912	1988	2588	43.4
1918	2940	1403	67.7	1916	3891	3145	55.3
1922	3943	3280	54.6	1920	6572	2905	69.3
1926	3963	1487	72.7	1924	7266	2208	76.7
1930	5070	3742	57.5	1928	9445	4353	68.4
1934	7494	4447	62.7	1932	6884	5171	57.1
1938	9931	5913	62.7	1936	9745	6520	59.9
1942	6695	3781	63.9	1940	9520	5383	63.9
1946	7737	3094	71.4	1944	8819	4212	67.7
1950	8154	3951	67.4	1948	7945	3621	68.7
1954	7455	4965	60.0	1952	10,529	3653	74.2
1958	8976	5300	62.9	1956	10,752	4293	71.5
1962	9992	5366	65.1	1960	10,201	5760	63.9
1966	8553	4548	65.3	1964	6567	7838	45.6
1970	7120	4484	61.4	1968	8705	4364	66.6
1974	7569	4345	63.5	1972	9476	4154	69.5
1978	8054	3763	68.2	1976	8331	6075	57.8
1982	6999	4313	61.9	1980	8994	4660	65.9
1986	6668	5237	56.0	1984	10,566	4471	70.3
1990	3204	6655	32.5	1988	9077	4871	65.1
1994	7499	3973	65.4	1992	7356	5368	57.8
1998	9330	2830	76.7	1996	7354	5912	55.4
Mean			61.9	Mean			62.7
Classification: Strongly Republican				Classification: Strongly Republican			

Table A.59 Tioga County

Gubernatorial elections				Presidential elections			
Year	Rep.	Dem.	% Rep.	Year	Rep.	Dem.	% Rep.
1902	4724	2635	64.2	1900	7458	2638	73.9
1906	4680	3061	60.4	1904	7410	1536	82.8
1910	3204	480	87.0	1908	6947	2321	74.9
1914	2921	3202	47.7	1912	1895	1901	49.9
1918	3921	684	85.1	1916	5347	2294	70.0
1922	3952	1569	71.6	1920	9718	1258	88.5
1926	4488	886	83.5	1924	8452	1271	86.9
1930	6944	2002	77.6	1928	11,774	1688	87.5
1934	8573	3971	68.3	1932	9583	3004	76.1
1938	11,846	4993	70.3	1936	12,567	5442	69.8
1942	7727	2238	77.5	1940	11,645	4434	72.4
1946	8779	2117	80.6	1944	10,381	3248	76.2
1950	8678	3360	72.1	1948	10,016	2986	77.0
1954	7471	3841	66.0	1952	11,203	3006	78.8
1958	8470	4112	67.3	1956	10,827	3280	76.7
1962	9865	4418	69.1	1960	11,082	4047	73.3
1966	8429	3643	69.8	1964	7064	7415	48.8
1970	6615	3953	62.6	1968	9298	3488	72.7
1974	7274	3866	65.3	1972	10,028	3733	72.9
1978	8371	2827	74.8	1976	8417	5795	59.2
1982	6998	4233	62.3	1980	8770	4273	67.2
1986	6392	4835	56.9	1984	10,532	4060	72.2
1990	4270	5737	42.7	1988	9471	4807	66.3
1994	7939	3417	69.9	1992	7823	4868	61.6
1998	7000	2071	77.2	1996	7382	4961	59.8
Mean			69.3	Mean			71.1
Classification: Strongly Republican				Classification: Strongly Republican			

Table A.60 Union County

	Gubernatorial elections				Presidential elections		
Year	Rep.	Dem.	% Rep.	Year	Rep.	Dem.	% Rep.
1902	2159	1551	58.2	1900	2810	1359	67.4
1906	1789	1480	54.7	1904	2548	1631	61.0
1910	1113	279	79.9	1908	2547	1154	68.8
1914	1463	1497	49.4	1912	470	1126	29.4
1918	11,938	658	74.6	1916	1902	1272	59.9
1922	1930	2343	45.2	1920	3305	1155	74.1
1926	3099	493	86.3	1924	3707	1209	75.4
1930	3641	1306	73.6	1928	5708	765	88.2
1934	3546	2303	60.6	1932	3534	1948	64.5
1938	5925	2394	71.2	1936	5589	2946	65.5
1942	3798	1454	72.3	1940	5612	2220	71.6
1946	4185	1468	74.0	1944	5585	1704	76.6
1950	4283	1886	69.4	1948	5058	1442	77.8
1954	4417	2517	63.7	1952	6558	1610	80.3
1958	5609	2167	72.1	1956	6620	1844	78.2
1962	7031	2199	76.2	1960	7466	1993	78.9
1966	5906	2055	74.2	1964	4944	4262	53.7
1970	4533	2475	64.7	1968	6422	2178	74.7
1974	4905	2434	66.8	1972	6905	2278	75.2
1978	6079	1944	75.8	1976	6309	3405	64.9
1982	4791	3564	57.3	1980	6798	2687	71.7
1986	4882	2810	63.5	1984	7792	2747	73.9
1990	2440	4694	34.2	1988	7912	3163	71.4
1994	5539	2445	69.4	1992	6362	3623	63.7
1998	5395	1700	76.0	1996	6570	3658	64.2
Mean			66.5	Mean			68.5
Classification: Strongly Republican				Classification: Strongly Republican			

Table A.61 Venango County

	Gubernatorial elections				Presidential elections		
Year	Rep.	Dem.	% Rep.	Year	Rep.	Dem.	% Rep.
1902	4163	3564	53.9	1900	5931	4014	59.6
1906	3659	2439	60.0	1904	5892	1740	77.2
1910	2417	892	73.0	1908	4868	2815	63.4
1914	2692	2694	50.0	1912	1660	2507	39.8
1918	3252	1573	67.4	1916	3856	3938	49.5
1922	4696	2992	61.1	1920	7718	2669	74.3
1926	6611	1523	81.3	1924	10,841	1886	85.2
1930	9392	4707	66.6	1928	17,450	4531	79.4
1934	12,646	7997	61.3	1932	12,230	6174	66.4
1938	17,944	6501	73.4	1936	17,676	9212	65.7
1942	9770	3707	72.5	1940	17,728	6873	72.1
1946	11,697	3595	76.5	1944	14,916	6426	69.9
1950	11,395	5076	69.2	1948	11,920	5144	69.8
1954	11,085	6846	61.8	1952	17,006	6356	72.8
1958	13,098	7021	65.1	1956	17,107	5594	75.4
1962	14,244	7100	66.7	1960	17,193	8064	68.1
1966	11,655	7226	61.7	1964	9873	13,065	43.0
1970	8311	8351	49.9	1968	12,323	8319	59.7
1974	10,221	6040	62.9	1972	13,991	6302	68.9
1978	8515	8479	50.1	1976	12,270	8653	58.6
1982	10,399	7659	57.6	1980	11,547	7800	59.7
1986	8530	8480	50.1	1984	13,507	9114	59.7
1990	4899	9999	32.9	1988	11,468	8624	57.1
1994	10,682	4796	69.0	1992	8545	8230	50.9
1998	9643	3595	72.8	1996	8398	8205	50.6
Mean			63.0	Mean			63.2
Classification: Strongly Republican				Classification: Strongly Republican			

Table A.62 Warren County

Gubernatorial elections				Presidential elections			
Year	Rep.	Dem.	% Rep.	Year	Rep.	Dem.	% Rep.
1902	3545	2304	60.6	1900	5609	2500	69.2
1906	3409	2560	57.1	1904	4737	1215	79.6
1910	1890	512	78.7	1908	4672	2054	69.5
1914	2062	2834	42.1	1912	1564	1686	48.1
1918	3058	1200	71.8	1916	3413	2628	56.5
1922	4379	2998	59.4	1920	7791	2180	78.1
1926	4688	1184	79.8	1924	8502	2161	79.7
1930	5991	3471	63.3	1928	12,077	2835	81.0
1934	6527	6381	50.6	1932	7872	5254	60.0
1938	10,830	6125	63.9	1936	9440	8495	52.6
1942	6490	2693	70.4	1940	11,016	5825	65.4
1946	7477	2540	74.6	1944	9276	4440	67.6
1950	8110	4058	66.6	1948	8378	4103	67.1
1954	7679	4829	61.4	1952	11,555	4442	72.2
1958	8760	5330	62.2	1956	12,145	4463	73.1
1962	9445	5083	65.0	1960	11,611	6525	64.0
1966	8104	5123	61.3	1964	5965	10,598	36.0
1970	5816	5710	50.5	1968	8889	6368	58.3
1974	6669	4285	60.9	1972	10,018	4877	67.3
1978	7561	4584	62.3	1976	8508	7412	53.4
1982	7049	4716	59.9	1980	9165	5560	62.2
1986	7641	5527	58.0	1984	10,838	6244	63.4
1990	4153	9260	31.0	1988	8991	6790	57.0
1994	9194	3643	71.6	1992	6585	6972	48.6
1998	6760	2301	74.6	1996	7056	7291	49.2
Mean			62.7	Mean			62.3
Classification: Strongly Republican				Classification: Strongly Republican			

Table A.63 Washington County

Gubernatorial elections				Presidential elections			
Year	Rep.	Dem.	% Rep.	Year	Rep.	Dem.	% Rep.
1902	8499	5994	58.6	1900	10,408	6380	62.0
1906	8934	6771	56.9	1904	11,530	4866	70.3
1910	7473	742	91.0	1908	11,430	7018	62.0
1914	7920	7949	49.9	1912	4297	5563	43.6
1918	8769	4113	68.1	1916	10,367	7747	57.2
1922	10,234	8281	55.3	1920	18,514	8827	67.7
1926	17,048	5210	76.6	1924	22,315	6706	76.9
1930	20,091	12,368	61.9	1928	31,099	17,149	64.4
1934	19,462	31,245	38.4	1932	21,447	28,934	42.6
1938	30,281	35,720	45.9	1936	23,342	52,878	30.6
1942	24,089	27,425	46.8	1940	29,066	50,829	36.3
1946	27,748	32,054	46.4	1944	27,615	47,023	37.0
1950	28,025	39,634	41.1	1948	26,860	46,327	36.7
1954	26,220	47,702	35.5	1952	36,041	55,725	39.3
1958	30,211	40,713	42.6	1956	39,465	48,052	45.1
1962	39,235	41,043	48.9	1960	38,348	53,729	41.6
1966	29,953	41,574	41.9	1964	24,167	63,482	27.6
1970	20,273	42,982	32.0	1968	28,023	47,805	37.0
1974	26,721	35,330	43.1	1972	42,587	34,781	55.0
1978	22,796	44,491	33.9	1976	32,827	49,317	40.4
1982	29,322	39,398	42.7	1980	32,532	45,295	41.8
1986	23,033	37,308	38.2	1984	34,782	50,911	40.6
1990	13,734	40,354	25.4	1988	28,651	47,527	37.6
1994	25,852	30,856	45.6	1992	21,977	46,143	32.3
1998	22,825	20,050	53.2	1996	27,777	40,952	40.4
Mean			49.2	Mean			46.0

Classification:
  Became More Democratic

Classification:
  Became More Democratic

Table A.64 Wayne County

Gubernatorial elections				Presidential elections			
Year	Rep.	Dem.	% Rep.	Year	Rep.	Dem.	% Rep.
1902	2360	2978	44.2	1900	3229	2647	54.9
1906	2008	2440	45.1	1904	3386	2093	61.8
1910	1293	798	61.8	1908	3650	2438	59.9
1914	1610	2610	38.1	1912	659	1924	26.5
1918	2373	1235	65.8	1916	2869	2019	58.7
1922	3944	2626	60.0	1920	5164	1589	76.5
1926	4837	1959	71.2	1924	5578	1477	79.1
1930	6935	2280	75.2	1928	8576	3148	73.1
1934	6998	3200	68.6	1932	6215	3666	62.9
1938	9492	3803	71.4	1936	9347	4864	65.8
1942	5753	2373	70.8	1940	9203	3460	72.7
1946	6853	2041	77.0	1944	8242	2793	74.7
1950	7378	2852	72.1	1948	7708	2284	77.1
1954	7744	3335	69.9	1952	9623	2530	79.2
1958	8181	4118	66.5	1956	9658	3092	75.7
1962	9175	3799	70.7	1960	9360	4425	67.9
1966	7908	3092	71.9	1964	6512	5781	53.0
1970	6669	2920	69.5	1968	7827	3176	71.1
1974	6204	3121	66.5	1972	8948	2733	76.6
1978	7016	2584	73.1	1976	7811	4244	64.8
1982	6396	3264	66.2	1980	8468	3375	71.5
1986	5718	4886	53.9	1984	10,061	3155	76.1
1990	3503	5882	37.3	1988	9926	3775	72.4
1994	7430	3862	65.8	1992	8184	4817	62.9
1998	8692	2892	75.0	1996	8077	5928	57.7
Mean			64.1	Mean			66.2
Classification: Strongly Republican				Classification: Strongly Republican			

Table A.65 Westmoreland County

Gubernatorial elections				Presidential elections			
Year	Rep.	Dem.	% Rep.	Year	Rep.	Dem.	% Rep.
1902	11,657	10,040	53.7	1900	16,014	11,010	59.2
1906	10,950	8186	57.2	1904	17,239	7991	68.3
1910	7365	2374	75.6	1908	15,429	11,101	58.1
1914	12,908	11,710	52.4	1912	4298	9262	31.7
1918	11,037	8571	56.3	1916	15,283	13,829	52.5
1922	16,762	13,110	56.1	1920	27,077	12,845	67.8
1926	29,491	7510	79.7	1924	34,522	10,223	77.2
1930	34,416	22,516	60.4	1928	51,760	30,587	62.8
1934	26,171	41,899	38.4	1932	30,426	45,436	40.1
1938	46,433	49,827	48.2	1936	36,079	73,574	32.9
1942	29,664	31,714	48.3	1940	42,643	64,567	39.8
1946	42,916	43,272	49.8	1944	43,202	61,057	41.4
1950	42,497	50,330	45.8	1948	41,709	61,901	40.2
1954	39,901	75,379	34.6	1952	58,923	80,008	42.4
1958	51,867	68,282	43.2	1956	66,580	72,616	47.8
1962	68,876	66,009	51.1	1960	68,825	85,641	44.6
1966	53,013	70,497	42.9	1964	41,493	107,131	27.9
1970	34,695	75,493	31.5	1968	52,206	81,833	38.9
1974	45,550	57,951	44.0	1972	75,085	59,322	55.9
1978	39,398	76,049	34.1	1976	59,172	74,217	44.4
1982	56,645	61,450	48.0	1980	63,140	68,627	47.9
1986	40,719	63,473	39.1	1984	71,377	79,906	47.2
1990	24,039	71,922	25.1	1988	61,472	76,710	44.5
1994	46,089	48,045	49.0	1992	47,315	69,817	40.4
1998	44,331	32,375	57.8	1996	62,058	63,686	49.4
Mean			49.4	Mean			47.4
Classification: Became More Democratic				Classification: Became More Democratic			

Table A.66 Wyoming County

Gubernatorial elections				Presidential elections			
Year	Rep.	Dem.	% Rep.	Year	Rep.	Dem.	% Rep.
1902	1892	2046	48.0	1900	2247	1875	54.5
1906	1549	1522	50.4	1904	2308	1575	59.4
1910	976	335	74.4	1908	2234	1629	57.8
1914	1220	1638	42.7	1912	480	1505	24.2
1918	1298	557	70.0	1916	1698	1444	54.0
1922	1972	1985	49.8	1920	3208	1247	72.0
1926	3254	877	78.8	1924	3213	1194	72.9
1930	4201	1738	70.7	1928	5321	906	85.4
1934	4144	2829	59.4	1932	3968	2728	59.2
1938	5518	2581	68.1	1936	5321	3269	61.9
1942	3604	1583	69.5	1940	5273	2548	67.4
1946	3796	1588	70.5	1944	4581	1982	69.8
1950	4288	2198	66.1	1948	4332	1674	72.1
1954	3875	2511	60.7	1952	5772	1815	76.1
1958	4979	2739	64.5	1956	5906	2120	73.6
1962	6079	2399	71.7	1960	6188	2726	8914
1966	5337	2020	72.5	1964	3864	4268	47.5
1970	4279	2460	63.5	1968	5207	2366	68.8
1974	4817	2476	66.0	1972	6423	2112	75.3
1978	5389	2108	71.9	1976	5705	3628	61.1
1982	4737	2851	62.4	1980	5919	2766	68.2
1986	4002	3583	52.8	1984	7230	2518	74.2
1990	1969	4434	30.8	1988	6607	2797	70.3
1994	5074	2481	67.2	1992	5143	3158	62.0
1998	6965	1682	80.5	1996	4888	4049	54.7
Mean			63.2	Mean			63.8
Classification: Strongly Republican				Classification: Strongly Republican			

Table A.67 York County

Gubernatorial elections				Presidential elections			
Year	Rep.	Dem.	% Rep.	Year	Rep.	Dem.	% Rep.
1902	110,368	12,894	44.6	1900	12,237	13,732	47.3
1906	11,062	13,361	45.3	1904	14,837	12,973	53.4
1910	8017	8178	49.5	1908	14,610	15,171	49.0
1914	10,726	13,255	44.7	1912	5251	14,979	25.9
1918	12,335	9787	55.7	1916	12,276	16,314	42.9
1922	13,592	18,939	41.8	1920	19,879	14,396	58.0
1926	18,284	8822	67.4	1924	23,044	15,600	59.6
1930	24,437	16,200	60.1	1928	45,791	11,216	80.3
1934	25,253	29,635	46.0	1932	25,430	29,313	46.4
1938	35,182	32,879	51.7	1936	29,233	45,142	39.3
1942	21,362	20,757	50.7	1940	30,228	39,543	43.3
1946	28,543	28,962	49.6	1944	32,617	38,226	46.0
1950	29,847	31,134	48.9	1948	32,494	33,321	49.4
1954	27,619	46,029	37.5	1952	44,489	39,508	53.0
1958	33,635	40,047	45.6	1956	48,176	38,743	55.4
1962	46,045	34,505	57.2	1960	55,922	39,164	58.8
1966	42,842	32,832	56.6	1964	33,677	58,787	36.4
1970	34,292	35,786	48.9	1968	51,631	33,328	60.8
1974	35,799	36,447	49.6	1972	63,606	27,520	69.8
1978	44,759	28,621	61.0	1976	56,912	41,281	58.0
1982	48,364	31,853	60.3	1980	61,098	33,406	64.7
1986	45,733	30,301	60.1	1984	75,020	33,359	69.2
1990	23,440	57,394	29.0	1988	72,408	37,691	65.8
1994	49,278	31,013	61.4	1992	60,130	46,113	56.6
1998	62,657	16,825	78.8	1996	65,188	49,596	56.8
Mean			52.3	Mean			53.3
Classification: Became More Republican				Classification: Became More Republican			

References

Alderfer, H. F., and Fannette H. Luhrs. 1946. *Gubernatorial Elections in Pennsylvania, 1922–1942*. State College, Pa.: Pennsylvania Municipal Publications Service.

Alderfer, H. F., and Robert M. Sigmund. 1940. *Presidential Elections by Pennsylvania Counties, 1920–1940*. State College: Pennsylvania State College Press.

Alford, John, and John Hibbing. 1981. Increased incumbency advantage in the House. *Journal of Politics* 43:1042–61.

Almanac of the 50 States: Basic Data Profiles with Comparative Tables, 2000. 2000. Burlington, Vt.: Information Systems.

American Electronic Association. *Cyberstates 2002: A State-by-State Overview of the High-Technology Industry*. Accessed at www.aeanet.org/PressRoom/idmk_cs2002_Pennsylvania.asp.

Andersen, Kristi. 1979. *The Creation of a Democratic Majority, 1928–1936*. Chicago: University of Chicago Press.

Bartels, Larry M. 2000. Partisanship and voting behavior, 1952–1996. *American Journal of Political Science* 44:35–50.

Beck, Paul Allen, Lawrence Baum, Aage R. Clausen, and Charles E. Smith, Jr. 1992. Patterns and sources of ticket splitting in subpresidential voting. *American Political Science Review* 86:916–28.

Beck, Paul Allen, and Marjorie Randon Hershey. 2001. *Party Politics in America*. New York: Longman.

Beers, Paul B. 1980. *Pennsylvania Politics Today and Yesterday*. University Park: Pennsylvania State University Press.

Born, Richard. 1979. Generational replacement and the growth of incumbent margins in the U.S. House. *American Political Science Review* 73:811–17.

Bradley, Martin B., Norman M. Green, Jr., Dale E. Jones, Mac Lynn, and Lou McNeil. 1992. *Churches and Church Membership in the United States, 1990*. Atlanta: Glenmary Research Center.

Breaux, David. 1990. Specifying the impact of incumbency on state legislative elections: A district level analysis. *American Politics Quarterly* 18:270–86.

Breaux, David, and Anthony Gierzynski. 1996. Running for reelection in American state legislatures. In *Politics in the American States and Communities: A Contemporary Reader*, ed. Jack R. Van Der Slik. Boston: Allyn and Bacon.

Burden, Barry C., and David C. Kimball. 1998. A new approach to the study of ticket-splitting. *American Political Science Review*. 92:533–44.
Burnham, Walter Dean. 1970. *Critical Elections and the Mainsprings of American Politics*. New York: Norton.
Carey, John M., Richard G. Niemi, and Lynda W. Powell. 2000. Incumbency and the probability of reelection in state legislative elections. *Journal of Politics* 62 (2000): 691–700.
Collie, Melissa. 1981. Incumbency, electoral safety, and turnover in the House of Representatives. *American Political Science Review* 75:119–31.
Commonwealth of Pennsylvania. *Pennsylvania Statistical Abstract*. Selected vols. Harrisburg, Pa.: Pennsylvania State Data Center.
Commonwealth of Pennsylvania. *The Pennsylvania Manual*. Selected vols. Harrisburg, Pa.: Department of General Services.
Commonwealth of Pennsylvania. 1901. *Smull's Legislative Hand Book and Manual of the State of Pennsylvania*. Harrisburg, Pa.: Printer of the Commonwealth.
Cover, Albert. 1977. One good term deserves another: The advantage of incumbency in congressional elections. *American Political Science Review* 21:523–41.
Cover, Albert D., and David R. Mayhew. 1977. Congressional dynamics and the decline of competitive congressional elections. In *Congress Reconsidered*, ed. Lawrence C. Dodd and Bruce I. Oppenheimer. New York: Praeger.
Cox, Gary W. 1997. *Making Votes Count*. Cambridge. Cambridge University Press.
Crotty, William J. 1977. *Political Reform and the American Experiment*. New York: Thomas Y. Crowell.
DeVries, Walter, and V. Lance Tarrance. 1972. *The Ticket-Splitter: A New Force In American Politics*. Grand Rapids, Mich.: William B. Eerdmans.
Dran, Ellen M., Robert B. Albritton, and Mikel Wyckoff. 1991. Surrogate versus direct measures of political culture: Explaining participation and policy attitudes in Illinois. *Publius* 21:15–30.
Dunaway, Wayland F. 1948. *A History of Pennsylvania*. New York: Prentice-Hall.
Elazar, Daniel. 1984. *American Federalism: A View from the States*. 3d ed. New York: Harper and Row.
Erikson, Robert. 1971. The advantage of incumbency in congressional elections. *Polity* 3:395–405.
———. 1976. Is there such a thing as a safe seat? *Polity* 9:623–32.
Evans, Frank B. 1966. *Pennsylvania Politics, 1872–1877: A Study in Political Leadership*. Harrisburg, Pa.: Pennsylvania Historical and Museum Commission.
Federal Election Commission. 1997. *The Impact of The National Voter Registration Act of 1993 on the Administration of Elections for Federal Office, 1995–1996*. Washington, D.C.: U.S. Government Printing Office.
Ferejohn, John. 1977. On the decline of competition in congressional elections. *American Political Science Review* 71:166–76.
Fitzpatrick, Jody L., and Rodney E. Hero. 1988. Political culture and political characteristics of the American states: A consideration of some old and new questions. *Western Political Quarterly* 41:145–53.
Flanigan, William H., and Nancy H. Zingale. 2002. *Political Behavior of the American Electorate*. 7th ed. Washington, D.C.: Congressional Quarterly Press.
Garand, James C. 1991. Electoral marginality in state legislative elections, 1968–86. *Legislative Studies Quarterly* 16:7–28.

Garand, James C., and Donald Gross. 1984. Change in the vote margins for congressional candidates: A specification of historical trends. *American Political Science Review* 78:17–30.
Garand, James C., Kenneth Wink, and Bryan Vincent. 1989. "Marginality and the uniformity of inter-election vote swings in U.S. congressional elections: A diachronic extension of Jacobson's thesis." Paper presented at the annual meeting of the Southern Political Sciences Association. Memphis.
Gordon, Dianna. 1994. Citizen legislators—alive and well. *State Legislatures*, January, 24–27.
Herzig, Eric B. 1985. The legal-formal structuring of state politics: A cultural explanation. *Western Political Quarterly* 38:413–23.
Hinsdale, B. A., and Mary L. Hinsdale. 1899. *History and Civil Government of Pennsylvania*. Chicago: Werner School Book Company.
Information Publications. 2000. *Almanac of the 50 States*. Burlington, Vt.: Information Publications.
Jacobson, Gary C. 1987. The marginals never vanished: Incumbency and competition in elections to the U.S. House of Representatives, 1952–82. *American Journal of Political Science* 31:126–41.
———. 1997. *The Politics of Congressional Elections*. 7th ed. New York: Longman.
Jewell, Malcolm E. 1994. State legislative elections: What we know and don't know. *American Politics Quarterly* 22:483–509.
Jewell, Malcolm E., and David Breaux. 1988. The effect of incumbency on state legislative elections. *Legislative Studies Quarterly* 13:495–514.
Jewell, Malcolm E., and Sarah M. Morehouse. 2001. *Political Parties and Elections in American States*. 4th ed. Washington, D.C.: Congressional Quarterly Press.
Jewell, Malcom E., and David M. Olson. 1988. *Political Parties and Elections in the American States*. 3d ed. Chicago: Dorsey.
Johnson, Charles A. 1976. Political culture in American states: Elazar's formulation examined. *American Journal of Political Science* 18:331–45.
Joslyn, Richard A. 1980. Manifestations of Alazar's political subcultures: State public opinion and the content of political campaign advertising. *Publius* 10: 37–58.
Keefe, William J., and Morris Ogul. 1997. *The American Legislative Process*. Upper Saddle River, N.J.: Prentice Hall.
Keith, Bruce E., David B. Magleby, Candice J. Nelson, Elizabeth Orr, Mark C. Westlye, and Raymond E. Wolfinger. 1992. *The Myth of the Independent Voter*. Berkeley and Los Angeles: University of California Press.
Keller, Richard Calvin. 1960. *Pennsylvania's Little New Deal*. Ann Arbor, Mich.: University Microfilms.
Kennedy, John. 1999. *The Contemporary Pennsylvania Legislature*. New York: University Press of America.
Key, V. O., Jr. 1955. A theory of critical elections. *Journal of Politics* 17:3–18.
———. 1956. *American State Politics: An Introduction*. New York: Knopf.
———. 1959. Secular realignment of the party system. *Journal of Politics* 21:198–210.
Klein, Philip S., and Ari Hoogenboom. 1973. *A History of Pennsylvania*. University Park: Pennsylvania State University Press.
Kurtz, Karl T. 1992. *Understanding the Diversity of American State Legislatures*. Denver, Colo.: National Conference of State Legislatures.

Lieske, Joel. 1993. Regional subcultures of the United States. *Journal of Politics* 55: 888–913.
Lilley, William III, Laurence J. DeFranco, and William M. Diefenderfer III. 1994. *The Almanac of State Legislatures.* Washington, D.C.: Congressional Quarterly Press.
Lowery, David, and Lee Sigelman. 1982. Political culture and state public policy: The missing link. *Western Political Quarterly* 35:376–84.
Mayhew, David. 1974. Congressional elections: The case of the vanishing marginals. *Polity* 7:295–317.
Miller, Warren E., and J. Merrill Shanks. 1996. *The New American Voter.* Cambridge: Harvard University Press.
Morgan, David R., and Sheilah S. Watson. 1991. Political culture, political system characteristics, and public policies among the American states. *Publius* 21:31–48.
Nardulli, Peter F. 1990. Political subcultures in the American states: An empirical examination of Elazar's formulation. *American Politics Quarterly* 18:287–315.
Nelson, Candice. 1978–79. The effect of incumbency on voting in congressional elections, 1964–1974. *Political Science Quarterly* 93:665–78.
Nie, Norman H., Sidney Verba, and John Petrocik. 1976. *The Changing American Voter.* Cambridge: Harvard University Press.
Niemi, Richard G. 1981. *Generations and Politics.* Princeton: Princeton University Press.
Niemi, Richard G., Simon Jackman, and Laura R. Winsky. 1991. Candidacies and competitiveness in multimember districts. *Legislative Studies Quarterly* 16:91–110.
Parker, Glenn. 1980. The advantage to incumbency in House elections. *American Politics Quarterly* 8:449–64.
Partin, Randall W. 1995. Economic conditions and gubernatorial elections. *American Politics Quarterly* 23:81–95.
Patterson, Samuel C. 1996. Legislative politics in the states. In *Politics in the American States,* 6th ed., ed. Virginia Gray and Herbert Jacob. Washington, D.C.: Congressional Quarterly Press.
Pennsylvania Statistical Abstract. See Commonwealth of Pennsylvania.
Pennsylvania Manual. See Commonwealth of Pennsylvania.
Pennsylvania State Data Center. 1993. *1990 Census of Population and Housing.* Harrisburg, Pa.: Pennsylvania State Date Center.
Rae, Douglas W. 1967. *The Political Consequences of Electoral Laws.* New Haven: Yale University Press.
Ray, David, and John Havick. 1981. A longitudinal analysis of party competition in state legislative elections. *American Journal of Political Science* 25:119–28.
Rosenthal, Alan. 1998. *The Decline of Representative Democracy.* Washington, D.C.: Congressional Quarterly Press.
Sharkansky, Ira. 1969. The utility of Elazar's political culture: A research note. *Polity* 2:66–83.
Schlitz, Timothy D., and R. Lee Rainey. 1978. The geographic distribution of Elazar's political subcultures among the mass population: A research note. *Western Political Quarterly* 31:410–15.
Smith, Reed. 1964. *State Government in Transition: Reforms of the Leader Administration, 1955–1959.* Philadelphia: University of Pennsylvania Press.
Smull's Legislative Hand Book. See Commonwealth of Pennsylvania 1901.

Sorauf, Frank. 1963. *Party and Representation*. New York. Atherton Press.
Squire, Peverill. 1992. Legislative professionalism and membership diversity in state legislatures. *Legislative Studies Quarterly* 17:69–79.
———. 1998. Uncontested seats in state legislative elections. Typescript.
Stanley, Harold W., and Richard G. Niemi, eds. 2000. *Vital Statistics on American Politics*. Washington, D.C.: Congressional Quarterly Press.
StateNet. 1995. *Guidebook to Pennsylvania Legislators*. Sacramento, Calif.: StateNet.
Stevens, Sylvester K. 1964. *Pennsylvania: Birthplace of a Nation*. New York: Random House.
Sundquist, James L. 1983. *Dynamics of the Party System: Alignment and Realignment of Political Parties in the United States*. Rev. ed. Washington, D.C.: Brookings Institution.
Tanger, Jacob, and Harold F. Alderfer. 1939. *Pennsylvania Government*. Harrisburg, Pa.: Pennsylvania Book Source.
Tanger, Jacob, Harold F. Alderfer, and M. Nelson McGeary. 1950. *Pennsylvania Government*. State College, Pa.: Penns Valley Publishers.
Teixeira, Ruy A. 1992. *The Disappearing American Voter*. Washington, D.C.: Brookings Institution.
Tidmarch, Charles, Edward Lonergan, and John Sciortino. 1986. Interparty competition in the U.S. states: Legislative elections, 1970–1978. *Legislative Studies Quarterly* 11:353–74.
Tucker, Harvey J., and Ronald E. Weber. 1985. Electoral change in U.S. states: System versus constituency competition. Presented at the Annual Meeting of the American Political Science Association, New Orleans, La.
U.S. Bureau of the Census. 1900. *1900 Census of the Population, Pennsylvania, General Population Characteristics*. Washington, D.C.: U.S. Government Printing Office.
———. 1998a. *Statistical Abstract of the United States: 1998*. Washington, D.C.: U.S. Government Printing Office.
———. 1998b. Voting and registration in the election of November 1996. *Current Population Reports*, ser. P-20, no. 504. Washington, D.C.: U.S. Government Printing Office.
———. 2001. *Census 2000 Summary File*. Accessed at www.census.gov/prod/cen2000.
Van Dunk, Emily, and Ronald E. Weber. 1997. Constituency-level competition in the United States, 1968–1988: A pooled analysis. *Legislative Studies Quarterly* 22:141–60.
Wattenberg, Martin P. 1994. *The Decline of American Political Parties*. Cambridge: Harvard University Press.
Weber, Ronald E., and William R. Shaffer. 1972. Public opinion and American state policy-making. *Midwest Journal of Political Science* 16:683–99.
Weber, Ronald E., Harvey J. Tucker, and Paul Brace. 1991. Vanishing marginals in state legislative elections. *Legislative Studies Quarterly* 16:29–47.
Wolfinger, Raymond E., and Steven J. Rosenstone. 1980. *Who Votes*. New Haven: Yale University Press.
Yost, Berwood A. 2003. Disappearing Democrats: Rethinking partisanship within Pennsylvania's electorate. *Commonwealth* 12:77–86.

Index

Adams County, 128
agriculture, 8–9
Allegheny County
    2000 presidential election, 213
    African American population, 5
    Competition Index (CI) in
        gubernatorial elections, 174, 176
    current partisanship, 121
    Democratic support, 1970–1998, 133,
        134, 135
    gubernatorial elections, 97, 100, 104,
        105, 106
    Home counties of office holders, 185,
        186, 187, 191, 197, 198, 199
    least Republican in presidential
        elections, 128
    malapportionment, 14, 15
    most Republican in gubernatorial
        elections, 125
    most Republican in presidential
        elections, 125
    population growth, 3
    presidential elections, 110, 111, 114, 116
    urbanism and Democratic vote, 170, 206
Allentown, 150, 151
Andersen, Kristi, 28, 193

Ballot Reform Act of 1892, 18
Beaver County, 127, 128, 133, 135
Beidelman, Edward E., 155
Berks County
    Competition Index (CI) in
        gubernatorial elections, 175, 176
    current partisanship, 121
    gubernatorial elections, 101, 106

income level, 7
independents, 28, 31
least Republican in gubernatorial
    elections, 127, 128
least Republican in presidential
    elections, 128
malapportionment, 16
Berry, William H., 44, 45, 46, 201
Bethlehem Steel, 8
Blair County, 125, 209
Bonniwell, Eugene C., 39, 98, 99
Brace, Paul, 52
Bradford County, 122, 125, 134, 209
Breaux, David, 51, 53
Brumbaugh, Martin G., 45, 97
Bucks County, 6, 28, 29, 121, 193
Burnham, Walter Dean
    legislative competition, 50, 52, 59, 70, 76
    partisan realignment 159, 160, 161
Bush, George H.W., 119, 120
Bush, George W., 213
Butler County, 209

California, 86
Cambria County
    Competition Index (CI) in
        gubernatorial elections, 176
    least Republican in gubernatorial
        elections, 127, 135
    least Republican in presidential
        elections, 128, 130, 135
    presidential elections, 120
Cameron County, 124, 125
Cameron, Donald, 12, 13
Cameron, Simon, 11, 12, 13, 88

Carbon County, 108, 128, 173
Carey, John M., 86
Carnegie Steel Corporation, 8
Carter, Jimmy, 117, 119
Casey, Robert P., 45, 68, 106, 107, 180, 198
caucus. *See* nominations
Chester County, 5, 6, 121
City Party, 44
Clarion County, 128
Clark, Joseph S., 130, 132
Clinton, Bill, 46, 120
coal mining, 14–15
Collie, Melissa, 51
Columbia County, 128, 173, 177, 180, 182, 209
Competition Index (CI), 172–73
constitution(s)
   of 1874, 13, 14, 15, 16, 17, 20
   of 1968, 16–17
county interparty competition
   gubernatorial and presidential elections, 181–82, 191
   gubernatorial elections, 173–77, 190–91, 199
   presidential elections, 177–81, 191, 199
conventions. *See* nominations
Crawford County, 18
Crawford County System, 18
Cumberland County, 30, 193
Curtin, Andrew Gregg, 12

Dauphin County, 5, 30, 125, 193
Delaware County, 5, 6, 121, 125, 173, 209
Democratic Party
   success in statewide elections, 130–34, 135
   under Republican machine, 11–12
   U. S. Senate elections, 130–34, 135
Dewey, Thomas E., 115, 166
direct primary. *See* nominations
Dole, Bob, 120
Dukakis, Michael S., 119

Earle, George H., 101, 198
economy, transformation of, 9–10
Eisenhower, Dwight D., 115, 166
Elazar, Daniel, 31–33
Elk County, 125, 128, 173, 178, 181
Erie County
   Comparison of Competition Index (CI) in gubernatorial and presidential elections, 181
   Competition Index (CI) in presidential elections, 176, 178, 180
   gubernatorial elections, 1950–58, 104
   most Republican in gubernatorial elections, 124, 125
Erikson, Robert, 51
ethnicity, 3–4

Fayette County
   coke production, 8
   Competition Index (CI) in gubernatorial elections, 174, 176
   Democratic support, 1970–98, 133
   least Republican in gubernatorial election, 126, 127, 134
   least Republican in presidential elections, 128, 129, 134, 135
   presidential elections, 118,
Fine, John S., 102, 176, 198
Fisher, John S., 97, 155, 198
Fisher, Mike, 210, 214
Flinn, William, 56
Ford, Gerald R., 117
Forest County, 124, 125
Franklin County, 28, 29, 164, 193, 209
Fulton County, 128, 173, 180

Garand, James C.
   decline in congressional competition, 50, 70, 71
   incumbent reelection rates, 51
   meaning of marginality, 52, 63, 65, 73
Gekas, George, 212
General Assembly
   careerism among members, 82–84, 94–95, 204–5
   careerism compared with Pennsylvania members of U.S. House of Representatives, 85–86, 94–95, 205
   categorized as professional legislature, 81
   contested elections, 62–63, 76, 202–3, 211
   electoral marginality and incidence of defeat, 63–65, 76, 197
   historical comparison of legislators' backgrounds, 86–93, 95, 204–5
   incidence of marginal districts, 58–61, 76, 77–78, 195–97, 211
   incumbents running for reelection, 55, 75, 202, 210
   malapportionment, 14–16
   reelection success of incumbents, 55–58, 75–76, 195, 211
   Republican and Democratic districts compared, 182–85, 191
   vote share versus seats, 65–69, 76–77, 203–4, 211–12

Gierzynski, Anthony, 51, 53
Gore, Al, 213, 214
Gormley, Ken, 61
Greene County
  Competition Index (CI) in
    gubernatorial elections, 173, 177
  Competition Index (CI) in presidential
    elections, 178, 180
  gubernatorial elections, 99, 102,
  least Republican counties in gubernatorial elections, 126, 127, 190
  least Republican counties in presidential elections, 128, 129
  presidential elections, 111, 118
  realignment, 168
Grim, Webster, 44, 97
Gross, Donald, 50, 70, 71
Grundy, Joseph R., 163–64
gubernatorial elections
  1900–1908, 97
  1910–18, 97
  1920–28, 97–100
  1930–38, 101–2
  1940–48, 102
  1950–58, 102–4
  1960–68, 105
  1970–78, 105–6
  1980–88, 106
  1990–98, 106–8
  2002, 214
  counties won, 121, 123
  least Republican counties, 126–28, 134–35
  most Republican counties, 121–25, 134
Guffey, Joseph F., 131–32

Hafer, Barbara, 68,
Harding, Warren G., 111
Harrison, Benjamin, 12
Havick, John, 52, 58, 59
Heinz, John, 130, 132
Hemphill, John M., 164
Holden, Tim, 212
home counties of officeholders
  composite, 187–88, 191
  governor, 186, 191
  statewide office, 187, 191
  U.S. senator, 186–86, 191
Hoover, Herbert, 111, 112
Hughes, Charles Evans, 111
Humphrey, Hubert, 116
Huntingdon County, 124, 125

Idaho, 81
Independent Republicans (Lincoln Party), 44, 45
independents
  explanation of, 29–33
  incidence by county, 28–29
  percentage of national electorate, historical, 25–27
  percentage of Pennsylvania electorate, historical, 27–28
  political culture and, 31–33
Indiana County, 124, 125
Itkin, Ivan, 68

Jacobson, Gary C., 51, 52, 73
James, Arthur H., 101, 154, 166, 198
Jewell, Malcolm E., 51
Johnson, Lyndon Baines, 116
Juniata County, 164

Kennedy, John, 136, 150
Kennedy, John F., 116
Key, V.O., 137, 138, 144, 148, 150, 159
Keystone Party, 45

Labor Party, 27, 28
Lackawanna County
  Competition Index (CI) in
    gubernatorial elections, 176, 177
  Competition Index (CI) in presidential
    elections, 180, 181
  gubernatorial elections, 105, 108
  least Republican in gubernatorial
    elections, 127, 135
  least Republican in presidential
    elections, 128, 129, 135
  malapportionment, 16
  presidential elections, 117, 120
  realignment, 170
Lancaster County
  Competition Index (CI) in
    gubernatorial elections, 173
  Competition Index (CI) in presidential
    elections, 179
  current partisanship, 121
  independents, 28, 31
  malapportionment, 16
  most Republican in gubernatorial
    elections, 122, 124, 134, 190
  most Republican in presidential
    elections, 125, 134
  nominations, 18
Lawrence, David L., 103

Lawrence County, 125
Leader, George M., 103, 198
Lebanon County, 28, 31, 125, 193
legislative careerism. *See* General Assembly and U.S. House of Representatives
Lehigh County
  Competition Index (CI) in gubernatorial elections, 175
  gubernatorial elections, 101, 106
  income, 7
  independents, 28, 31,
  least Republican in gubernatorial elections, 128
  partisan realignment, 164
Liberal Party, 164
Libertarian Party, 27
Lieske, Joel, 32
Lincoln Party. *See* Independent Republicans
Lonergan, Edward, 52
Louisiana, 81
Luzerne County
  Competition Index (CI) in gubernatorial elections, 176, 177
  Competition Index (CI) in presidential elections, 178, 181
  gubernatorial elections, 105, 108
  malapportionment, 16
  partisan realignment, 170
Lycoming County, 128, 182

manufacturing, 9–11
Martin, Edward, 102, 198
Massachusetts, 81
McCormick, Vance C., 45, 97
McGovern, George, 117
McKean County, 122, 125
McKinley, William, 110
Mondale, Walter, 119
Monroe County
  Competition Index (CI) in gubernatorial elections, 175, 176
  gubernatorial elections, 99, 101
  least Republican in gubernatorial elections, 128
  least Republican in presidential elections, 128
  political culture, 31
  population growth, 1990–2000, 3
Montgomery County, 5, 6, 121, 164
Montour County, 128, 175, 182, 209
Morgan, J. P., 8
Myers, Francis J., 132

National Conference of State Legislatures, 81
National Voter Registration Act of 1993, 22, 25, 41–42, 48, 210
Niemi, Richard G., 86
Nineteenth Amendment, 20
Nixon, Richard, 117
nominations, 17–19
Northampton County
  Competition Index (CI) in gubernatorial elections, 173, 176
  Competition Index (CI) in presidential elections, 178, 180
  gubernatorial elections, 101, 102, 106,
  independents, 28, 31
  least Republican in gubernatorial elections, 127
Northumberland County, 128, 173, 177, 182

O'Donnell, John, 12
Oregon, 81
Oregon v. Mitchell (1970), 20

Palmer, A. Mitchell, 45
partisan realignment
  concept of, 159–60
  1890s realignment, 160–61, 189
  New Deal realignment, 161–66, 190
  relationship between Republican vote and urbanization, ethnicity, and racial diversity, 166–71
Partisanship Consistency Index (PCI)
  and voting behavior, 43–47, 48, 201, 210
  defined, 42–43
Pennsylvania, population characteristics of,
  African American population, 4–5
  ethnicity, 3–4
  income, 6–7
  population below poverty level, 7
  population growth, 2–3
  religious diversity, 5–6
  senior population, 3
  urban population, 3
Pennsylvania Association of Manufacturers, 163
Pennypacker, Samuel W., 97
Penrose, Boise, 11, 13, 45, 88, 198
People's Bank of Philadelphia, 12
Pepper, George Wharton, 155, 156
Perry County, 209
Philadelphia County
  2000 presidential election, 213
  African American population, 5

Competition Index (CI) and gubernatorial elections, 174, 176, 177
Competition Index (CI) and presidential elections, 180,
current partisanship, 121
gubernatorial elections, 97, 100, 102, 104, 105, 106, 107, 108, 135
home counties of officeholders, 185, 186, 187, 191, 197, 198, 199
least Republican counties in gubernatorial elections, 127
least Republican counties in presidential elections, 128
malapportionment, 14, 15, 16
most Republican counties in gubernatorial elections, 125
most Republican counties in presidential elections, 125
partisan realignment, 160, 161, 162, 163, 164
presidential elections, 110, 111, 114, 115, 116, 117, 120, 135
U.S. Senate elections, 133, 134, 135
urbanism and Democratic vote, 169, 206
Philadelphia Inquirer, 164
Philadelphia metropolitan area
home areas of officeholders, 186, 187, 191, 197, 198, 214
population growth, 2–3
Philadelphia North American, 2
Philadelphia Public Ledger, 2
Pike County, 3, 31, 128, 175, 176
Pinchot, Gifford, 99, 101, 155, 163, 164, 175, 198
Pittsburgh, 2, 22, 150, 151, 161, 198
Pittsburgh metropolitan area
home areas of officeholders, 186, 187, 191, 197, 198, 214
population growth, 2–3
Pittsburgh Post-Gazette, 164
Powell, Lynda W., 86
presidential elections
1900–1908, 109–10
1910–18, 110–11
1920–28, 111–12
1930–38, 112–14
1940–48, 115
1950–58, 115–16
1960–68, 116
1970–78, 116–18
1980–88, 118–20
1990–98, 120
2000, 213–14
counties won, 121
least Republican counties, 128–30
most Republican counties, 125–26
primary election competition
contested primaries and general election vote, 148–50
correlates of, 137–39
gubernatorial and senatorial primaries, 139–43
Pennsylvania General Assembly and U.S. House or Representatives, 143–48
urban-rural differences, 150–54
Progressive Party, 110

Quay, Matthew, 11, 12, 13, 88, 198

Ray, Douglas W., 52, 58, 59
Reagan, Ronald, 118, 119
Registry Act of 1869, 21
Rendell, Ed, 214
Republican Party
pre-1932 dominance, 11
state machine, 11–13
Ridge, Tom, 68, 107, 154, 198
Roosevelt, Franklin D., 57, 113, 115, 166
Roosevelt, Theodore, 56, 110, 111

Santorum, Rick, 132, 133
Schnader, William A., 101
Schuylkill County, 16, 176
Schweiker, Richard, 132
Sciortino, John, 52
Scott, Hugh, 132
Scranton, 22
Scranton, William, 105
senatorial elections. *See* Democratic Party; primary election competition
Shafer, Raymond P., 105, 198
Shapp, Milton J., 105, 198
Snyder County, 122, 125, 134
Socialist Party, 27, 28
Somerset County, 124, 125
Sorauf, Frank
multimember districts, 15
primary elections, 136, 137, 138, 144, 148, 150, 156
split-ticket voting, 42–47, 48–49, 201–2, 210
Sproul, William C., 39, 97, 198
Squire, Peverill, 81
steel industry, 8
Stone, William A., 13
Stuart, Edwin S., 97

Sullivan County, 128, 182
Susquehanna County, 125

Taft, William Howard, 56, 110
Tener, John K., 97, 198
term limits, 81
Thornburgh, Dick, 105, 106, 130
Tidmarch, Charles, 52
Tioga County, 122, 125, 134, 173, 179
Tucker, Harvey J., 52
Turnout-Loyalty Index (TLI), 35–37, 194
Twenty-Sixth Amendment, 20

Uniform Elections Act of 1874, 21
Union County, 122, 125, 134
U.S. House of Representatives
  careerism among members, 84–85, 94, 204–5
  careerism compared with members of the General Assembly, 85–86, 94–95, 205
  contested elections, 72, 78–79, 202–3, 213
  electoral margin and incidence of defeat, 72–73, 79, 197, 213
  incidence of marginal districts, 70–71, 78, 195–97, 213
  incumbents running for reelection, 69–70, 78, 202, 212
  reelection success of incumbents, 70, 78, 195, 212
  vote share versus seats, 73–75, 79, 203–4, 213
Utah, 81

Van Valkenburg, Edwin, 56
Vare, William S., 12, 155, 163, 164
Venango County, 124, 125,
Vincent, Bryan, 73
voter registration
  as percentage of voting age population, historical, 25, 26, 208
  history of, 21–22
  partisan registration, historical, 33, 34
  partisan vote and, 33–38, 193–94
voter qualifications, 20
voter turnout
  as percentage of registered voters, historical, 40–42, 48, 200–201
  as percentage of voting age population, historical, 38–40, 47, 200
  decline of, 38–41, 48
  impact of National Voter Registration Act on, 41–42, 48, 200–201
  impact of women's suffrage on, 39–40, 200
  impact of youth suffrage on, 39, 200
  in primaries, 154–56, 157, 206
  presidential versus gubernatorial elections, 38–39, 200
Voting Rights Act of 1970, 20

WAMs (Walking Around Money), 57
Warren County, 28, 29, 124, 125, 193, 209
Washington, 81
Washington County
  presidential elections, 118
  least Republican in gubernatorial elections, 127, 135
  least Republican in presidential elections, 128, 130, 135
  Competition Index (CI) in gubernatorial elections, 174, 176
Washington Party, 56, 110
Wayne County, 3, 31, 122, 125, 134
Weber, Ronald E., 52
Westmoreland County
  coke production, 8
  Competition Index (CI) in gubernatorial elections, 174, 176
  current partisanship, 121
  least Republican in gubernatorial elections, 127, 135
  least Republican in presidential elections, 128, 130, 135
  malapportionment, 16
Wilson, William B., 155
Wilson, Woodrow, 44, 46, 36, 111, 201
Wink, Kenneth, 73
Wofford, Harris, 130, 131
Wyoming, 81
Wyoming County, 125

York County
  Competition Index (CI) in gubernatorial elections, 175, 177
  current partisanship, 121
  gubernatorial elections, 104
  independents, 28, 31
  least Republican in gubernatorial elections, 128
  least Republican in presidential elections, 128
  New Deal realignment, 164
  presidential elections, 115
Yost, Berwood, 37, 194

www.ingramcontent.com/pod-product-compliance
Lightning Source LLC
Chambersburg PA
CBHW021354290426
44108CB00010B/241